OTHER A TO
THE SCAREC

The A to Z of Existentialism

Stephen Michelman

The A to Z Guide Series, No. 162

The Scarecrow Press, Inc.
Lanham • Toronto • Plymouth, UK
2010

Published by Scarecrow Press, Inc.
A wholly owned subsidary of
The Rowman & Littlefield Publishing Group, Inc.
4501 Forbes Boulevard, Suite 200, Lanham, Maryland 20706
http://www.scarecrowpress.com

Estover Road, Plymouth PL6 7PY, United Kingdom

British Library Cataloguing in Publication Information Available

Library of Congress Cataloging-in-Publication Data

The hardback version of this book was cataloged by the Library of Congress
as follows:

Michelman, Stephen, 1962–
  Historical dictionary of existentialism / Stephen Michelman.
    p. cm. — (Historical dictionaries of religions, philosophies, and movements ;
no. 82)
  Includes bibliographical references.
  1. Existentialism–Dictionaries. 2. Existentialism–History. I. Title.
B819.M53 2008
142'.7803–dc22   2007042697

ISBN 978-0-8108-7589-0 (pbk. : alk. paper)

∞™ The paper used in this publication meets the minimum requirements of
American National Standard for Information Sciences—Permanence of Paper
for Printed Library Materials, ANSI/NISO Z39.48-1992.
Printed in the United States of America

For Karen, Isabella, and Theo

Contents

Editor's Foreword

Few recent philosophical movements have aroused as much interest and stirred up as much controversy as existentialism. Its impact has been felt beyond the academy, in literature, politics, and art, and in fields as diverse as psychotherapy, theology, and Asian thought. After World War II, it was closely identified with the work of Jean-Paul Sartre and Simone de Beauvoir and its definition grew uncertain, for while Sartre and Beauvoir embraced the existentialist label, others like Albert Camus, Martin Heidegger, and Karl Jaspers distanced themselves from it. To make matters worse, critics derided existentialism as postwar pessimism, while the media confused it with a bohemian fashion. However, this did not prevent the message of existentialism from quickly spreading far and wide, from Europe to the United States, Japan, and Latin America. Thus, though the golden age of existentialism has passed, it still influences the way we think about the world and ourselves, and existentially inspired concepts of freedom, alienation, absurdity, and even death have become part of our common vocabulary.

The A to Z of Existentialism explains the claims of existentialist philosophy and the contexts in which it developed. It documents the rise of German and French "philosophy of existence" in the 1920s and 1930s and its transformation into "existentialism" in the 1940s and 1950s. Thankfully, much of the uncertainty of "existentialism" has been removed by circumscribing its activity historically, roughly between 1919 and 1950, and identifying its chief philosophical proponents. At the same time, its diversity has been preserved by accounting for predecessor movements as well as an impressive array of writers and thinkers who played a part in its development. Essential contributions of figures like Sartre, Heidegger, Martin Buber, and Maurice Merleau-Ponty are recognized with detailed summaries of their lives, philosophies, and relations to other thinkers. Nineteenth-century forerunners of existentialism are discussed along with various religious existentialists, as well as critics of existentialism, and readers will appreciate entries on selected works of existentialist fiction. Throughout the substantial dictionary section, key concepts are explained with an eye to the unity of existentialist thought. The chronology shows where existentialism fits in historically, and the introduction places it in its philosophical setting. The bibliography then permits readers to engage in further study or reading on those philosophers and topics that attract them most.

This was not an easy volume to write, considering the diversity of philosophers and others who come under the existentialist heading and the ongoing controversy over its contents and terminology, but it was certainly worth the wait. Its author, Stephen Michelman, is an associate professor of philosophy at Wofford College. He has devoted over two decades to the study and teaching of existentialism and phenomenology and has published articles, reviews, and translations on these subjects. His broad knowledge of the French and German intellectual traditions and his sensitivity to the social and political contexts of ideas have served him well here. Readers should be pleased to have a work on existentialism that explains its claims and historical environment so clearly.

Jon Woronoff
Series Editor

Preface

The subject of this dictionary is the philosophy of human existence that flourished first in Germany in the 1920s and 1930s and then in France in the decade following the end of World War II. The operative meaning of *existentialism* here is thus broader than it was around 1945, when the term first gained currency in France as a label for the philosophy of **Jean-Paul Sartre**. However, it is considerably less broad than the view proposed by commentators in the 1950s and 1960s who, in an attempt to overcome Sartre's hegemony, discovered the seeds of existentialism far and wide—in Shakespeare, Saint Augustine, and the Old Testament prophets. In this dictionary, existentialism is understood as a decidedly 20th-century phenomenon, though with roots in the 19th century. Effort has been made to understand the philosophy of existentialism, as all philosophies should be understood, as part of an ongoing intellectual tradition: an evolving history of problems, concepts, and arguments. To take one salient example, existentialism would not have been possible without a prior philosophical endeavor formulated by **Edmund Husserl** in the early 1900s called *phenomenology*. Without Husserl's phenomenology, the philosophy of existence would have taken a radically different form. Its major theoretical statements, **Martin Heidegger**'s *Being and Time* and Jean-Paul Sartre's *Being and Nothingness*, would perhaps never have been written.

Happily, the risk is no longer very great that readers will conflate existentialism with a postwar malaise, a godless nihilism, or a bohemian lifestyle, as detractors in the 1940s and 1950s frequently did. Still, it bears repeating that existentialism is first and foremost a type of philosophy, not a style of literature or an aesthetic attitude. While many French existentialists chose to express themselves through literature as well as philosophy, existentialist fiction was for the most part "the pursuit of philosophy by other means," not an attempt at literary expression as an end in itself or an effort merely to *épater les bourgeois*.

The majority of entries in this dictionary concern the life and thought of eight major existentialists: **Martin Buber**, **Karl Jaspers**, Martin Heidegger, **Gabriel Marcel**, Jean-Paul Sartre, **Simone de Beauvoir**, **Maurice Merleau-Ponty**, and **Albert Camus**. Readers who consult entries on these eight figures will receive a fairly comprehensive overview of existentialist philosophy in the 20th century. Jaspers and Heidegger were the chief representatives of German "**philosophy of existence**," while Buber was the foremost Jewish existentialist writer and thinker. Marcel, Sartre, Beauvoir, and Merleau-Ponty were the principal architects of French existentialism. Albert Camus, while he was not strictly speaking an existentialist, was and still often is linked to existentialism. Thus Camus is accorded coverage commensurate with his reputation and historical importance.

Significant attention as well is devoted to the Danish Christian writer **Søren Kierkegaard**, the chief 19th-century precursor of existentialism. Entries for many core existentialist concepts, including **anxiety**, **authenticity and inauthenticity**, **choice**, **commitment**, **freedom**, and **responsibility**, refer readers to Kierkegaard's seminal formulation of these ideas and indicate, when appropriate, how his statements served as templates for future existentialist accounts. Entries are also dedicated to individual works by Kierkegaard, such as *The Concept of Anxiety* and *Fear and Trembling*, whose influence was particularly clear and important.

Friedrich Nietzsche is the second major 19th-century precursor of existentialism. Nietzsche's influence on existentialism, while significant, is, however, more diffuse and harder to pinpoint. His concepts of the "**death of God**," **nihilism**, the "Overman," the "**will to power**," and the "transvaluation of all values" cast a spell over *most* European intellectuals of the early 20th century, including many existentialists. Moreover, Nietzsche's status as an existentialist, or protoexistentialist, philosopher is subject to debate (his status as an existentialist is addressed in the entry for him). When appropriate, the specific nature of Nietzsche's influence is noted—for example, his understanding of "the death of God" and of European nihilism and how it is to be overcome. Many aspects of Nietzsche's thought, though, are beyond the scope of this inquiry and are not treated in this dictionary.

I have tried to convey a sense of the diversity and richness of other philosophical currents that contributed to existentialism. Entries on philosophers and philosophical movements instrumental to the development of existentialism include those on **Henri Bergson, Wilhelm Dilthey, G. W. F. Hegel**, Edmund Husserl, **Karl Marx** and **Marxism, neo-Kantian philosophy**, phenomenology, **philosophical anthropology, philosophy of life**, and **Max Scheler**. A discussion of **philosophy of existence** explains the character and provenance of existentialist thought in Germany and France in the 1920s and 1930s, prior to the emergence of Sartre's existentialism. I have also acknowledged important instances in which existentialism was exported to disciplines outside of philosophy. These developments are noted, inter alia, in entries on **Rudolph Bultmann** and **Paul Tillich**, theologians who developed the field of existential theology, as well as in a discussion of **existential psychotherapy** as practiced by the psychiatrists and psychoanalysts Medard Boss, Ludwig Binswanger, and **Victor Frankl**, among others. The relationship between existentialism and psychoanalysis is further assessed in entries on **existential psychoanalysis, Sigmund Freud, Jacques Lacan, psychoanalysis**, and Jean-Paul Sartre.

A spectrum of the ideas referred to under the umbrella category "religious existentialism" (i.e., *theistic* existentialism) is conveyed through entries on **Abraham, the absurd**, Martin Buber, **Catholicism, faith**, Karl Jaspers, Søren Kierkegaard, **Emmanuel Levinas**, Gabriel Marcel, and **Franz Rosenzweig**. Entries on **Hannah Arendt**, Emmanuel Levinas, and **Raymond Aron** document thinkers whose concerns and careers paralleled and at times overlapped with those of existentialist philosophers. Fields in which existentialist influence has been more contingent and episodic, such as feminism and race theory, receive proportionally less attention. Readers interested in these areas may consult the sections devoted to them in the bibliography.

As a historical dictionary, this work is also attentive to the political and cultural contexts in which existentialism developed. Two of the most important political episodes are Martin Heidegger's involvement with German National Socialism (*see* HEIDEGGER AND NAZISM) and Sartre and Merleau-Ponty's relationship with Marxism and Communist polemics (*see* COMMUNISM; MARXISM; POLITICS). The reader is left to decide to what degree these episodes represent authentic instances of existential "commitment." Entries devoted to **World**

War I, **World War II**, **Nazism**, and the **French Resistance** help to fill in the historical background of existentialist philosophy.

As noted, in a way perhaps unrivaled since the dialogues of Plato, and staunchly opposed by Anglo-American philosophers of the period, existentialism was intimately linked with literary modes of expression. Individual works of fiction by existentialists are documented in entries on Sartre's novel *Nausea* and his *The Roads to Freedom* trilogy, his plays *No Exit* and *The Flies*, and Beauvoir's novel *She Came to Stay*. (Camus's novel *The Stranger*, widely considered a classic of existentialist fiction, is discussed under philosophy of the **absurd**. Both *The Stranger* and *The Plague* are discussed in the entry for Camus.) Other literary and artistic topics include Leo Tolstoy's **The Death of Ivan Ilyich**, **existentialist literature**, **surrealism**, **theater of the absurd**, and **jazz**.

Critics of existentialism are accounted for in entries for **logical positivism** (Rudolph Carnap and A. J. Ayer), **Theodor Adorno**, **Karl Löwith**, and **Georg Lukács**, among others. Entries devoted to important scholars of the subject, especially authors of early commentaries that first brought the idea to the attention of American readers in the 1940s and 1950s, include those for **William Barrett**, **Wilfred Desan**, **Marjorie Grene**, **Walter Kaufmann**, Paul Tillich, and **Jean Wahl**, as well as for those who further developed these ideas in the 1960s and 1970s, such as **John Macquarrie** and Frederick Olafson (Olafson's work is discussed under **ethical voluntarism**). Among recent commentators, **David E. Cooper** is singled out for discussion in the dictionary as well as at the end of the introduction.

Finally, I have felt obligated to acknowledge certain popular myths and attitudes associated with existentialism, however erroneous. Some of the more sensationalized aspects of postwar French existentialism are documented in entries on Beauvoir, Sartre, and Camus; on figures associated with Sartre's circle like **Juliette Gréco** and **Boris Vian**; and on the **café existentialists** and places they haunted in Paris in the late 1940s—**Saint-Germain-des-Prés**, the **Café de Flore**, and the Café les Deux Magots. Popular misconceptions of existentialism are also discussed in the introduction.

Perhaps the greatest interpretive challenge in composing *The A to Z of Existentialism* has been to assign the concept of existentialism an extension broad enough to capture its varied expressions and yet narrow enough to retain its coherence as a form of philosophy. Commentators long ago abandoned the idea that existentialism can be understood historically as a single "school" or "movement." Nonetheless, the question remains of how one is to characterize the unity of existentialist philosophy. I have briefly suggested how this may be done in the dictionary entry for **existence** and in the introduction. It is hoped that, by consulting the entries on core existentialist concepts, such as **alienation**, anxiety, authenticity and inauthenticity, commitment, freedom, and responsibility, as well as on the major existentialists, readers will grasp for themselves how the unity of the philosophy of existence (i.e., existentialism) may plausibly be construed.

Acknowledgments

I want to thank my friend James Clarke for introducing this project to me many years ago, and series editor Jon Woronoff for his patience during those same years. Discussions with Clayton Whisnant helped me understand the significance of "conservative revolutionaries" in Weimar Germany. Chris Strauber gave valuable advice in composing the bibliography, and Paul Jones showed kindness and forbearance in managing my library books. Finally, I want to thank my wife, Karen Goodchild, for her support and understanding over the many summers I was engaged in writing this book.

Abbreviations

The following is a list of works abbreviated in the dictionary. Primary sources are cited by initials, secondary sources by last name of author or editor. Details of publication are given in the bibliography.

Bair	Deirdre Bair, *Simone de Beauvoir*
Barrett	William Barrett, *Irrational Man*
BEM	Jean-Paul Sartre, *Between Existentialism and Marxism*
BH	Gabriel Marcel, *Being and Having*
BMM	Martin Buber, *Between Man and Man*
BN	Jean-Paul Sartre, *Being and Nothingness*
BPW	Karl Jaspers, *Basic Philosophical Writings*
BT	Martin Heidegger, *Being and Time*
BW	Martin Heidegger, *Basic Writings*
CA	Søren Kierkegaard, *The Concept of Anxiety*
Cohen-Solal	Annie Cohen-Solal, *Sartre: A Life*
Contat & Rybalka	Micheal Contat and Michel Rybalka, eds., *The Writings of Jean-Paul Sartre Vol. I: A Bibliographical Life*
Cooper	David E. Cooper, *Existentialism*
CUP	Søren Kierkegaard, *Concluding Unscientific Postscript*
EA	Simone de Beauvoir, *The Ethics of Ambiguity*
EHE	Jean-Paul Sartre, "Existentialism" in *Existentialism and Human Emotions*
FC	Simone de Beauvoir, *Force of Circumstance*
FT	Søren Kierkegaard, *Fear and Trembling*
HC	Hannah Arendt, *The Human Condition*
HV	Gabriel Marcel, *Homo Viator*

IM	Martin Heidegger, *An Introduction to Metaphysics*
IT	Martin Buber, *I and Thou*
KA	Søren Kierkegaard, *A Kierkegaard Anthology*
Kaufmann	Walter Kaufmann, ed., *Existentialism from Dostoevsky to Sartre*
LCE	Albert Camus, *Lyrical and Critical Essays*
Lottman	Herbert Lottman, *Albert Camus: A Biography*
LPE	Jean-Paul Sartre, *Literary and Philosophical Essays*
MMA	Karl Jaspers, *Man in the Modern Age*
MS	Albert Camus, *The Myth of Sisyphus and Other Essays*
PE	Karl Jaspers, *Philosophy of Existence*
PEM	Gabriel Marcel, *The Philosophy of Existentialism*
PKJ	Karl Jaspers, *The Philosophy of Karl Jaspers*, Paul Schilp, ed.
PL	Simone de Beauvoir, *The Prime of Life*
PP	Maurice Merleau-Ponty, *Phenomenology of Perception*
PrP	Maurice Merleau-Ponty, *The Primacy of Perception*
R	Albert Camus, *The Rebel*
RE	Karl Jaspers, *Reason and Existenz*
Safranski	Rüdiger Safranski, *Martin Heidegger: Between Good and Evil*
SM	Jean-Paul Sartre, *Search for a Method*
SNS	Maurice Merleau-Ponty, *Sense and Non-Sense*
SP	Jean-Paul Sartre, *The Writings of Jean-Paul Sartre Vol. II: Selected Prose*
Stewart	Jon Stewart, ed., *The Debate between Sartre and Merleau-Ponty*
TE	Jean-Paul Sartre, *The Transcendence of the Ego*
TWB	Gabriel Marcel, *Tragic Wisdom and Beyond*
Wahl	Jean Wahl, *A Short History of Existentialism*
WD	Jean-Paul Sartre, *War Diaries*
Young-Bruehl	Elizabeth Young-Bruehl, *Hannah Arendt: For Love of the World*

Chronology

1813 Birth of Søren Kierkegaard.

1831 Death of G. W. F. Hegel.

1844 Birth of Friedrich Nietzsche.

1855 Death of Kierkegaard.

1856 Birth of Edmund Husserl.

1878 Birth of Martin Buber.

1883 Birth of José Ortega y Gasset. Birth of Karl Jaspers.

1889 Birth of Martin Heidegger. Birth of Gabriel Marcel.

1900 Death of Nietzsche.

1901 Husserl publishes *Logical Investigations*.

1905 Birth of Jean-Paul Sartre.

1908 Birth of Simone de Beauvoir. Birth of Maurice Merleau-Ponty.

1909 A complete German edition of Kierkegaard's works is begun.

1913 Birth of Albert Camus. Husserl publishes *Ideas: General Introduction to Pure Phenomenology*. Miguel de Unamuno publishes *The Tragic Sense of Life*.

1914–1918 World War I.

1919 Publication of Jaspers's *Psychology of Worldviews*.

1921   Heidegger sends Karl Jaspers an extended review of *Psychology of Worldviews*, initiating a philosophical friendship that lasts through the 1930s.

1922–1926   Heidegger develops an original existential interpretation of philosophy in his university lectures.

1923   Martin Buber publishes *I and Thou*.

1927   Publication of Heidegger's *Being and Time*. Marcel publishes *Metaphysical Journal*.

1929   Heidegger gains attention for his lecture "What Is Metaphysics?" Kierkegaard is translated into French. The Wall Street stock market crashes, setting off a worldwide Depression.

1931–1932   Jaspers publishes *Philosophy,* in three volumes, elaborating his conception of *Existenzphilosophie*.

1933   Adolph Hitler is appointed Chancellor of Germany.

1933–1934   Heidegger joins the Nazi Party and serves for 12 months as rector of Freiburg University. Sartre studies Husserl's phenomenology in Berlin.

1933–1939   Alexandre Kojève lectures on Hegel in Paris.

1935   Publication of Marcel's *Being and Having*.

1938   Sartre publishes *Nausea*.

1939–1945   World War II.

1940–1944   Nazi Germany occupies France.

1942   Camus publishes *The Stranger* and *The Myth of Sisyphus*.

1943   Publication of Sartre's *Being and Nothingness*. Publication of Beauvoir's novel *She Came to Stay*.

1944   Sartre's play *No Exit* is produced in Paris.

1945   Merleau-Ponty publishes *Phenomenology of Perception*.

1945   September: Sartre publishes *The Age of Reason* and *The Reprieve*, the first two novels of *The Roads to Freedom* trilogy. **15 October:** First issue of the journal *Les Temps modernes*, coedited by Sartre and Merleau-Ponty, the main forum of expression for French existentialism. **29 October:** Sartre's lecture "Is Existentialism a Humanism?" inaugurates the "existentialist era" in France and abroad.

1947 Heidegger is banned from teaching; publishes *Letter on Humanism*. Camus publishes *The Plague*. Beauvoir publishes *The Ethics of Ambiguity*. Jaspers publishes *The Question of German Guilt*.

1948 Sartre's work is placed on the Vatican's Index of Forbidden Books.

1949 Beauvoir publishes *The Second Sex*.

1950 A papal encyclical, *Humani Generis*, condemns existentialism as a "false opinion threatening to undermine the foundations of Catholic doctrine."

1950–1953 The Korean War.

1951 Camus publishes *The Rebel*, which criticizes Joseph Stalin's state-sponsored terror in the Soviet Union.

1952 *Les Temps modernes* publishes a negative review of Camus's *The Rebel*, hastening a break between Camus and Sartre.

1952–1956 Sartre is "converted" to communism but becomes disillusioned after the Soviet invasion of Hungary.

1953 Merleau-Ponty breaks with Sartre and resigns from *Les Temps modernes*.

1954 Beauvoir's *The Mandarins* wins the Prix Goncourt.

1955 Death of Ortega y Gasset.

1957 Camus is awarded the Nobel Prize for Literature.

1960 Sartre publishes *The Critique of Dialectical Reason*. Camus dies in an automobile accident.

1961 Merleau-Ponty dies of a heart attack.

1964 Sartre refuses the Nobel Prize for Literature.

1965 Death of Martin Buber.

1969 Death of Karl Jaspers.

1973 Death of Gabriel Marcel.

1976 Death of Martin Heidegger.

1980 Death of Jean-Paul Sartre.

1986 Death of Simone de Beauvoir.

Introduction

Existentialism takes its name from a philosophical reference to human *existence*, that is, to the uniquely self-conscious and self-determining character of a human life as it is lived, enjoyed, and suffered in the first person rather than described or explained from an ostensibly neutral third-person perspective. The attempt to provide a philosophical account of the distinctive features of human existence that distinguish a human life from the nominally similar "existence" of other animals, plants, and things is the common goal of existentialist philosophers. These features include a lived awareness of time and a relationship to death; a more or less explicit understanding of the freedom to act and to interpret the world according to one's own lights and of one's responsibility for doing so; and a fundamental concern over the character of one's life, whether it will be lived *authentically*, as deliberately one's own, or *inauthentically*, as something for which one is not ultimately responsible.

By bringing these features into focus, existentialists have a corollary objective: to correct the picture of the human being as a disembodied "knower" promoted by traditional philosophy and science. The view of the person as an autonomous mind or consciousness is deeply rooted in the philosophical tradition. Its defining expression was given in the 17th century in **René Descartes**'s conception of the human being as *res cogitans*, a "thinking substance" independent of body and world. For existentialists, the Cartesian view is particularly pernicious because it underwrites the belief that mind and world are not intrinsically connected, that the human being is a spectator rather than an actor in the play of existence, an autonomous mind contemplating a mindless "external world." It also disconnects one mind from another, enclosing each person in the theater of his or her own mental representations. As a rule, existentialists have attacked both of these premises. For them, human

1

existence is essentially *embodied*, *situated* in a *world*, and lived in *relation to others*. For these reasons, they insist that existence cannot be predicated on an isolated consciousness. In the distinctive idiom of existentialist philosophers, existence is simultaneously *being-for-self*, *being-with-others*, and *being-in-the-world*.

The first phase of existentialism took place in Germany after World War I, when in the 1920s and 1930s an original "philosophy of existence" was developed by the philosophers Karl Jaspers and Martin Heidegger. A parallel development in religious thought was undertaken by the Jewish religious thinker Martin Buber and by the Protestant theologians Rudolph Bultmann and Paul Tillich. The second phase of existentialism occurred when the thought of Heidegger and Jaspers, along with the phenomenology of Edmund Husserl, the dialectical philosophy of G. W. F. Hegel, and the radical subjectivism of Søren Kierkegaard and Friedrich Nietzsche, were absorbed into French intellectual life during the 1930s and 1940s.

The chief figure of the second phase of existentialism was the French writer and philosopher Jean-Paul Sartre. Because Sartre achieved international acclaim after World War II, it is with his name that existentialism was and still is most frequently identified. However, care should be taken not to equate Sartre's philosophy with existentialism as a whole. His views represent one version of the existentialist project, one extreme of a spectrum of philosophical opinion.

In 1945 Sartre was catapulted to fame as the "leader" of a newly baptized "existentialist movement." With fellow philosophers Simone de Beauvoir and Maurice Merleau-Ponty, Sartre launched *Les Temps modernes*, a leftist journal of ideas and letters, which became the public platform for Sartrean existentialism. Albert Camus, already famous in his own right as a novelist and as editor of the popular newspaper *Combat*, befriended Sartre for a time and became linked to the movement, at least in the public eye. French Catholic philosopher Gabriel Marcel, one of Sartre's harshest critics, claimed precedence as the first French philosopher of existence and became associated with the movement as Sartre's antithesis. Henceforth Marcel, Jaspers, and Kierkegaard would be recognized as representatives of religious or theistic existentialism, a perspective Sartre took pains to distinguish from his own pronounced atheism. In Spain in the 1930s and 1940s, an existentialist philosophy similar to Sartre's was developed independently by the philosopher

José Ortega y Gasset. In Italy in the 1940s and 1950s, a divergent strand of existentialism developed around the work of the philosopher **Nicola Abbagnano**.

In the 1950s, 1960s, and 1970s, existentialism was exported to the United States and to countries around the world. Existentialist ideas were developed in disciplines as diverse as psychiatry, psychotherapy, theology, literary theory, and race and gender theory. Existentialist by-words like "anxiety," "absurdity," and "the meaning (or meaningless-ness) of life" crept into everyday language. The image of the existential "hero," abandoned and yet defiant in a meaningless universe, found resonance in art and literature of the Cold War era.

However, as existentialism entered popular culture, it became increasingly diffuse and ill-defined. Boosters like Paul Tillich hailed existentialism as "the great art, literature, and philosophy of the 20th century."[1] Yet critics called it a bohemian fad, a religious sect, a bout of "nihilism" brought on by World War II. Commentators traced its roots back to Pascal, Saint Augustine, Socrates, and the Old Testament prophets. To borrow a phrase from the French philosopher Maurice Merleau-Ponty, existentialism by the mid-1950s seemed to be "everywhere and nowhere": an "atmosphere," an "attitude," a "tendency," visible in all areas of human endeavor yet definable in none. The problem of defining such an amorphous entity was summed up in 1967 by the American philosopher Alasdair MacIntyre: "It has been alleged in our time to be the doctrine of writers as various as Miguel de Unamuno and Norman Mailer. . . . That two writers both claim to be existentialists does not seem to entail their agreement on any one cardinal point. Consequently . . . any formula sufficiently broad to embrace all the major existentialist tendencies would . . . be so general and so vague as to be vacuous. . . ."[2]

Existentialism fell out of favor in the 1970s, when it was replaced by interest in more recent philosophical trends from Europe, in particular French poststructuralism and postmodernism. A new breed of French philosophers trained in the 1950s and 1960s, postmodernists, such as Michel Foucault, Jacques Derrida, and Gilles Deleuze, rejected phenomenology and existentialism as naive "philosophies of the subject," which, they held, uncritically accepted the centrality of human experience in the constitution of the world. The postmodernists announced instead the "death of the subject" and advocated a "posthumanist" mode of thought sensitive to the linguistic and historical forces that shape individual consciousness. Ironically, most of the French poststructuralists were substantively indebted to Heidegger's philosophy. Thus they contributed to the dogma that Heidegger was not, even in his early thought, an "existentialist." This epithet they reserved for Sartre and Beauvoir, and, to a lesser extent, Merleau-Ponty. Through the passage of time, existentialism and phenomenology had come to represent the philosophical establishment in France. By the 1980s, in France as well as the United States, intellectuals generally regarded existentialism as an obsolete mode of thought, perhaps a viable topic for intellectual historians but no longer a viable philosophy.

GERMAN PHILOSOPHY OF EXISTENCE

Existenzphilosophie, or philosophy of existence, evolved in the unstable environment of Weimar Germany after World War I. Its main proponents were the phenomenological philosopher Martin Heidegger and the theologically oriented philosopher and psychiatrist Karl Jaspers. The Protestant theologians Rudolph Bultmann and Paul Tillich, Heidegger's university colleagues in the 1920s, were attracted to Heidegger's bold and original analysis of historical existence. They applied Heideggerean concepts to theological and biblical interpretation to create the field of "existential theology." An alternative religious vision of existence was defended by the Jewish philosopher Martin Buber. For Buber, the drama of existence was not waged primarily within the self but in a quest to achieve "dialogue" with the other, and through the other with God.

The earliest expression of German philosophy of existence was Jaspers's **Psychology of Worldviews**, published in 1919. Written in an accessible style, Jaspers's book became an intellectual best seller, and on the basis of its success he was offered a chair of philosophy at Heidelberg University in 1922. Strictly speaking, however, it was not a work of philosophy (Jaspers had not yet completed his move from psychiatry to philosophy) but a hybrid expression of psychology and a philosophy of **worldviews** inspired by the philosopher Wilhelm Dilthey and the sociologist **Max Weber**, as well as by Kierkegaard and Nietzsche. Still fumbling for his philosophical footing, Jaspers attempted to describe various ways in which the basic attitudes of personal existence are shaped into specific, rigid types. Of particular importance was his idea of **"limit situations"** (*Grenzsituationen*), extreme experiences of guilt, death, suffering, and chance through which the fundamental features of existence come into focus for the individual. (Jaspers's account of death as a limit situation later served as a model for Heidegger's account of "being-towards-death" in *Being and Time*. Jaspers may have influenced Heidegger in other ways; one of Heidegger's earliest formulations of his own existential position occurred in an extended critical review of *Psychology of Worldviews*, which he sent to Jaspers in 1921.[3])

Jaspers incorporated the notion of the limit situation into his mature philosophical position, which he published as *Philosophy*, in three volumes (1930–1932). In limit situations, the individual confronts an unfathomable truth and is thrown into a kind of cognitive suspense: Knowledge "founders"; rigidified habits and prejudices become useless. By living through the intensity of a limit situation, the individual may experience an expansion of awareness and self-awareness, a heightened sense of freedom and possibility, which Jaspers refers to as **Existenz**. *Existenz* is one's "authentic being." It is not a given state but emerges through acts of inner "struggle," "anxiety," and "decision." *Existenz* is not a self-sufficient condition. Rather, it necessarily opens out upon "transcendence," the ultimate reality or "Being itself," which stands beyond the self and "encompasses" its limited perspective. Jaspers's view that the self emerges as truly individualized only when it "knows itself before transcendence" became a central premise of religious existentialism.

Heidegger too stressed the encounter with finitude, or "being-towards-death," as a defining feature of human existence. In Heidegger's philosophy, however, the human being is thrown back on its own "nothingness" without appeal to a transcendent power. By confronting death and accepting the "groundlessness" of one's being, Heidegger maintained, the person receives a sense of his or her essential freedom and finitude, entering into "authentic" existence. Heidegger is considered by many to be the founding figure of atheistic existentialism.

The publication of *Being and Time* in 1927 confirmed Heidegger's status as a revolutionary thinker and earned him a national reputation in Germany. In the book, Heidegger's account of the urgency of authentic existence was coupled with a penetrating and original analysis of everyday experience, which Heidegger derived from the phenomenology of Edmund Husserl, his former teacher, to whom the book was dedicated. Heidegger's account of what he termed *"Dasein"* or "being-in-the-world" was widely recognized for its depth and originality; on its basis Sartre and Merleau-Ponty arrived later at their own versions of **existential phenomenology**. Among other effects, it also provided the foundation for a modern reformulation of hermeneutics by Heidegger's student, **Hans-Georg Gadamer**.

Jaspers and Heidegger initiated an intense philosophical friendship in the early 1920s, which lasted in diminished form until 1933. In that year, Heidegger joined the Nazi Party, and Jaspers broke off correspondence with his former friend, whose views he no longer recognized. Initially, however, they saw themselves as kindred spirits, young philosophy professors linked in the desire to revolutionize German philosophy. Both expressed disdain for conventional academic philosophy, which, they believed, reduced the concrete historical individual to an ahistorical "knowing subject." Both men also inveighed against the domination of the natural and mathematical sciences, which since the 17th century had sought to objectify human behavior and reduce the world to an array of neutral facts. Independently, each pursued his own path toward a philosophy of *existence*: a mode of thought directed toward the historical, practical, and emotional dimensions of human life that had been obscured by tradition. By attending to concrete historical existence, they believed, philosophy might be saved from bloodless rationalism and idealism and might reestablish its priority over the natural sciences.

Like many of their contemporaries, Jaspers and Heidegger each drew considerable inspiration from the 19th-century Danish Lutheran writer Søren Kierkegaard. After languishing in relative oblivion in Denmark for half a century, Kierkegaard's writings were translated into German beginning around 1909 and had a profound effect on a generation of German theologians and philosophers who reached maturity around the time of World War I, including Jaspers, Heidegger, and the Protestant theologian Karl Barth. Kierkegaard's appeal to subjectivity and his critique of Hegelian rationalism struck a chord with German intellectuals disillusioned with the abstract character of neo-Kantian philosophy and with the reductive program of materialist science.

Kierkegaard had produced the first philosophical treatment of existence in the relevant sense: the irreducibly particular, immediate, and subjective character of a human life as it is lived by the individual in time. In his writings of the 1840s, Kierkegaard stressed that human subjectivity cannot be reduced to objective form by philosophy or science. He maintained that genuine subjectivity is deepened through acts of ethical and religious commitment and is obscured by the "speculative philosopher," who seeks to subsume the individual within universal categories, e.g., to reduce the subject to an expression of objective "spirit," as Hegel had attempted. Kierkegaard held that the highest form of subjectivity is religious faith. Authentic faith is beyond reason; it is predicated on "the absurd."

Jaspers and Heidegger transposed many of Kierkegaard's insights into secular philosophical guise. For Jaspers, Kierkegaard represented the first truly existential thinker, the first "exception" to the rule of rational philosophical discourse. Because he fully invested himself in his thinking rather than hiding behind a mask of neutrality and objectivity, Kierkegaard, along with Friedrich Nietzsche, was for Jaspers the exemplary philosophers of *Existenz;* instead of merely theorizing about the world, they placed their most profound personal experience at the center of their thought. Jaspers was the first in the existentialist tradition to posit Kierkegaard and Nietzsche as forebears of 20th-century existentialism.

Heidegger was substantially indebted to Kierkegaard's concept of the "moment" as well as to his metaphysical account of anxiety and guilt. Following Kierkegaard, Heidegger in *Being and Time* described guilt and anxiety not merely as psychological states but as fundamental moods that reveal deep truths about the human being. While Heidegger fully appreciated the religious view of existence as a personal struggle for redemption from sin—at the time he was immersed in the study of Martin Luther, and as a youth he had trained to become a Jesuit priest— he had lost his faith toward the end of World War I. Now he effectively transposed Kierkegaard's religious concerns into a secular quest for "authenticity": a struggle to extricate oneself from the "fallenness" of everyday social life; to seize hold of historical possibilities offered by one's tradition; and to grasp oneself as a finite, free, and "anxious" "being of possibility." Kierkegaard's account of anxiety in *The Concept of Anxiety* was particularly influential. There Kierkegaard observed that, while fear is directed to a particular threatening object in the world, anxiety has no apparent object: It appears to be anxiety "over nothing." Following Kierkegaard, Heidegger argued that the elusive object of anxiety is existence itself, human "being-in-the-world." Some of the most vivid passages of *Being and Time* described the anxiety of "being-towards-death." In the face of death, the authentic individual accepts the groundlessness of its being—its "thrownness" into time and culture—and yet takes responsibility for shaping itself according to its own choices.

POLITICS AND EXISTENCE: HEIDEGGER AND NATIONAL SOCIALISM

Heidegger's decision in April 1933 to serve as the Nazi rector of Freiburg University is the darkest and most controversial chapter in the history of existentialism. Heidegger's actions invite comparison with Plato's ill-fated association, 2,300 years prior, with Dionysius the Younger, the tyrant of Syracuse. Like Plato, Heidegger placed philosophy on a pedestal above more mundane forms of human inquiry, and like the Greek philosopher he apparently saw himself as a "philosopher-king" who could employ his wisdom for political ends. At the height of his involvement Heidegger wrote to Karl Jaspers that his goal in undertaking the rectorship was to "lead the Leader (*"den Führer zu führen"*),"[4] that is, to guide Hitler in the spiritual reawakening of the German people. In retrospect, Heidegger's beliefs were exceedingly naive. He seemed to have been convinced that his own philosophical vision was necessary to direct the development of national socialism toward its proper fulfillment, a true awakening of the "spiritual community" of the German *Volk*.

Heidegger resigned from the rectorship in February 1934 and made no further ventures into politics. However, he remained at his teaching post at Freiburg University throughout World War II. In 1946, he was banned from teaching for five years by a French denazification committee, and, in 1951, he retired with emeritus status. Heidegger's tenure as rector and his subsequent explanations and evasions of his behavior have been the subject of a score of critical studies that have appeared since the late 1980s.[5] While the naiveté and hubris of Heidegger's behavior are not generally disputed, there is a variety of opinion among scholars about the degree to which Heidegger's philosophy is linked to, and hence contaminated by, the ideology of Nazism.

Heidegger himself affirmed that he was convinced at the time of the potential greatness of the National Socialist movement. However, he apparently understood the movement as an attempt to unify the German *Volk* around its intellectual, literary, and philosophical past, not as a biologically based racism. Such hopes for a "spiritual rebirth" of Germany were shared by various German intellectuals around the time of World War I, including the philosopher Max Scheler and the psychologist Wilhelm Wundt. It appears to have been this "spiritual" nationalism that guided Heidegger's actions in the early 1930s, not the biological racism and anti-Semitism of the Nazis.[6]

This interpretation is consistent with Heidegger's philosophical statements of the time. In a 1935 lecture course, "Introduction to Metaphysics," Heidegger's described the contemporary situation in terms that echoed the nihilistic judgments of other cultural and political conservatives of the period:

> The spiritual decline of the earth is so far advanced that the nations are in danger of losing the . . . energy . . . to see the decline . . . and to appropriate it as such (. . .) the darkening of the world, the flight of the gods . . . the transformation of men into a mass, the hatred and suspicion of everything free and creative, have assumed such proportions throughout the earth that such childish categories as pessimism and optimism have long since become absurd.[7]

Heidegger concluded that the solution to this global spiritual crisis lay in the hands of Germany, "the most metaphysical of nations." He announced that "this nation [*Volk*: people], as a historical nation, must move itself and thereby the history of the West . . . into the primordial realm of the powers of being" (IM, 38). Hence Heidegger's nationalism was profoundly philosophical and metaphysical. He believed that the German people's unique "spirituality"—their rootedness in the German language and German intellectual tradition—could provide the "spiritual energy" to lead Europe beyond the impasses of communism and capitalism by which it was threatened on both sides. Perversely, he believed that national socialism represented just such a renaissance of German spirit, the best chance of combating forces of alienation and modernization that had set Europe on the path to ruin.

However deluded Heidegger's views may appear to us today, it should be recalled that his presentiment of global decline was shared by many Germans of the time because Germany in the 1920s and early 1930s was subject to constant social upheaval, political unrest, and economic uncertainty. After the shock and humiliation of defeat in World War I and the reparations exacted by the Versailles Treaty, many Germans regard the fledgling Weimar government (a parliamentary democracy) as weak and ineffectual. In a wave of industrialization accelerated by the war, workers from the countryside flocked to the cities, and traditional rural life was disrupted. Communism remained an ongoing threat as the Russian Revolution risked being exported to the West. Conservatives hoped that a return to authoritarian governance could produce a stronger, united Germany. Perhaps, some thought, coming to the brink of the abyss could provoke a "rebirth" of German greatness.

The word "crisis" was thus frequently on the lips of the writers and demagogues of the period. The best known of these, Oswald Spengler, author of the best-selling *The Decline of the West*, warned that the conditions in Germany represented the epicenter of a "world-historical" crisis that signaled the end of Western civilization. The First World War, Spengler announced, had been "only the first lightning and thunder from the cloud passing across our century heavy with destiny. The form of the world is being recreated from the ground up."[8] While the details of Spengler's loosely Hegelian argument were criticized by German historians and philosophers, including Heidegger, his perception that a worldwide crisis was at hand was widely accepted; Spengler's diagnosis became more plausible after Germany entered the Great Depression in 1930. Other influential voices included the reactionary jurist and political theorist Carl Schmitt, who as a successful university professor defended the need for authoritarian dictatorship to achieve national strength and unity. (Schmitt went on to become the chief legal theorist of the Nazi regime.) Ernst Jünger, a highly decorated World War I veteran, described the quasi-religious experience of the soldier immersed in battle. In his widely read book *The Worker*, Jünger heralded an age of "total mobilization" in which the forces of mass technological society (communism in the East, capitalism in the West) would wage a struggle for world domination, and the individual, subsumed within the mass, would be forged into a new human "type," a selfless worker-soldier.

Given his conservative background and temperament, Heidegger was susceptible to such nihilistic prognoses. Raised in a small rural town in a conservative Catholic family of humble means, he disliked the anonymous hustle and bustle of big cities and, it seems, longed for a return to preindustrial forms of life. At heart, Heidegger was antimodern and antidemocratic—he distrusted the factionalism of modern politics and envisioned Germany as a single, cooperative society unified around shared customs, character, and intellectual traditions. For these reasons, it is not hard to imagine why the symbolism of National Socialism in the early 1930s, in particular its appeal to the value of work, cooperation, and natural living, and its rejection of alienated urban life, would have been compelling for him.

PHENOMENOLOGY AND
FRENCH PHILOSOPHY OF EXISTENCE

Another species of 20th-century German philosophy, phenomenology, was of immense importance for the development of 20th-century existentialism. Without it, in fact, neither Heidegger, nor Sartre, nor Merleau-Ponty would have arrived at their mature philosophical positions. Phenomenology was a philosophy of human consciousness developed by Edmund Husserl, a German philosopher trained in mathematics and logic. Husserl conceived phenomenology as a method for the description of consciousness that resisted the reduction of the mind to physiological or material causes, a prime goal of 19th-century materialist science. By attending carefully to the process by which things become meaningful for human beings, Husserl believed it possible to identify invariant "essences" or essential patterns that govern all types of human awareness. Such essences, he surmised, provide a necessary and universal foundation for the activity of any human consciousness whatsoever. Hence the various modes of consciousness by which humans relate to the world—thinking, perceiving, imagining, remembering, feeling, and so forth—cannot be reduced to merely subjective processes within the individual mind or brain; they admit of an invariant universal structure, true for all human subjects at all times. Husserl thus saw phenomenology as a "rigorous" "foundational science" that, in describing the essential structures of consciousness, would clarify the basis of all human knowledge.

For young French philosophers in the 1930s, Husserlian phenomenology held out a further ideal: the promise of a return to "concrete existence." Phenomenology was understood to offer a mode of access to
the world not mediated by theoretical constructions, a manner of directly *describing* experience in its variety and richness rather than explaining it on the basis of suspect metaphysical postulates. In 1932,
when Sartre learned from his friend Raymond Aron that a phenomenologist could philosophize about an apricot cocktail or a glass of beer, he
"turned pale with emotion" because this was precisely the concrete approach to philosophy he was looking for. Sartre's early philosophical
work on imagination, emotion, and consciousness, though it diverged
significantly from Husserl in several respects, was conducted under the
aegis of Husserlian phenomenology. Merleau-Ponty immersed himself
in the study of Husserl's unpublished manuscripts during World War II,
leading to the formulation of his mature views in *Phenomenology of
Perception* (1945).

Thus, in the concrete existential setting of France in the 1930s, as in
Germany in the 1920s, Husserl's rationalist, ahistorical phenomenology
was transformed into *existential* phenomenology: an exploration of the
world as it is disclosed in emotional, practical, and social experience, not
merely of the "essences" that ostensibly govern this disclosure. Heidegger's *Being and Time* was the principal model for this transformation,
and Husserl's phenomenology was often perceived through the lens of
Heidegger's philosophy of existence.[9] Other key factors were the
philosophies of Hegel and Kierkegaard, which entered French thought at
this time through the work of philosophers like Jean Wahl, **Jean Hyppolite**, Gabriel Marcel, and **Alexandre Kojève**. In addition, the writings
of Nietzsche and of the German phenomenologist Max Scheler were also
influential among the vanguard of Parisian intellectuals.

In this way, prior to the emergence of "existentialism," Sartre, Beauvoir, and Merleau-Ponty came to maturity in an atmosphere of existential thought. Like the Germans who inspired them, French philosophers
of existence championed a return to personal, historical human existence as a corrective to academic abstraction. At the same time, they developed a distinctive focus on embodiment and interpersonal relations,
which was continued in the later work of Sartre, Beauvoir, and Merleau-
Ponty. A further important difference was the significance of Marxism
for French intellectual of the day. After World War II, Marxist philoso-

phy played an important role in Sartre and Merleau-Ponty's development, and, in the 1950s, in the subsequent dissolution of existentialism in France.

SARTRE AND THE FRENCH EXISTENTIALIST MOVEMENT

The term *existentialism* first gained currency as a label for Sartre's philosophy in the politically charged atmosphere of France following the Liberation of Paris in August 1944. With the successful production of two plays, renewed interest in his prewar fiction, and publication of a philosophical tome, *Being and Nothingness*, Sartre had become a minor celebrity in Paris during the German occupation. Sartre's popularity raised the concerns of the French Communist Party, which perceived existentialism as a threat to the hegemony of Soviet ideology among French youth. Attacked by the communist press,[10] Sartre responded on 29 December 1944 in an article published in the communist newspaper *Action,* entitled "Concerning Existentialism: A Clarification" ("*A Propos de l'existentialisme: mise au point*"), in which he affirmed his commitment to "class struggle" and rejected the accusation that existentialist philosophy was an expression of decadent Western individualism and "idealism." Like many French intellectuals of the day, Sartre had discovered Marxism and was uncomfortable being portrayed as the leader of a movement that opposed it. He firmly resisted the existentialist label that had been pinned on him. As late as August 1945, Simone de Beauvoir recalled in her memoirs, "Sartre had refused to allow Gabriel Marcel to apply [the existentialist] adjective to him: 'My philosophy is a philosophy of existence; I don't even know what Existentialism is'."[11] The new term had been minted with pejorative intent; it suggested a monolithic system where none existed. Moreover, it stirred associations with other subversive "isms" of the day—communism, socialism, fascism, surrealism—that risked misrepresenting Sartre's ideas.

Everything changed in the autumn of 1945. Autumn is the time of year the French call *la rentrée*, the annual return from summer vacation, when life in Paris starts once again. The *rentrée* of 1945 was exceptional in that it was France's first experience of freedom after four years of German occupation. Dozens of new newspapers and journals appeared; new political parties were formed and vied for power; and the

French press, unrestrained by German censors, hungered after stories to report. In this atmosphere of uncertainty and excitement, Beauvoir and Sartre came to understand that "existentialism" could be an asset and not just a liability; they decided to embrace the term and "use it" for their "own purposes." These purposes had been suggested in *Being and Nothingness*, but the book, at over 600 pages and written in dense, technical language, found few readers when published in 1943. The goals of existentialism were more clearly conveyed through Sartre and Beauvoir's novels and plays and through articles and editorials published in their journal, *Les temps modernes*. Within the span of only one month in the fall of 1945, the first two novels of Sartre's *Roads to Freedom* trilogy, Beauvoir's novel *The Blood of Others*, and the first issue of *Les temps modernes* announced to the public Sartre's existentialist agenda. Existentialism was a philosophy of radical individual freedom, responsibility, and social commitment; it sought to expose the hypocrisy of traditional, "serious" values and to replace them with a doctrine of individual choice and creation. By compelling people to confront their "duplicities" and to "assume responsibility" for themselves "without excuses," Sartre and Beauvoir would seek to make French society more free.

A decisive event was Sartre's public lecture of 29 October 1945, entitled "Existentialism Is a Humanism." In direct language Sartre set forth the tenets of his position and defended existentialism from both conservative Catholic and communist critics. In the process, he advanced a pithy formula, the claim that "existence precedes essence," which became existentialism's most famous definition. When the lecture was published as a short book, it sold thousands of copies and was quickly translated into several languages. While Sartre regretted the book's hasty formulations, he accepted the recognition it brought. At this moment the "existentialist era" was born.

In the lecture, Sartre underlined an ideal of existential "honesty" or "authenticity" derived from Heidegger and from Kierkegaard. He observed that existence is suffused with "anguish" (*angoisse*, anxiety) over the responsibility we must assume for our freedom. Anxiety, in turn, along with the freedom and responsibility it heralds, may be embraced with "honesty" or, more commonly, it may be denied and "fled from" with "dishonesty." Existential dishonesty consists in acting as if one were determined by circumstances or by one's emotions, or as if one's choices were ordained by preexisting values. Existential honesty consists in acting in full awareness of one's freedom to create value and meaning without reference to external authority. Moreover, Sartre insisted, it requires the realization that one's freedom "depends entirely on the freedom of others, and that the freedom of others depends on ours."[12]

Sartre's picture of existence—responsible yet free, obligated to others yet concerned with self, "anguished" yet optimistic and creative—was meant to appeal to the "European of 1945," whom he invoked in the lecture. It announced to French men and women morally and physically compromised by the events of the war that the past does not determine the present, because the present is continually being remade through human choice and action. It stressed taking responsibility for the past but at the same time held open the possibility of future renewal. In Sartre's hands, existentialism was a reminder that human life is an ongoing project of self-creation, not a performance of preexisting roles or a repetition of the past.

In the wake of Sartre's notoriety, popular images of existentialism spread through European and American culture. The sculptures of Alberto Giacometti, the plays of Samuel Beckett and Eugene Ionesco, even, some said, the works of the American abstract expressionist painters, evinced an "existentialist ethos" of alienation, anxiety, and absurdity. Camus's novel *The Stranger* became a classic of "existentialist fiction." At the start of the Cold War, the idea of the forlorn, heroic individual confronting a meaningless world captured the spirit of the times, regardless of its philosophical accuracy.

A parallel, sensationalized image of existentialism as a bohemian fad was constructed by the Parisian press. As Beauvoir recalled:

> The Existentialist label had been applied to all our books—even our pre-war ones—and to those of our friends . . . also to a certain style of painting and a certain sort of music. Anne-Marie Cazalis had the idea of profiting from this vogue . . . she baptized . . . the young people who prowled between the Tabou and Pergola, as Existentialists.[13]

According to this myth, existentialists were frivolous hipsters who loved to drink and to jitterbug in the *caves* of Saint-Germain-des-Prés. Sartre and Beauvoir were the "High Priest" and "Priestess" of Existentialism, frequenting the bars and cafés and holding forth during drunken orgies. The grain of truth in these stories was that Sartre and Beauvoir did live in the neighborhood of Saint-Germain, and they did befriend some of the self-appointed "existentialists," notably the actress and singer Juliette Gréco. Beauvoir later lamented that the image of bohemian decadence was used by Sartre's enemies to discredit him: "What confidence could one have in a philosopher whose teachings inspired orgies . . . whose disciples lived for nothing more than having a good time?"[14]

Sartre's fame rose precipitously throughout the late 1940s and early 1950s and with it the notoriety of existentialism. To the French Communist Party, controlled directly by Moscow, Sartre remained a dangerous Western decadent. To mainstream Catholic critics, he was a corruptor of Gallic youth. In 1948, Sartre's works were placed on the List of Forbidden Books by the Vatican; in 1950, Pope Pius XII issued an encyclical identifying existentialism as one of the "false opinions threatening to undermine the foundations of Catholic doctrine."[15] The end of the French existentialist era was signaled in the early 1950s when Sartre became increasingly involved with political polemics concerning Marxism and communism, and he broke off relations with Merleau-Ponty and with Camus over political differences.

EXISTENTIALISM IN THE WAKE OF SARTRE

Despite his intention of speaking for all existentialists, Sartre's definition of existentialism remained a definition of *Sartre's* existentialism. It admirably translated core tenets of Sartre's own perspective—the primacy of individual freedom and responsibility, the importance of action and involvement, the frequency of self-deception—into nontechnical language. Yet it did not always reflect the views of the other existentialists whom Sartre claimed to represent. In the end, Sartre's emphasis on creation and self-creation, choice as the source of value, and "the complete arbitrariness and complete freedom . . . of existence" in a world without God,[16] by the same token that it may have attracted the average European of 1945, alienated other philosophers of existence, prompting them, as well as many commentators, to reassess the meaning of existentialism.[17]

The most momentous repudiation of existentialism prompted by Sartre's lecture was Martin Heidegger's 1947 *Letter on Humanism*.[18] To gauge the import of this repudiation, one must recall that Heidegger was considered by Sartre and by other French thinkers to be the father of 20th-century existentialist philosophy. Some, like the French phenomenologist Emmanuel Levinas, even went so far as to claim that Heidegger was in fact "the only true existentialist."[19]

Following the publication of *Existentialism Is a Humanism* in 1946 and in response to questions posed by French philosopher **Jean Beaufret**, Heidegger published a 50-page text in which he denied any connection between his own thought and that of Sartre.[20] According to Heidegger, while Sartre places the human subject at the creative center of the world to the exclusion of any extra-human dimension, his own thought casts humans in a receptive and responsive relationship with thought, language, and tradition, with the "Being" that "claims" us:

> Man does not decide whether and how beings appear, whether and how God and the gods or history and nature come forward into the lighting of Being. . . . The advent of beings lies in the destiny of Being. . . . Man is the shepherd of Being.[21]

Sartre's "humanism," in turn, remained for Heidegger a classical "metaphysics of the subject," exalting the powers of the human being to know, act upon, create, and control an encompassing reality. In Heidegger's view, true humanism would have to begin by rethinking the meaning of the human being not as the subject of action and thought, ranging over a world of external objects, but rather as an "openness to Being." This Heidegger now calls **"ek-sistence,"** an attentive and receptive "standing in the lighting of Being."

It would be hasty to conclude, as have some commentators, that Heidegger's rejection of Sartre's existentialism can be taken as proof that Heidegger was not an existentialist. For one thing, the *Letter on Humanism* was written in 1947, 20 years after the publication of *Being and Time*, Heidegger's major existentialist work. As his postwar judgment clearly reflects a shift in philosophical outlook, it should not be taken as authoritative in regard to his earlier work. What is more, Heidegger's assessment of Sartre and of the disparity between their philosophies may not always be accurate. Sartre's account of consciousness in *Being and Nothingness*, for example, may be made out to be consistent with Heidegger's notion of being-in-the-world.

Nonetheless, Heidegger's *Letter on Humanism* did reinforce the assumption that existentialism was primarily Sartre's creation and was to be judged on Sartre's terms. This idea was confirmed by a series of defections subsequent to 1945 by many notable writers associated with existentialism. Albert Camus, closely allied with Sartre in the minds of critics and whose literary reputation rivaled Sartre's after the war, adamantly rejected the existentialist label. In Germany, Karl Jaspers felt that Sartre's existentialism marked the death of true philosophy of existence, of which he counted himself the prime representative.[22] In similar fashion, in France the Catholic philosopher Gabriel Marcel became a staunch critic of Sartre's philosophy, especially for his atheism and his overemphasis on individual choice. At the same time, Marcel claimed that he himself had "first formulated" "the main lines of this new [existentialist] development" in France, starting in 1925.[23]

Maurice Merleau-Ponty, whose philosophical background and perspective closely resembled Sartre's, and who served as political editor and coeditor in chief at *Les Temps modernes,* was hesitant to associate his name with Sartre's. Merleau-Ponty chose not to have his name appear on the journal's masthead and signed his articles with the initials "T.M." Though his philosophy was a close cousin to Sartre's in many respects, he, too, was ambivalent about the existentialist label. Like Heidegger, he questioned Sartre's emphasis on the absolute character of individual freedom and choice. Do not freedom and choice presuppose a background of cultural and historical meaning that is effective precisely because it is *not* chosen? If the human being is truly "thrown" into time, can it ever fully extricate itself from history? Merleau-Ponty thus preferred to characterize the postwar period of French existentialism as continuous with the "philosophy of existence" that had begun in France in the 1930s. In his assessment, Marcel, Husserl, Heidegger, and Jaspers were necessary precursors to Sartre's existentialism as well as to his own thought, and both he and Sartre could be properly understood only with reference to their prior accomplishments.[24]

The cycle of repudiations was completed toward the end of the 1950s when Sartre himself broke ranks with his former identity:

> I do not like to talk about existentialism. It is the nature of an intellectual quest to be undefined. To name it and define it is to wrap it up and tie the

knot. What is left? A finished, already outmoded mode of culture, something like a brand of soap—in other words an idea.[25]

Sartre's disparaging remarks are to be placed in the context of his later affiliation with Marxism. The "idea" of existentialism, while it had functioned in part as a marketing tool—one that aided his popular success—was not reducible to its media "packaging." Its substance was the philosophy of radical individual freedom and responsibility he had derived from his reading of Heidegger. Despite his misgivings, this remained Sartre's major contribution to 20th-century thought.

EXISTENTIALISM TODAY

The prospects for existentialism today are more sanguine than Sartre had predicted in 1960. An introductory course in existentialism is offered by many philosophy as well as literature and foreign language departments to undergraduates across the United States, while advanced classes in existentialist philosophy are taught in many American philosophy graduate programs. The Society for Phenomenology and Existential Philosophy, founded in 1962, retains a sizable membership among American philosophers. Heidegger, Sartre, and Merleau-Ponty have philosophical societies dedicated to them in the Unites States.

Individual studies of the thought of Heidegger, Jaspers, Beauvoir, Sartre, Merleau-Ponty, and other philosophers associated with existentialism increased markedly throughout the 1980s and 1990s. Today, there is a voluminous literature on each of the major existentialists. Preparing the way for these were the English translations of *Being and Time* in 1962 and *Being and Nothingness* in 1965. A host of important posthumous texts by Sartre and Heidegger have also appeared in English in recent years, shedding new light on the development and substance of existentialist philosophy. These include Sartre's *War Diaries* (1984) and *Notebook for an Ethics* (1992) and Heidegger's *The Basic Problems of Phenomenology* (1982), *Kant and the Problem of Metaphysics* (1990), and *The Fundamental Concepts of Metaphysics* (1995). In addition, a complete translation of Heidegger's writings, including dozens of his university lecture courses, has been underway since 1976. It is expected to fill 100 volumes.[26]

General studies of existentialism have nonetheless been rare since the early 1970s. A happy exception is David E. Cooper's *Existentialism: A Reconstruction*, first published in 1990.[27] Cooper's book has helped rekindle interest in the general problematic of existentialist philosophy. Following the path forged by earlier commentators like Frederick Olafson and John Macquarrie,[28] Cooper synthesized the views of Heidegger, Sartre, Merleau-Ponty, and other existentialists into a single "rational reconstruction" of the existentialist viewpoint. By avoiding the temptation, to which many critics have succumbed, of devoting individual chapters to each existentialist and thus losing sight of the forest for the trees, Cooper succeeded in presenting a picture of existentialism as a "coherent, definable philosophy—no less, though perhaps no more, homogenous than logical positivism or . . . pragmatism."[29] To this end, one of the book's most important contributions was its spirited defense of Sartre and Heidegger as complementary rather than opposed in their conceptions of human existence.

As British philosophers have traditionally held existentialism in low esteem, it is instructive to recall that Cooper's book would have been unthinkable in Great Britain only 30 or 40 years ago. Today, the British attitude toward continental philosophers like Heidegger, Nietzsche, Sartre, and Merleau-Ponty has improved dramatically, and there appears to be growing interest in the issues of existential phenomenology, though still considerably less than in the United States. In Canada, philosophers like Charles Taylor have helped to kindle interest in existentialist thought. Taylor has succeeded in incorporating ideas from Heidegger, Sartre, and Merleau-Ponty and developing them in the context of his own philosophy. His work on ethics and on the formation of the self has been particularly influential. American philosophers who have recently helped to refocus attention on the philosophical claims of existentialism include Stanley Cavell, Hubert Dreyfus, Charles Guignon, Richard Rorty, and Robert Solomon.[30]

In France today, the existentialism of Sartre, Beauvoir, and Merleau-Ponty is treated somewhat as a philosophical dinosaur. It continues to be overshadowed by the philosophy of Heidegger, who, as noted above, is generally not placed in the existentialist category but is treated as a thinker sui generis. Virtually every major French thinker associated with poststructuralism and postmodernism over the past 30 to 40 years has expressed his or her debt to Heidegger in some fashion, as well as to the thought of Friedrich Nietzsche. In Germany, interest in Heidegger's philosophy remains high, though, as in France, he is generally not regarded as an existentialist. **Jürgen Habermas**, the greatest living German philosopher, has been a formidable critic of Heideggerean existentialism. Generally, however, Heidegger is accepted as the major German philosopher of the 20th century, whose stature, many believe, rivals that of Fichte, **Schelling**, or Hegel.

The influence of existentialist philosophy continues to be felt in other parts of the world as well, particularly in Japan and Latin America. In universities throughout Latin America, the philosophy of Heidegger, Sartre, and José Ortega y Gasset is broadly influential, and existentialism and phenomenology are accepted as mainstream philosophical paradigms. In Japan, philosophers have been conversant with the thought of Nietzsche, Heidegger, Sartre, and Merleau-Ponty since the 1950s. Following in the path of thinkers like **Keiji Nishitani**, philosophers continue to explore the relationship between traditional Asian thought and existentialism, facilitating communication and exchange between Eastern and Western philosophical traditions.

NOTES

1. Paul Tillich, *The Courage to Be* (New Haven: Yale University Press, 1952), 143.

2. "Existentialism," in *The Encyclopedia of Philosophy*, Volume 3, ed. Paul Edwards, 147 (New York: Macmillan, 1967).

3. Published as "Comments on Karl Jaspers's Psychology of Worldviews," trans. John van Buren, in Martin Heidegger, *Pathmarks*, ed. William McNeill (Cambridge: Cambridge University Press, 1998), 1–38.

4. Cited in Julian Young, *Heidegger, Philosophy, Nazism* (Cambridge: Cambridge University Press, 1997), 17.

5. A list of these publications is given in the bibliography.

6. For a detailed defense of this position, see Young, *Heidegger, Philosophy, Nazism*.

7. Heidegger, *An Introduction to Metaphysics*, trans. Ralph Manheim (New Haven: Yale University Press, 1959), 38.

8. Cited in Hans Sluga, *Heidegger's Crisis: Philosophy and Politics in Nazi Germany* (Cambridge, Mass.: Harvard University Press, 1993), 55.

9. See, e.g., Emmanuel Levinas, *The Theory of Intuition in Husserl's Phenomenology*, trans. André Orianne (Evanston, Ill.: Northwestern University

Press, 1998; first published 1930). Levinas's book played a decisive role in introducing Sartre to phenomenology. Because Heidegger was still known as Husserl's student, their perspectives were not always clearly distinguished at the time.

10. See, e.g., the criticisms of Henri Lefebvre, a Marxist sociologist, in *Action* (June 8, 1945).

11. Simone de Beauvoir, *Force of Circumstance,* trans. Richard Howard (New York: G. P. Putnam's Sons, 1964), 38. Gabriel Marcel may have been the first to coin the term "existentialism" as a label for Sartre's philosophy, sometime after the publication of *Being and Nothingness* in 1943.

12. Jean-Paul Sartre, "Existentialism," in *Existentialism and Human Emotions*, trans. Bernard Frechtman (New York: Philosophical Library, 1957), 46.

13. Beauvoir, *Force of Circumstance*, 141.

14. Beauvoir, *Force of Circumstance*, 142. Beauvoir's worst fears were confirmed by the 1957 Hollywood movie musical *Funny Face*, in which, in Paris for a fashion shoot, Audrey Hepburn falls under the spell of the sex-crazed "Émile Flostre," the founder of "empathicalism."

15. *Humani Generis* (August 12, 1950).

16. Sartre, "Existentialism" in *Existentialism and Human Emotions*, 46. Sartre's atheism is asserted throughout.

17. Sartre's views nonetheless continue to leave their mark on dictionary definitions of existentialism. A case in point is *The Oxford English Dictionary On-line,* which defines existentialism as follows: "A doctrine that concentrates on . . . the individual, who, being free and responsible, is held to be what he makes himself by the self-development of his essence through acts of the will . . ." (http://dictionary.oed.com/).

18. Published in Martin Heidegger, *Basic Writings*, ed. David Farrell Krell (San Francisco: Harper Collins, 1993), 190–242.

19. Levinas made this claim in a 1946 roundtable discussion about the meaning of existentialism that is reproduced in Jean Wahl, *A Short History of Existentialism*, trans. Forrest Williams and Stanley Maron (New York: Philosophical Library, 1949), 48.

20. In the lecture, Sartre had declared Heidegger and himself to belong to the same camp of "atheistic" existentialism (*Existentialism and Human Emotions*, 13).

21. Heidegger, *Basic Writings*, 234.

22. Cited in Jean Wahl, *A Short History of Existentialism*, 2. Jaspers made the claim that, "Viewed historically . . . my *Psychology of World Views* is the first work of what later came to be called modern existentialism." Jaspers, "Philosophical Memoir" in *Philosophy and the World*, trans. E. B. Ashton (Washington: Regnery Gateway, 1963), 221.

23. Gabriel Marcel, *The Philosophy of Existentialism* (New York: Citadel Press, 1984), 5.

24. See Merleau-Ponty, "The Philosophy of Existence," in *The Debate Between Sartre and Merleau-Ponty*, ed. Jon Stewart (Evanston, Ill.: Northwestern University Press, 1998).

25. Jean-Paul Sartre, Preface, *Search for a Method*, trans. Hazel E. Barnes (New York: Vintage Books, 1968), xxxiii. By the late 1950s Sartre's philosophical concerns had shifted to political and sociological problems, specifically, the task of reconciling existentialism and Marxism, attempted in *Critique of Dialectical Reason* (1960).

26. *Martin Heidegger: Gesamtausgabe*, ed. F. W. von Herrmann (Frankfurt-on-Main: Klostermann, 1977).

27. David E. Cooper, *Existentialism: A Reconstruction*. 2nd ed. (Oxford: Blackwell Publishers, 1999).

28. Frederick Olafson, *Principles and Persons: An Ethical Interpretation of Existentialism* (Baltimore: Johns Hopkins Press, 1967); John Macquarrie, *Existentialism* (Philadelphia: Westminster Press, 1972).

29. Cooper, *Existentialism*, 6.

30. Relevant works by these authors are listed in the bibliography.

The Dictionary

– A –

ABBAGNANO, NICOLA (1901–1990). Italian philosopher and leading proponent of **Italian existentialism**. Abbagnano's existentialist philosophy focused on a critical analysis of the concept of possibility. In his early thought, he was influenced by American **pragmatism**, especially the work of John Dewey, and was critical of the philosophical idealism of Giovanni Gentile and Benedetto Croce, which dominated Italian philosophy at the time. In the 1930s, he discovered the existentialism of **Martin Heidegger, Søren Kierkegaard, Karl Jaspers,** and **Gabriel Marcel,** as well as the **phenomenology** of **Edmund Husserl**; after **World War II** he encountered the work of **Albert Camus** and **Jean-Paul Sartre**. On this basis he proposed a synthesis and critique of European existentialism in a series of books—*La Struttura dell'esistenza* (*The Structure of Existence*), 1939; *Introduzione all'esistenzialismo* (*Introduction to Existentialism*), 1942; and *Esistenzialismo positivo* (*Positive Existentialism*), 1948—which brought European existentialism to the attention of Italian philosophers.

The focus of Abbagnano's critique was what he perceived to be a repeated misuse of the concept of possibility. While the centrality of possibility is recognized by Jaspers, Heidegger, Sartre, and Camus, the essential indeterminacy, uncertainty, and problematic nature of true existential possibility is, he claimed, ultimately lost in their respective accounts of human **existence**. In the case of Jaspers and Heidegger, he argued that human existence is understood in terms of an *inevitable* failure of human **projects**: for example, the failure to attain **transcendent** knowledge, or the failure to live **authentically**. Thus, the idea of possibility tends to be reduced to that of *impossibility*.

In the case of **Christian** existentialists like Marcel, he maintained that existence is understood in terms of the inevitable *success* of human endeavors, since those possibilities understood as most authentic, such as the quest for love or moral value, are guaranteed by God, who has the power to realize them. Here Abbagnano maintained that the idea of possibility is conflated with that of *potentiality,* in that existence becomes a natural development of preexisting dispositions. True existential possibility, in contrast, must be understood in terms of a *situation* that both limits and establishes **choices** for **action**; an authentically *possible* choice must be **freely** made and yet uncertain—neither guaranteed to succeed nor guaranteed to fail. Moreover, a normative criterion termed "transcendental possibility" must be fulfilled: the possibility must continue to "remain possible"; that is, a chosen course of action must be sustainable and allow for future growth in the same direction.

ABRAHAM. For **Søren Kierkegaard**, the biblical story of Abraham and Isaac (Genesis 22) exemplifies the **absurd** nature of **authentic** religious **faith**. Abraham is ordered by God to sacrifice his only son, Isaac, and he is set to obey God's command when an angel intervenes to stop him. Kierkegaard's interpretation of the story, given in *Fear and Trembling*, is that Abraham's willingness to obey God's command demonstrates a type of suprarational **commitment** essential to faith. Abraham shows that a "**teleological suspension of the ethical**" is possible for his act that cannot be justified according to shared **ethical** norms: The nature of his decision remains irreducibly personal and cannot be communicated to others. Put another way, Abraham illustrates how faith must be understood as issuing from individual conscience rather than from adherence to general rules or principles. While Abraham's faith is not the result of rational deliberation, it is important for Kierkegaard that it not be understood simply as the result of an act of will: Abraham's faith depends as much on God's grace as on Abraham's intentions. In this sense, Abraham is not presented as a model to be understood, let alone emulated, but as a "wonder," beyond comprehension. Kierkegaard's treatment of Abraham is intended in various ways to oppose the rationalist **metaphysics** of **G. W. F. Hegel**, according to which faith can be rationally articulated and justified. As Kierkegaard observes, "Abraham had faith . . . by virtue of the absurd, for all human calculation ceased long ago" (FT, 36). *See also* KNIGHT OF FAITH AND KNIGHT OF INFINITE RESIGNATION.

ABSTRACT EXPRESSIONISM. Movement in American painting that flourished in the 1950s in and around New York City, emphasizing the spontaneous creation of abstract forms and patterns. Abstract expressionism was sometimes associated with existentialism, though there is little to suggest any substantive link between the endeavors. The critic Harold Rosenberg used existentialist-flavored vocabulary to describe abstract expressionist painting, which he named "action painting." In action painting, he wrote, the canvas becomes "an arena in which to act" rather than a "space in which to reproduce, re-design, analyze, or 'express' an object, real or imagined." What appears on the canvas is thus "not a picture but an event," the record of an "encounter" between painter and canvas, which is "genuine" when it preserves the "dialectical tension" ingredient in its creation. The genuine work of the action painter involves "risk," "will," and "decision" (*The Tradition of the New*, 25, 32). Leading abstract expressionist painters included Willem de Kooning, Jackson Pollock, Lee Krasner, Clifford Still, Robert Motherwell, Mark Rothko, and Barnett Newmann.

ABSURD, THE. The concept of the absurd in existentialism admits of two distinct lines of interpretation. One account, developed primarily in **existentialist literature**, understands by *the absurd* a sense of the radical **contingency** of all things that exist: the sense that everything might be otherwise than it is because there is no ultimate plan or purpose according to which things might be justified. The other, more explicitly philosophical conception of absurdity is limited to **actions** and **choices** of human beings. These are said to be absurd to the extent that, as they issue from human **freedom**, they lack a foundation outside of themselves. The latter view of absurdity was first elaborated by **Søren Kierkegaard** in the context of **Christianity**, and was developed diversely by **Martin Heidegger** and **Jean-Paul Sartre**. A literary **understanding** of the absurd was expressed by Sartre in his first novel, *Nausea*, and explored by **Albert Camus** in his extended "essay on the absurd," *The Myth of Sisyphus*.

In its literary guise, the absurd is tied to an experience of radical contingency in which the **world**, myself, and the universe as a whole reveal themselves as lacking intrinsic meaning or purpose, as "superfluous" or "gratuitous" in the sense that they could just as well *not* exist. Roquentin, the protagonist of Sartre's *Nausea*, describes such an experience in which the linguistic veneer of things is peeled away to reveal their brute physical "existence": "[M]ounting up as high as the sky, spilling over . . . I could see . . . as far the eye could reach. . . . I knew it was the world, the naked World suddenly revealing itself . . . this gross, absurd being . . . . It didn't make sense" (*Nausea*, 134). Camus's account of the absurd also underlines the experience of the physical world as alien or "inhuman": "[A] stone is foreign and irreducible to us. . . . At the heart of all beauty lies something inhuman . . . that denseness and that strangeness of the world is the absurd" (MS, 14).

A distinct conception of absurdity grounded in the problematic of existential **freedom** and choice was first articulated by Kierkegaard. In regard to **faith**, Kierkegaard specifies the absurd in terms of the "crucifixion of the understanding" effected by the **Christian** belief that God has become incarnate in human form, for it is not rationally comprehensible how the eternal could enter into time. Kierkegaard stresses that the **authenticity** of this belief is lost once probable reasons and arguments for it are adduced; it becomes a matter of rational calculation rather than passionate **commitment**. A related sense of absurdity in Kierkegaard is illustrated by the biblical story of **Abraham**. Abraham is considered the father of faith precisely because he is willing to follow God's command to sacrifice his son despite the fact that it is contrary to his personal desire and to the moral law. Abraham's ability to maintain two contradictory beliefs—that he must sacrifice Isaac and yet that Isaac will not be lost—is evidence for Kierkegaard of his genuine religious faith. He submits to God's command at the same time that he believes he will win Isaac back "by virtue of the absurd," that is, by virtue of his belief in God's infinite love and wisdom, a belief that cannot be rationally justified. Kierkegaard's understanding of the absurd thus places the standard pejorative meaning of the terms "ridiculous" or "nonsensical" in a positive light. The absurd reveals the limits of objective reason and expresses the tension-ridden nature of authentic selfhood.

In *Being and Nothingness*, Sartre employs the absurd in a sense that harkens back to Kierkegaard's idea of commitment to a belief or cause without rational foundation. **Freedom**, the choice I make of myself through my "fundamental **project**," is absurd, Sartre writes, because it is "made without base of support and dictating its own causes to itself . . . . This is because freedom is a *choice* of its being but not the *foundation* of its being" (BN, 479). Freedom requires choosing between alternatives within the limits of one's **situation**; but at the same time one cannot justify one's choice by reference to an external standard, since standards themselves are meaningful and binding only by the attitude one chooses to take toward them. Thus, Sartre concludes, authentic choice "is lived in the feeling of unjustifiability; and it is this which is expressed by the fact of the *absurdity* of my choice and consequently of my **being**" (BN, 480).

ABSURD, PHILOSOPHY OF THE. *See* PHILOSOPHY OF THE ABSURD.

ABSURD HERO. *See* PHILOSOPHY OF THE ABSURD.

ABYSS. *See* NEGATION/NOTHINGNESS.

ACTION. A voluntary or intentional human behavior, usually but not necessarily the result of conscious **choice** or decision. French existentialists, especially **Jean-Paul Sartre**, tend to regard action as determinative of a person's identity. A person is defined by what he or she does more than by what he or she says, believes, or wishes, and thoughts, wishes, and beliefs often reflect what one would like to be, or to have others believe, more than what one is. Sartre also maintained that behaviors that do not appear to be within conscious control, in the sense that we are normally not aware of choosing them (e.g., **emotions**), are nonetheless actions for which we are responsible. They are, or stem from, basic existential attitudes that each of us chooses to assume. In this view, virtually all human behavior is a form of intentional, though not necessarily self-conscious, action, and all that one does, feels, thinks, or imagines expresses the fundamental **project** one has chosen.

ACTION PAINTING. *See* ABSTRACT EXPRESSIONISM.

ADORNO, THEODOR (1903–1969). German philosopher and a founding member of the **Frankfurt School** of critical theory. Adorno studied at the University of Frankfurt and was active there, along with Max Horkheimer and **Herbert Marcuse**, in the Institute for Social Research (which came to be called "the Frankfurt School") during the late 1920s and early 1930s. In 1934, after the **Nazis**' rise to power, he immigrated to Oxford, and in 1938 to New York. He returned to Frankfurt in the early 1950s and was the director of the revived Institute for Social Research from 1958 to 1969.

Adorno was critical of existentialism at the same time that he shared certain existentialist concerns and influences. Along with **Karl Jaspers** and **Martin Heidegger**, he was critical of the dehumanizing effects of modern technology and sensitive to the dangers of mass movements like Soviet **communism**, which compromised individual **freedom** and **conscience** in the name of obedience to authority. His interest in **Søren Kierkegaard**, expressed in his postdoctoral thesis, "Kierkegaard: Construction of the Aesthetic" (1965), suggested another common denominator. Adorno developed a critique of **Edmund Husserl**'s **phenomenology** in *Against Epistemology: A Metacritique* (1972).

Adorno's main criticism of existentialism was its perceived disregard for social and political realities in favor of a naïve esteem for individual **freedom** and **authenticity**. In *The Jargon of Authenticity* (1965), a highly polemical book, he criticized the obscure language of Heideggerean philosophy as a veil for what he perceived as an antisocial and reactionary politics. Adorno held that Heidegger's philosophy of individual "authenticity" and "**resoluteness**" cannot be divorced from his support for German nationalism, evidenced by his involvement with Nazism in the early 1930s. In an essay entitled "**Commitment**" (*The Essential Frankfurt School Reader*, 300–318), Adorno also criticized **Jean-Paul Sartre**'s conception of **committed literature**. Citing as evidence Sartre's own plays and novels, Adorno maintained that committed writers tend toward a predictable "thesis-art" that expounds ideas in the manner of a philosophical treatise and at the expense of attention to form and style. Thus he concluded that artworks produced out of Sartrean commitment backfire in their intention to awaken their readers's sense of **freedom**. By conforming to established norms rather than calling them into question, committed works encourage readers to preserve the aesthetic, moral, and political status quo. Adorno's major philosophical works include *The Dialectic of Enlightenment* (1947, with Max Horkheimer) and *Negative Dialectics* (1973).

AESTHETIC, THE. *See* KIERKEGAARD, SØREN.

AESTHETICS, EXISTENTIALIST. *See* COMMITTED LITERATURE; POETRY AND PHILOSOPHY.

ALGREN, NELSON (1909–1981). American novelist. Algren was **Simone de Beauvoir**'s lover between 1947 and 1951. Beauvoir and Algren met during her first lecture tour of the United States, and they fell for each other instantly, as "'each was the most exotic thing the other had ever seen'" (Bair, 333). In his native Chicago, Algren introduced his "French school teacher" to the underside of American life: "'I introduced her to stickup men, pimps, baggage thieves, whores and heroin addicts . . . . I took her on a tour of the County Jail and showed her the electric chair'" (Bair 335–336). Beauvoir later described Algren as "'the only true passionate love in my life'" (Bair, 344) and claimed to have mastered English thanks to the 350 love letters she subsequently wrote to him. Algren is memorialized as the character "Lewis Brogan" in Beauvoir's novel *The Mandarins*.

ALIENATION. For existentialists, to be alienated is to be divorced from one's true nature as a human being. In general terms, this means lacking a clear sense of oneself as a "**being** of possibility," that is, a being who is essentially **finite**, **free**, and **responsible**. Gaining such a sense of oneself is tantamount to attaining **authenticity**, while remaining alienated is synonymous with existing "inauthentically," in a manner that is "not one's own." Alienation is thus a central problem of existentialism, and it receives diverse treatment from different existentialists. Generally, the accounts of human **existence** proposed by existentialist philosophers can be understood as attempts to identify the deep sources of alienation and to sketch a vision of authenticity through which it is overcome.

A significant antecedent to the existentialist view was propounded in the 19th century by **G. W. F. Hegel** and **Karl Marx**. However, where Hegel and Marx stressed **historical** conditions of alienation and the circumstances under which these may be overcome, existentialists tend to see alienation as a condition endemic to existence itself. Nonetheless, Hegel and Marx's influence was profound, and their views set the parameters for many existentialist discussions. Marx's account of alienation in *Economic and Philosophical Manuscripts of 1844* was particularly important for **Maurice Merleau-Ponty** and **Jean-Paul Sartre** after **World War II**.

Existentialists generally concur with Hegel and Marx that alienation is a collective and not solely an individual condition, one that affects individuals in and by means of their social setting. At times they describe alienation in terms analogous to those of Marx, as life in a dehumanized world in which people collectively lose sight of their nature as human beings and tend to treat themselves, others, and beings of the natural world as "objects" to be used and manipulated. This they recognize as the world relegated to us by modern science and industrial capitalism. In the words of **Martin Buber**, it is a world of "things and processes . . . bounded by other things and processes and capable of being measured . . . and compared . . . an ordered world, a detached world" (IT, 82). For **Martin Heidegger**, in contrast, modern technology and capitalism are expressions of a deeper **metaphysical** alienation, a turning away from the **mysterious** character of being itself, coincident with the origins of Western philosophy.

A tension within existentialism is the question of whether alienation is to be overcome individually or (also) by collective means. The classic conception of authenticity proposed by Heidegger in *Being and Time* is, on its standard reading, highly individualistic, as it suggests that one must extricate oneself from alienating social conventions and seize hold of life's possibilities on one's own, through a solitary confrontation with **death** and **anxiety**. At the same time, there is an awareness in Heidegger as well as in other existentialists of the interpersonal and social dimensions of authenticity. These are captured in the idea of **reciprocity**, the notion that self-understanding is necessarily bound up with one's understanding of others. The claims of reciprocity do not disburden the individual of the challenge of coming to terms with freedom and finitude. They do, however, add the requirement that freedom cannot be authentically grasped apart from recognition of the freedom of others, and this deepens and complicates the problem of existential alienation.

ALTHUSSER, LOUIS (1918–1990). French political philosopher best known for his "antihumanist" interpretation of **Marxism** that draws on structuralist theory and **Lacanian** psychoanalysis. Althusser taught at the **École Normale Supérieure** in Paris in the 1960s and 1970s. His views became an influential reference point in the wake of the May 1968 student uprisings in Paris. A lifelong **communist**, Althusser developed a critical interpretation of **Karl Marx**'s philosophy that distinguished between early, humanist writings, such as the *Economic and Philosophical Manuscripts of 1844*, and Marx's mature work, especially *Capital*, which, according to Althusser, abandoned a humanist perspective in favor of a more rigorously objective science of social and economic reality. Althusser argued that Marx's theory of dialectical materialism avoids naïve economic determinism by acknowledging a principle of "overdetermination" whereby political and ideological, as well as economic, factors are seen as explanatory of human affairs, each being accorded a degree of autonomy.

Like Claude Lévi-Strauss's structural anthropology and Michel Foucault's "archaeology of knowledge," Althusser's reading of Marx militated against existentialism and **phenomenology**; these were seen as naïve forms of humanism that focused on individual **consciousness** and hence ignored unconscious conditions of behavior and knowledge. Specifically, Althusser rejected the view of individual *praxis* developed by **Jean-Paul Sartre** in *Critique of Dialectical Reason* (1960).

AMBIGUITY. From a traditional standpoint, ambiguity results from a lack of clarity or precision in linguistic expression and is considered a fault to be avoided, as entities are assumed to have one set of properties that exclude opposite or contrary properties: being healthy excludes being sick, being close by excludes being far away, being black excludes being white, and so forth. In contrast, some existentialists recognize a positive sense in which entities, especially human beings, cannot be exclusively described in terms of one or the other of a pair of properties, like activity and passivity, or subjectivity and objectivity, but must be said to participate in both and thus to exist in ambiguity.

Maurice Merleau-Ponty places emphasis on ambiguity as a deep feature of the **world** and of human experience, especially the experience of embodiment. The human **body** for Merleau-Ponty is exemplarily ambiguous: Passive in its reflexes and autonomic responses, at the same time the body plays an active, unifying role in perception, memory, and the use of language and gesture. Furthermore, while my body is experienced by me subjectively, to the point that I tacitly identify myself with it, I also observe it and touch it like an object in the world. For Merleau-Ponty, language and history are also essentially ambiguous. Language is both an external, social form and the immediate expression of subjective thought and experience. History too is ambiguously objective and subjective, for events of the past come to be understood only in light of particular human interpretations, and these in turn influence future events. In the end, Merleau-Ponty understands ambiguity as expressive of a deep **ontological** truth about the world as it bears on human experience, one that is falsified by the (Cartesian) assumption that the world consists of discrete **substances** whose properties may be clearly and univocally enumerated.

In similar fashion **Simone de Beauvoir** points to ambiguity as a defining feature of the human condition. In her analysis in *The Ethics of Ambiguity*, the manner in which humans exist, as suspended between **freedom** and **nature**, mind and matter, self and other, becomes a "tragic ambiguity" only when one of the two poles of existence is denied or suppressed. The ethics of ambiguity require that ambiguity be "assumed" as constitutive of our condition. One consequence of the recognition of ambiguity is an insight into the **reciprocity** of freedom, that is, that "[my] freedom can be achieved only through the freedom of others" (EA, 156).

ANGUISH. *See* ANXIETY.

ANNIHILATE. *See* NEGATION/NOTHINGNESS.

ANTHROPOLOGY. *See* PHILOSOPHICAL ANTHROPOLOGY.

ANXIETY. A central concept of existentialist philosophy, alternately rendered as "dread," as "anguish" (a translation of the French term *angoisse*), or left in the original German as *Angst.* The concept of anxiety receives a range of distinct treatments by different existentialists. Nonetheless, there is general agreement that anxiety is not merely a psychological state that reflects the personality of the individual but an **ontological** or **metaphysical phenomenon** that reveals a deep truth about the nature of human beings. The core of the idea is that anxiety is a reckoning of the self with its essential **freedom** to choose what it shall be, and in the face of its radical **responsibility** for that **choice**. The idea is expressed well by **Jean-Paul Sartre**: "In anxiety I apprehend myself at once as totally free and as not being able to derive the meaning of the world except as coming from myself" (BN, 40).

An existentialist conception of anxiety was first formulated by **Søren Kierkegaard** in *The Concept of Anxiety* (1844). Subsequent accounts by existentialists are variously indebted to Kierkegaard, in particular that of **Martin Heidegger** in *Being and Time*. Heidegger assigns the concept of anxiety a major role in the analysis of *Dasein*, where it is linked to the **possibility** for **authentic** existence. The link between anxiety, freedom, and authenticity established by Heidegger is elaborated in a distinct manner by Sartre in *Being and Nothingness*.

Kierkegaard proposes his view of anxiety in a religious context, where the cause of anxiety is ultimately a concern for the salvation of the soul. Still, his ideas set the parameters for future discussion. *The Concept of Anxiety* is a developmental account of the subjective experience of sin; here Kierkegaard portrays anxiety as emergent in progressive stages of spiritual self-awareness, where the self becomes increasingly conscious of its freedom to choose and to act and of its responsibility for its choices. Underlying the various experiences of anxiety, Kierkegaard writes, is thus a certain "dizziness of freedom" (CA, 61) peculiar to human beings and "not found in the beast" (CA, 42). Kierkegaard establishes several assumptions preserved by later accounts. Anxiety is an index of human freedom, a metaphysically positive phenomenon expressive of a deep truth about human beings, and as such it cannot be reduced to a "negative" **emotion**. Anxiety confirms that the human being lives in a mode of deep-seated existential concern for the self, and not solely as a **knowing subject** or a pleasure-seeking animal.

Heidegger's account of anxiety in *Being and Time* cleaves closely to the Kierkegaardian model in several respects. For Heidegger, anxiety is a "fundamental **mood**" (*Grundstimmung*) that discloses a deep truth about the human being in its relation to the world: "Anxiety discloses Dasein as *being-possible* . . . " That is, anxiety "makes manifest . . . its *being-free for* the freedom of choosing itself and taking hold of itself" (BT, 232). In anxiety, **everyday concerns** and involvements with others, through which an average, standardized understanding of the world is sustained, "sink away," for "[a]nxiety . . . takes away from Dasein the possibility of understanding itself . . . in terms of the 'world' and the way things have been publicly interpreted" (BT, 232). Removed from the tranquilizing interpretations of *das Man*, *Dasein* is forced to confront itself apart from the roles assigned to it by others and so becomes aware of itself as a pure "being of possibility," an "authentic potentiality-for-being-in-the-world." For this reason Heidegger insists that "[a]nxiety **individualizes** Dasein and thus discloses it as '*solus ipse*'" (BT, 233). In other words, in anxiety it is brought home to me that it is *I*, not "they" or "anyone," who am responsible for interpreting the world, and that I cannot avoid the freedom of choosing certain possibilities over others.

What Sartre in *Being and Nothingness* calls "*l'angoisse*" is a conscious development of Heidegger and Kierkegaard's concept of anxiety, and to avoid confusion should be called by the same name. Like Kierkegaard, Sartre defines anxiety as "the consciousness of freedom," and he likens this to an experience of vertigo (*vertige*). Hiking near a precipice, I am seized with anxiety "to the extent that I am afraid not of falling over . . . but of throwing myself over" (BN, 29). Anxiety thus arises from consciousness of radical freedom, which is normally suppressed: No drive to self-preservation or other psychological motive *prevents* me from throwing myself off. In another example, Sartre describes the anxiety of a gambler who, having resolved never to gamble again, passes a gaming table and realizes that nothing prevents him from breaking a promise made in the past. In each case, anxiety is a recognition of the "constantly renewed obligation to remake the Self" (BN, 35). Alternately, it is the realization that the self is, at bottom, radical "nothingness": a lack of substantive causes or content that might provide a foundation for one's choices and **values**.

APOLLONIAN AND DIONYSIAN. The terms of this distinction, introduced by **Friedrich Nietzsche** in his first book, *The Birth of Tragedy Out of the Spirit of Music* (1872), designate antagonistic principles of human **action** and artistic **creation**. According to Nietzsche, the grandeur of ancient Greek tragedy resulted from an exceptional coalition of the two principles. The Apollonian principle represents the drive toward order, reason, and restraint evident in classical Greek sculpture and architecture; the Dionysian principle represents the tendency toward passion, intoxication, and destruction evident in ancient Greek music and ritualistic dance. In Nietzsche's analysis, Dionysian ritual subsumes the individual within the group, while Apollonian art allows individuality to be recognized and to flourish. The genius of classical tragedy, represented by the plays of Aeschylus and Sophocles, was to create an art form combining Apollonian and Dionysian elements in a productive tension. From Plato on, however, Nietzsche maintained, Greek philosophy was premised on a denial of the Dionysian element and as a consequence an unhealthy overestimation of the powers of intellect and reason.

Though existentialists make little explicit reference to Nietzsche's distinction, **Martin Heidegger**'s interpretation of the origins of early Greek philosophy is loosely analogous. In his later thought, Heidegger discerned in the fragmentary texts of pre-Socratic philosophers like Heraclitus and Parmenides an "originary" and "primordial" **understanding** of **being** as emergent, dynamic, and **mysterious**. In Heidegger's view, this understanding deteriorated by the time of Plato, when being was conceived in terms of unchanging "ideas" that underly the changing world of **nature** and sense perception, and are known only by intellection.

ARAGON, LOUIS (1897–1982). French poet and novelist. Originally affiliated with the **surrealists**, Aragon joined the French **Communist** Party in 1927, and from that date on was a staunch supporter of

Joseph Stalin's Soviet Union. With his wife, the Russian-born writer Elsa Triolet (1896–1970), Aragon maintained a literary salon and monitored the French literary scene, encouraging young authors to join the Communist Party. Although **Jean-Paul Sartre** never joined the Party, he remained on friendly terms with Aragon and Triolet.

ARENDT, HANNAH (1906–1975). Jewish German **political** philosopher whose life and thought paralleled and at several points intersected the development of 20th-century existentialism. Arendt was a highly independent scholar who never identified herself with an intellectual movement. Nonetheless, her work can be seen as a creative extension of insights of **existential phenomenology** into the political realm, in particular those of her teacher, **Martin Heidegger**.

Life. Born in **Immanuel Kant**'s hometown of Königsberg, in Eastern Prussia, Arendt studied philosophy with Heidegger and with **Edmund Husserl** before taking her doctoral degree with **Karl Jaspers**, who remained her lifelong friend and mentor. Fleeing **Nazi** persecution, she moved to Paris in 1933 and worked for a Zionist organization. In 1940, she immigrated to the United States, where she remained officially stateless until becoming a U.S. citizen in 1951. She lived and worked in the United States as a journalist and professor of philosophy, at Bard College and at the New School for Social Research, until her **death** in 1975. Her major works, published in English, include, *The Origins of Totalitarianism* (1951), *The Human Condition* (1958), *Between Past and Future* (1961), *Eichmann in Jerusalem* (1965), *On Revolution* (1965), *Men in Dark Times* (1968), and *The Life of the Mind* (1978), a posthumous, incomplete work in two volumes. Arendt was an early commentator on existentialism in the United States. Her articles of interest include "French Existentialism" (1946) and "What Is Existenz Philosophy?" (1946).

A formative period for Arendt began during the 1924–1925 academic year, when she enrolled as a student at Marburg University. Her initial intention was to study theology, which she did briefly with **Rudolph Bultmann**. But soon she was won over to philosophy by the teaching of Martin Heidegger, who enjoyed a reputation as the rising star of the new phenomenological movement centered around Edmund Husserl. Heidegger's lectures on Aristotle and on Plato's *Sophist*, which would become integral parts of *Being and Time*, were perceived as brilliant and difficult. The 18-year-old Arendt was taken by the young professor, and they began a passionate love affair, documented in a series of love letters, which they agreed would be published only after their deaths. Arendt went on to write her doctoral dissertation, "The Concept of Love in Saint Augustine" (*Der Liebesbegriff bei Augustine*, 1929), under Karl Jaspers and gradually to distance herself from Heidegger, whose questioning of **being** and analysis of ***Dasein***, she thought, left little room for social and political concerns. Later she came to see Heidegger as "the last German Romantic" (Young-Bruehl, 69), whose distrust of modernity and yearning for preindustrial existence led him to align himself with the folly of German National Socialism. By the early 1930s, she had broken with Heidegger and begun a lifelong association with Jaspers, who, although a German nationalist, was suspicious of Nazi rhetoric.

An Engaged Intellectual. Arendt's experience as a German, a Jew, and a refugee during **World War II** prompted her to address the historical origins of modern European anti-Semitism and totalitarianism. *On Totalitarianism* (1951) is a book of great historical erudition, in which Arendt describes the "totalitarian state" as the novel form of social and political organization exemplified by Nazi Germany and Soviet Russia. Arendt became known to the public, however, for her controversial coverage of the trial of the Nazi Adolf Eichmann in Jerusalem in 1961. Published in 1963, *Eichmann in Jerusalem: A Report on the Banality of Evil* grapples with the question of how a German bureaucrat of middling intelligence could have organized the death of thousands of innocent people without believing he had done anything wrong. As the book's subtitle suggests, Arendt finds Eichmann's mind and character normal to the point of banality; he speaks only in cliches and never has an original thought. What is exceptional about him, she maintains, is his inability to distinguish right from wrong and truth from half-truth, and his lack of consistency in his personal beliefs. Eichmann often bragged to coworkers, "I'll go to my grave laughing because I know that I'm responsible for the death of five million people," yet he also prided himself on not being a brutal anti-Semite and for developing "friendships" with the Jewish functionaries with whom he "negotiated." For Arendt, that he sees no inconsistency in these statements is a sign of the peculiar perversity of the Nazi regime: More than merely a tyrannical government, the

Nazis used totalitarian methods to transform a civilized nation into a dehumanized twilight world, without consistent standards of truth and falsity and right and wrong.

Although Arendt did not question Eichmann's guilt and the need for punishment, her book was perceived by many Jewish leaders and intellectuals as anti-Jewish and was widely criticized. The book cost Arendt a long-standing friendship with noted Jewish scholar and philosopher Gershom Scholem, who saw her position as a betrayal of Israel's interests and ideals.

Phenomenology of the Human Condition. Like that of her mentors Heidegger and Jaspers, Arendt's work is stamped with a concern for overcoming human **alienation**. However, while Arendt maintained ties to Jaspers throughout her life and even renewed her friendship with Heidegger after World War II, she can be categorized neither as an existentialist nor as a phenomenologist in any strict sense. Generally, she employs resources of existential phenomenology, mainly derived from Heidegger, in the service of an original philosophy of politics. Arendt's key insight concerns the crucial status of "public space" (*der öffentliche Raum*) as a necessary condition for human action. For Arendt, public space was exemplified in the life of the ancient Greek *polis*, where individuals "revealed themselves" to their peers through speech and action judged by common standards, and where the goals of the community were subject to continual debate. Living and acting together, the Greeks came to distinguish between an impermanent and unpredictable "realm of appearances," corresponding to the world of public affairs and action, and an unchanging realm of being, corresponding to intellectual thought. Arendt detects in the work of Plato and Aristotle a withdrawal from the vicissitudes of political life, the *vita activa*, to the reassuring permanence of contemplation. The subsequent history of Western philosophy in the **Christian** era is for Arendt a story of the valorization of "theory" over "praxis." Arendt's analysis thus parallels Heidegger's view of the history of philosophy as the valorization of being **present-at-hand**.

Arendt provides a historical and philosophical foundation for her perspective in *The Human Condition* (1958). Like the existentialists, Arendt rejects the idea of an unchanging **human nature** : "[N]othing entitles us to assume that man has a nature or essence in the same sense as other things" (HC, 10). Instead, she understands by "human condition" something similar to what Heidegger calls the "existentialia" of *Dasein*, those basic features of existence that give life its human character. Proceeding through a careful interpretation of Aristotle's *Nichomachean Ethics* and *Politics*—again much like Heidegger, with whom she had studied Aristotle in the 1920s—Arendt identifies "natality," "mortality," **worldliness**," "plurality," and "the earth" as key components of the human condition. Among these, plurality and natality may be singled out for their unique contribution. Plurality is the condition of "being among others," understood as definitive for political life. At the same time, it refers to the fact of human diversity, that individuals are irreducibly plural in their viewpoints rather than repetitions of a universal type. Natality is the condition of being born as an instance of "beginning something new"; "[W]ith each birth something uniquely new comes into the world" (HC, 178). While natality corresponds to action, "the capacity of beginning something new," plurality corresponds to "speech," the capacity to reveal "who one is" to others. Arendt's treatment of the distinction between "who one is" and "what one is" parallels the existentialist distinction between "existence" and "essence." Action and speech form a complementary whole. Speech is required to elucidate the meaning of one's acts, and both are required to reveal "who one is" to others. In Arendt's analysis, the degradation of action into mere "labor" or "work," and the reduction of speech to the mere communication of information, are major symptoms of modern alienation.

ARON, RAYMOND (1905–1983). French political philosopher, sociologist, and journalist. Aron was **Jean-Paul Sartre**'s fellow student at the **École Normale Supérieure** in Paris in the mid-1920s and maintained a friendship with his better-known counterpart through about 1947, when they had a falling out over political differences. While associated with Sartre, **Maurice Merleau-Ponty**, and *Les Temps modernes* in the mid- to late 1940s, Aron was not an existentialist. His politics were more conservative than Sartre's, and he was a critic of what he perceived as the conformity of French intellectuals who hastened to embrace **Marxism** and Soviet **communism**. Aron's *The Opium of the Intellectuals* (1955) stirred up controversy in France and abroad for its criticism of the way intellectuals (such as Sartre) naïvely supported political revolution while they condemned democracy. Nonetheless, Aron was influential in the development of Sartre's thought. He was among the first French intellectuals to have firsthand contact with German **phenomenology** and **philosophy of existence**, represented by **Edmund Husserl**, **Martin Heidegger**, and **Karl Jaspers**. From 1931 to 1933, Aron was a fellow at the French Institute in Berlin, and he persuaded Sartre to apply for the same fellowship the following year. A famous anecdote recounts that it was Aron who first sparked Sartre's interest in Husserl. In 1932, seated at a café with Sartre and **Simone de Beauvoir**, Aron remarked, "'if you are a phenomenologist, you can talk about this cocktail and make philosophy out of it!'" Beauvoir reports in her memoirs that Aron's remark had considerable impact on Sartre. "Sartre turned pale with emotion . . . . Here was just the thing he had been longing to achieve" (PL, 112). Aron also helped to introduce Sartre to the philosophy of history, the subject of Aron's doctoral thesis, which Sartre read around 1938. In addition to contributing to *Les temps modernes*, Aron was for a time an editorialist for Albert Camus's *Combat*. From the mid-1950s until his **death** he maintained a dual career, teaching at the Sorbonne and later at the Collège de France, while at the same time writing influential political editorials for *Le Figaro* and *L'Express*. Although she disagreed with his political positions, **Hannah Arendt** respected Aron for helping German communists flee to France in 1933 during his stay in Berlin.

ATHEISTIC EXISTENTIALISM. In his lecture "**Existentialism Is a Humanism**," **Jean-Paul Sartre** makes a distinction between "two kinds of existentialist; first, those who are **Christian**, among whom I would include **[Karl] Jaspers** and **Gabriel Marcel** . . . and on the other hand the atheistic existentialists, among whom I class **[Martin] Heidegger**, and then the French existentialists and myself" (EHE, 13). The defining feature of atheistic existentialism, according to Sartre, is acceptance of the idea that there is no human **essence** prior to human **existence**, because there is no God to create such an essence. Alternately put, it is the idea that a human being is "nothing else but what he makes of himself." *See also* RELIGIOUS EXISTENTIALISM.

AUTHENTICITY AND INAUTHENTICITY. A central tenet of existentialism is that selfhood is not naturally given but must be "won over" from a state of complacency, conformity, and self-forgetfulness. Winning oneself, or authenticity, amounts to accepting one's essential **finitude, freedom**, and **responsibility** and applying this insight in one's actions. Losing oneself, or inauthenticity, amounts to "fleeing from" one's freedom and continuing to regard one's **existence** impersonally, as something for which one is not ultimately responsible.

The term "authenticity" (*Eigentlichkeit*) was introduced by **Martin Heidegger** in *Being and Time*, though the idea derives from **Søren Kierkegaard**. Kierkegaard was the first in the existentialist tradition to insist that authentic selfhood must be wrested away from the average anonymity of social life and from "aesthetic" diversions and distractions. Kierkegaard thus speaks of the process of "becoming a self" rather than "being a self." One becomes "singular" and "particular" (in contrast to remaining generic and universal) through deliberate **ethical** and religious **choice** and **commitment**. Selfhood emerges in the act of commitment and increases with the intensity or "inwardness" of that commitment. The highest level of commitment is occasioned by religious **faith**, for faith is intensely subjective and yet objectively uncertain; thus, the self that emerges in faith cannot fall back into complacency, nor can it attain self-satisfaction and self-certainty.

Heidegger's account of authenticity exploits the etymology of the German term *Eigentlichkeit*, derived from the word *eigen*, "own"— in the sense of "a room of one's own"— similar to how the English word *authentic* derives from the Greek word *autentes*, "author or originator of an action," one who does something on his or her own authority. For the most part, ***Dasein*** exists in a manner that is *not* its own; it neither thinks nor acts for itself, but conforms to the expectations of others and accepts the ready-made meanings and **values** of its **world**. Heidegger insists that the subject of **everyday** existence is thus not the individual but ***das Man***, an impersonal "one" or "anyone" to which individuals collectively conform. The **project** of authenticity begins when *Dasein* is displaced from this mode of existence, which requires a shock, a confrontation with finitude that Heidegger calls **being-towards-death**. In the **moment** when **death** is grasped not as an abstract possibility that happens to anyone and everyone but as "my death," my "ownmost (*eigenst*) possibility," the everyday world sinks away, leaving me with an acute awareness of my self as a "being of possibility," that is, a being who is **thrown** into existence yet remains free to choose itself. Authenticity for Heidegger results from a coordinated "owning up" to facticity and a making "one's own" of the possibilities present in one's **situation**.

Jean-Paul Sartre provides the most detailed account of the psychology of inauthenticity, which he analyzes in terms of the phenomenon of **bad faith**. Pursued by diverse strategies, the goal of bad faith is to "escape oneself," to avoid acknowledging one's freedom and responsibility as a self-determining being. Sartre presents a series of typical portraits: the café waiter who tries to assume the "being" of his social role, to actually "be" a waiter and not merely "play at" being one; the homosexual who accepts society's judgment that he is determined to act according to a specific human "type"; the idealistic woman who evades her sexuality by dissociating her true self (her mind) from her body (her hand) being caressed by a suitor. In each case, bad faith is a strategy for avoiding the realization that one "makes oneself" through one's choices and commitments, and that these are without external justification or foundation. Sartre has less to say about *authentic* existence. Generally, authenticity is defined by Sartre in terms close to Heidegger's: "To be authentic is to realize fully one's being-in-situation" he writes in 1940 (WD, 54). However, concrete illustration of authentic existence is lacking in ***Being and Nothingness***. Sartre's subsequent study of the writer **Jean Genet**, *Saint Genet: Actor and Martyr* (1952), suggests a growing appreciation for the complexity of authenticity and the degree to which it is never untarnished by elements of bad faith.

AVAILABILITY (Fr. *disponibilité*). Gabriel Marcel describes the normative goal of interpersonal relations in terms of my availability to the other person. I am available to the other when I listen and respond with my whole self, mentally, spiritually, and emotionally, rather than with only part of myself: "[T]he person who is available to me is the one who is capable of being with me with the whole of himself when I am in need" (PE, 40). Furthermore, availability involves **reciprocity**: I remain open and receptive to another person to the extent that I perceive the other to be open and receptive to me. Marcel's notion of availability bears similarities to **Martin Buber**'s notion of **dialogue** between I and You.

AWAKENING. For many existentialists, the activity of philosophy aims not only to *describe* what is true, but at the same time to *awaken* individuals to the truth of their **existence**, namely, to the essential character of human being as finite, free and self-determining, and **situated** in a **world**. The phenomenon of awakening is clearly present in **Karl Jaspers'** conception of **philosophizing** as an appeal that arouses in others a sense of **freedom** and possibility. **Martin Heidegger** can be seen to share a similar view of the transformative power of philosophical thinking. The scenario at the start of *Being and Time* is that the "question of the meaning of being" has been "forgotten": The nature of human being and of **being** in general have long been taken for granted—and Heidegger's first task is thus "to *reawaken* an understanding for the meaning of the question" (BT, 19). Heidegger's description of **authenticity** itself, moreover, depends on a type of awakening from an "average" "tranquillized" state, in which we complacently accept social roles and **values**, to an awareness of existential freedom according to which we take **responsibility** for our decisions and make certain possibilities our own.

AYER, A. J. *See* LOGICAL POSITIVISM.

– B –

BACHELARD, GASTON (1884–1962). French philosopher of science and influential professor of philosophy. Bachelard taught at the Sorbonne from 1940 to 1954, where his students included Michel Foucault and **Louis Althusser**. He is best known for his later works on poetic imagination, in which he proposed a "**psychoanalysis**" of the four elements, that is, a description of the images and beliefs associated with the "primitive" experience of earth, air, water, and fire. Bachelard's careful **phenomenological** descriptions were acknowledged by **Jean-Paul Sartre** and **Maurice Merleau-Ponty**; Merleau-Ponty refers to Bachelard in an essay on literature, "Indirect Language

and the Voices of Silence" (*Signs*, 57). Bachelard's insights into poetry and literature, as well as his unique synthesis of philosophy, cultural history, and literary theory, were praised and emulated by literary theorists like Roland Barthes.

Bachelard's work on imagination was of keen interest to Sartre in
particular, and Sartre discusses his work approvingly in *Being and
Nothingness* (BN, 600–604). **Simone de Beauvoir** confirmed this
interest in her memoirs: "In *L'eau et les rêves* (1942) (*Water and
Dreams*), Bachelard investigated the imaginative processes in terms
of something very much like **existential psychoanalysis** . . . the book
interested [Sartre and I] a great deal" (PL, 425). Initially Bachelard
approached poetic experience as a stubborn obstacle to scientific objectivity (for example, in *The Psychoanalysis of Fire* [1938]). In *The
Poetics of Space* (1957), however, Bachelard sought to develop a philosophy of poetic imagination as an autonomous mode of apprehending the world, to be judged by its own standards, independent of
the rules of scientific cognition. The method for apprehending these
standards he found in phenomenology, which he described as a "consideration of the *onset of the image* in an individual consciousness"
(*The Poetics of Space*, Introduction, xv).

In contrast, Bachelard's early research concerned the history and
development of science and the relationship between scientific advance and philosophy. In such books as *Le nouvel esprit scien-
tifique* (1938) (*The New Scientific Spirit*), Bachelard argued that
philosophical views of reality are derived from scientific discoveries, and that philosophy must periodically revise its assumptions to
keep pace with scientific advances. Scientific theories, in turn,
cannot be separated from the tools and technologies that make
them real and concrete. Bachelard introduced the concept of the
"epistemological break" (*coupure épistémologique*) to explain
leaps in scientific development, anticipating the ideas of Thomas
Kuhn and Michel Foucault.

After about 1940, Bachelard turned his attention to the role of the
"unconscious of the scientific mind": recurring images and beliefs
about the natural world that originate often in states of trancelike
reverie, like sitting before a blazing fire. While he accepted Carl
Jung's view that these images attest to primitive archetypes stored in
a collective unconscious, Bachelard was not interested in psycho-

analysis per se, drawing his examples from literature and scientific belief rather than from psychoanalytic observation. In the end, he regarded poetic images as radically novel creations that defy psychological or psychoanalytic explanation, a view not dissimilar to Sartre's view of imagination.

BAD FAITH (Fr. *mauvaise foi,* **"dishonesty," "deception," "hypocrisy").** This ordinary French expression is employed as a technical term by **Jean-Paul Sartre** to designate various strategies of avoidance and self-deception that lie at the root of inauthentic **existence.** Sartre's discussion of bad faith in *Being and Nothingness*, one of the most vivid and influential passages of his philosophy, is an attempt to rethink the **psychoanalytic** concept of the unconscious in terms consistent with an existentialist theory of **freedom.** If it is possible to "lie to oneself" and "deceive oneself," is one not still the source of the deception and thus in some sense **responsible** for it? The goal of bad faith is to avoid acknowledging one's freedom and responsibility, most commonly by construing oneself as causally determined (by heredity, temperament, or social circumstances) or by conforming oneself to social norms and the opinions of others. The **project** of bad faith, however, remains for Sartre highly unstable and ultimately unrealizable, because **consciousness** always transcends its objectifications, that is, each false self-interpretation deployed is at the same time held at arm's length and called into question as an object of consciousness. Sartre conveys the psychology of bad faith through a series of typical portraits. There is the young woman on a date who idealizes the sexual advances of her suitor, construing his words and gestures as addressed to her mind rather than her body. There is the café waiter who tries to "disappear" into his social role. There is the homosexual man who sees himself as determined by the "type" of person he is. These portraits add a **concrete** dimension to the account of inauthenticity presented by **Martin Heidegger**. *See also* AUTHENTICITY AND INAUTHENTICITY.

BARNES, HAZEL (1915–). American philosopher and translator of **Jean-Paul Sartre**'s *Being and Nothingness*. In *An Existentialist Ethics* (1967), Barnes defends the **ethical** implications of Sartre's philosophy and attempts to show that Sartrean existentialism is uniquely capable of responding to the ethical dilemmas of the Cold War.

BARRETT, WILLIAM (1913–1992). American philosopher and one of the earliest American interpreters of existentialism. In 1947, *Partisan Review*, of which Barrett was then the editor, published an extended essay by Barrett entitled "What Is Existentialism?" which was one of the first treatments of the subject in the United States. Barrett's *Irrational Man: A Study in Existential Philosophy* (1958) was widely read in the 1950s and 1960s and helped to popularize existentialism among the American reading public. Barrett later authored *The Illusion of Technique* (1979), a critical analysis of modern technology that explores **Martin Heidegger**'s philosophy.

BARTH, KARL (1886–1968). Swiss Protestant theologian, often considered the most influential theologian of the 20th century. Barth's *The Epistle to the Romans* (*Der Römerbrief*, 1919; revised 1922) was one of the first books to introduce the thought of **Søren Kierkegaard** to German-speaking intellectuals. Like Kierkegaard, Barth insisted that **Christian faith** cannot be reduced to rational terms and that religion suffers when understood as a species of philosophical inquiry. Barth criticized the **historicism** and "subjectivism" of **G. W. F. Hegel** and the liberal theologians who, he believed, overly humanized **Christianity** by focusing on the human experience of religious striving rather than on the nature of divine revelation. For Barth, God is radically **transcendent** to human life, and the radical otherness of the divine must be respected as the core of theology. In this sense, Barth, though affiliated with Kierkegaard in his early work, was opposed to the tendency of **existential theologians** like **Rudolph Bultmann** and **Paul Tillich** to place human experience at the center of theology. During **World War I**, Barth was angered by theologians and church leaders who saw Germany's pursuit of victory as divinely sanctioned. He referred to his own perspective as a "theology of crisis," a description of the catastrophic state of human affairs when a culture has strayed from the path of true religious understanding. In the 1920s and 1930s, he taught theology at several German universities, where he was the center of an intellectual movement known as "dialectical theology." Barth was a vocal opponent of the **Nazi**

regime and in 1935 was removed from his teaching post after he publicly refused to swear allegiance to Aldolf Hitler. Barth then moved back to Switzerland, where he continued to teach at the University of Basel until 1962.

BATAILLE, GEORGES (1897–1962). French novelist, essayist, and philosopher, sometimes mistakenly identified as an existentialist. Bataille broke with André Breton and the **surrealists** in the early 1930s to pursue his own inquiries into the nature of violence, transgression, and the experience of the sacred. Between 1937 and 1939, he formed a discussion group in Paris with the anthropologist Roger Caillois and the surrealist writer Michel Leiris, called the *Collège de sociologie*. In 1946, Bataille founded the important French intellectual journal *Critique*. While Bataille was at times labeled an existentialist, thanks especially to his raw, pornographic novel *The Story of the Eye* (1936), he was openly critical of **Jean-Paul Sartre**'s philosophy, which he saw as an attempt to rationalize the irrational. Sartre in turn criticized Bataille's celebration of violence and the sacred as a type of "new mysticism." **Gabriel Marcel** was harsher in his judgment. For Marcel, Bataille's work represented either "a perverse and fascinating game, or . . . the end of a process of self-destruction . . . within a doomed society, within a humanity which has broken . . . its **ontological** moorings" (HV, 211).

BEAT MOVEMENT. Countercultural trend in American literature in the 1950s and 1960s. The Beats were precursors of the hippie movement of the late 1960s. The Beat movement was incubated in New York City in the 1950s and flourished in the bars and coffee houses of San Francisco in the 1960s and 1970s. Though there was no direct link with existentialism, Beat writers and poets were sometimes characterized as "existentialists" due to their repudiation of middle-class **values**, celebration of individuality, and experimentation in art and living. Principal East Coast Beats were William Burroughs, Gregory Corso, Alan Ginsberg, and Jack Kerouac. The West Coast Beats, centered around the publishing efforts of City Lights Books owned by poet Laurence Ferlinghetti, included Michael McClure, Kenneth Rexroth, and Gary Snyder. Kerouac's novel *On the Road* (1957) and Ginsberg's collection *Howl and Other Poems* (1958) were two pieces of Beat literature at times described as existentialist, for reasons noted above.

BEAUFRET, JEAN (1907–1982). French philosopher, among the first in France to embrace German existentialist philosophy, in particular the work of **Martin Heidegger**. Beaufret befriended Heidegger in 1946, around the time of Heidegger's denazification hearings, and he endeavored to help strengthen Heidegger's image in France during the time that Heidegger was banned from teaching in German universities (1947–1951). Beaufret became a dedicated disciple and leading French interpreter of Heidegger's philosophy. A question he posed to Heidegger in a letter of 1946, "How can we restore meaning to the word *humanism*?" prompted Heidegger's *Letter on Humanism*.

BEAUVOIR, SIMONE DE (1908–1986). French philosopher, novelist, and essayist. Beauvoir was **Jean-Paul Sartre**'s lifelong companion, and she and Sartre were the leading advocates of French existentialism after **World War II**. Beauvoir collaborated with Sartre and **Maurice Merleau-Ponty** as editor of the journal *Les Temps modernes* and was an active voice in political and cultural debates of the time, embodying alongside Sartre the ideal of the "**committed** writer." Her longest work, *The Second Sex*, published in 1949, was a groundbreaking analysis of sexism and feminine identity that drew conceptual resources from existentialism; today it is recognized as a founding work of modern **feminism**. Beauvoir had a modest opinion of her own philosophical talents, and her purely philosophical writings are few. After an early essay, "Pyrrhus and Cineas" (1944), and a short book on existentialist **ethics**, *The Ethics of Ambiguity* (1947), she devoted herself primarily to articles for *Les temps modernes*, novels, and a series of autobiographical works documenting the major phases of her life. Her literary work, however, was guided by philosophical intentions. Her novels offer concrete illustrations of existential **freedom** and **bad faith**, and her memoirs document the process whereby an individual **transcends** the **facticity** of her social and **historical situation**.

Life. A great deal is known about Beauvoir's life, as she recorded its details in four autobiographical books, published between 1958 and 1972. The eldest child in a conservative, upper-middle-class family, as a young girl Beauvoir accepted the role of "dutiful daughter." She was provided with a live-in nanny, attended private **Catholic** schools, and was taken to church by her mother three times a week for communion. The situation changed after **World War I**, when a downturn in her family's finances required a move to a smaller apartment and cast into doubt her chances of marriage, as her father could no longer afford a dowry. Subsequently, as an adolescent Beauvoir lost her religious faith and, despite opposition from her parents, devoted herself to academic studies, which she pursued with determination. As a high school student she studied mathematics, ancient Greek, and literature before discovering her love for philosophy. Beauvoir entered the Sorbonne in 1927, where her diligent work ethic earned her the nickname "Castor" ("Beaver"), which she kept her whole life. She studied Gottfried Wilhelm Leibniz with **Léon Brunschvicg** and made the acquaintance of fellow philosophy students Merleau-Ponty and Sartre. In 1929, Beauvoir became only the ninth French woman to pass the national *agrégation* exam in philosophy, placing a close second behind Sartre in a virtually hung jury; though Sartre's oratory was brilliant, "everybody agreed that, of the two, she was the real philosopher" (Cohen-Solal, 74).

Rejecting marriage because it was perceived as too conventional, Beauvoir and Sartre made a "pact" with each other, to be renewed every few years, that they would be equals in everything and hide nothing from one another. Remarkably, they maintained this relationship for over 50 years, becoming one of the world's most famous literary and philosophical couples. After taking up with Sartre, Beauvoir was able to make a break with her bourgeois past and begin to define herself as a nonconformist intellectual and writer. In the 1930s, she taught high school philosophy in Marseille, Rouen, and then Paris, developing strong relationships with her female students, who admired her greatly. One of her students, Olga Kosakievicz (later Olga Bost), entered into a love triangle with her and Sartre, which is dramatized in Beauvoir's first novel, ***She Came to Stay*** (*L'invitée*, 1943). Beauvoir took on the **responsibility** of editing Sartre's literary and philosophy **projects**, a service he came to depend on. However, she doubted her ability to be a philosopher like Sartre—that is, one who creates his own "philosophical system"— and she dismissed a career of scholarship as merely "[e]xpounding other people's beliefs." Consequently, Beauvoir decided to dedicate herself to writing: "I wanted to communicate the element of originality in my own experience . . . to do this successfully I knew it was literature toward which I had to orientate myself" (PL, 178).

Transformed by the experience of the German occupation, Beauvoir and Sartre emerged from World War II with strong commitments to radical leftist politics and social causes. In the fall of 1945, they launched *Les Temps modernes,* which through the 1970s served as the main vehicle of expression for their shared **Marxist** politics and existentialist philosophy. The publication of Beauvoir's first novel was followed quickly by two others, *The Blood of Others (Le sang des autres,* 1945) and *All Men Are Mortal (Tous les hommes sont mortels,* 1946), which established her literary reputation in France. *The Ethics of Ambiguity* (1947), her sole book of philosophy, was a defense of an existentialist concept of **freedom.** *The Second Sex* (1949) established her status as an intellectual independent from Sartre, and as a feminist.

By the late 1940s and early 1950s, Beauvoir and Sartre had become internationally famous. They visited Cuba in 1960 as guests of Fidel Castro, and the Soviet Union in 1962, where they were hosted by Nikita Khrushchev. In the early 1960s, she and Sartre became vocal critics of French policy in Algeria and supporters of the Algerian revolution, resulting in **death** threats against them. In this same period, Beauvoir published the main volumes of her autobiography, *Memoirs of a Dutiful Daughter (Mémoires d'une jeune fille rangée,* 1958), *The Prime of Life (La force de l'âge,* 1960), and *Force of Circumstance (La force des choses,* 1963), which document her life in Paris between 1944 and 1963 and won her a wider readership. A final volume, *All Said and Done (Tout compte fait),* was published in 1972. Beauvoir's feminist commitments deepened in the 1960s, and she became sought after as a leading figure in the nascent feminist movement. She addressed issues of death and aging in *A Very Easy Death (Une mort très douce,* 1964), which recounts her mother's death; *The Coming of Age (La viellesse,* 1970), a critique of society's attitude toward the elderly; and *Adieux: A Farewell to Sartre (Les cérémonies des adieux,* 1981), a wrenching account of Sartre's death.

Freedom and Situation. Beauvoir's philosophical reflections are often presented as clarifications and elaborations of Sartre's thought.

At the same time, they also offer important correctives to Sartre, especially to certain formulations of the concept of freedom. In *Being and Nothingness*, freedom is defined as absolute, constrained by nothing beyond itself. The physical world, history, other people, even one's own body, take on meaning according to one's projects and thus do not represent intrinsic constraints on who one is and how one thinks or acts. Beauvoir takes up two problems raised by the notion of absolute freedom. First, if freedom is absolute, what is the basis for ethical obligation to others? The second problem is related to the first: If freedom is absolute, how are we to make sense of the relation to the **other**, the social relation, in the construction of identity? Beauvoir tackles the first problem in *The Ethics of Ambiguity*. The second problem is addressed in *The Second Sex*.

Like Sartre's reflections in **"Existentialism Is a Humanism,"** *The Ethics of Ambiguity* seeks to defend existentialism against charges of solipsism and moral relativism by clarifying the notion of existential freedom. As in Sartre's account, freedom is postulated as "the ultimate . . . end to which man should destine himself" (EA, 49). Thus, Beauvoir holds out the hope that "by turning towards this freedom we are going to discover a principle of action whose range will be universal" (EA,23). Unlike Sartre in *Being and Nothingness*, however, Beauvoir conceives of the actual exercise of freedom as dependent on others and thus socially constrained: "[T]he existence of others as a freedom defines my situation and is even the condition of my own freedom" (EA, 91). Alternately, "[my] freedom can be achieved only through the freedom of others" (EA, 156) because I depend on others for confirmation of my freedom and "no existence can be validly fulfilled if it is limited to itself" (EA, 67). When this confirmation is withheld, however, I am reduced to an unfree being, a mere thing devoid of transcendence. Thus, "It is this interdependence [of self and other] which explains why oppression is possible" (EA, 82). Beauvoir is here groping toward a conception of **reciprocal** freedom, freedom as an interpersonal and social accomplishment and not merely an individual power. This is the conclusion that Sartre will reach later, in the 1950s, through a deepened appreciation of Marxism. Yet, as Beauvoir recounts in her memoirs, she was inclined in this direction already in 1940. She reports a discussion with Sartre in which she had argued that not all situations are equal, that some circumstances may in themselves limit the exercise of freedom: "What sort of transcendence could a woman shut up in a harem achieve? Sartre replied that even such a cloistered existence could be lived in several quite different ways. I stuck to my point . . . Basically I was right. But to defend my attitude I should have had to abandon the plane of individual, and therefore idealistic, morality on which we had set ourselves" (PL, 346).

Freedom and the Other. The *Second Sex* represents just such an abandonment of the individual perspective. In this work, Beauvoir confronts a defining aspect of her own facticity: that she is a woman, and that her consciousness as a woman is not an **ontological** given but is deeply informed by the attitudes of a society governed by men. Grounded in her experience as a French woman in the first half of the 20th century, and not simply in an ostensibly universal human perspective, Beauvoir's study thus provides an exemplary instance of existential concreteness.

Beauvoir observes that the social constraints on woman's freedom are clear: "[H]umanity is male and man defines woman not in herself but as relative to him; she is not regarded as an autonomous being" (*The Second Sex*, xxii). In the language of **Hegelian** dialectics, woman is "the other" to man—natural as opposed to spiritual, emotional as opposed to rational, identified with the body as opposed to the mind. On Beauvoir's analysis, the project of **authenticity**, of accepting and exercising or of masking one's freedom, thus takes on a social dimension. If women tend to accept their unequal status it is because the entire social world conspires against them, not simply because they have embarked as individuals on a project of "bad faith."

Beauvoir's inquiry gives specificity to the generic analyses of consciousness offered in *Being and Nothingness*. If consciousness is gendered, it is because society is gendered, and consciousness is socially constituted. The struggle for freedom and authenticity is accordingly posed on a social plane: Women's acquiescence to their plight as well as their potential transcendence of it are for Beauvoir collective concerns in which both men and women are implicated. If the project of authentic existence is a collective enterprise, it is because others reflect back an image of one's own freedom, and genuinely free actions require the participation and acknowledgment of others, who carry on one's project indefinitely into the future. This is approximately the position that Sartre comes to in the ***Critique of Dialectical Reason***. If Beauvoir reaches it sooner, it is perhaps because, as a woman, she was more tellingly aware of social inequity and non-reciprocity.

BECKETT, SAMUEL (1906–1989). Irish novelist, playwright, and poet. Beckett lived in Paris from 1937 on and was a close friend of James Joyce. After **World War II**, he became a leading voice in modernist literature, receiving the Nobel Prize for Literature in 1969. Beckett's work is often linked to the **theater of the absurd** for its portrayal of human **alienation** and **anxiety** and its pessimism regarding meaningful **communication**; for similar reasons it is also sometimes characterized as "existentialist," but this term should not be taken in the strict sense. It may be more accurate to say that Beckett's plays, such as *Waiting for Godot* and *Endgame*, poetically express a problem—the alienation of self and other, mind and **body**, humans and **nature**, and present and past—that existentialism seeks to analyze, and in part to remedy, philosophically. *See also* EXISTENTIALIST LITERATURE.

BEING (Ger. *Sein*). The notion of being in existentialism is tied primarily to the essential role it plays in the philosophy of **Martin Heidegger**. For Heidegger, the "question of the meaning of being," that is, inquiry into the guiding historical and metaphysical presuppositions according to which a thing can be said to "be" at all, is the most pressing task for philosophy. A major claim of Heidegger's ***Being and Time*** is that a renewed understanding of *human* being is a necessary point of departure for a renewed understanding of being in general. While other existentialists generally do not share Heidegger's preoccupation with **ontology**, they do agree that analysis of human **existence** is the central task of philosophy.

Heidegger observes that being is the most universal and apparently most abstract concept. It applies to everything that is, everything that can be said to exist. But what does it mean to be, and what does it mean to exist? For Heidegger the ordinary understanding of being is internally guided by the categories of Western **metaphysics**, according to which being in the highest sense is **substance**. Substance is

conceived as that which is unchanging and self-subsistent; the sub-
stantiality of things thus cannot be perceived through the senses but
can be grasped only through a pure, detached beholding of what remains unchanged and self-subsistent. Related metaphysical concepts
such as **"essence,"** "soul," "subject," "actuality," "God," and "reality" are for Heidegger variations on the central notion of substantial
presence; they are subject to similar criticism for applying a single
static conception of being to all things that exist.

The central tenet of Heidegger's existentialism is that an **authentic** understanding of being must be sought in existence itself. Analysis of existence reveals a different set of guiding categories, which
Heidegger calls "existentialia"—not merely rules governing thought
but basic manners of existing common to all human beings. They include **mineness, facticity, mood, thrownness, falling,** being-possible, **historicality,** and **being-towards-death.** These existential categories provide the **horizon** for an authentic understanding of human
Dasein. And it is only by attending to such authentic self-understanding of the human being that philosophy can arrive at a renewed
understanding of being in general, that is, as dynamic, historical, and
temporal rather than as static atemporal presence.

BEING AND NOTHINGNESS (*L'Être et le néant*, **1943**). **Jean-Paul
Sartre**'s major philosophical work and, after **Martin Heidegger**'s
Being and Time, the most influential statement of existentialist philosophy. Sartre conceived and wrote the book between 1939 and
1942, significant portions being composed while he served in the
French army between September 1939 and June 1940 and while interned in a German prisoner-of-war camp from June 1940 to March
1941. Upon his release, he continued work on the project in Paris and
completed the manuscript in 1942. At more than 600 pages, the book
found few readers when first published in 1943.

In contrast to Sartre's earlier **phenomenological** studies, *Being
and Nothingness* presents itself as a work of "phenomenological **ontology**," an analysis of basic categories and structures of **being** as
they are given in human experience. In its systematic scope, it is self-
consciously modeled after Heidegger's *Being and Time*, which also
approached the question of being through analysis of the categories
of human **existence.** Following Heidegger, its existentialist character

is confirmed by the centrality assigned to themes of **authenticity and inauthenticity**, **freedom**, **anxiety**, **responsibility**, and **choice**.

Consciousness and Freedom. Being and Nothingness is an extended reflection on the nature of **consciousness** as freedom. The analysis is centered on the power of consciousness to withdraw from the **world** and to "**negate**" (*néantiser*) what is "given." The negating power of consciousness is applied not only to circumstances in the physical and social world but also, importantly, to the self. The nature of consciousness is to continually reassess the past in light of future aims, such that past decisions are not binding for the future but require continual reevaluation. Because "consciousness continually experiences itself as the nihilation of its past being," (BN, 28) to be conscious is to re-create oneself and one's situation through an ongoing choice of goals and **projects**. The dynamic and evanescent character of consciousness leads Sartre to designate its ontological status as "nothingness."

While consciousness is not a thing and cannot grasp itself as object, there is nonetheless "an immediate, non-cognitive relation of the self to itself" (BN, liii) operative in ordinary awareness. This becomes less paradoxical when we realize that ordinary awareness is not the self-reflective state imagined by philosophers and psychologists but a type of **prereflective** involvement in tasks that absorb us. Consciousness is aware of itself immediately through its involvements in the world. For example, when absorbed in the task of counting my cigarettes, I am explicitly aware of the cigarettes but at the same time implicitly aware that I am counting them. This is confirmed when someone asks me what I am doing and I answer without hesitation or self-scrutiny, "counting" (BN, liii). To take another example, pleasure exists only as "consciousness of pleasure"; I may be engrossed in the music I am hearing, but my enjoyment is obviously being felt, if only "prereflectively." Because consciousness involves both intrinsic self-awareness and the power to relate to itself explicitly, Sartre calls it "**being-for-itself**." Nonconscious things to which consciousness is primarily directed have, in contrast, the character of "being-in-itself." That which has being-in-itself—a table, a chair, a mountain—"is what it is": solid, permanent, unchanging; it is identical with itself and cannot be other than what it is. A paradox of the category of being-in-itself is that it defies further characterization or comparison, for apart from human (conscious) schemes of meaning, all we can say of nonconscious entities is that they *are*, they *exist*. That they exist is purely **contingent** and thus **absurd.** Sartre's analysis of the relationship between these two basic ontological categories is developed throughout the rest of the book. His main contentions are, first, that consciousness (being-for-itself) introduces a sense of nonbeing and possibility into reality (being-in-itself) and, second, that human beings are motivated by a desire to achieve a synthesis of being-for-itself and being-in-itself, that is, to attain the identity and permanence of a thing and yet remain free and conscious beings. This desire is unrealizable, however, because a free and conscious being can construe itself as permanent and necessary only at the cost of repudiating its freedom.

The Project of Bad Faith. Sartre follows **Søren Kierkegaard** (and Heidegger) in his characterization of freedom as something unsettling from which humans tend to flee. Concretely, human beings are prone to a strategy of self-evasion, which Sartre calls bad faith. In bad faith, one tries to hide one's freedom from oneself by interpreting oneself as causally determined by one's past, temperament, social role, or the judgments of others. Bad faith is thus a kind of prereflective self-deception. In its most common form, it appears to be a by-product of social expectations and conformism. The café waiter "acts like" a waiter, and the grocer "acts like" a grocer because it is expected of them: "A grocer who dreams is offensive to the buyer . . . as if we lived in perpetual fear that he might escape from [his condition]" (BN, 59). Society imagines that the grocer has a fixed identity, a kind of being-in-itself. Yet, try as they might, neither grocers nor waiters can fully "be" what they "are" because they remain conscious of their roles and to this degree always "exceed" or "transcend" them. Put slightly differently, one's **factical** situation (profession, race, class, gender, and so forth) exists only to the extent that one confers meaning on it, yet one cannot at the same time acknowledge this fact and treat it as ready-made and given independently of one's attitude toward it: I am both author and actor of my existence, but I cannot be fully both at the same time. For this reason, Sartre says that consciousness in bad faith is **ambiguous** and "metastable," continually shifting between the position of being-in-itself and that of being-for-itself, facticity and transcendence. At bottom it is motivated by the anxiety of coming to terms with freedom and responsibility, for Sartre, the weighty task of continually conferring meaning on the world and on ourselves. This expresses Sartre's basic moral conception of the human being: "[T]o be is to *choose oneself* . . . entirely abandoned to the intolerable necessity of making [oneself] be—down to the slightest detail" (BN, 440–441).

To the extent they portray human behavior as causally determined, traditional psychology and philosophy act as accomplices to bad faith. In Sartre's view, **psychoanalysis** is especially pernicious in this regard because it absolves individuals of responsibility for themselves by attributing thoughts and behaviors to unconscious motives. Sartre does acknowledge the truth of **Sigmund Freud**'s discoveries; however, he proposes an alternate manner of interpreting them, one intended to avoid the problems posed by the idea of "unconscious mind," which he takes to be contradictory. In place of the psychoanalytic focus on the unconscious, Sartre proposes an "**existential psychoanalysis**" founded on the notions of bad faith and the **fundamental** project. A fundamental project is the most basic attitude one assumes toward the world, oneself, and others. Paradoxically, Sartre characterizes the fundamental project as "chosen," but by this he does not mean that it is the product of deliberate decision. Rather, one's character and one's most basic outlook on life are "chosen" in the sense of being freely and consciously developed and not causally determined. The temptation of bad faith is to construe one's fundamental project in terms of pregiven character, heredity, or fate.

Ethics and Authenticity. Sartre has a great deal less to say about the nature of authentic existence and, generally, about the theoretical justification for an existentialist ethics. While in the closing sentence of *Being and Nothingness* Sartre promises to address **ethical** concerns "in a future work," this work never appeared. Sartre's notebooks on this topic, written in 1947 and 1948 and published posthumously as *Notebooks for an Ethics*, suggest his deepening appreciation of the difficulties of such a project. Chief among these is the problem of abstraction: If, from an existentialist perspective, ethics is necessarily concrete and situational, then a general theory of ethics, applicable regardless of situation, is ill-advised. In fact, Sartre suggests, consideration of ethical problems in abstraction from the social and **historical** situation of actual individuals may itself be an act of bad faith, to the extent that it serves to absolve one of the need to confront real moral conflicts and dilemmas. In the *Notebooks*, Sartre appears to realize that the abstract ontological categories of *Being and Nothingness* are ill-suited to the task of such a concrete analysis. Sartre's less narrowly philosophical works, such as his study of the writer **Jean Genet**, may come closer to a concrete elaboration of his ethical position at the time.

BEING AND TIME (*Sein und Zeit*, **1927**). **Martin Heidegger**'s magnum opus and the seminal statement of existentialist philosophy. *Being and Time* provided the theoretical blueprint for subsequent existentialist philosophers, most notably for **Jean-Paul Sartre** in *Being and Nothingness*. It was also indispensable to a range of intellectual endeavors, including **existential theology** and **existential psychotherapy**. Material for the book derived from Heidegger's university lecture courses on **phenomenology** and the history of Western philosophy, in particular his study of the philosophy of Aristotle, between about 1920 and 1926. According to Heidegger, the analysis of **being** in Aristotle's *Metaphysics* was the last great attempt to grapple with the defining problem of Western philosophy, the problem of being. The problem of being, the central problem Heidegger's philosophy seeks to address, may seem an unlikely point of departure for existentialism. However, it is Heidegger's central contention in *Being and Time* that **ontology**, the study of being in general, can be properly pursued only through an appropriate understanding of *human* **existence**.

The Question of Being. The introduction to *Being and Time* sets out as that work's primary aim a re**awakening** of the "question of the meaning of being," which, after initial treatment by the Greeks, effectively disappeared from view in the philosophical and scientific traditions for over 2,000 years. This "forgetting" of the question of the meaning of being is not, however, merely a theoretical oversight. It is a profound loss that has impoverished our understanding of the world and ourselves. The strategy of *Being and Time* is to conduct a thorough reappraisal of the meaning of "human being" that in its radicality will allow for a corresponding reappraisal of the meaning of being in general, that is, a renewed understanding of the ontology of the natural and human sciences and a deeper understanding of the ontological **commitments** of philosophy.

The root of this impoverishment, Heidegger maintains, is the hegemony of the theoretical attitude, according to which reality consists in an "external world" of physical objects to be known or manipulated and which stands over against the "internal world" of human **consciousness**. From the perspective of theoretical observation as it has been determined since Aristotle, the basic constituents of reality are **substances**, essentially mental things and physical things, which stand in no intrinsic relation to each other nor to any broader context of meaning. The forgetting of the question of being thus amounts to a distortion and "covering over" of a more basic relation to the world, the immediate practical engagement with things and other people, which Heidegger calls "**being-in-the-world**."

Dasein. An essential component of the task of recovering the meaning of existence as being-in-the-world is a critical reappraisal of the language of traditional philosophy. Not the least of Heidegger's accomplishments is to have forged an original vocabulary of human existence, one that exploits etymological relationships of ordinary German in an attempt to avoid the biases of conventional philosophy. Rejecting traditional concepts such as "soul," "mind," "body," and "person," Heidegger refers to human beings as *"Dasein"* ("existence" in ordinary German; sometimes written in hyphenated form, *Da-sein*, to reflect the etymological meaning, "being-there"). *Dasein* does not designate the "what" of human beings in the sense of essential properties such as "rationality" or "morality" that stand at the heart of classical definitions. Rather, it expresses the "how"of human being: a distinctive openness toward a world and "anxious" concern for the self that Heidegger calls "existence" (*Existenz*).

Being and Time endeavors to frame the question of human existence at a deeper level than previous thinkers devoted to the subject such as **Wilhelm Dilthey, Karl Jaspers**, and **Max Scheler**, to whom Heidegger is nonetheless clearly indebted. In contrast to Dilthey's **philosophy of life**, Scheler's **philosophical anthropology**, and Jaspers's *Existenzphilosophie*, the framework of *Being and Time* is sensitive to both the history of Western metaphysics and its own methodological assumptions. The former thinkers Heidegger criticizes for uncritically employing traditional metaphysical concepts such as "man," "person," "soul," "mind," "body," "spirit," and "life," which, he maintains, are infected with the biases of substance ontology.

To avoid these prejudices, Heidegger not only creates a nontraditional conceptual vocabulary but also submits the history of Western philosophy to an internal critique referred to as the "**destruction**" of the history of metaphysics. The goal of this critique is to clear the way for a reappraisal of the "meaning of being in general," without which any account of human being would, he believes, remain mired in metaphysical prejudices.

Heidegger also criticizes previous philosophers for failing to properly distinguish the function of philosophy from that of "regional" sciences like psychology, anthropology, history, and theology, which presuppose ontological categories of "nature," "culture," "reason," and "life" yet leave unexamined the question of the "unity" of the concept of being underlying each regional ontology. "**Fundamental ontology**" is the name Heidegger gives to the endeavor of elucidating the unity of being underlying its various modalities. The two-pronged thesis of *Being and Time* is that analysis of human existence constitutes the core of such a fundamental ontology and that time provides the "**horizon** for the **understanding** of being" (BT, 39), that is, time grasped not as an abstract entity but through the existential **temporality** of *Dasein*.

Being-in-the-World. Division One of *Being and Time* is an account of the basic structures of existence as being-in-the-world (*In-der-Welt-sein*). Not only are these structures obscured by the philosophical tradition, but they are also so mundane as to be passed over by ordinary understanding. *Dasein* is "in" the world not in the sense a plate is "in" the cupboard or my car is "in" the driveway, but in the sense of being actively engaged with things and situations that matter to it. *Dasein* thus relates to things not as a range of unrelated physical objects but as networks of "equipment," tools to be used for specific human purposes. The being of a water glass is understood not through theoretical observation but when it is taken out of the cupboard and filled with cold water to drink; the being of a hammer is understood when it is picked up to hammer in a nail. This immediate pragmatic character of things in the world Heidegger calls "**readiness-to-hand**" (*Zuhandenheit*) and *Dasein*'s attitude toward them Heidegger names "**concern**" (*Besorgen*). Only when one stands back from concernful engagement in the world and "just looks" at things do they take on the character of isolated "objects" to be known, which Heidegger calls "**presence-at-hand**" (*Vorhandenheit*). From the traditional theoretical perspective presence-at-hand is taken as the underlying character of being. Yet mere occurrent presence is not a fundamental mode of being: It is an abstraction from the nexus of lived meanings and purposes that constitute a human **world**. Without prior nontheoretical understanding of the world as a **life-world**, no individual objects could emerge for philosophical and scientific inspection. Such objects are things ready-to-hand that have been isolated and neutralized, their lived meanings pared away.

Being-with-Others. Because an understanding of other people is intrinsic and not merely incidental to human existence, being-in-the-world is at the same time also a being-with-others. Others are copresent with me in the world in an original sense and need not be constituted by analogy to myself or otherwise indirectly inferred. They are "given" not only indirectly, through concern with things ready-to-hand, but also directly, in the specific stance I assume toward them, which Heidegger names "solicitude." *Fürsorge*, solicitude or "caring for" others, along with *Besorgen*, concernful preoccupation with things, is an essential feature of *Dasein*'s most basic manner of being as *Sorge*, "care."

Just as everyday concern involves a "fascination" with the world of practical tasks, everyday being-with-others involves an "absorption" in the social world. In everydayness, *Dasein* exists primarily *just like everyone else*, conforming its thoughts and actions to the average mode of understanding and judging that dictates social behavior. Thus Heidegger concludes that everyday *Dasein* exists not as a self but as an instance of "*das Man*," an anonymous "anyone," an impersonal "they." The insidious effect of *das Man* is to "tempt" one into a manner of existence that effectively "disburdens" one of one's being. By settling all questions in advance, *Das Man* "**levels** down" "the possible options of **choice** to what lies within the range of the familiar, the attainable, the respectable," removing the need for *Dasein* to make choices for itself. *Dasein* thus "becomes blind to its possibilities, and tranquillizes itself with that which is merely 'actual'" (BT, 239). In this manner, *Das Man* is the foundation of inauthentic existence. By disburdening *Dasein* of its **freedom** and responsibility, it ensures that the individual exists in **alienation** from its genuine human possibilities. Not only does *Das Man* provide *Dasein* with certain false interpretations of itself and the world; by treating all things as factual givens, it obscures the way in which the world exists as the correlate of human activities and interpretations, that is, the way in which *Dasein* is an active being-in-the-world rather than a passive recipient of data and stimuli.

Anxiety and Authenticity. The path from inauthentic to authentic existence *Dasein* must find on its own, as the result of its own decision; to put its trust simply in the guidance of others would be to reaffirm the hegemony of *das Man*. The first step on this path is occasioned by the experience of **anxiety** (*Angst*). Anxiety is not a pathological psychological phenomenon but a basic affective attunement to the world Heidegger calls "**mood**" (*Stimmung*) and "state-of-mind" (*Befindlichkeit*)—colloquially, "how one is" (literally, "how one finds oneself"). *Dasein* always finds itself in a certain mood which, "*prior* to all cognition and volition" (BT, 175), discloses the world in a certain light. In a striking reversal of traditional theories, Heidegger argues that mood is not a subjective projection onto an emotionless world, but a "disclosive submission to the world, out of which we can encounter something that matters to us" (BT, 177). For example, a mood of apprehension allows the silhouette of a mountain to appear as threatening; a mood of elation allows the blue sky to appear as joyful. In each case, mood discloses something about the world and cannot be reduced to a merely "subjective" occurrence. The world always appears under some affective aspect, and this disclosure is effected by *Dasein*'s mood.

Anxiety is a "fundamental mood" (*Grundstimmung*), one that discloses a deep truth about human being in its relation to the world. Specifically, "[a]nxiety discloses Dasein as *being-possible*"; it "makes manifest . . . its *being-free for* the **freedom** of choosing itself and taking hold of itself . . . the **authenticity** of its being" (BT, 232). This fundamental possibility of "choosing itself" has been obscured by the tranquilizing power of *das Man*, which has deflected *Dasein*'s intrinsic self-concern into a fascination with things and people. In anxiety, everyday concerns and involvements with others, through which an average understanding of the world is sustained, "sink away." "Anxiety . . . takes away from Dasein the possibility of understanding itself . . . in terms of the 'world' and the way things have been publicly interpreted" (BT, 232). Thus removed from the tranquilizing interpretations of *das Man*, *Dasein* is forced to confront itself apart from the roles and meanings assigned to it by others. For the first time, it becomes aware of itself as a pure "being of possibility," an "authentic potentiality-for-being-in-the-world." For this reason, Heidegger insists that "[a]nxiety **individualizes** Dasein and thus discloses it as '*solus ipse*'" (BT, 233). In other words, in anxiety it is brought home to me that it is *I*, not "they" or "anyone," who is responsible for interpreting the world and that I cannot avoid the freedom of choosing certain possibilities over others. Accordingly, in anxiety the comfortable and familiar "being-at-home" of everyday life "collapses" in an experience of "not-being-at-home" or "**uncanniness**" (*Unheimlichkeit*) as *Dasein* is torn away from its everyday concerns and left to confront itself.

Death. Division Two of *Being and Time*, entitled "Dasein and Temporality," develops the analysis of authentic existence broached at the end of Division One. The most unsettling experience of anxiety is connected to the possibility that is closest to myself (*eigenst*): the possibility of my own death. Heidegger devotes the first chapter of Division Two—some of the densest passages of *Being and Time*—to the phenomenon he calls **being-towards-death** (*sein zum Tode*). Being-towards-death is contrasted with the mundane fear of dying and with morbid preoccupation with one's demise or the demise of others. Its object is not the actuality of death, real or imagined, but death as a possibility. Heidegger's claim is that human beings relate to "death as a possibility" in the sense that a tacit preconceptual apprehension of **finitude** underlies and gives shape to a human life. Authentic being-towards-death involves an awareness of finitude as the temporal **horizon** against which life's plans and projects take on meaning and are judged. In Heidegger's terms, authentic *Dasein* "anticipates" death as a "possibility not to be outstripped"; death is the ultimate possibility, which "discloses also all the possibilities which lie ahead" (BT, 309) and thus gives *Dasein* a sense of its existence "as a whole." Death provides life with its finite measure, allowing one to gauge the importance of current concerns against the totality of one's life as it is grasped in anticipation. Authentically apprehended, death stirs *Dasein* out of everyday "untroubled indifference" and provides it with a sense of urgency and self-responsibility. *Das Man*, however, acts in various ways to suppress the experience of anxiety and the self-awareness it engenders. Everyday being-to-wards-death transforms death into an event to be feared and avoided yet at the same time into something whose inevitability should be countenanced with "indifference," not reflected on seriously. *Das Man* pacifies *Dasein* with the thought that "everyone dies." Thus it alienates *Dasein* from a proper understanding of its own existence.

Historicality and the Moment of Vision. Heidegger complements his analysis of authentic being-towards-death with a chapter devoted to *Dasein*'s understanding of the past, the uniquely human manner of grasping history that he names "**historicality**" (*Geschichtlichkeit*). Just as *Dasein* relates to the future as more than an abstract category of what is "not yet actual," it grasps the past as something other than what is "no longer present." In order for the past to become an object of study for historians and anthropologists, it must first be tacitly understood in terms of possibilities to be appropriated by the individual. The authentic past is not a dead abstraction but consists of living possibilities, both personal and collective, that must be taken hold of and responded to. Heidegger calls *Dasein*'s distinctive manner of existing in a constant relation to its past and its future "historizing" (*Geschehen*). Historizing is the process of "stretching between birth and death" that characterizes *Dasein*'s lived understanding of time; this understanding thus should not be assumed to be centered around the present moment as it is in traditional accounts, for the view of the present as a succession of passing "now points" derives from the metaphysical conception of time as something present-at-hand. "Dasein does not exist as the sum of momentary actualities of experiences which come along successively and disappear" (BT, 426). Instead, *Dasein* enacts the authentic present through an attitude of decisive "**resoluteness**" (*Entschlossenheit*) that issues in the "**moment** of vision" (*Augenblick*).

Heidegger's account of the moment of vision is an attempt to respond to the problem of how *Dasein* can both be "**thrown**" into—and thus constrained by—its past, and yet at the same time be able to extricate itself from past interpretations of itself and its world. Authentic being-towards-death clarifies for *Dasein* its relation to its past: "Only being-free *for* death . . . pushes existence into its finitude . . . snatches one back from the endless multiplicity of possibilities which offer themselves . . . and brings Dasein into the simplicity of its *fate*

[*Schicksal*]" (BT, 435). The moment of vision is achieved when, through anxious anticipation of death, one becomes clear about the finite historical possibilities that constitute one's situation—the circumstances one has inherited, the relationships into which one has been "thrown"—and at the same time one resolves deliberately to choose certain of these possibilities as one's own. Authentic awareness and action in the present is thus tantamount to authentic appropriation of the past, guided by authentic understanding of the future. *See also* HEIDEGGER AND NAZISM.

BEING-FOR-ITSELF AND BEING-IN-ITSELF (Fr. *être-pour-soi* and *être-en-soi*). Central concepts in the philosophy of **Jean-Paul Sartre**. Being-for-itself designates the type of being of human **consciousness**; being-in-itself designates the type of being of nonconscious things. In Sartre's account in ***Being and Nothingness***, the two categories are interrelated in the following manner. Being-for-itself refers to the power of consciousness to turn back on itself and continually "**negate**"—revise, reassess, reinterpret—the meaning of that which it apprehends. Nonconscious things—a table, a chair, a book, a mountain—to which consciousness is primarily directed, have the character of being-in-itself. They are experienced as independent of consciousness and as purely factual and self-identical. Consciousness exists in the manner of actively interpreting and using things that have being-in-itself; being-in-itself exists in the manner of not being reducible to the activity of consciousness.

BEING-IN-THE-WORLD (Ger. *In-der-Welt-sein*). A central concept of **Martin Heidegger**'s *Being and Time*. For Heidegger, the human being cannot be understood apart from its immediate practical **concern** with things and people; conversely, the idea of **world** cannot be understood apart from an intrinsic relation to human activities and purposes. Being-in-the-world designates the reciprocal relationship between *Dasein* and world, which for Heidegger is definitive of human being and of **being** itself.

A crucial premise of Heidegger's account is that things in the world are normally apprehended in terms of their immediate practical significance, or **readiness-to-hand**, rather than as "external objects," "sense data," or other theoretical constructs, which have the character of **presence-at-hand**. Things taken as present-at-hand are derivative upon things ready-to-hand; the bare physical properties assumed by science and traditional philosophy to be the primary constituents of reality are abstractions from the concrete world of human purposes. In Heidegger's example, a hammer is **understood** as a tool for driving nails to the extent that it is immediately manipulated for that purpose. The hammer as a brute physical object emerges only when one stands back from the practical task and "just looks" at it, removing it from the context of significance within which it is normally understood. Theoretical contemplation thus transforms the world of immediate involvements into an array of objects present-at-hand, a neutral assortment of things defined by location in space rather than by belonging to specific "places" and "regions" of human experience. The water is "in" my glass in the sense of spatial location. Human beings, however, are "in" the world in quite a different sense: We "dwell" in and are "familiar with" the world; we become immersed and absorbed in it.

The world is thus not to be conceived as an object of experience; it is an a priori whole. It is the condition for meaningful experience, the totality of purposes and meanings out of which particular things and activities emerge and to which they refer. The individual does not constitute the meaning of the world but presupposes it as the background of relations against which things are perceived and used. This is the sense of Heidegger's remark that "[t]he world is something 'wherein' Dasein as an entity already *was*" (BT, 106). A similar thought is expressed by Heidegger's insistence that *Dasein* exists as "**thrown**" into the world, finding itself within an already meaningful social and historical **situation**. Finally, the concept of being-in-the-world may be understood as Heidegger's recasting of **Edmund Husserl**'s idea of **intentionality**. The interpretation of intentionality as a relationship between the human being and world rather than between **ego** and the meanings it intuits is the foundation of **existential phenomenology**.

BEING-THERE. *See DASEIN.*

BEING-TOWARDS-DEATH (Ger. *Sein zum Tode*). Technical term in the vocabulary of **Martin Heidegger**'s *Being and Time*. Being-towards-**death** designates the uniquely human awareness of death that for Heidegger is crucial to the emergence of **authenticity**. Heidegger contrasts being-towards-death with the mundane fear of dying and with morbid preoccupation with one's own demise or the demise of others. The object of being-towards-death is thus not the actuality of death, real or imagined, but death as a possibility. Heidegger's claim is that human beings relate to "death as a possibility" in the sense that a tacit preconceptual apprehension of **finitude** underlies and gives shape to a human life.

Authentic being-towards-death involves an awareness of finitude as the temporal **horizon** against which life's plans and **projects** take on meaning and are judged. In Heidegger's terms, authentic *Dasein* "anticipates" death as a "possibility not to be outstripped"; death is the ultimate possibility, which "discloses also all the possibilities which lie ahead" (BT, 309) and thus gives Dasein a sense of its existence "as a whole." Death provides life with its finite measure, allowing one to gauge the importance of current concerns against the totality of one's life as it is grasped in anticipation. Authentically apprehended, death stirs *Dasein* out of everyday "untroubled indifference" and provides it with a sense of urgency and self-**responsibility**.

BEING-WITH-OTHERS. In the vocabulary of **Martin Heidegger**'s *Being and Time*, *Mitsein*, "being-with" or "being-with-others," is constitutive of *Dasein*; relations to other people are intrinsic and not merely incidental to **existence**. In Heidegger's account, other people are copresent with me in the world in an original sense and need not be constituted by analogy to myself or otherwise indirectly inferred. Others are "given" not only indirectly through my **concern** with things **ready-to-hand** but also directly in the specific stance I assume toward them, which Heidegger names "**solicitude**." *Fürsorge*, solicitude or "caring for" others, along with *Besorgen*, concernful "preoccupation" with things, is an essential feature of *Dasein*'s most basic manner of being as *Sorge*, "**care**." *See also* OTHER, THE.

BERDYAEV, NIKOLAI (1874–1948). Russian philosopher of religion. Berdyaev was a professor of philosophy at the University of Moscow when he was exiled in 1922 during one of Joseph Stalin's purges of the intelligentsia. He established the Academy of Philosophy and Religion in Berlin and moved it to Paris in 1924, where he remained until his **death**. Berdyaev is often classed, along with **Lev Shestov**, as a "Russian **Christian** existentialist." However, he may also be described as a Christian personalist philosopher with an affinity for existentialist themes like radical individual **freedom** and the critique of abstract thought. Berdyaev was a devout follower of the Russian Orthodox Church. His understanding of existentialism was narrowly wedded to **Søren Kierkegaard**'s insight that individual **existence** cannot be adequately expressed in objective or universal terms. "Existentialism," he maintained, is "a philosophy which will not accept objectifying knowledge. Existence cannot be the object of knowledge" (*Truth and Revelation*, 11). Thus he rejected **Martin Heidegger**'s and **Jean-Paul Sartre**'s formal **phenomenological** analyses of existence, while he accepted the more inconclusive approaches of **Gabriel Marcel** and **Karl Jaspers**: "[W]hatever may be the desire of Heidegger and Sartre to construct an **ontology** by bringing into service the concept, they are in the grip of objectifying knowledge and fail to break with the tradition" (*Truth and Revelation*, 12).

BERGSON, HENRI (1859–1941). Bergson was the preeminent French philosopher of the first quarter of the 20th century, and his influence on the ideas of the time was profound and wide-ranging. His status as a philosophical radical was at its peak in the early 1900s but had diminished by the 1930s, when the **philosophy of existence** began to emerge as a distinctive avenue of thought for French intellectuals like **Jean-Paul Sartre** and **Maurice Merleau-Ponty**. Thus, while Sartre and Merleau-Ponty, like other young French philosophers of the time, had studied Bergson's philosophy as university students, they make few references to Bergson in their mature works.

At the core of Bergson's philosophy is a radical theory of lived time or "duration" (*durée*), introduced in his first book, *Time and Free Will* (*Les données immédiates de la conscience*, 1889). In contrast to the abstract, objective time of physics—time as a series of discrete, quantifiable moments—the lived experience of time is an "intuition of duration," a continuous, ever-changing flow in which the past is carried forward into the present while the present presses forward into the future. A paradigmatic example of the intuition of duration is the perception of a musical melody, where each note is experienced as part of an evolving, organic whole and never simply as a discrete tone, such that there is "a mutual penetration, an interconnexion and organization of elements, each one of which represents the whole, and cannot be distinguished or isolated from it except by abstract thought" (*Time and Free Will*, 101). Similarly, time as revealed in duration is characterized by a continual interpenetration, rather than a static juxtaposition, of past, present, and future, such that it is impossible to identify a particular mental event as "cause" and a subsequent event as "effect." The illusion that there are discrete units of time, some present, some past, and the correlative illusion that the mind consists in discrete mental states, is produced when, for purposes of communication and survival, intellectual concepts are applied to the living flow of reality, breaking it down into what appear to be distinct, self-contained objects. Only when time and reality are "frozen" into discrete bits, for example, in abstract theories of philosophy and science, does it seem possible that one bit (existing in the past) can determine another bit (existing in the present), as in associationist theories of the self.

From the perspective of durational experience, Bergson argues, the self appears as it truly is, a dynamic process of becoming rather than a static entity; crucial to his argument is the claim that such a "living," interpenetrating process is not susceptible to causal analysis. Thus, for Bergson the clearest instance of a "free act" is one that springs from the "deep self" (*moi profond*), the self that is not reducible to deterministic mechanisms but that continually creates itself, assimilating new experiences and thoughts from moment to moment, never coming to rest in a fixed state or character. For Bergson, the problem of determinism arises only when, from an objectifying perspective, consciousness is falsely broken down into discrete states, and the self is misidentified as a static, unchanging thing.

It is clear that Bergson's account of consciousness as lived duration and his defense of **freedom** are complementary to primary concerns of existentialism. Parallels with Sartre's conception of **consciousness** and freedom are particularly apparent. Further, Bergson's treatment of the **body** as an "instrument of action," presented in his second book, *Matter and Memory* (*Matière et mémoire,* 1896), anticipates and complements the views of Merleau-Ponty. Yet Bergson's relationship to existentialism was one of missed opportunity, not fruitful partnership. Sartre traces his earliest moment of philosophical inspiration as a college student to his reading of Bergson's *Time and Free Will*; however, soon afterward his interest in Bergson was overshadowed by what he perceived as more revolutionary—i.e., existentially oriented—philosophers such as **G. W. F. Hegel**, **Martin Heidegger**, and **Edmund Husserl**. Merleau-Ponty reported a similar experience in his observation that, had it not fallen out of favor in the 1930s, Bergson's philosophy of duration might have provided the approach to **concrete** experience that he and Sartre hungered after as young philosophers: "[I]f we had been careful readers of Bergson . . . we would have been drawn to a much more concrete philosophy. . . . But since Bergson was hardly read by my contemporaries . . . we had to wait for the philosophies of existence in order to learn much of what he would have been able to teach us" (Stewart, 495). Heidegger was familiar with Bergson's theory of time as lived duration, but he dismissed it somewhat peremptorily as beholden to traditional conceptions of time. A more successsful encounter with Bergson is noted by **Gabriel Marcel**, the eldest of the French existentialists. Marcel followed Bergon's lectures at the Collège de France for two years in the 1910s, and he testified to Bergson's extraordinary charisma and power as a teacher: "Everytime we went there, it was somehow with a beating heart and with a kind of hope of hearing a revelation . . . the feeling really was that Bergson was in the process of discovering something . . . of revealing to us certain deeper and more secret aspects of our own reality" (TWB, 219).

BEYOND GOOD AND EVIL. *See* NIETZSCHE, FRIEDRICH.

BINSWANGER, LUDWIG. *See* EXISTENTIAL PSYCHOTHERAPY.

BLANCHOT, MAURICE (1907–2003). Modernist French novelist, critic, and literary theorist. Blanchot's fiction and criticism explore themes of interiority, **death**, and the limits of **communication** as these are embodied in the act of writing. His work was instrumental in the development of the French *nouvel roman* in the 1960s and was a leading influence on the development of deconstruction in the

1970s and 1980s. A highly secretive man who refused to be photographed or to speak in public, Blanchot maintained close friendships with **Georges Bataille** and especially with **Emmanuel Levinas**, with whom his writing bears similarities of style and thematic interest. Blanchot and **Jean-Paul Sartre** respected each other's literary work, and in the 1950s Blanchot contributed to Sartre's journal, *Les Temps modernes*. As a literary critic Blanchot wrote on Sartre as well as on **Albert Camus**. However, Blanchot's view of writing as an autonomous act unrelated to the social and political **world** and to the personal life of the author was diametrically opposed to Sartre's conception of **committed literature**. Sartre's review of Blanchot's early novel *Aminadab* (1942), "*Aminadab* or the Fantastic Considered as a Language" (1947), treated Blanchot as a young "writer of the fantastic" akin to **Franz Kafka**, but one still searching for his own style. In 1960, Blanchot composed the final draft of a manifesto in opposition to the Algerian War, the "Manifesto of 121," signed by 121 French writers and intellectuals, including Sartre.

BODY AND MIND. Traditionally Western philosophy has tended toward a dualist view, which holds that mind and mental events are distinct from and irreducible to physical objects and events, including the human body. From a dualist perspective, while the body passively receives sense impressions from the world, it is the mind that actively organizes these impressions, abstracting from them to form general ideas, drawing inferences and conclusions, and eventually attaining knowledge. Apart from its receptive role in cognition, the body tends to be of little interest to traditional philosophy; it is an unthinking array of physiological processes, including instincts and appetites that may interfere with objective knowledge, and these have no significant part in a philosophical account of human **understanding**.

Existentialists have tended to reject traditional mind/body dualism and have endeavored in various ways to rehabilitate the philosophical status of the human body. The key to this rehabilitation is a distinction, respected by most existentialists, between the "objective body"—the body observed externally and as an object of scientific knowledge—and the "lived body"—the body as experienced immediately but **prereflectively** in the first person. Once the lived body is distinguished from the objective body, it becomes clear that the body is not normally an object or tool manipulated by the mind, just as the mind is not a disembodied power. Mental acts generally have a bodily component, just as bodily behaviors generally express intentions, attitudes, and desires. From an existentialist perspective, "lived body" and "embodied mind" are alternate descriptions of the human being; the existentialist concepts of "**consciousness**," "*Dasein*," and "**existence**" also assume the primary experiential unity of mind and body.

French existentialists, especially **Gabriel Marcel** and **Maurice Merleau-Ponty**, elevate the body to a topic of primary philosophical concern. Building upon **Henri Bergson**'s earlier treatment of embodiment in *Matter and Memory*, Marcel's starting point, sketched somewhat impressionistically, is the insight that the human body is experienced as a tacit, pregiven, and nonobjectifiable background for perception and action rather than as a mechanical instrument subservient to the mind. This idea is developed systematically by Merleau-Ponty in *Phenomenology of Perception*. For Merleau-Ponty, the lived body (*corps propre*) is a dynamic complex of prereflective habits and dispositions that underlie our perception of the **world** and render perception a projective and interpretive activity rather than a passive transcription of sense data or a purely mental process of categorizing objects. "The lived body is in the world as the heart is in the organism: it keeps the visible spectacle constantly alive, it breathes life into it and sustains it inwardly, and with it forms a system" (PP, 203, translation slightly altered). While the lived body thus shares attributes of both the mental and the physical, it is an **ambiguous** third term, reducible to neither. As such, Merleau-Ponty distinguishes it from Sartre's notion of consciousness as well as from materialist views of the organism guided by instinct, reflex, or conditioned response.

A distinct treatment of embodiment focused on the body as objectified by others is offered by **Jean-Paul Sartre** in *Being and Nothingness*. For Sartre, the body is objectified by the look of the **other**, who sees me and judges me, alienating me from my sense of myself as nondetermined and provoking my shame. German existentialism is less eloquent on the subject of the body. **Martin Heidegger** takes an extreme position, opting to avoid traditional distinctions between body and mind altogether, because he perceives such language as harboring illicit metaphysical assumptions about the nature of human beings: "When . . . we come to the question of man's being, this is not something we can simply compute by adding together those kinds of being which body, soul, and spirit respectively possess . . . [s]ome idea of the being of the whole must be presupposed" (BT, 74).

BOREDOM (Ger. *Langeweile*). In *Being and Time*, Heidegger focuses on **anxiety** as the **mood** most revelatory of *Dasein*'s finite character. In his 1929–1930 lecture course, published as *The Fundamental Concepts of Metaphysics*, Heidegger amends this analysis by identifying *boredom* as a basic **ontological** mood, the mood that most reveals the historical **situation** of post–**World War I** Germany. Heidegger analyzes the phenomenon of boredom from several perspectives. The etymology of the German *Langeweile*, "long while," points to an experience of time passing slowly, hence of being "burdened" by time. Heidegger exploits the link between time and boredom. Experientially, boredom is felt when time "drags" because there is nothing of interest to do, nothing to preoccupy one. A superficial understanding is that boredom may be overcome by occupying oneself with some task or distraction. A more penetrating view, for Heidegger, sees boredom as an index of a deeper malaise, an apprehension of the superficiality of **existence** itself, its lack of weight and **mystery**. Recognizing boredom is thus, for Heidegger in 1929, a necessary step in the **awakening** of philosophy to the historical situation.

BOSS, MEDARD. *See* EXISTENTIAL PSYCHOTHERAPY.

BOUNDARY SITUATION. *See* LIMIT SITUATION.

BRACKETING. *See* PHENOMENOLOGICAL REDUCTION.

BRASILLACH TRIAL. When the young French writer and journalist Robert Brasillach (1905–1945) was sentenced to **death** in 1945 for his collaborationist journalism during the German occupation of France, French writers were divided over his fate, and his trial in the winter of 1945 became the most visible and controversial of the postwar "purification" trials of French intellectuals. A petition of appeal organized by novelist and journalist François Mauriac and signed by many distinguished writers and intellectuals, including Paul Valéry, Jean Anouilh, **Gabriel Marcel**, and **Albert Camus**, failed to sway Charles de Gaulle, and Brasillach was executed on 6 Feburary 1945. When asked to sign the petition, Camus, who throughout the autumn of 1944 had argued in his *Combat* editorials for the need for justice against collaborators—battling against Mauriac's pleas for compassion voiced in his editorials for the conservative *Figaro* newspaper— had paced the floor all night. His decision to sign the petition marked a turning point for Camus, as it committed him to a condemnation of capital punishment from which he never wavered.

BRENTANO, FRANZ (1838–1917). German philosopher and psychologist who first proposed the concept of **intentionality** as an essential feature of human **consciousness**. Brentano was a teacher of **Edmund Husserl** and is thus essential to the development of **phenomenology**. In 1907, Martin Heidegger received a copy of Brentano's dissertation, "On the Several Senses of Being in Aristotle." This work, which outlined the notion of "intentional objects," was Heidegger's first glimpse of a phenomenological perspective, and it aroused his interest in Husserl's philosophy. Significantly, it was also Heidegger's first exposure to the problem of **being**, which became the focus of his mature thought.

BRUNSCHVICG, LÉON (1869–1944). French idealist philosopher and historian of philosophy. Brunschvicg was a highly regarded philosopher and professor who taught philosophy at the Sorbonne from 1900 until 1939. For **Jean-Paul Sartre** and **Maurice Merleau-Ponty** as young philosophers in Paris in the 1930s, Brunschvicg's "critical idealism" was overly abstract, rationalistic, and prejudiced toward science—precisely the type of philosophy that the **philosophers of existence** sought to overcome. In the late 1930s, Sartre characterized Brunschvicg's idealism as a type of "digestive thinking," which swallows and assimilates things to the mind, denying their independent, **concrete** reality. In contrast, **Gabriel Marcel** spoke highly of Brunschwicg both as a philosopher and as a person.

BUBER, MARTIN (1878–1965). Jewish Austrian social and religious philosopher, Talmudic scholar, and translator. A prolific writer and editor, Buber was the leading figure of the Jewish cultural renaissance in Germany in the 1920s. His accomplishments extend also into politics and education: He was a leader in the Zionist movement, was an organizer of Jewish adult education in Germany prior to **World War II**, and later participated in the formation of the Hebrew University of Jerusalem. Though not exclusively an existentialist philosopher, his contribution to existentialism is substantial. Buber's poetic essay *I and Thou* (1923) is among the first statements of 20th-century existentialism and was highly influential in the subsequent development of the **philosophy of existence** in Germany and France. Beginning with this book, Buber developed the core insight of his philosophical thought, the idea of the encounter (*Begegnung*) or of **dialogue** (*Zwiesprache*) with the **other**. Genuine dialogue is described as a relationship between "I" and a personal "You" (*Du*), a relationship between subject and subject that is contrasted with the relation of subject to object, or "I–It" relation, required by philosophical and scientific thinking. The *telos* and ultimate guarantor of human I–You relationships is relationship to the "absolute You," God. Accordingly for Buber, the core of **authentic existence** is not found in any particular doctrine or practice, religious or otherwise, but in the experience of an absolute, undelimitable You that nourishes and pervades the experiences of ordinary life.

Life. Buber was born in Vienna, the son of two assimilated Jews, and his early education reflects the refined intellectual culture of the late Austro–Hungarian Empire, which produced such brilliant thinkers and writers as **Ludwig Wittgenstein**, **Sigmund Freud**, and Hugo Von Hofmannsthal. After his parents separated in 1882, he was raised by his grandparents, wealthy Jewish philanthropists who participated in the Enlightenment movement to modernize eastern European Jewry. While Buber learned Hebrew with his grandfather, he was drawn initially to secular German culture rather than to Judaism, studying philosophy and art at the Universities of Vienna, Berlin, and Zurich, and writing a doctoral dissertation on the mystical thought of Nicholas of Cusa and Jacob Böhme. Like many German-speaking intellectuals of his generation, for a time Buber was strongly impressed by **Friedrich Nietzsche**, and the influence of Nietzsche's rejection of a transcendent world and his affirmation of the earth, as well as his notion of the "eternal recurrence of the same," can be detected in

Buber's mature writing. Other influences include the social philosophy of Georg Simmel and Fernand Tönnies and the **philosophy of life** of **Wilhelm Dilthey**.

In 1901, at the behest of Theodor Herzl, Buber briefly served as editor of the Zionist monthly *Die Welt*. He continued to be an active voice in the Zionist movement, stressing the need for Jewish "spiritual renewal" in the establishment of a Jewish homeland. In 1916, he founded the monthly journal *Der Jude*, which became the leading intellectual forum for German-speaking Jews in Europe. In keeping with his philosophy of dialogue, as editor Buber advocated a binational (Arab and Jewish) solution to the situation in Palestine, a dissenting opinion that estranged him from other Zionist leaders. In 1925, Buber and his friend **Franz Rosenzweig** undertook a translation of the Bible into modern German, which was completed after World War II, after Rosenzweig's **death**. Praised for its direct, poetic language, Buber and Rosenzweig's translation is still widely used by **Christian** ministers in Germany today. In 1916, with his wife, Paula Winckler, and their two children, Buber moved to a small town outside of Frankfurt, Germany, where he lived and worked as an editor until, under mounting pressure from the **Nazis**, he immigrated to Palestine in 1938. The rest of his life was spent mainly in Jerusalem, where he taught anthropology and sociology at the Hebrew University.

Overcoming Alienation. In similar fashion to other existentialists of the time, Buber identifies the problem of **alienation** as the starting point for philosophical inquiry. Human beings are alienated to the extent that they relate to the **world** and to others as objects to be known and manipulated rather than as subjects to be encountered. This is the world of I–It (*Ich–Es*) relations. It is substantially the world relegated to us by modern science and industrialized capitalism, of "things and processes that are bounded by other things and processes and capable of being measured against and compared . . . an ordered world, a detached world" (IT, 82). In such a dehumanized world, human beings also become alienated from themselves. Reductive theories of the human being, such as Darwinian biology and Freudian **psychoanalysis**, encourage us to see ourselves as determined by biological, psychological, and historical forces, to the point that "[i]t is considered foolish to imagine any **freedom**" (IT, 105).

The alienated world of I–It relations is, thankfully, not self-suffi-cient. Rather, it is interwoven with a network of I–You (*Ich–Du*) re-lationships, human relationships in which one feels oneself "ad-dressed" by another living being. To be addressed by the other is to feel oneself called on to respond to the other's "presence," to enter into "dialogue" with the other. It is to be personally addressed, by "first and last name," and thus forced out of the perspective of anony-mous observer into that of engaged and responsible agent. In this way, through dialogical relationship one comes to an experience of one's own freedom in conjunction with recognition of the freedom of the other who addresses one. Buber asserts that the I–You relation-ship is not controlled by any preconception, purpose, or communica-tion of information between self and other. It transpires in the simple experience of saying "you" to another and of being recognized as "you" in turn; it is immediate, reciprocal, and occurs wholly in the present. At its highest fulfillment in religious experience, the rela-tionship of I and You extends not only to other persons but also to other animals and to the entire natural and human world. Experienced as "unique" Yous, as "signs" to which one is called on to respond rather than as mechanical "things and processes," all things become "heavy with meaning" (IT, 158). The culmination of Buber's vision is the point at which one becomes aware of the fundamental truth that "we live in the currents of universal **reciprocity**" (IT, 67).

Religion in Dialogue. As a young man Buber was drawn to mysti-cism, yet it is crucial for his mature thought that religious experience not be construed as mystical union with God or as transport to an-other world. For Buber, religious revelation always takes the form of being addressed by a You, yet it is an "absolute You" that cannot be objectively described or known. Thus Buber rejects the doctrinal claims of religion, including Judaism, that specify God's nature and dictate human rules of worship; these he sees as objectifications of genuine religious encounter, which remains unspecifiable and unpre-dictable. Moreover, to know God is not to renounce the **world**. Rather, it is to "grasp everything in him," to experience ordinary life as sacred, shot through with **mystery** and presence: "[W]hen you consecrate life you encounter the living God" (IT, 128). In this sense, Buber's philosophy of religion remains faithful to the existentialist thesis of the primacy of **concrete** human experience. God is not encountered in contemplation but in **action**, decision, and living.

Further, Buber rejects the idea that God may or even must be encountered in solitude, apart from one's relations and **commitments** to other human beings. In a 1936 essay, "The Question to the Single One" (BMM, 46–97), Buber attributes this idea to **Søren Kierkegaard** and submits it to extensive criticism. For Buber, Kierkegaard exemplifies the life of the "single one" who renounces marriage and ordinary commerce with others in order to free himself for God. This is a perennial temptation of religion but, Buber argues, ultimately an error, for it is based on renouncing the very human relationships through which God is primarily encountered. Alternately put, it is a view of **faith** centered in "monologue" rather than dialogue:

> All the enthusiasm of the philosophers for monologue, from Plato to Nietzsche, does not touch the simple experience of faith that speaking with God is something *toto genere* different from 'speaking with oneself'; whereas, remarkably, it is not something *toto genere* different from speaking with another human being. (BMM, 58)

Dialogue with another thus exemplifies and instantiates faith; "worldly" relations to others are not to be excluded from one's relation to the divine, for they are expressive of it. "Creation is not a hurdle on the road to God, it is the road itself. . . . Creatures are placed in my way so that I, their fellow-creature, by means of them and with them find the way to God" (BMM, 60).

Buber's view of religion consequently requires human reciprocity at the collective as well as the individual level. True collective existence, however, requires not only shared beliefs and **values** but also a "concrete togetherness," a life of shared work, love, and worship. Buber thus espouses a type of utopian, humanistic socialism in which concrete communities, rather than anonymous "collectivities" such as a class or a nation, form the basis of society and the state, a vision realized in the communal life of Jewish settlers in Palestine and later in the Israeli Kibbutzim. Even if secular in nature, a true community is for Buber essentially religious, in that it is founded on real I–You relationships: "All real relationship points to God; and all craving for God points to real community. . . . Men search for God but cannot

find Him, for He is 'not there'. . . . He does not want to be possessed
but to be realized. Only when men want God to be will they practice
community" (*The Martin Buber Reader*, 251).

   Buber's Critique of Heidegger. Buber extends his criticism of
Kierkegaard to the "new philosophy" Kierkegaard's thought engen-
dered in Germany in the 1920s and 1930s, namely, the "philosophy
of existence" represented by **Martin Heidegger**. Just as
Kierkegaard's understanding of religious faith remains for Buber essentially solitary, Heidegger's philosophy of human existence remains fundamentally "monological": "[I]n Heidegger's view, the true
significance . . . of [the categories of existence] is disclosed only in
the realm of the individual's relation to himself" (BMM, 195). According to Buber, this is particularly clear in the **ethical** phenomena
analyzed by Heidegger, such as "guilt" and "conscience." In Heidegger's analysis in *Being and Time*, the "call of conscience" draws *Dasein* away from its ordinary relations to others and calls it to take up
its own authentic possibilities. Yet, Heidegger insists, the call comes
ultimately not from God, a moral tradition, or another person, but
from *Dasein* itself. Buber sees Heidegger's account of conscience,
and more generally his philosophy of **authenticity**, as fundamentally
monological. He offers a contrasting account: "If a . . . present being
move[s] past me, and I was not really there, then . . . out of its disappearance, comes a . . . cry. . . : 'Where were you?' *That* is the cry of
conscience. It is not my existence which calls to me, but the being
which is not I" (BMM, 197). Buber's criticism of Heidegger exemplifies the general criticism leveled by religious existentialists such as
Gabriel Marcel and **Karl Jaspers** against "atheistic" existentialism,
that it is unjustifiably skewed toward the solitary individual. Because
thinkers like Heidegger and **Jean-Paul Sartre**, it is alleged, ignore
the reality of positive relationships to other persons, and because they
dogmatically deny the experience of the divine, their accounts of existence are hopelessly incomplete and one-sided. "Heidegger turns
away not merely from a relation to a divine unconditioned being, but
also from a relation in which man experiences another than himself
in the unconditioned. . . . Heidegger's 'existence' is monological"
(BMM, 199). In the existentialist tradition, Buber's critique of monological thinking is elaborated later by the French philosopher **Emmanuel Levinas**.

BUDDHISM. *See* NISHITANI, KEIJI.

BULTMANN, RUDOLPH (1884–1976). German Protestant theologian and biblical scholar. Along with **Paul Tillich** and Karl Barth, Bultmann was a principal proponent of **existential theology**. Bultmann was a colleague of **Martin Heidegger**'s at Marburg University in the 1920s. There they attended each others' lectures and participated together in a weekly reading group on ancient Greek literature and philosophy. This interaction played a role in Bultmann's most influential and controversial work, the project of "demythologizing" the New Testament, translating the "mythical" notions of early **Christianity** into modern terms to render them intelligible to a contemporary audience. In "New Testament and Mythology" (1941), Bultmann contended that the essential message of the New Testament—that God has become revealed in Christ—is independent of the mythical world picture within which it was originally framed. The conception of a three-tiered cosmos of earth, heaven, and hell, and of an ongoing battle between spirits of darkness and light, demons and angels, Satan and God, issuing in an apocalyptic end of the world, is not credible for modern readers. Hence the message must be reformulated in terms that preserve its essential truth. These Bultmann found in existentialist philosophy—specifically, the philosophy of Heidegger's *Being and Time*. In a creative and often compelling fashion, Bultmann reinterpreted New Testament ideas in light of Heidegger's existentialism. *Sin* is understood as inauthentic **existence**, absorption in the **world** of **everyday** concerns; the *life of the spirit* or *faith* is seen as **authentic** existence, the state we achieve when we "die to the world" and, in an act of **resolute** decision, become aware of our essential **nothingness**. Faith, like authentic existence, requires letting go of a false "sense of security"; thus it is described as a "readiness for **anxiety**."

In response to critics, Bultmann defended demythologizing as a means to reveal the existential truth of Christianity, not to reduce Christianity to existentialism. Heidegger's analysis of existence was not, he insisted, invoked as an authority higher than religion. Rather, it was understood to be "only a profane philosophical presentation of the New Testament view of who we are" (*New Testament and Mythology and Other Basic Writings*, 23). In the 1950s, **Karl**

Jaspers engaged with Bultmann in a debate over the meaning of demythologizing that was published in a series of articles and responses.

– C –

CAFÉ EXISTENTIALIST. This term, coined by **David Cooper**, refers to young denizens of **Saint-Germain-des-Près** during the late 1940s and 1950s, who embodied the style but not the substance of existentialism. Dressed in what Simone de Beauvoir described as the "new 'Existentialist' uniform . . . of black sweaters, black shirts and black pants" (FC, 142), these bohemian artists, actors, writers, and musicians had little to do with existentialist philosophy but were commonly identified as "existentialists" by the French press. An icon of café existentialism was the actress and singer **Juliette Gréco**, who knew **Jean-Paul Sartre** and **Simone de Beauvoir** personally.

CAMUS, ALBERT (1913–1960). French Algerian novelist, journalist, and playwright, often classified as an existentialist due to his association with **Jean-Paul Sartre** in the mid- and late 1940s. Camus's 1942 novel *The Stranger* is commonly read as a classic of existentialist literature, and his essay of the same year, ***The Myth of Sisyphus***, is frequently cited as an exemplary existentialist treatment of the **absurd**. However, on closer scrutiny Camus's status as an existentialist is not assured. Camus considered himself first and foremost a writer, not a philosopher. While he was attracted to philosophical problems, he avoided analyzing them in a sustained or systematic way. Moreover, Camus resented having his work assimilated to that of Sartre, and he rejected the existentialist label when applied to his own endeavors, preferring instead the "**philosophy of the absurd**" as a more accurate description of his early viewpoint. It should also be recalled that Camus's conception of the absurd developed independently from the main currents of existentialist thought in France at the time. He avoided serious engagement with the philosophy of **G. W. F. Hegel** or **Martin Heidegger** and the **phenomenology** of **Edmund Husserl**, as well as with Sartre's philosophy as expounded in ***Being and Nothingness***. Camus modeled himself instead on figures like Blaise Pascal and **Friedrich Nietzsche**, who combined considerable literary talent with a strong moral agenda, and who held the activity of philosophy in low esteem. Thus, while his criticism of philosophical abstraction and his treatment of themes of absurdity, mortality, **freedom**, and revolt offer clear parallels with existentialism, his identity as an existentialist is open to question.

Life. Camus was born and raised as a "*pied-noir*," or French national, in Algeria when it was still a colony of France. Unlike the existentialists, Camus's background was relatively poor and lower middle class, and throughout his career he enjoyed an "outsider" status vis-à-vis the Parisian cultural and intellectual elite. Camus's father, a cellerman for an Algerian vineyard, was killed in **World War I** when Camus was eight months old; his mother, who could neither read nor write, subsequently worked as a maid. After his father's **death**, Camus, his mother, and his older brother moved to Algiers to live with his maternal grandmother, who became the de facto head of the household. Together with an uncle, they shared a three-room apartment in a working-class neighborhood, in a building that lacked electricity or running water. Camus, his brother, and his mother slept together in one room crowded with furniture and beds. Still, his childhood was happy: "Poverty was . . . never a misfortune for me: it was radiant with light . . . my family . . . who lacked almost everything . . . envied practically nothing . . . their silence . . . their natural sober pride . . . taught me the most valuable and enduring lessons" (LCE, 6–7). Among those lessons learned were to avoid envy and resentment of others and "a certain fidelity and silent tenacity" (LCE, 10).

Camus attended high school in Algiers as a scholarship student. His passion for soccer and swimming was curbed when he contracted tuberculosis at age 17, an illness that plagued him for for the rest of his life. Soon after he enrolled as a philosophy student at the university of Algiers, where he came under the tutelage of his philosophy professor, Jean Grenier, who encouraged his interest in literature and philosophy and remained a lifelong friend. Camus was attracted to thinkers like Nietzsche, Pascal, Socrates, and Spinoza for their clear moral vision. He completed a master's thesis on Plotinus and Saint Augustine before deciding not to pursue a teaching career. In the 1930s, Camus began a lifelong relationship with the theater, working as a director and actor with the Théâtre du Travail, producing leftist plays for boisterous working-class audiences, and in 1934–1935 he briefly joined the Algerian **Communist** Party. In the late 1930s, Camus emerged as a leading figure in Algiers's intellectual community, writing for the leftist newspaper *Alger Républicain*, where his book reviews included a critical assessment of Jean-Paul Sartre's first novel, **Nausea**. While Camus admired Sartre's book, he found it a failure as a work of art due to a "lack of balance between . . . ideas . . . and the images that express them" (LCE, 201). Camus pursued his writing in private, working on plays, essays, and a novel.

Moving to Paris in 1940, Camus made a splash in the Parisian literary world in 1942 with the publication of his first novel, *L'Etranger* (*The Stranger*), which was praised for its austerity and "classicism" by reviewers, including Sartre, and criticized for its "pessimism" and lack of "meaningful **values**" by more conservative critics. Later in the year *The Myth of Sisyphus* also appeared, providing a philosophical complement to *The Stranger* in which Camus explained his philosophy of the absurd. Camus's play *Caligula*, also dealing with the theme of absurdity, was produced in 1944. In these wartime years, Camus befriended Sartre and Beauvoir but tended not to discuss ideas with them. Late in 1943, he joined the clandestine resistance group **Combat**, agreeing to serve as editor of a bimonthly newssheet. After the liberation of Paris in August 1944, *Combat* became a regular daily newspaper, and Camus stayed on as editor. His editorials for *Combat* from 1944 to 1947, in which Camus passed judgment on and sought to influence affairs of the day, made him one of the most respected intellectuals in France.

Camus's second novel, *La Peste* (1947) (*The Plague*), heralded a political turn in his thought, brought about by his experience under the German occupation. Conceived as an allegory for human resistance to evil, and in particular for European resistance to the Nazis, the novel chronicles a small Algerian town's response to an outbreak of bubonic plague. Camus presented his critical reflections on the concept of political and moral revolt in *L'Homme révolté* (1951) (**The Rebel**), which provoked heated controversy over its critique of Soviet **communism** and precipitated the end of his relationship with Sartre and Beauvoir. In *The Rebel*, Camus introduced a universal humanist **ethics** that forms the basis of his mature political position, including the condemnation of torture and capital punishment. Through the 1950s, Camus became increasingly disillusioned with politics. He was criticized for remaining neutral during the Algerian War, but refused to condone the use of violence on either side and hoped for a negotiated settlement. Camus's third novel, *La Chute* (*The Fall*), published in 1957, is an extended confessional monologue that turns away from political issues. That same year he was awarded the Nobel Prize for literature. Camus died in a car accident in the south of France in 1960, at the age of 47.

Nihilism and the Limits of the Absurd. Camus's understanding of the absurd may be illuminated by comparison to Nietzsche's analysis of **nihilism**, to which it is indebted. Nietzsche understands nihilism, the denial of the value of life, as a perennial human temptation aggravated by the "**death of God**," the loss of belief in transcendent **values** occasioned by the demise of religion as a social force in Europe during the 18th and 19th centuries. Similarly, in *The Myth of Sisyphus* Camus portrayed his own era as a time of crisis haunted by nihilism, an era defined by the failure of classical systems of science, philosophy, and religion to make sense of the world and give direction to human life. The result of this failure, Camus maintains, is a prevailing experience of "absurdity" or "meaninglessness" reflected in the philosophy, art, and literature of the day; in such "absurd thinkers" as **Martin Heidegger**, **Karl Jaspers**, and **Søren Kierkegaard**, Camus notes, metaphysical "illusions" are peeled away, and the world is revealed to exist without transcendent purpose or meaning. But removing metaphysical illusions, such as divine providence or universal reason, by which the world has traditionally been propped up, is not ultimately cause for despair; this is the fault of "existential" philosophers like Heidegger and Jaspers who, Camus asserts with little argument, resign themselves to a kind of nihilism. Rather, confrontation with the absurd allows human beings to attain their true "dignity" by choosing to live despite the meaninglessness of their condition. Camus's value-perspective is thus close to Nietzsche's: Human grandeur and nobility emerge in the struggle to act and to create in a world indifferent to human purposes.

If Camus's view, like Nietzsche's, has often been misinterpreted as a type of radical nihilism, an endorsement to "do whatever you want" because in the end "nothing matters," it is in large part because Meursault, the hero of *The Stranger*, his best-known work, gives credence to this interpretation. Meursault seems oblivious to the feelings of others and refuses to express remorse about killing an Arab man, going only so far as to say that "it was on account of the sun," that he wished it hadn't happened, and that he wished the man were still alive. But again, Camus's intention is not to celebrate absurdity but to indicate a means of moving beyond it, to show that "within the limits of nihilism it is possible to find the means to proceed beyond nihilism" (MS, v). Thus, while Meursault is a murderer (a dramatic choice whose necessity may be questioned), he is not an absolute nihilist. His realization at the novel's end is that life has irreducible value despite its apparent absurdity. Alternately put, through the absurd he realizes that the value of life is immanent to the experience of life itself and does not depend on **metaphysical** justification.

In the course of the 1940s, Camus became increasingly aware of the limits of the absurdist view. For one thing, to speak (with Meursault or Sisyphus) of the "value of life" is to speak of the value *my* life affords *me*, yet says nothing about the value of others' lives and how I ought to behave toward them. If the absurd hero is engaged in a solitary struggle against the conditions of his existence, the role of others in this struggle remains dangerously unspecified. Like Sartre and Beauvoir, Camus learned during the German occupation that real-life struggles depend on the collaboration of others. Moreover, he came to see that in the social and political domain, value questions cannot be so easily relativized. Personally, Camus was deeply opposed to Nazism and to all forms of political oppression and violence. Yet absurdism remained an ethic of individual fulfillment and thus an inadequate basis for a social ethics. Consequently, in the next phase of his work Camus turned to politics and history in an attempt to find a basis for a more universalist perspective.

An Ethics of Rebellion. The mature phase of Camus's thinking, documented in *The Plague* and *The Rebel*, attempts to move beyond the absurdist position to a humanistic stance where issues of **responsibility** and obligation to others replace issues of individual **authenticity**. The foundation of this stance is the notion of "rebellion" (*révolte*). In *The Rebel*, Camus understands rebellion as the refusal of conditions perceived as unjust. Thus, in contrast to the absurd, rebellion is essentially a moral concept. Moreover, it is also a political concept, for overcoming conditions of injustice and oppression is essentially a collective endeavor, never solely an individual undertaking. In Camus's analysis, rebellion has historically tended to deteriorate into "metaphysical rebellion," paradigmatic instances of which are the state-sponsored terrorism following the French and Russian Revolutions. Metaphysical rebellion is an expression of modern hubris that seeks to remake the imperfect world of human affairs in the service of a utopian ideology. Thus it is ultimately a revolt "against the human condition itself" rather than against particular circumstances of oppression affecting human beings. Consequently, Camus links the problem of rebellion to the question of "murder," of whether killing another human being can be justified in the name of a "higher"political or moral end. This, Camus notes, referring to Soviet totalitarianism as well as to **Nazism**, is "the question put to us by the blood and strife of our century" (R, 12).

Camus's conclusion, that killing another person is never morally justified, clearly moved him beyond absurdism; the value of human life, "the dignity common to all men," is recognized as "a primary value" (R, 245), universally binding. Genuine (nonmetaphysical) rebellion, Camus maintained, is motivated by recognition of human dignity and by a sense of solidarity with others. At the same time, it is constrained by an awareness of limits and a pragmatic moral realism, for a morally perfect world is not attainable, and the illusion of attaining it leads to moral excess. Camus's mature stance of pragmatic humanism is exemplified by Dr. Rieux, the protagonist of *The Plague*, who organizes "sanitation squads" to alleviate people's suffering from the plague, not to save humanity from evil once and for all. It is also evident in Camus's attitude toward the Algerian crisis in the 1950s, where he condemned the violence of both the French military and the Algerian nationalists and hoped for a negotiated settlement that would allow for continued association between French and Arab peoples. By shifting his emphasis from the individual struggle against absurdity to shared struggles against injustice, Camus was able to posit courage, compassion, and respect for human dignity as universal human goods.

CARE (Ger. *Sorge*). In *Being and Time*, **Martin Heidegger** rejects traditional attempts to define human beings in terms of universal properties such as "rationality" or "spirituality." For Heidegger such definitions misinterpret humans as entities **present-at-hand**. Instead, Heidegger characterizes the **being** of *Dasein* at its most general level as *care*. Heidegger's conception is intended to capture the sense in which to **exist** is to be intimately concerned with oneself, to see one's life as "an issue" requiring **choice** and decision. Heidegger is also sensitive to etymological considerations: Care (*Sorge*) manifests itself in human **concern** (*Besorgen*) for things and **solicitude** (*Fürsorge*) toward others. Care is especially manifest for Heidegger in the **phenomenon** of **conscience**, which is described as "the call of care" (BT, 322).

CARNAP, RUDOLPH. *See* LOGICAL POSITIVISM.

CASSIRER, ERNST (1874–1945). German philosopher and key figure in the Marburg School of **neo-Kantian philosophy**. In the 1920s and 1930s, Cassirer, a leading interpreter of the philosophy of **Immanuel Kant**, became one of the best known philosophers in Germany and a well-known public intellectual. His *The Philosophy of Symbolic Forms* (1922) was particularly influential. Cassirer's significance to the history of existentialism stems from a historic debate held with **Martin Heidegger** at Davos, Switzerland, in 1929, focused on the meaning of Kant's philosophy. Heidegger, who had just published his controversial study *Kant and the Problem of Metaphysics* (1929), was on the rise as a philosophical radical. In pitting the young Heidegger against the older Cassirer, the debate highlighted differences between mainstream German philosophy and the **philosophy of existence** that sought to usurp it.

Cassirer's philosophical project was to show how Kant's a priori categories of experience may be extended beyond the domain of natural science to all aspects of human culture. According to Cassirer, Kant's categories are specific instances of a more general capacity for "symbolization," which is definitive of human **consciousness**. Symbolization is evident not only in scientific reasoning but also in myth, art, and religion; in each case, general organizing concepts are applied to make sense of perceptual and sensory experiences. In contrast to Kant, Cassirer held that these concepts or "symbolic forms" evolve over time. For example, the symbolic **world** of myth evolved over time into the perspective of common sense, and from out of the perspective of common sense developed the symbolic outlook of science. Human culture is an ongoing evolution and preservation of symbolic forms. In all its aspects—language, science, art, myth, literature, philosophy, history, and religion—culture is an ideal creation that adds a dimension of depth and significance to the natural world. While Heidegger accepted Cassirer's emphasis on social and historical dimensions of experience, he rejected the conception of the human being as rational consciousness. For Heidegger, Cassirer's philosophy inadvertently legitimized the **metaphysical** prejudice that treats the human being as a subject with unchanging properties.

CATHOLICISM. The Catholic Church's opposition to existentialism was in large part a reaction to the militant atheism of **Jean-Paul Sartre**'s philosophy. In "**Existentialism Is a Humanism**," Sartre had asserted that belief in the nonexistence of God was a core component of "atheistic existentialism." Moreover, politically Sartre defended a version of **Marxist** socialism and was hostile to conservative and centrist positions supported by most French Catholics. In 1948, his books were placed on the List of Forbidden books by the Vatican. In 1950, an encyclical of Pope Pius XII identified existentialism as one of the "false opinions threatening to undermine the foundations of Catholic doctrine." In these same years one of Sartre's harshest critics was the French Catholic philosopher **Gabriel Marcel**. Marcel accused Sartre of dogmatically asserting his atheism and of ignoring positive human relationships like love and friendship in his account of the relation of self and **other**. Marcel defended a version of the **philosophy of existence** based in essential religious experiences of **hope**, love, and fidelity. He was the preeminent French Catholic philosopher of existence. A subsequent French philosopher who combined Marcel's interests in Catholicism and existentialism with a concern for **phenomenology** was **Paul Ricoeur**. Another prominent Catholic critic of Sartre's existentialism was the French neo-Thomist philosopher Jacques Maritain.

In Germany, the relationship between existentialism and Catholicism was somewhat less antagonistic. **Martin Heidegger** received his early education within the Catholic Church, studying medieval theology and even training briefly to become a Jesuit priest. He abandoned Catholicism definitively for philosophy after **World War I**. However, in his philosophy he retained an appreciation for the awe and **mystery** of the **Christian worldview**. One of Heidegger's students at the University of Freiburg in the mid-1930s, Karl Rahner (1904–1984), went on to become the leading 20th-century German Catholic theologian. Like **Paul Tillich**, Rahner was attracted to Heidegger's existential interpretation of the history of philosophy, and he applied Heideggerean concepts like **being-in-the-world** to his **understanding** of the Christian faith.

CAU, JEAN (1925–1993). Jean-Paul Sartre's personal secretary from 1946 until 1957. From Sartre's apartment on the rue Bonaparte in Paris, Cau managed Sartre's professional life, making appointments, opening mail, and managing finances every morning while Sartre wrote.

CHESTOV, LEON. *See* SHESTOV, LEV.

CHOICE. The existentialist notion of choice has sometimes been misconstrued as "being able to choose whatever one wants," which has led some to mistake existentialism for a philosophy of irrationalism and personal whim. The existentialist notion of choice rests, rather, on the connection between choice and personal **freedom**. The idea received two distinct formulations, one from **Søren Kierkegaard**, the other from **Jean-Paul Sartre**.

For Kierkegaard choice is essentially **ethical** choice, a personal decision that, because it is made with "the whole inwardness of [the] personality" draws the **individual** out of the waywardness of **aesthetic** existence into awareness of freedom and **responsibility** that constitutes the ethical. The crucial element in choice is thus not correctness, but **commitment**, the properly subjective and personal manner in which it is made: "[I]t is not so much a question of choosing the right as of the energy, the earnestness, the pathos with which one chooses. Thereby the personality announces its inner infinity . . . and . . . the personality is consolidated" (KA, 106).

Here the question arises, might one not earnestly choose wrong over right, evil over good? In Kierkegaard's view, which is an attempt to clarify **Christian** thought, the sense of freedom that emerges in ethical choice is at the same time an awareness of one's "inner in-finity," that is, that one possesses a soul and that one's life is con-nected to a higher being. Thus the heightened self-awareness entailed by authentic choice is itself a guarantee of its ethical nature: "[E]ven if a man were to choose the wrong, he will nevertheless discover, pre-cisely by reason of the energy by which he chose, that he has chosen the wrong" (106). Because human beings are essentially free, they are in one sense free to choose to do wrong, for example, to live self-ishly in pursuit of pleasure; but if such a life-choice is to be genuine, then commitment to it must be made explicit—it must be recognized as consciously chosen rather than externally compelled—and once this occurs, the choice of wrongdoing leads inevitably to guilt and, ultimately for Kierkegaard, to repentance.

Sartre's understanding of choice is also linked to his conception of existential freedom and responsibility. For Sartre, **consciousness** is essentially free; undetermined by the past, at every moment it re-mains open and unconstrained. Hence, one is responsible not only for one's **actions** and beliefs but also for one's emotions, attitudes, and character, to the extent that these all result from the activity of con-sciousness. Why then do people appear to be disposed to act in cer-tain ways and to have relatively fixed characters? Sartre postulates that a person's beliefs and attitudes are expressions of an "original choice," a fundamental stance toward the world and others "which originally creates all causes and motives which can guide us to par-tial actions . . . which arranges the world with its meaning" (BN, 465). Original choice is not the result of conscious deliberation, yet it is not unconscious. It is "coincident with" consciousness itself.

Critics have been quick to point out problems with the idea of orig-inal choice. Can we make sense of a choice that is absolutely original—made without any prior establishment of alternatives or criteria for choosing? Does not choice make sense only within a hori-zon of a preestablished meaning, within a given **situation**? Further, if original choice is entirely unconditioned by personal history and en-vironment, in what sense can one be said to "make it"? Such an event would seem indistinguishable from a random occurrence, and hence no real choice at all. Criticism of Sartre's conception of original choice was proposed by **Maurice Merleau-Ponty** in the last chapter of his ***Phenomenology of Perception***. Merleau-Ponty argued that the meaning of the world is not initially chosen but *given* through the individual's social and historical situation. He maintained that our most basic apprehension of meaning is not the product of choice but rather serves as the precondition for choice.

CHRISTIAN EXISTENTIALISM. *See* CHRISTIANITY; EXISTENTIAL THEOLOGY; RELIGIOUS EXISTENTIALISM.

CHRISTIANITY. **Søren Kierkegaard**, the principal 19th-century forerunner of existentialism, was a staunch apologist for the purity of the Christian **faith** as defined by the teachings of the New Testament. In his later work, Kierkegaard became a critic of the Danish Lutheran Church and of the social and political institution of Christianity, which he called "Christendom." Kierkegaard was the originator of the range of religious and philosophical perspectives that are sometimes placed under the heading "Christian existentialism." Philosophers who have been classified under this heading include **Nikolai Berdyaev**, **Karl Jaspers**, and **Gabriel Marcel**. However, because existentialists who, like Jaspers and Marcel, recognized the role of the divine in human experience, also tended to avoid **commitment** to specific religious doctrines in their philosophies, it is perhaps more accurate to call them **religious existentialists**.

The other major 19th-century forerunner of existentialism, **Friedrich Nietzsche**, was a determined atheist and vocal critic of Christianity both as an institution and as a system of belief. For Nietzsche, Christianity was "Platonism for the people": a **metaphysical** system centered on the illusion of an all-powerful God and the promise of eternal life. Like Plato's realm of perfect, unchanging Forms, Christian beliefs were for Nietzsche an attempt to compensate for the inevitability of **death** and the perceived deficiencies of earthly **existence**. They were also an opportunity for the weak and disenfranchised to control the actions of stronger, "noble" individuals through the instrument of morality.

Existentialists in the 20th century were less clearly divided according to their acceptance or denial of Christianity. Some, like **Jean-Paul Sartre** and **Simone de Beauvoir**, were strict atheists. Others, like **Martin Heidegger** and **Maurice Merleau-Ponty**, remained open in their philosophical perspectives to the possibility of religious experience. **Albert Camus**, though closely affiliated with Nietzsche's viewpoint in many respects, was skeptical or agnostic in regard to religion: While the **absurd** "does not lead to God," Camus wrote, neither does it lead to the denial of God (MS, 40 n.7). Sartre famously defined his own perspective in contrast to the theistic (Christian) viewpoint. He asserted that "there is no **human nature**, since there is no God to conceive it," and that "if God does not exist, there is at least one being in whom **existence precedes essence**, a being who exists before he can be defined by any concept, and that being is man" (EHE, 15). *See also* CATHOLICISM; EXISTENTIAL THEOLOGY.

CIPHER (Ger. *Chiffer* **or** *Chiffre*). In the philosophy of **Karl Jaspers**, a cipher is a sign or symbol used to intimate a **transcendent** truth, that is, one that cannot be objectively known but can be suggested by the language of philosophy and religion. "God," "soul," "**freedom**," and "truth" are examples of ciphers in philosophy. In contrast to concepts that can be analyzed and understood objectively, ciphers must be grasped existentially, from the perspective of the existing individual. "When I read ciphers I am **responsible** because I read them only through my self-being [. . .] the reading of the cipher-script takes place in inner action" (BPW, 310).When treated otherwise, as they often and perhaps inevitably are, ciphers revert back to neutral concepts.

CLUB MAINTENANT. Host organization for **Jean-Paul Sartre**'s 1945 lecture, "**Existentialism Is a Humanism**," which inaugurated the existentialist era in France. In 1946, the Club Maintenant sponsored another lecture, by the philosopher **Jean Wahl**, entitled "Short History of Existentialism." This lecture was followed by a discussion with the philosophers **Nikolai Berdyaev**, Maurice de Gandillac, Georges Gurvitch, **Alexandre Koyré**, **Emmanuel Levinas**, and **Gabriel Marcel**. Both lecture and discussion were representative of the intellectual debates concerning existentialism in France at the time. They were published in book form by Jean Wahl as *A Short History of Existentialism* (1949).

***COGITO ERGO SUM* (Lat. "I think, therefore I am").** This famous dictum of French philosopher **René Descartes** is meant to suggest the indubitability of the first-person perspective: While I can doubt the existence of all external things, Descartes reasoned, including my own **body**, I cannot doubt my own **existence** as a "thinking thing," for the act of doubting is itself an instance of thought, and I must exist as the subject of thought. The *cogito* argument claims to provide a firm foundation for philosophical inquiry, a starting point that cannot be doubted and that depends on no other assumptions beyond the experience of **consciousness**.

Jean-Paul Sartre accepted the foundational aspect of the *cogito* argument. Along with Descartes, Sartre saw consciousness as the sole possible starting point for philosophy: *I think, therefore I am* is "the absolute truth of consciousness becoming aware of itself . . . before there can be any truth whatever . . . there must be an absolute truth . . . it's a matter of grasping it directly" (EHE, 36–37).

In contrast, **Martin Heidegger** regarded the Cartesian *cogito* as an uncritical assertion of the primacy of the **knowing subject** and an exemplary expression of philosophy's neglect of the question of the meaning of **being**. For Heidegger, consciousness, or mere "knowing," is founded on **prereflective** practical understanding of things and people, or **being-in-the-world**. The disparity between their views reflects a difference between French and German philosophical traditions, the latter founded on the work of **Immanuel Kant**, the former on the work of Descartes. Following Descartes, Sartre accepts the data of consciousness as irreducible. Following Kant, Heidegger approaches human experience through underlying "transcendental" conditions not immediately present to consciousness.

A point of agreement between Sartre and Heidegger is that the *cogito* misrepresents the nature of human being to the extent that it suggests a self-enclosed sphere of subjectivity. Consciousness for Sartre is not a substantial "thinking thing" but rather continually "**negates** itself" and "surpasses itself" toward the **world**. Alternately, *Dasein* for Heidegger exists not in the manner of a **substance** but as essentially "ahead of itself," in a continual **projection** of possibilities.

COMBAT. French Resistance group in which **Albert Camus** participated from the fall of 1943 until the liberation of France in August 1944, editing a clandestine anti-German newssheet. After the war, *Combat* continued as a daily newspaper, with Camus as editor. With his friend and colleague Pascal Pia, Camus built *Combat* into a significant voice in French politics and culture, left-leaning but critical of both the rigid Soviet **Marxism** embraced by many French intellectuals as well as Charles de Gaulle's more conservative nationalism. Camus's editorials for *Combat* between 1944 and 1947 made him one of the most influential writers in France at the time. Criticizing other French papers for pandering to popular taste, Camus set a high moral tone for the paper and insisted that its writing remain independent of the viewpoint of any organized political party. For a time, **Raymond Aron** shared the editorial page with Camus.

COMMITMENT. An existentialist concept of commitment was first specified by **Søren Kierkegaard**. For Kierkegaard, deliberate **ethical** and religious **choice** and commitment are the primary means through which a human being "becomes an individual." That is, by making serious commitments—to raise a family, join the priesthood, or become a writer, for example—one specifies who one is and gains a sense of one's individuality. In this manner selfhood emerges in the act of commitment and increases with the intensity or "inwardness" and "passion" of that commitment. Only through commitment is one saved from the generic indifference of social life, where one is pressured to conform to the expectations of others and discouraged from expressing one's individuality.

For Kierkegaard, ethical commitments to other persons point ultimately toward commitment to God, for without a religious foundation ethical relationships remain **contingent** and transitory. The highest level of commitment is thus occasioned by religious **faith**, which is intensely personal and subjective and yet objectively uncertain. The self that emerges through genuine religious commitment accordingly exhibits the highest level of inwardness and passion; it cannot fall back into complacency, nor can it attain self-satisfaction and self-certainty. **Jean-Paul Sartre** develops a related notion of commitment (Fr. *engagement*) as engagement in a social and **historical situation**. This idea is illustrated by the protagonists of many of Sartre's plays and novels, who are transformed only once they are able to commit themselves to a particular cause or relationship. Sartre's claim is that commitment provides necessary weight to **existence**, in that it allows for a **concrete** experience of **freedom**. Without commitment, freedom remains a metaphysical abstraction—merely the idea of not being constrained. Commitment gives ethical content and direction to life, making one *free for* the undertakings one deems meaningful. *See also* COMMITTED LITERATURE.

COMMITTED LITERATURE (Fr. *littérature engagée***).** In his Introduction (*Présentation*) to the first issue of *Les Temps modernes* (October 1945), **Jean-Paul Sartre** announced the ideal of "committed literature" or "engaged writing," to which his journal would attempt to conform by confronting social and political issues of the day. The idea drew immediate criticism from **André Gide**, among others, who likened Sartre's view to the **communist** requirement that art should serve the interests of the revolution. Sartre subsequently defended and elaborated on the idea of committed literature in a series of articles, published initially in *Les Temps modernes* and in book form as *What Is literature?* (1947). While the book is often polemical in tone, in it Sartre advances an account of the **reciprocity** of human **freedom** that responds to the criticism that his view of freedom in *Being and Nothingness* is overly individualistic, even solipsistic.

Sartre's guiding premise is that literature in the postwar period has entered a phase in which it is, or ought to be, aware of its social and political significance, that is, where writers have become aware of writing as a social and political act and not merely an an aesthetic expression. Sartre's analysis begins with a distinction between the aims of prose and those of poetry. While poetry disinterestedly contemplates and manipulates words as objects of interest in themselves, prose is essentially utilitarian, using words to convey extralinguistic truth, truth about the **world**. Prose writing, both fiction and nonfiction, is thus in a sense a form of **action**: The writer pursues a particular purpose, for example, to defend, explain, criticize, or persuade. While different writers may have diverse personal motives for writing, and while writing in past historical epochs may have been directed to different purposes than in our own, Sartre argues that contemporary writers (circa 1947) share a common purpose: to appeal to and elicit the reader's freedom. That is, the committed writer presents the reader with **situations** and problems requiring the reader's own reflection and decision; in reflecting on the work and **imaginatively** living through its dramatic situations, readers may actualize powers of evaluation and interpretation essential to human freedom.

Consequently, committed writing should not manipulate or constrain the reader by narrowly defending a particular thesis or point of view. Rather, it should "[appeal] to the reader's freedom to collaborate in the production of the work" (*What Is Literature?* 46). Committed writing is thus premised on a reciprocity of writer and reader: The more freedom the writer allows, the more the reader experiences, and the more freedom the reader experiences in an imaginative reconstruction of the meaning of the work, the more freedom he or she is disposed to grant the writer who created it.

Sartre insists committed writing is not abstractly universal but rather **concrete** and historical, in that it necessarily addresses a particular audience that shares a common social and historical social experience. For example, **Richard Wright**'s novel *Black Boy* is primarily addressed to African Americans who have suffered from racism, while Sartre's plays and novels are primarily addressed to middle-class French intellectuals. In each case, however, the writer's task is to bring into focus through the lens of his or her individual subjectivity issues of collective importance, and these for Sartre are primarily issues of social injustice and oppression. In the end, Sartre thus holds out committed literature as a kind of utopian socialist ideal: "[T]he reflective self-awareness of a classless society" (*What Is Literature?* 158). Moreover, it is not some final statement of truth but "the subjectivity of a society in permanent revolution" (*What Is Literature?* 159).

Sartre's other works from the time clearly reflect the ideal of committed writing. In particular, the novels in the trilogy ***The Roads to Freedom*** encourage readers to imaginatively experience various ways freedom may be won or lost. *Anti-Semite and Jew* in turn forces readers of 1948 to confront anti-Semitism as constitutive of their own historical situation. More generally, French existentialism after World War II is characterized by its social engagement. Other French existentialists, while they may differ with the details of Sartre's view, subscribe to the premise that philosophy ought to be engaged with the issues of its time and pursued, in a nontechnical way, in a public arena rather than among university professors. Thus **Simone de Beauvoir**, **Albert Camus**, and **Maurice Merleau-Ponty** write as novelists, playwrights, and journalists as well as philosophical theorists, and **Gabriel Marcel** is an accomplished playwright and literary critic as well as a philosopher. *See also* COMMITMENT.

COMMUNICATION. Karl Jaspers maintains that unrestrained, **reciprocal** communication between individuals is a condition for the emergence of **ethical**, philosophical, and religious truth. Outside of an **authentically** communicative relationship, truth remains abstract and existentially empty. A related and even stronger thesis is that communication with another *brings into being* an authentic self: "[Communication proper] obtains only . . . in mutual reciprocity . . . the process . . . in which the self properly becomes itself . . . in its relation with the other self" (PKJ, 785). For Jaspers, unrestrained existential communication, rather than justification of the truth of specific propositions, is the aim of philosophy. Through such communication alone may philosophers elicit a genuine existential response in the reader, a response that heightens their own awareness of *Existenz*. Jaspers's notion of philosophy as existential communication bears comparison with **Søren Kierkegaard**'s notion of "**indirect communication**." Jaspers's emphasis on the importance of interpersonal communication in turn may be fruitfully compared to **Martin Buber**'s notion of **dialogue** between I and You.

COMMUNISM. Economic and social theory developed in the mid-19th century by **Karl Marx**. According to Marx's analysis of European history and political economy, the inequities of capitalism can be resolved only through a revolution of the working classes that inaugurates a wholly egalitarian and classless, hence "communist," society. In the 1920s and 1930s, communism exercised strong appeal for many workers and intellectuals in Western Europe. The ideal of communist society held out hope for a solution to the problems of war, economic depression, and political instability that seemed endemic to capitalism in the years following **World War I**.

As a political ideal, communism is highly utopian. In a true communist society, Marx predicts that human **alienation** will be overcome; thanks to the abolition of private property and the restitution of meaningful human work, envy, greed, and social conflict will come to an end, economic resources and means of production will be held in common, and the resultant increase in productivity will create a society free from economic need. Ideal communism is thus for Marx a form of humanism: To be freed from want and social strife is to be free to develop fully one's senses and one's mind in association with others. As a historical political reality, however, communism falls far short of the ideal. The Russian Revolution of 1917 was an attempt to realize the ideal of a communist society, but under the leadership of Vladimir Lenin and that of his successor, Joseph Stalin, it deteriorated into a regime of state-sponsored repression and terror.

Communism in both real and ideal forms played an increasingly important role in French society beginning in the 1920s and continuing through the 1940s and 1950s. The French Communist Party, controlled directly by Moscow, was the central organizing force behind the **French Resistance**, and it emerged from **World War II** as the most powerful political party in France. French intellectuals and writers in the 1930s and 1940s as a rule sympathized with causes of the Left; many, like André Malraux, joined or were intimately associated with the Communist Party. French existentialists too were attracted to the ideal of communism, though with the exception of **Albert Camus** in 1934–1935, they hesitated to join the Communist Party. After World War II, **Simone de Beauvoir**, **Maurice Merleau-Ponty**, and **Jean-Paul Sartre** each advocated a form of socialism closely aligned with **Marxist** ideals.

In Germany, communism represented a potent social and political force from the 1910s and 1920s through Adolf Hitler's rise to power in 1933. German communists were the best organized of any European nation; in several instances communist-led workers' insurrections threatened the fragile German government. As in France, many German intellectuals were strongly sympathetic to communist ideals, among them **Theodor Adorno**, **Hannah Arendt**, and **Herbert Marcuse**; some, like the playwright Bertolt Brecht, were members of the Communist Party. However, among German existentialists, communism was not as significant a political or intellectual influence. **Martin Buber** advocated a kind of utopian socialism in the 1920s and 1930s, but he is an exception. The two main German **philosophers of existence**, **Martin Heidegger** and **Karl Jaspers**, were rather conservative in political temperament and more closely aligned with the conservative institution of the German universities. Neither embraced socialist or communist political ideals in his philosophy.

CONCEPT OF ANXIETY, THE (*Begrebet Angest*, 1844). This book, authored by **Søren Kierkegaard** under the pseudonym Virgilius Haufniensis, concerns the nature of original sin as it manifests itself through various forms of **anxiety**. While Kierkegaard's aims are ultimately religious, his treatment of anxiety is particularly significant to the history of existentialism in its linking of anxiety to human **freedom** and possibility. Kierkegaard's account provides the conceptual basis for **Martin Heidegger**'s analysis of anxiety in *Being and Time*. It is also influential on **Jean-Paul Sartre**'s understanding of the subject, notably Kierkegaard's description of anxiety as "the dizziness of freedom" (CA, 61), an image Sartre reprises in *Being and Nothingness* (BN, 29–32).

Kierkegaard portrays anxiety as an **ambiguous** and haunting phenomenon whose ultimate cause is the human awareness of sin. His point of departure is the account of original sin in the book of Genesis, where Adam is awakened out of innocence by God's command not to eat from the tree of the knowledge of good and evil: "The prohibition induces in him anxiety, for the prohibition awakens in him freedom's possibility [. . .] the anxious possibility of *being able*" (CA, 44). God's prohibition puts Adam for the first time in a position to grasp that he has the power to choose, to obey or to disobey—in a word, that he is free. It is a dawning awareness of his own freedom, and not fear of some external threat, that evokes his anxiety. Kierkegaard underlines this point by remarking that, since Adam is still in a state of innocence in regard to concepts of knowledge, good, and evil, God's command is not initially understood; thus, the source of Adam's anxiety is not a rational fear of punishment for disobeying God, but rather a dawning awareness of his own freedom. Unlike the threat of punishment, which is simply feared, the awareness of freedom that occasions anxiety is essentially "ambiguous," both attractive and repellent. It has often been correctly noted that Heidegger and Sartre secularized Kierkegaard's account, preserving key psychological and philosophical insights while removing reference to sin and God. This is particularly true in the case of Heidegger, who makes a point of recasting anxiety, along with related concepts of **guilt** and **conscience**, in philosophical rather than religious terms.

CONCEPT OF IRONY, THE (*Om Begrebet Ironi med stadigt Hensyn til Socrates*, 1841). Søren Kierkegaard's doctoral thesis at Copenhagen

University was entitled "On the Concept of Irony with Constant Reference to Socrates." Based on his dissertation, *The Concept of Irony* deals with Socratic irony as well as irony in the work of the German Romantic author A. W. Schlegel. According to Kierkegaard, Socrates used irony to undermine the authority of his own statements and those of his interlocutors; what counts for Socrates is not the transfer of objective information to another, but the process of questioning deeply held beliefs to arrive at deeper self-understanding.

CONCERN (Ger. *Besorgen*). A central concept of **Martin Heidegger**'s *Being and Time*. *Besorgen*, rendered as "concern," designates *Dasein*'s immediate preoccupation with things in the **world**. Concern is thus an important expression of *Dasein*'s fundamental character as *Sorge*, "**care**." Things engaged with through concern are characterized by Heidegger as **ready-to-hand**: they are understood immediately in terms of their practical function and value. Heidegger observes that objects of concern, such as a hammer, are items of "equipment" (*Zeug*) situated within broader equipmental contexts and never simply isolated things. When, for example, I pick up a hammer to help frame a house, I **understand** immediately but non-thematically its relation to nails, wood, planes, and other tools; I also understand it in terms of the purpose of my activity, to build a house, which Heidegger characterizes in Aristotelian terms as the ultimate "for-the-sake-of-which" of hammering.

My grasping of the various "networks" of significance of hammering also in turn implies an immediate understanding of the natural world. The natural world is grasped as something from which I need shelter as well as something toward which I must orient myself, which I do by facing the windows of the house toward the south to let in more sunlight, for example. As evidenced in the mundane example of framing a house, the contexts of concern fan out to include our relations to others, to **nature**, society, and tradition—all of these are dimensions of *Dasein*'s basic manner of existing, which Heidegger terms **being-in-the-world**. Connections between the various dimensions of being-in-the-world are reflected in Heidegger's vocabulary: *Besorgen* is linked etymologically to *Fürsorge*, **solicitude**, *Dasein*'s intrinsic relations to others. Both are instances of *Sorge*, care, *Dasein*'s fundamental attitude toward itself, the world, and others.

It is crucial to recall that, for Heidegger, in apprehending things through concern we are not foisting subjective interpretations onto some preexisting "world-stuff." Rather, we are *disclosing* the **being** of things as they are in themselves, their primary and fundamental manner of being. In Heidegger's example, the south wind is immediately understood by the farmer as a sign of rain; it is not first apprehended as a "flow of air," onto which the value of being a warning signal is subsequently appended. A weather station may detect the direction of an air flow in a definite geographical direction, but this type of understanding of the wind as something **present-at-hand** is derivative on the farmer's type of concern. Thus Heidegger maintains that the world disclosed by concernful dealings is the world as it is in itself and not merely a subjective coloring of it (BT, 111–112).

CONCRETE, TOWARDS THE (*Vers le concret*, 1932). This book by French philosopher **Jean Wahl** was one of the first in France to identify the trend toward **concrete existence** as a unifying theme of contemporary philosophy. Wahl juxtaposes the work of **William James**, Alfred North Whitehead, and **Gabriel Marcel**, suggesting that, at this early stage, French intellectuals did not yet recognize the specific identity of existentialist philosophy—the drama of personal **authenticity** with its attendant **anxiety**, the struggle to confront existential **freedom** and **responsibility**. This identity emerged clearly in French understanding only at the start of the 1940s. In 1932 Wahl identifies a broader trend characterized by a concern for the givenness of experience and a correlative critique of philosophical abstraction, a general orientation in philosophy that he calls a "vast movement directed 'towards the concrete'" (19). In Wahl's judgment, the movement toward the concrete is evident in "[**Søren**] **Kierkegaard**'s profound influence on contemporary German thought and . . . that dialectical theology largely inspired by him" (19)—that is, the work of **Karl Barth, Rudolph Bultmann**, and **Paul Tillich**. It includes as well the older generation of **Henri Bergson, James**, and Whitehead. **Martin Heidegger**, too, is praised throughout Wahl's footnotes for his unique marriage of Kierkegaard's concern for personal existence with **phenomenology**'s concern for the givenness of ordinary experience (**being-in-the-world**). Wahl's book documents the broad perspective of French **philosophy of existence** prior to the emergence of French existentialism after **World War II**. The book was influential for young French philosophers in the 1930s, like **Jean-Paul Sartre**, eager to overthrow the rationalist idealism of their professors. Sartre observes that at the time Wahl's book was read by everyone he knew: "[It] pleased us, for it embarassed idealism by discovering in the universe paradoxes, ambiguities, conflicts, still unresolved" (SM, 19).

CONCRETE EXISTENCE. In the 1920s and 1930s, German and in particular French **philosophers of existence** advocated a "return to the concrete" as a corrective to reductive science and abstract philosophy. Concrete existence refers to the irreducible subjective immediacy and particularity of human experience; their contention was that concrete existence is overlooked or distorted by scientific and traditional philosophical accounts of the human being. A tendency toward the concrete can be discerned earlier in the century in **Henri Bergson**'s theory of time as lived duration and, in American **pragmatism**, in such ideas as **William James**'s "stream of **consciousness**" and Alfred North Whitehead's "fallacy of misplaced concreteness."

Jean-Paul Sartre is representative of young French philosophers in the 1930s whose hunger for concrete existence propelled them beyond the confines of academic philosophy, which earlier figures like Bergson had more or less respected. Case studies from **psychopathology** and **psychoanalysis**, characters from modernist literature, as well as recent historical events and experiences of everyday life were exploited as raw material for philosophical description and analysis. Sartre was initially drawn to **phenomenology** for its promise to provide access to concrete existence unavailable to the sciences. In this regard, he subscribed to **Martin Heidegger**'s interpretation of phenomenology as **existential phenomenology**. **Alexandre Kojève**, **Emmanuel Levinas**, and **Jean Wahl** were philosophers similarly guided by a desire for concrete existence, which they elaborated through existential interpretations of **G. W. F. Hegel**, Heidegger, **Edmund Husserl**, and **Søren Kierkegaard**. *See also CONCRETE, TOWARDS THE.*

CONSCIENCE. In **Martin Heidegger**'s analysis in *Being and Time*, the "call of conscience" draws *Dasein* away from its **everyday** relations to others and to things and motivates it to take up its own **au-**

thentic possibilities: "[Conscience] summons the Self to its potentiality-for-being-a-Self, and thus calls Dasein forth to its possibilities" (BT, 319). Heidegger insists that conscience does not derive from an external source, such as God, society, or other persons, but ultimately from *Dasein* itself. *Dasein* is both caller and called; in its authenticity it "summons itself" out of inauthenticity. Crucial to his perspective is the idea that the phenomenon of conscience cannot be understood objectively from an external perspective, for example, as the voice of universal reason or as a psychological mechanism. Rather, conscience only comes into focus within the lived first-person perspective inhabited by *Dasein*. **Martin Buber** criticized Heidegger's account of conscience as fundamentally "monological." Buber offered a contrasting account: "If a . . . present being move[s] past me, and I was not really there, then . . . out of its disappearance, comes a . . . cry . . . : 'Where were you?' *That* is the cry of conscience. It is not my existence which calls to me, but the being which is not I" (BMM, 197). For Buber, Heidegger's view of conscience denies the essentially **dialogical** nature of **ethics**.

CONSCIOUSNESS. According to **Jean-Paul Sartre**, consciousness is the defining characteristic of the human being. In Sartre's analysis consciousness is not simply a state of mental awareness, or even self-awareness, though the latter is a crucial aspect of it. It is more importantly an interpretive and evaluative activity ingredient in all forms of human awareness, from **perception** to **emotion**, imagination, conceptual thought, and physical **action**. Sartre stresses the practical aspect of consciousness: It is not a passive beholding but a type of doing, of acting on things. In this way, consciousness is also aligned with **freedom**; to be conscious of something is to freely interpret and evaluate it in the light of one's goals and desires.

While consciousness is traditionally thought of as an inner, mental power, Sartre follows **Edmund Husserl** in insisting that consciousness is essentially relational or **intentional**, as it requires objects external to it for its exercise: "All consciousness," Sartre writes, "transcends itself in order to reach an object, and it exhausts itself in this same positing" (BN, li). Thus, paradoxically, consciousness is nothing apart from its directedness to a **world**; it is most emphatically, for Sartre, not a self-enclosed subjective sphere, an **ego** or mental

substance that produces thoughts. Nor is it to be identified with any other psychological structure, such as "character" or "personality," which is determined by the past. Rather, it is best conceived as a type of pure "spontaneity" that "creates itself" anew at each moment. Consequently when Sartre speaks of consciousness as "freedom," "translucence," and, more paradoxically, "**nothingness**," he is asserting its essential non-thing-like character.

A further feature of Sartrean consciousness is that it entails **prereflective** self-awareness, what Sartre describes as "an immediate, noncognitive relation of the self to itself" (BN, liii). That is, while ordinary consciousness is not reflective and deliberate but "tacit" and "non-positional," absorbed in the world and not in itself, Sartre argues that consciousness must always be able to become aware of itself. The only other option, he reasons, would be to acknowledge the concept of the unconscious, which Sartre takes to be inadmissible: "[A] consciousness ignorant of itself, an unconscious . . . is absurd" (BN, lii). *See also* BEING-FOR-ITSELF AND BEING-IN-ITSELF.

CONTINGENCY. Traditionally in philosophy, the opposite of necessity. An entity exists contingently if its **existence** is not necessary. It could be otherwise than it is, or could not exist at all. In ancient and especially medieval philosophy, material things are assigned contingent existence because they are "corruptible," coming into being and passing away in time; nonmaterial things like mathematical concepts, God, and the human soul are said to have necessary existence because they are noncorruptible, remaining unchanged through time. In existentialism, the notion of contingency plays a major role in the early thought of **Jean-Paul Sartre**. Sartre reports that his first original philosophical idea, which preoccupied him throughout the 1930s and into the 1940s, was the idea of contingency: the realization that nothing in the world enjoys necessary existence. Sartre's first novel, *Nausea*, whose working title was "factum on contingency," is a celebration of the varieties of contingent experience. Prominent among them is the protagonist's experience of the contingency of his own **body**. Roquentin experiences his body as a brute physical thing. When he stares at himself in the mirror, it is "flaccid," "swollen," "inhuman," a sheerly objective body detached from the **consciousness** that perceives it. In *Being and Nothingness*, Sartre develops the thesis that the deep motive of human being, or "**being-for-itself**," is to try to escape from the condition of contingency that "haunts" it. The paradox of human **freedom**, however, makes this escape impossible, for each free thought and act "**negates**" the past, rendering an unchanging identity unattainable. Moreover, truly free acts have no foundation outside of themselves and thus could always be otherwise than they are.

COOPER, DAVID E. (1942–). English philosopher and commentator on existentialism. In *Existentialism: A Reconstruction* (1999), Cooper offered a reconstruction of the existentialist position derived by synthesis of the views of major existentialist philosophers. In his reading, the unifying goal of existentialist philosophy is to overcome **alienation**. One important way this is accomplished is by "dissolving" false metaphysical dualisms—between mind and **body**, self and **world**, and self and **other**—that alienate us from our most genuine human possibilities. Cooper's books related to existentialism include *The Measure of Things: Humanism, Humility, and Guilt* (2002), *Heidegger* (1996), and *Authenticity and Learning: Nietzsche's Educational Philosophy* (1983).

CORBIN, HENRI (1903–1978). French philosopher of religion, theologian, and orientalist. Corbin was the first French translator of **Martin Heidegger**. His 1938 collection *Qu-est-ce que la métaphysique?* included, in addition to Heidegger's essay ("**What Is Metaphysics?**"), chapters from ***Being and Time*** and a preface authored by Heidegger himself. It was through Corbin's translations that many French intellectuals, including **Jean-Paul Sartre** and **Maurice Merleau-Ponty**, were introduced to Heidegger's work. Corbin's rendering of ***Dasein*** as "*réalité humaine*" was preserved by Sartre and other French writers of the time.

CREATION. In the philosophy of **Gabriel Marcel**, creation is conceived as a power of receptivity and response to **being**, not primarily as an act of the self. For Marcel, productive making, for example, of art or music, is creative to the extent that it is inspired by something beyond the self, that is, in the **world**, in **others**, or in God. **Albert Camus** shared **Friedrich Nietzsche**'s high estimation of the creative artist. For Camus, as for Nietzsche, the act of artistic creation, paradigmatically that of the writer or poet, affirms life's meaning in the face of its apparent **absurdity**.

CREATIVE EVOLUTION. See BERGSON, HENRI; *ÉLAN VITAL.*

CREATIVE FIDELITY. See MARCEL, GABRIEL.

CRITICAL THEORY. *See* FRANKFURT SCHOOL.

CRITIQUE OF DIALECTICAL REASON **(*Critique de la raison dialectique*, 1960).** **Jean-Paul Sartre**'s second major theoretical work was an attempt to reconcile an existentialist view of **freedom** with a **Marxist** theory of history. The book was conceived and written in the late 1950s, after Sartre had distanced himself from existentialism. However, the degree to which the *Critique* necessitates revision or rejection of Sartre's former positions is open to debate.

The book is the culmination of a decade of reflection on social and **political** questions, history, and **ethics**. In the late 1940s, Sartre had struggled to formulate an existentialist ethics, which he was unable to do to his satisfaction. A substantial problem left unresolved from his earlier work was the relationship between the individual and society and the individual and history. Gradually he came to realize that an account of existential freedom required an account of how individuals interact with and are conditioned by their social class and by history. By the 1950s, Sartre was convinced that **Karl Marx**'s theory of **historical materialism** represented the only viable approach to these problems. Since his rise to fame in the 1940s, Sartre had been antagonized by Marxist critics and philosophers who criticized existentialism as a form of bourgeois individualism. Sartre in turn chided Marxist philosophers like **Georg Lukács** for their dogmatism and naïve reductionism. Still, he defended Marxism as a heuristic program. Between 1952 and 1956, Sartre set aside his reservations about Marxism and aligned himself with the **Communist** Party. In the mounting tensions of the Cold War, he perceived capitalists (led by the United States) as aggressors and **communist** states (including the Soviet Union) as victims. After the second Soviet invasion of Hungary in 1956, he became disillusioned with **communism** but remained dedicated to a Marxist vision of social change.

Critique of Dialectical Reason was Sartre's attempt to articulate a **philosophical anthropology** appropriate to such a vision. In contrast to existentialism, which had focused on the irreducible nature of individual **existence**, Sartre's new "dialectical" perspective endeavored to take account of historical "totalities": individuals in an evolving relationship with their historical circumstances, social and economic class, and the physical world. The introductory volume to the *Critique*, published separately in English as *Search for a Method*, and based on a 1957 lecture entitled "Marxism and Existentialism," set forth Sartre's general intentions. It begins with a critical account of the development of existentialism from **Søren Kierkegaard** through **Karl Jaspers**. Sartre observes, self-critically, that while existentialism started as a critique of Hegelian idealism, it remained idealistic in that it naïvely privileged the individual subject in isolation from history and society. Marxism, in contrast, effected a more **concrete** critique of **G. W. F. Hegel** in that it recognized the primacy of the material world and of the activity of human labor that transforms it. Sartre concludes that Marxism as a general heuristic program represents the only living philosophy of the 20th century, one that "cannot be surpassed." Existentialism in turn he describes as "an enclave inside Marxism," no longer an autonomous philosophy. Nonetheless, he maintains that existentialism can expand the horizons of Marxist inquiry as it brings to Marxism an appreciation of the open-ended nature of historical events insofar as they depend on ongoing human interpretation. Existentialism also teaches the importance of the lived experience of social and economic facts, and of the decisive role played by childhood, when these facts are most profoundly experienced.

Sartre summarizes his view of Marxism with a phrase attributed to Marx: "Men themselves make their history but in a given environment that conditions them." *Praxis* is the term Sartre assigns to the action of "making history," and praxis is one of the major concepts analyzed in the *Critique*. Crucial to Sartre's view is the idea that the praxis of an individual or a group is never simply caused by its economic conditions but always "goes beyond them while conserving them" (SM, 85). Sartre thus retains in the *Critique* a core component of existentialism, namely, the affirmation of human **freedom**. At the same time, praxis has a necessary social and historical dimension: It is **action** and work accomplished on the basis of collective effort in relation to material scarcity.

– D –

DADAISM. Modernist protest movement in art and literature sparked by **World War I**. Beginning in Zurich in 1916, Dada spread to Paris and New York. The Dadaists rejected conventional **values** of progress, reason, and beauty, which they felt were travestied by the horrors of the war. Instead, they celebrated an art of random occurrences and "nonsense," ridiculing middle-class conformity, patriotism, and militarism as well as the institution of art itself. Leading Dadaists included Tristan Tsara, Hans Arp, Hugo Ball, and Marcel Duchamp. In Paris in the early 1920s, Dadaism evolved into **surrealism**. Like French existentialism after **World War II**, Dadaism was both reviled and celebrated by the media. This explains **Jean-Paul Sartre**'s remark in 1947 that the vogue of existentialism is like "*le nouveau Da-Da*" (cited in Marjorie Grene, *Introduction to Existentialism*, 49).

DAS MAN **(Ger. "the one," "the they").** In the vocabulary of **Martin Heidegger**'s *Being and Time, das Man* designates the average, **everyday** manner of *Dasein*'s **existence**. Heidegger observes that the ordinary trend of human life is to think and behave *just like everyone else*, conforming one's thoughts and actions to the expectations of others. Thus, Heidegger concludes, the standard subject of existence is not an **individualized** self but an average "anyone," a collective, impersonal manner of being. While *das Man* is the standard mode of *Dasein*'s existence, it is the mode in which *Dasein* is decidedly "not itself": It lives without awareness of the necessity of **choice** and decision, and thus without awareness of **freedom**. *Das Man* **levels** down "possible options of choice to what lies within the range of the familiar, the attainable, the respectable." Settling all questions in advance, it removes the need for *Dasein* to make choices for itself. *Dasein* thus "becomes blind to its possibilities, and tranquillizes itself with that which is merely 'actual'" (BT, 239). In this manner, *das Man* is the foundation of inauthentic existence: By disburdening *Dasein* of its freedom and **responsibility**, it ensures that it exists in **alienation** from its genuine human possibilities. *See also* AUTHENTICITY AND INAUTHENTICITY.

DASEIN. This expression, the ordinary German word for "being" or "existence," is employed by **Martin Heidegger** as the philosophical term for human being. It plays a crucial role in the philosophy of *Being and Time*, which offers a detailed analysis of *Dasein*'s unique mode of being as **existence**. Critical to Heidegger's conception is the idea that *Dasein* is not a "subject" in the sense of a preformed mental, physical, or spiritual entity that subsequently comes into contact with a **world**. Rather, *Dasein* is essentially **being-in-the-world**, and what it is cannot be specified apart from its involvement in the world and with others; through this involvement, and not prior to or independently of it, *Dasein* comes to know itself and to take up a stance toward its own **being**. A correlate to this idea is that the world, and indeed being itself, are not preextant realities but emerge in conjunction with *Dasein*. The world and being are that toward which *Dasein* comports itself, that toward which it "**transcends.**"

Heidegger emphasizes the nonsubjective character of *Dasein* in various ways. *Dasein* is not a specific type of thing to be defined by essential properties, such as rationality or spirituality. It is not a **substance**, mental or physical, with unchanging properties. *Dasein* designates the *how* of human being rather than the *what* or **essence**, for human beings do not have an essence in the same sense as objects like a table, a planet, or a triangle. *Dasein*'s being is always "an *issue* for it" and never merely an occurrent state that it contemplates objectively. *Dasein* is not a thing on a par with other things but rather the being in relation to which all other things exist. Accordingly, *Dasein* must be approached not through an enumeration of objective properties but through an elucidation of its distinctive manner of existing. This is the sense of Heidegger's statement that "*The 'essence' of Dasein lies in its existence*" (BT, 67). *Dasein*'s essence can be described by identifying the basic possibilities that organize any human life. These Heidegger calls *Existentialien* (existentialia), distinguishing them from the traditional philosophical concept of categories. The enumeration of *Dasein*'s existentialia constitutes one of the most original aspects of Heidegger's philosophy. They include **being-towards-death**, **facticity**, **falling**, **historicality**, **mineness**, and **thrownness**. Heidegger suggests that *Dasein*'s being at the most general level may be qualified as **care**.

Heidegger sometimes employs the term in hyphenated form, *Da-sein*, to exploit its constitutive meaning, "being (*sein*) there (*Da*)." The "there" that is constitutive of *Dasein*'s being is in effect the world itself, for *Dasein* exists spatially and temporally "outside of itself," in and through its engagements with things and among others. The there of *Dasein* is decidedly not a type of **consciousness**, which Heidegger assumes to be a self-sufficient mental awareness on the model of the Cartesian **cogito**. *Dasein*'s there is described, rather, as a space of "disclosure" for other beings as well as for itself. One of Heidegger's chief insights is that the range of human **projects** and activities—building, farming, calculating, performing scientific experiments, making art, and so forth—discloses a range of different possibilities in things, or alternately, a range of distinct modes of being. *Dasein* is thus described as a uniquely **ontological** being in that, through its various projects, **moods**, and involvements, it reveals the diversity of ways in which things, including human beings, can be said to be. As *Dasein*'s mode of being comprises all other possible modes of being, the analysis of *Dasein* is referred to as **fundamental ontology**. Finally, because *Dasein* is distinguished by a fundamental self-concern, it exists either in the mode of "not being itself" or of "being itself": that is, either inauthentically, uncritically accepting the possibilities dictated by tradition and society, or **authentically** taking hold of existence in terms of possibilities consciously chosen and affirmed. *See also DAS MAN*; EGO.

DASEIN **ANALYSIS.** *See* EXISTENTIAL PSYCHOTHERAPY.

DEATH. The subject of death receives scant attention in the history of philosophy. In certain respects, existentialists are the first philosophers in modern times to recognize its importance and propose a philosophical treatment. For existentialists, death is not a physical event or biological process but the awareness that one is going to die. Varying interpretations of this awareness are offered by different writers; it is generally agreed, however, that awareness of death is constitutive of **existence**, not merely a psychological state that may or may not be present, and that it is linked to an awareness of **freedom**, and thus to the exercise of **authenticity**. **Martin Heidegger**'s analysis of *Dasein* assigns central importance to the experience of death, though a similar emphasis can be found in other German philosophers of existence. For example, the Jewish German existentialist **Franz Rosenzweig** begins *The Star of Redemption* (1922) with these words: "All cognition of the All originates in death, in the fear of death. Philosophy takes it upon itself . . . to rob death of its poisonous sting" (3). Similarly, **Karl Jaspers** speaks of death as one of the **limit situations** that occasion the emergence of *Existenz*. Common to the existentialist view is the idea that death is dimmed down when treated simply as a natural fact or as an unproblematic passage to a "beyond" rather than an event that evokes fear and **anxiety**. In Heidegger's account, a full existential awareness of death is a necessary condition for authenticity, for death places the contents of one's life in a properly finite and first-person perspective: "Only by the anticipation of death is every accidental and 'provisional' possibility driven out. . . . Once one has grasped the **finitude** of one's existence, it snatches one back from the endless multiplicity of possibilities" (BT, 435). Thus, according to Heidegger, anxiety in the face of death shocks *Dasein* out of **everyday** complacency and allows it to understand itself as a "finite freedom," that is, as a power of **choice** that can be exercised only on the basis of the constraints of the **situation**. *See also* BEING-TOWARDS-DEATH; *DEATH OF IVAN ILYICH, THE*; ECSTASIS.

DEATH OF GOD. **Friedrich Nietzsche** understood the "death of God" as the loss of belief in **transcendent values** occasioned by the decline of religion in Europe in the 18th and 19th centuries. For Nietzsche, the core illusion of the Western tradition was its belief in an omniscient, omnipotent God, the source of **value** and purpose on earth and the guarantor of truth. The development of modern science and emergence of modern political institutions had, he thought, contributed to the demise of the religious **worldview**, including the decay of such metaphysical adjuncts to religion as the idea of the soul as distinct from the **body**. But what will humans propose to replace the religious view? The answer to this question was not clear. Nietzsche saw the death of God as heralding a period of **nihilism** in 19th-century Europe, when societies might succumb to "baser" values of self-preservation and utilitarian interest and lose sight of "nobler" values such as artistic creation. Ultimately, however, he had **faith** that the challenge of nihilism could be met by those resilient and "cheerful" enough to live and create in the absence of metaphysical illusions. For such "higher men," Nietzsche predicted, the death of God will be an occasion to affirm earthly existence: to redeem the value of the body and the senses and to enjoy the exercise of the creative drives free from the crippling constraints of morality and religion.

***DEATH OF IVAN ILYICH, THE* (1886).** This short novel by Leo Tolstoy (1828–1910) was significant to certain existentialists for its vivid portrayal of the experience of **death**. Ivan Ilyich is a magistrate in tsarist Russia, fond of cards and a glass of wine, and occasionally of reading "some book which was much talked about." He embodies the comfortable complacency that existentialists identify with inauthentic **existence**. One day, while arranging the curtains of his new apartment, he falls and injures himself. The injury does not appear serious, but gradually his pain increases. Doctors make vague diagnoses yet remain unconcerned; their chief interest is to suppress recognition of the reality of death. His family also encourages him in the illusion that he is merely sick and will get better. Only his servant, a peasant named Gerasim, is able to accept that he is dying and to provide him some comfort. Ilyich suffers physically, but nagging moral doubts (he wonders whether his entire life has not been a mistake) increase his pain immensely. Finally, only hours before dying, he is comforted by a vision of light, an apparent religious conversion.

Tolstoy's story was particularly influential for **Martin Heidegger**, who cited the story in a footnote to a discussion of **being-towards-death** in *Being and Time*. For Heidegger, *The Death of Ivan Ilyich* dramatized the difficulty of arriving at an **authentic** awareness of death in face of society's tendency to obscure and deny it.

DE BEAUVOIR, SIMONE. *See* BEAUVOIR, SIMONE DE.

DECISION. *See* CHOICE; MOMENT, THE.

DECISIONISM. Historically the term refers to a right-wing revolutionary political theory formulated in the 1920s by the German political philosopher and jurist Carl Schmitt, in response to the perceived weakness and ineffectualness of the Weimar parliamentary democracy. Schmitt's decisionism defined **authentic** political **choices** as "absolute decisions" "created out of nothingness," which gain their power from an abrogation of law and consensus and issue out of a kind of "dictatorship" rather than a "legitimacy." Schmitt's *Political Theology* (1922) drew an analogy between the "state of exception" or emergency in which political law is abrogated and true political sovereignty is revealed, and the divine miracle in which natural laws are abrogated and God's sovereignty is revealed.

In more general terms, decisionism is sometimes used to refer to a theory of moral choice or **action** that stresses the groundless, subjective, and arbitrary character of **ethical** decisions. **Martin Heidegger**, **Søren Kiekegaard**, and **Jean-Paul Sartre** have each been accused of a type decisionism. The criticism is tempered in the case of Heidegger and Sartre by their emphasis on the **situated** and hence socially and morally constrained nature of authentic decision. *See also* MOMENT, THE.

DESAN, WILFRED (1909–2001). Belgian American philosopher and early commentator on **Jean-Paul Sartre**'s philosophy. Desan studied philosophy in Belgium at the University of Lille before pursuing interests in cinematography. He met Sartre in Paris in the 1940s and developed a keen interest in existentialism. Immigrating to the United States in 1948, Desan earned a Ph.D. in philosophy at Harvard University. In 1954, he published *The Tragic Finale*, a penetrating early discussion of Sartre's argument in *Being and Nothingness*.

DESCARTES, RENÉ (1596–1650). French philosopher and mathematician, considered the father of modern Western philosophy. From an existentialist perspective, Descartes's philosophy is criticized for its strict mind/**body** dualism and for its rationalism. **Martin Heidegger** proposed an extensive critique of Descartes's view of self and **world**. According to Heidegger, Descartes's conception of the human being as a "thinking thing" (*res cogitans*) opposed in its being to the "extended things" (*res extensae*) that make up the physical world was a seminal expression of the theoretical prejudice of traditional **metaphysics**. By defining the person as a mental **substance** distinct from the world and from other people, Descartes reduced the human being to a **knowing subject** that manipulates and calculates a universe of objects **present-at-hand**.

Jean-Paul Sartre offered a more positive assessment. While he too rejected Descartes's **substance ontology**, he embraced Descartes's central idea that **consciousness** provides the necessary starting point for philosophy. In this, he remained at odds with Heidegger's understanding of consciousness as a derivative metaphysical concept. Sartre also followed Descartes in the assumption that consciousness remains **free** from causal determination.

DESPAIR. *See* KIERKEGAARD, SØREN.

DESTRUCTION (Ger. *Destruktion***).** **Martin Heidegger** refers to the necessity of an internal critique or "destruction" of the history of Western philosophy as a necessary component of **fundamental ontology**. However, destruction is not a purely negative attempt to eradicate the past. Such an attempt would be futile because philosophy is necessarily guided by inherited concepts and assumptions. The goal of destruction is rather to "stake out the positive possibilities" latent within ancient **ontology** and to bring them to fruition in a contemporary context. This was the general intention of Heidegger's *Being and Time*, which drew upon a renewed **understanding** of ancient Greek **metaphysics**, in particular the metaphysics of Aristotle, as well as a critical reappraisal of seminal texts like **Immanuel Kant**'s *Critique of Pure Reason*, in its revisionary account of human **existence**.

DEUX MAGOTS, CAFÉ LES. This café in the heart of **Saint-Germain-des-Près** was a central meeting place for **Jean-Paul Sartre**, **Simone de Beauvoir**, and other writers and artists associated with the existentialist movement in Paris in the 1940s and 1950s. After 1946, when tourists began to flock to the **Café de Flore** to catch a glimpse of Sartre at work, Sartre and Beauvoir moved their base of operations to the neighboring Café Les Deux Magots.

DIALECTIC. *See* HEGEL, G. W. F; KIERKEGAARD, SØREN.

DIALECTICAL MATERIALISM. *See* HISTORICAL MATERIALISM.

DIALOGUE (Ger. *Zwiesprache***).** In the philosophy of **Martin Buber**, dialogue denotes an **authentic**, open encounter between self and

other. In dialogue, the other person is recognized as subject rather than as object, as a source of **freedom** irreducible to my conception of him or her. **Reciprocally**, the self exists **authentically**, as a whole self, only in dialogue with another.

"The basic movement of the life of dialogue is the turning toward the other (*Hinwendung*)" (BMM, 25). This is accomplished in mundane acts like greeting another person, having a conversation, or simply exchanging meaningful glances. It is exemplified as well in the creation of art, music, and poetry, which for Buber derive their power from being addressed to the eyes and ears of another. At the highest level, dialogue becomes an encounter with the absolute other or God. Yet even here dialogue operates not on some **transcendent** plane or in a mystical union but in the action and suffering of **concrete existence**, "not above the struggle with reality but in it" (*The Martin Buber*, 227). Dialogue is ultimately an experience of the world's **mystery** and meaning through an encounter with otherness.

"Monologue," in contrast, is not simply a turning away from the other but "reflexion" (*Ruckbiegung*), literally, a "bending back" of the self on the self: "[R]eflexion [is] when a man withdraws from accepting with his essential being another person in his particularity . . . and lets the other exist only as his own experience" (BMM, 27). *See also* AVAILABILITY.

DILTHEY, WILHELM (1833–1911). German philosopher identified with the **philosophy of life** and influential particularly in the development of German **philosophy of existence**. Dilthey directed himself to understanding life in all its variety and richness, borrowing ideas from the philosophy of **Immanuel Kant** and **G. W. F. Hegel**. Where Kant had identified categories of the mind that organize our perception of the physical world, Dilthey proposed "categories of life" that organize our experience of ourselves, the **world**, and others. This experience is organized not only perceptually but also in terms of categories of "**value**," "meaning," and "purpose," which operate below the level of explicit awareness. Categories of life are combined to form different **worldviews**, generalized interpretations of reality akin to what Hegel had called "forms of spirit."

To gain a comprehensive picture of life requires broadening one's inquiry beyond the scope of philosophy. In particular for Dilthey, it required studying those "human sciences" (*Geisteswissenschaften*) that concern themselves with life as it is experienced and not merely as an object of scientific observation. Disciplines such as history, psychology, literary criticism, and comparative religion are distinguished by their intrinsic reference to the experience of conscious human beings, in contrast to the natural sciences, which seek to explain all phenomena, including **consciousness**, in terms of nonconscious physical processes. Dilthey thus advanced an important distinction between causal **explanation** (*Erklärung*) used in natural science and hermeneutical **understanding** (*Verstehen*) used in the human sciences. The method of *understanding* is required of the human sciences because it allows one to grasp the "lived meanings" (*Erlebnisse*) of words, ideas, and feelings experienced by individuals in different cultures and historical periods. Because lived meanings are constantly changing and developing in the lives of individuals and in the development of cultures, they cannot be formalized or placed in a final system. Dilthey held that a formal science of human life and culture modeled on natural science is a grievous mistake. At the same time, Dilthey recognized universal features of human life that allow an interpreter to empathetically grasp ideas, art, and literature of the past.

Dilthey's importance for existentialism lies primarily in his influence on **Martin Heidegger** and **Karl Jaspers**. In *Being and Time*, Heidegger accepted the thrust of Dilthey's analyses of "life" and "lived experience" while criticizing the language in which they were expressed as "ontologically undifferentiated" and "indefinite" (BT, 210). According to Heidegger, Dilthey's concept of "life" takes for granted a more basic understanding of "world" and of human being as essentially **being-in-the-world**. Nonetheless, Heidegger was clearly influenced by Dilthey's work. He acknowledged his debt to Dilthey's understanding of how life is bounded and defined by **death** (BT, 249, n.vi). More substantively, Heidegger recognized Dilthey's "pioneering work" (BT, 378) on the subject of historical time. Heidegger's discussion of human **historicality** (BT, §73–77) was intended as a clarification and amplification of Dilthey's views.

Karl Jaspers's *Psychology of Worldviews* was also in a sense an elaboration upon an idea of Dilthey. Dilthey had introduced the concept of *Weltanschauung*, or worldview, to designate the holistic attitude by which a person perceives, evaluates, and responds to the world. He identified three basic worldviews: naturalism, subjective idealism, and objective idealsm. Jaspers expanded this typology to include more psychological attitudes like narcissism, pessimism, and optimism. Dilthey's conception of history and of life were, finally, essential for the Spanish philosopher **José Ortega y Gasset**. Ortega acknowledged his debt by identifying Dilthey as "the most important thinker of the second half of the nineteenth century" (*History as a System*, 213). *See also* PHILOSOPHY OF LIFE.

DIONYSIAN. *See* APOLLONIAN AND DIONYSIAN.

DOS PASSOS, JOHN (1896–1970). American novelist and short-story writer whose experimental fiction, in particular his *U.S.A.* novel trilogy, translated into French in the 1930s, influenced the style of **Albert Camus**'s *The Stranger* as well as **Jean-Paul Sartre**'s *Nausea* and *The Roads to Freedom* trilogy. As a literary critic, Sartre had deep appreciation for Dos Passos. In a 1938 review, Sartre opined, "I regard Dos Passos as the greatest writer of our time" (LPE, 96).

DOSTOEVSKY, FYODOR (1821–1881). Russian novelist, one of the greatest novelists of the 19th century. His influence on literature in the late 19th and early 20th centuries was profound, and he is widely cited as a forerunner of the modern psychological novel. In the 1950s and 1960s, Dostoevsky's status as a forerunner of existentialism was promoted by the American philosopher and critic **Walter Kaufmann**. Kaufmann's judgment, in his popular anthology *Existentialism from Dostoevsky to Sartre*, that Dostoevsky's *Notes from Underground* is "the best overture for existentialism ever written" (Kaufmann, 14), confirmed for some Dostoevsky's existentialist credentials. Kaufmann placed importance on the fact that, toward the end of his life, **Friedrich Nietzsche** had discovered *Notes from Underground* and read it as the expression of "a kindred spirit." Yet Kaufmann also made clear that Dostoevsky was not an existentialist in a strict sense of the term, only a harbinger of existential themes such as the experience of **guilt**, suffering, and shame, and the rejection of the classical view of the human being as a **knowing subject**. Dostoevsky's stylistic influence can be detected in the early fiction of **Albert Camus** and **Jean-Paul Sartre**. *See also* EXISTENTIALIST LITERATURE.

DREAD. *See* ANXIETY.

DUALISM. *See* BODY AND MIND.

DURATION. *See* BERGSON, HENRI.

– E –

ECCE HOMO **(1888) (Lat. "Behold the man").** **Friedrich Nietz-sche**'s philosophical autobiography; the title refers to words suppos-edly pronounced by Pontius Pilate upon presenting Christ wearing a crown of thorns to the Jews. Throughout the book Nietzsche plays ironically with this identification. Like Christ, he too has been mis-understood by his contemporaries, and his works alone will achieve immortality after his **death**. At the same time, Nietzsche also under-stands himself as the antithesis of a religious leader, an "Anti-Christ" (as the title of another of one of his books puts it) who announces the **death of god** (the demise of belief in transcendent **values**), unmasks **Christian** morality as a sham, and derides the weakness of his would-be followers and believers.

ÉCOLE NORMALE SUPÉRIEURE. Most of the leading French philosophers of the 20th century graduated from this prestigious French institution of higher learning, including **Henri Bergson**, (class of 1881), **Maurice Merleau-Ponty** (class of 1930), and **Jean-Paul Sartre** (class of 1929). Located in Paris on the rue d'Ulm, in the heart of the Latin Quarter, the École Normale is one of a series of *grandes écoles* instituted by Napoleon as elite training centers for French professionals, scientists, and government officials. The École Normale Supérieure specializes in the humanities, and philosophy is traditionally highlighted in its curriculum.

ECONOMIC AND PHILOSOPHICAL MANUSCRIPTS OF 1844. These manuscripts, written when **Karl Marx** was in his midtwenties, provide an early outline of Marx's materialist theory of history as well as his analysis of human **alienation** under capitalism. Discov-ered posthumously in the late 1920s and published in German in

1932, the *Manuscripts* reveal the humanistic dimension of Marx's thought—his focus on the effects of alienated labor and on the overcoming of alienation and the fulfillment of human social and creative potential though **communism**. The humanistic tenor of the *Manuscripts* increased Marx's appeal among Western intellectuals, like **Maurice Merleau-Ponty**, who were wary of the reductive economic materialism of orthodox Soviet **Marxism**.

The *Manuscripts* were troubling to the communist orthodoxy in that they also revealed Marx to be clearly in the debt of the idealist and hence "bourgeois" philosophy of **G. W. F. Hegel**, particularly Hegel's idealist conception of alienation. Hegel had described history as a process in which mind or spirit (*Geist*) initially "alienates itself" in material **nature**, losing sight of its own creative role in constituting a **world** of meaningful objects. Gradually, through a dialectical process, spirit achieves self-recognition as human beings come to see themselves as actively and freely producing and not simply observing and contemplating their world.

Marx's analysis proceeds by a critical appropriation of Hegel's idea of the "self-alienation" of spirit in history. However, Marx locates the mechanisms of alienation in a materialist rather than an idealist setting, in which the production of physical objects takes precedence over the production of ideas. Productive activity and sociality are recognized as the essential attributes of human beings, production being necessarily realized in a social setting. Alienation occurs when in the course of human social and economic development a world of physical objects is produced by human labor, and these in turn become objects of ownership (private property), represented by money under capitalism. In capitalism, productive activity is assigned a monetary value, and as "wage labor" is reduced to a mechanical process whose human **essence** is forgotten. Consequently, what is most essential to human beings—the capacity to create and produce in concert with others—stands over against us as an "alien" force that controls us; this we inadvertently recognize when we speak of economic "forces" and the "power" of the free market. Under capitalism, workers and owners, poor and rich alike, are alienated from their true natures, for they see themselves as egoistic individuals who seek fulfillment in money and material advantage over others. Alienation is overcome only through the development of **communism**. By means of the abolition of private property and the consequent disappearance of economic exploitation, a communist society allows individuals to develop their creative and productive powers in self-conscious cooperation with others. The ideal of an unalienated socialist society articulated in the *Manuscripts* held sway over many French intellectuals after **World War II**, including Merleau-Ponty and **Jean-Paul Sartre**.

ECSTASIS (Ger. *Ekstase*). Derived from Greek words meaning "standing outside," *ecstasis* is a technical term introduced by **Martin Heidegger** in *Being and Time* to denote existential **temporality** in contrast to traditional philosophical and scientific conceptions of time. Heidegger's use of the term *ecstasis* is related to his understanding of *ek-sistence* as a process of "standing outside" oneself by one's involvements in the world, or, alternately put, of being "ahead of oneself" in a continual orientation toward future "possibilities" (goals and **projects**). Because the human being is primarily guided by future projects, which "stand out" as the **horizon** of present concerns without themselves being reducible to contents or experiences present in the mind, Heidegger observes that existential time is essentially futural rather than centered around the present or the "now point," as in traditional conceptions. It is through a relation to the future that the other two ecstases of time, the past and the present, are properly understood.

Existential time is also essentially related to **finitude** and to **death**: The ultimate future possibility, in relation to which both past and present come into focus, is the possibility of my own death. Heidegger speaks of **authentic** time as a kind of **being-towards-death**, a tacit recognition of one's own finitude that organizes past and present concerns. In authentic being-towards-death, each of the three ecstases—future, past, and present—is coimplicated in a process Heidegger calls "primordial **historizing**," whereby "**Dasein** *hands* itself *down* to itself . . . in a possibility which it has inherited and yet has chosen" (BT, 435).

L'ÉCUME DES JOURS (1947) ("Foam of Passing Days"). Humorous novel by French author and jazz trumpeter **Boris Vian**. The novel, a love story with **surrealist** elements, documents the bohemian life of **St. Germain-des-Prés** in postwar Paris. The book parodies, among other things, the cult of personality surrounding **Jean-Paul Sartre** in the late 1940s. Mocking the famously crowded conditions at Sartre's public lecture "**Existentialism Is a Humanism**," Vian's character "Jean-Sol Partre" (author of the book "La Lettre et le Néon") gives a lecture in which he has to fight his way to the stage with an axe.

EGO. In traditional philosophical parlance, the ego is the "I" or the self. Two classic views of the ego frame the existentialist conception. The first is expressed by **René Descartes**'s famous observation, *cogito ergo sum* — "I think, therefore I am" or "I am thinking, therefore I exist." Existentialists accept the immediacy and indubitability of first-person experience. However, they reject the equation of this awareness with the private mental experience of an ego cut off from the **world**. In the existentialist conception, self and world are **reciprocal** and complementary poles of **existence**.

The other view is expressed in **Immanuel Kant**'s observation that the 'I' must be capable of accompanying all mental representations, that is, that there must be a unified mental subject to whom experiences occur. Kant believed that the true nature of this subject could not be directly perceived or intuited but rather must be assumed as a transcendental condition for experience. Kant's **transcendental ego** is a necessary but nonobservable entity, distinct from empirical perceptions I may have of myself. The **phenomenology** of **Edmund Husserl** expanded upon Kant's conclusion. For Husserl, the contents of the empirical self (an individual's interests and desires relative to a real world that fulfills them) must be bracketed by the process of **phenomenological reduction**. What remains after this purifying process are essential structures of **consciousness** that have their **being** independent of the empirical world. Consciousness so purified is no longer attached to an existing self, yet it retains an essential unity and interconnectedness, and this must be attributed to a transcendental ego.

Existentialists generally reject the idea of an autonomous mental subject, whether empirical or transcendental. **Jean-Paul Sartre** maintains the extreme position that consciousness has no intrinsic ego-structure. For Sartre, an illusion of stability and permanence is conveyed by language, social roles, and other means of self-objecti-fication. Beneath these labels and illusions, consciousness remains a pure "spontaneity," a "**nothingness**." **Martin Heidegger** criticizes the traditional conception of the self as a **knowing subject**. The idea of a private sphere of mental representation is highly suspect for Hei-degger, as it distorts our ordinary experience of ourselves as agents immersed in a shared social world. Ordinarily, he maintains, the hu-man being exists "outside of itself," in the world and in relations with others. This primary level of shared engaged agency Heidegger calls **being-in-the-world**. *See also DASEIN.*

Maurice Merleau-Ponty expands upon Heidegger's account to highlight the role of the **body** in the formation of subjectivity. The body, with its perceptual powers and dispositions, constitutes a kind of "prepersonal" self that is the basis for more explicit mental and lin-guistic self-awareness.

EK-SISTENCE. Martin Heidegger employs the hyphenated form of this term to recall its original Greek and Latin meaning, "to stand out-side of" or "to stand out from." Heidegger's intention is to stress that human **existence** stands "ahead of" and "outside of" itself both tem-porally and spatially: temporally because the plans and **projects** that define who one is are continually being enacted and revised; spatially because **action** entails projecting oneself into a world and relating to things with which one is **concerned**. To say that *Dasein* "ek-sists" is thus to recall that human beings are dynamic, world-oriented, and self-interpreting entities rather than static, ahistorical, and self-suffi-cient **substances**.

ÉLAN VITAL **(Fr. "impulse of life").** In *Creative Evolution* (1907), **Henri Bergson** argued that the process of organic evolution can-not be understood in purely mechanical terms. Instead, to explain the emergence of life out on nonlife, as well as the creation of new organs and species, Bergson appealed to a **vitalistic**, nonmaterial cause referred to as the "impulse of life" or "*élan vital*." The *élan vital* is spontaneous, creative, and unpredictable in its results. Bergson maintained that appeal to such a nonmaterial principle is required to explain qualitative leaps in evolution from plants to an-imals, and from animals to humans. Humans, while still partially governed by instinct and habit characteristic of lower forms, are unique in their capacity for reason and, particularly, intuition, an empathic perception of the creative unfolding of life. While reason allows us to assimilate the world to unchanging laws and patterns, intuition allows us to grasp the overall intention or meaning of things, their creative "becoming." Intuition is thus both the means of access to and itself an expression of the impulse of life. **Friedrich Nietzsche**'s notion of the **will to power** is sometimes understood as a vitalistic principle similar to Bergson's *élan vital*. This is the basis for the classification of both Bergson and Nietzsche as "**philosophers of life**."

EMOTION. While few existentialists advance explicit theories of emotion, most agree that emotional experience is essential to human awareness rather then merely an irrational disturbance of an otherwise emotionless state. Moreover, **moods** and emotions like **anxiety**, shame, and love are understood not as subjective projections but as manners of disclosing substantial truths about the **world**. Anxiety discloses the self's concern for its own **freedom**, shame discloses our bond to **others**, while love reveals a person or thing as having intrinsic value and worth. In each case, the contention is that emotional awareness serves to reveal a truth that could not be otherwise accessed by "neutral" observation alone.

   In early writings **Jean-Paul Sartre** advanced a theory of emotion that stands in tension with the general existentialist view. *The Emotions: Outline of a Theory* (1939) proposed that emotions are **actions** we choose rather than passions we undergo. According to Sartre, an emotion is a spontaneous, **prereflective** attempt to transform a **situation** by "magic" when real action proves too difficult. Thus, one sobs "in order to" avoid having to face a disagreeable truth, and one faints in fear in order "not to see" the charging animal. The plausibility of Sartre's theory is stretched by the involuntary physiological effects of emotions like fear, as well as by the nonpurposive character of emotions like grief, shame, and guilt, where there is no apparent gain for the individual. Sartre's treatment is nonetheless significant for its criticism of reductive biological and psychological theories that portray emotions as internal events divorced from experience of the world and others. *See also* MOOD.

ENCOMPASSING, THE (Ger. *das Umgreifende*). A central notion in the philosophy of **Karl Jaspers**. Jaspers employs the phrase "the encompassing," or in some translations "the comprehensive," to express the sense in which particular acts of awareness and thought are experienced to be "encompassed" within a more general, total, or ultimate **horizon**, which itself cannot be experienced. We can extend the horizon of our awareness to a point, but then we necessarily come up against a limit. Nonetheless, we sense that beyond that limit possibilities remain indefinite and "inexhaustible." This intimation of participating in an indefinite totality of **being** is our sense of the encompassing.

To take an example considered by Jaspers, the nature of the human being may be studied from a number of scientific and **historical** perspectives, each of which places the person within a determinate horizon—biological, economic, sociological—and yields a certain body of objective knowledge. Yet the ultimate horizon for understanding the human being cannot be specified, as human possibilities for spontaneity and creativity remain indefinite and inexhaustible. Thus, in pursuing the question, "What is a human being?" to its limit, one arrives at an experience of the encompassing. Jaspers speaks of awareness of the encompassing as a "basic philosophical operation" through which "we free our sense of being from its connection with knowledge" (PE, 18). It is precisely the nonobjectifiable, and hence unknowable, features of reality—for Jaspers, the encompassing, **transcendence**, *Existenz*, and being—that are the highest concern of philosophy. Because these are not objects, nor even concepts in the strict sense, the goal of **philosophizing** is not to provide a determinate analysis or explanation of them but rather to **awaken** the sense that we participate in something greater than what we can know.

EPOCHÉ. *See* PHENOMENOLOGICAL REDUCTION.

ESPRIT. French Catholic journal of ideas, edited by the French personalist philosopher **Emmanuel Mounier**. *Esprit* published articles on existentialist philosophy in the 1940s and 1950s, most of which endorsed a **religious existentialist** viewpoint, such as that of **Gabriel Marcel**, and opposed **Jean-Paul Sartre**'s atheistic existentialism. *Esprit* was a rival to Sartre's journal, *Les Temps modernes*.

ESSENCE (Lat. *essentia*, Gk *eidos*). The concept of essence in traditional philosophy derives in large measure from the Platonic notion of unchanging, intelligible "forms" or "ideas" that underlie and bring unity and permanence to perceptual objects. The essence of a thing defines what the thing is, the properties it must exhibit in order to be a thing of that type. Mathematical concepts provide classical examples of essences in this sense. The essence of a triangle, "a three-sided figure the sum of whose angles equals 180 degrees," is instantiated by any perceived or constructed triangle; moreover, essences may be known intellectually, independent of empirical observation.

The existentialist dictum "**existence precedes essence**" is a rejection of the idea that human beings have an essence in the traditional sense, that is, that a person can be adequately understood as the instantiation of a set of universal properties. This is because a human being is not a self-contained object in the manner of a table, chair, mathematical equation, or planet. Rather, a human being is always in the process of becoming, of determining who it will be according to the **choices** and **actions** it takes and the **values** it **commits** itself to. Human **existence** is thus both dynamic and self-relational—self-interpreting and self-evaluating—in contrast to entities that appear to exist objectively.

ETHICAL, THE. *See* KIERKEGAARD, SØREN.

ETHICAL VOLUNTARISM. The version of **ethical** voluntarism that seems to apply to many existentialists is the view that volitional elements—will, **choice**, decision, **commitment**—in contrast to acts of intellect or theoretical reason, are the essential components of moral **action**. In *Principles and Persons: An Ethical Interpretation of Existentialism* (1967), Frederick Olafson makes the case that the existentialists' major contribution to ethical theory is precisely to have developed a nuanced understanding of how volition and choice are essential to ethics, and of how overly intellectualist views of human beings tend to obscure the true nature of ethical action.

In Olafson's reconstruction of the existentialist position, determining what ought to be done requires that certain features of a **situation** be evaluated as more important than others and that they be acted upon, not simply thought about or intellectually analyzed. In this account, moral actions are those that issue from an awareness of one's ability to choose between alternatives and one's **responsibility** for such choices. To see one's actions as based on evaluations of the **world**, and to see oneself in turn as responsible for these evaluations in some sense, is for Olafson the core of the existentialist notion of moral autonomy. From Olafson's perspective, existentialists' criticism of traditional ethics is directed against the idea of "objective **values**," values that ostensibly exist and can be known and taken into account through a purely intellectual operation independently of an agent's choices, rather than against the idea that some values may be universal, or that a person's choice of values should be internally consistent.

ETHICS. It has not escaped the attention of critics that what are perceived as core **values** of existentialism—**freedom**, individuality, rejection of social norms, passion, and **choice**—seem to conflict with core **ethical values** like obligation to others, cooperative action, impartiality, and respect for social norms. Each of the major 20th-century existentialists confronted this problem to a certain degree, though, for various reasons, none produced an "existentialist ethics" that fully answered these difficulties. In the end, the demand for individual **authenticity**, at the heart of the existentialist perspective, may be the core of its ethical contribution. At the same time, it is also the source of lingering tensions with traditional ethical concerns like obligation to others and respect for universal norms.

Søren Kierkegaard's critique of rationalist ethics set the stage for existentialists who broached the topic in the 20th century, especially **Jean-Paul Sartre**. Kierkegaard maintained that religious **faith** is sourced in an irreducibly personal decision that cannot be rationally justified to others: One has faith in virtue of the **absurd**, not as the outcome of any rational procedure. Ethical decisions, in contrast, may always be communicated and made reasonable to others, based on shared values and principles of right and wrong. Thus, Kierkegaard concluded, faith must be recognized as in a sense "higher" than ethical awareness, for the irreducibly individual nature of the person, the highest expression of human subjectivity, is realized in faith, but not in ethics. Thus in matters of faith a **teleological suspension** of ethical norms is possible.

Sartre's understanding of ethics also is framed by a hostility to rationalism and a valorization of individual freedom. To justify one's acts by appeal to external standards, such as standards of reasonableness, is to absolve oneself of **responsibility** and so to risk falling into **bad faith**. Authenticity requires recognizing that I am the origin of my acts, and that the values I choose to live by derive their authority from my decision to embrace them.

Sartre's ideal of authenticity based in individual freedom has prompted serious criticism. Can one freely and authentically choose to be a murderer? Are there limits to the pursuit of freedom? If so, how, within existentialism, are they to be justified? In his attempt to grapple with such questions, Sartre's thinking became less individualistic and moved in the direction of social ethics. Throughout the late 1940s and 1950s, he came to consider the project of individual freedom as a facet of a larger social endeavor, which may be described as a kind of revolutionary socialism. Only within a truly equitable and free society can I come to know myself as free, for my knowledge of myself depends significantly on how others view me. The **reciprocity** of freedom gives others the role of collaborators rather than rivals in the quest for personal autonomy.

An alternative within existentialism to the ethics of individual authenticity is what may be called the ethics of **dialogue**. Such an ethics was proposed most forcefully within the existentialist tradition by **Martin Buber**. For Buber, the highest human value is not freedom or autonomy, but *dialogue*, encounter with the **other**. Ethics is occasioned by the claim of another being who addresses me in a personal fashion, requiring a personal response. Only through dialogue, and never through solitary decision, is authentic subjectivity realized. A similar vision of ethics based in interpersonal **communication** is advocated by **Karl Jaspers** and **Gabriel Marcel**.

ETHICS OF AMBIGUITY, THE (Pour une morale de l'ambigüité, 1947). In this short work, her sole book of philosophy, **Simone de Beauvoir** attempts to clarify the claims of an existentialist **ethics**, a task that **Jean-Paul Sartre** at the end of *Being and Nothingness* had promised to address "in a future work" (BN, 628) that never materialized. While Beauvoir's effort is generally regarded as a failure in philosophical terms—an opinion shared by Beauvoir herself—it nonetheless opens up several suggestive avenues for thought.

Like Sartre, Beauvoir starts from the premise that **freedom** is the defining feature of the human being. It is Beauvoir's hope that "by turning towards this freedom we are going to discover a principle of **action** whose range will be universal" (EA, 23). The challenge she faces is how to square radical individual freedom with the claims of morality that would seem to limit it. Beauvoir and Sartre's appeal to universality recalls the position of **Immanuel Kant**, which recognizes the claims of reason as universally binding moral imperatives. However, if the individual is truly free in the existentialist sense, then the claims of reason cannot be binding in themselves but only because they are acknowledged as binding, in the individual's free **commitment** to them. To attempt to justify one's commitment by appeal to reason is to seek refuge from a responsibility that is in the end unjustifiable.

Beauvoir's most promising strategy is to insist on the ineluctably social nature of human **existence**: "[N]o existence can be validly fulfilled if it is limited to itself. It appeals to the existence of others" (EA, 67). If freedom is to be more than an abstract ideal, it must be acted on, and it may be acted on only in a social setting, where it becomes dependent on the judgment and action of others. Thus, she observes, "the existence of others as a freedom defines my situation and is even the condition of my own freedom" (EA, 91). Alternately put, "[my] freedom can be achieved only through the freedom of others" (EA, 156), because I depend on others for confirmation of my freedom: when this confirmation is withheld, I am reduced to an unfree being, a mere thing devoid of **transcendence**. Words and actions must be taken up by others "into an open future" or else they remain lifeless and their animating intention is lost. In this way, Beauvoir arrives at a positive statement of an existentialist moral position: in order to fully realize my own freedom, "the freedom of [others] must be respected and they must be helped to free themselves" (EA, 60). If *The Ethics of Ambiguity* does not provide a philosophically cogent defense of Sartre's ethics, it does offer one of the clearest statements of the existentialist concept of **reciprocal** freedom, freedom as an interpersonal and social accomplishment and not merely an individual power.

EVERYDAYNESS (Ger. *Alltäglichkeit*). According to **Martin Heidegger**, the basic structures of **existence** are not to be sought primarily in the "higher" intellectual, moral, and spiritual acts traditionally taken to define the human being but in *Dasein*'s "average everyday" manner of **being-in-the-world**. Heidegger's strategy in *Being and Time* is to "uncover" the mundane significance of practical and affective relations to things, other people, and ourselves as a guide to a more appropriate interpretation of human being than that provided by the philosophical tradition. One of Heidegger's most striking claims is that the meaning of things is initially revealed to us through **moods** rather than through reflective thought. Everydayness is also instrumental in *Dasein*'s tendency toward self-misinterpretation and **inauthenticity**. In everyday existence *Dasein* immerses itself in mundane **projects** and relations with others, losing sight of its essential **freedom** to determine itself. *See also* AUTHENTICITY AND INAUTHENTICITY.

EXCEPTION. There are two related uses of the concept of the "exception" in existentialism. For **Søren Kierkegaard**, a person becomes an exception when, as a test of **faith**, God requires him or her to commit an act that suspends the **ethical** standards of the community. In this case, the action appears as a rejection of or an "exception" to accepted standards. Moreover, the individual is unable to communicate reasons for acting in terms others will understand, since their reasons for acting are not universal but apply only to this individual in the state of exception. **Abraham** is the most extreme example Kierkegaard offers of such a state of exception.

In an obliquely related sense, **Karl Jaspers** proposes the category of the exception to describe the status of truly original thinkers whose viewpoints are genuine exceptions to the received views and expectations of their time. For Jaspers, Kierkegaard himself and **Friedrich Nietzsche** were exemplary exceptions:

> They were exceptions in every sense . . . . Those who knew them felt attracted in an enigmatic way by their presence, as though elevated for a moment to a higher level of being; but no one really loved them . . . . They have been called simply insane . . . . They cannot be classed under any earlier type . . . . With them, a new form of reality appears in history. They are . . . representative destinies, sacrifices whose way out of the world leads to experiences for others. (RE, 37–38)

Jaspers's concept of the exception is a liberal transformation of Kierkegaard modeled on the Romantic notion of *genius*. *See also* TELEOLOGICAL SUSPENSION OF THE ETHICAL.

EXISTENCE. The technical philosophical term for human existence, from which the expressions "**philosophy of existence**" and "**existentialism**" are derived. *Existence* refers to the distinctively self-conscious and self-determining character of a human life as it is lived from a first-person perspective and that becomes obscured when viewed from an external, objectifying perspective. Existentialists maintain that traditional definitions of the human being as a "rational animal," "thinking thing," or "created being," by reducing the individual to an instance of a universal **essence**, misconstrue the subjective and inherently relational character of existence. They insist that human existence is not thinglike or substantial—and thus not to be conceived according to objective definition—for several related reasons.

To begin, unlike things or **substances**, whose essential properties are "fixed" and "fully present" and so may be enumerated by the scientist or metaphysician, persons are always in the process of becoming, that is, of pursuing **projects** and possibilities yet to be realized and that cannot be specified in advance. **Karl Jaspers** expressed well the connection between the process-character of existence and the fact of human **freedom**: "Man is something more than what he knows of himself. He is not what he is simply once and for all, but is a process . . . not merely an extant life, but . . . endowed with possibilities through the freedom he possesses to make of himself what he will be by the activities on which he decides" (MMA, 146).

Another way existentialists have made the same point is to deny that humans have a fixed nature or essence. Things—a chair, a cabbage, a mathematical equation, a divine being—may be adequately identified by a set of properties common to all of the entities in that class. But there is no set of properties common to all humans that adequately describes *who* a person is, since who a person is emerges only through the choices she or he makes and the projects she or he pursues. For the individual, the process of existing itself provides the "form" of existence. This is the context of **Martin Heidegger**'s assertion, "*The 'essence' of Dasein lies in its existence*" (BT, 67). It is also the context for **Jean-Paul Sartre**'s famous definition of existentialism as the doctrine that "**existence precedes essence**," a reformulation of Heidegger's remark.

A further reason existence is not to be equated with the being of a thing or substance is that it is not merely occurrent or "**present-at-hand**." To say that a stone "exists" means that it is "present" or "actual" but says nothing about how the stone relates to other things or to itself. In contrast, human existence must be described in terms of an essential **concern** with itself, the **world**, and others. Heidegger calls this fundamental attitude of existential concern "**care**." Sartre captures something similar by speaking of existence as a "**being-for-itself**," that is, not only a self-conscious being but also one that continually *relates* to itself, the world, and others through its concerns and projects.

A related aspect of the uniqueness of existence is suggested by the etymology of the term. In Latin and in Greek, "to exist" means "to stand outside of." Martin Heidegger stresses this etymological meaning by sometimes hyphenating the word: "**ek-sistence**." The "ek-sisting" individual "stands outside of itself" in the sense that it is primarily a **being-in-the-world** and **being-with-others** and thus cannot be reduced to a sphere of autonomous subjectivity or private mental experience. We exist **ecstatically** in space in that, as bodies immersed in a physical world that concerns us, we are never a purely self-contained "here" but rather always also "somewhere else": "at the top of the next hill" when we are hiking, "toward the bottom of that shelf" when we are searching for a familiar book. We also exist ecstatically as "ahead-of-ourselves" in time, for even when we attempt to exist purely "in the moment," we are guided by what we aim to become in the future as well as by what we have been in the past. For these reasons, "existence" is unique to human beings. As Martin Heidegger observes, "The being that exists is man. Man alone exists. Rocks are, but they do not exist. Trees are, but they do not exist. Horses are, but they do not exist. Angels are, but they do not exist. God is, but he does not exist" (*Pathmarks*, 284).

EXISTENCE-PHILOSOPHY. *See* PHILOSOPHY OF EXISTENCE.

"EXISTENCE PRECEDES ESSENCE." Formula introduced by **Jean-Paul Sartre** in his essay "**Existentialism Is a Humanism**" to identify the philosophical core of existentialism. Though Sartre later distanced himself from it, it became existentialism's most widely cited definition. In the essay, Sartre's meaning is clarified by two further assertions: "Man is nothing else but what he makes of himself" and "there is no **human nature** since there is no God to conceive it" (EHE, 15). The formula thus means that human beings define themselves through their **actions** and **choices** in the process of **existing** rather than by being determined by a preestablished nature or **essence**, in the manner of human artifacts, mathematical objects, or a divine being.

Sartre's formula plays off of the distinction in traditional philosophy between *what* a thing is, its "essence," and *that* it is, its "existence." Traditionally an essence is the unchanging and universal form, nature, type, or category of which the particular existing thing is an instantiation. Essences are traditionally understood as the more appropriate object of philosophical inquiry, for they express necessary and unchanging aspects of reality, while existence is taken to express only what is **contingent** and transient. The triangle that exists because I draw it on the chalkboard is less real—less perfect, less complete, and more transient—than the essence of a triangle that I conceive in my mind. Like most things that exist, the chalkboard triangle is an imperfect instantiation of its essence.

Sartre explains how in the case of human beings, this situation is reversed. Humans differ from other things in that they have no fixed essence in the traditional sense, no predetermined purpose or nature, such as that which classical definitions of the human being, as "rational animal" or "created being," seek to capture. *What* a person is is rather the result of *how* he or she chooses to exist, the sum of his or her actions and decisions. "Existence precedes essence" thus means that my defining characteristics or "essence" cannot be known prior to existing, for the type of person I am will be decided by the **commitments** I choose to pursue in my life. Allegedly universal human characteristics like rationality or morality are for Sartre products but never causes of existence. Heredity and social circumstances, too, are in the end only "what I make of them" through my **projects** and commitments.

The provenance of Sartre's formula is most likely the proposition by **Martin Heidegger** in *Being and Time* that "*the 'essence' of* **Da-**

sein lies in its existence" (BT, 67). However, it should be noted that Heidegger did not share Sartre's understanding of existence, which he took to be misguidedly anthropocentric and subjectivistic. He clearly dissociated himself from Sartre's existentialism in *Letter on Humanism*.

EXISTENTIAL ANALYSIS. *See* EXISTENTIAL PSYCHOTHERAPY.

EXISTENTIAL FREEDOM. *See* FREEDOM.

EXISTENTIAL NOVEL. *See* EXISTENTIALIST LITERATURE.

EXISTENTIAL PHENOMENOLOGY. Since the 1950s, this phrase has been used to describe the thought of existentialist philosophers whose accounts of human **existence** draw on insights of **phenomenology**. In particular, it is applied to the philosophy of **Martin Heidegger**, **Jean-Paul Sartre**, and **Maurice Merleau-Ponty**, three of the most important existentialist thinkers of the 20th century. Each saw his work as a variant of phenomenology derived from **Edmund Husserl**. But all clearly distinguished their work from Husserl's: They rejected the attempt to give an account of **consciousness** purified of reference to the empirical **world**, and they argued that human experience is necessarily that of an embodied agent in an already-meaningful social and **historical** world. This entailed a significant revision of the phenomenological concept of **intentionality**.

Heidegger was Husserl's teaching assistant from 1919 to 1923. While he accepted Husserl's central view of the mind as intrinsically directed toward or "intending" objects and states of affairs outside of itself, he interpreted intentionality as a relation between existing individual and world rather between mental subject (or **ego**) and its objects. By reducing human experience to the intellectual processes of an autonomous ego, Heidegger maintained, Husserlian phenomenology deprived itself of the means to understand practical and emotional experiences, such as **moods**, that are essential to existence, and that exemplify an engaged, nonspectatorial relation to a world. Consequently, Heidegger rejected Husserl's goal of **phenomenological reduction** as an impossibility, for to bracket the external world is to lose sight of the range of practical, linguistic, and emotional involvements that form the basis of human existence. Heidegger recast the concept of intentionality as **being-in-the-world**; he replaced Husserl's method of phenomenological intuition with a method of **hermeneutical** analysis that assumes a rich, tacit "pre-understanding" of the world as its point of departure. "Hermeneutic phenomenology" is an alternative characterization of Heidegger's thought.

Sartre and Merleau-Ponty followed Heidegger in rejecting the idea of phenomenological reduction and in insisting on intentionality as a lived relation between self and world. To an extent, they arrived at these conclusions independently through their study of Husserl. In the case of Sartre, however, this was strongly colored by the Heideggerean reading of Husserl proposed by **Emmanuel Levinas**. Merleau-Ponty was among the first philosophers to seek access to Husserl's unpublished manuscripts in the early 1940s, and he maintained an active interest in Husserl's thought throughout his life. In his reading, Husserl's thought evolved toward a position that accords greater importance to historical, cultural, and affective dimensions of consciousness, and thus is not incompatible with the viewpoint of existential phenomenology, though it stands in tension with it.

EXISTENTIAL PSYCHIATRY. *See* LAING, R. D.

EXISTENTIAL PSYCHOANALYSIS. Jean-Paul Sartre used this term in the last chapter of ***Being and Nothingness*** to refer to his own version of **Sigmund Freud**'s **psychoanalysis**, purged of what Sartre takes to be a strict causal determinism of conscious behavior by unconscious desires. In this chapter, Sartre presents a philosophical critique of psychoanalysis and more generally of empirical psychology. He explicitly rejects basic tenets of Freud's theory, such as the theory of the unconscious and the notion that the past, especially childhood memories, is determinative of the present. For Sartre, Freud's theories undercut the **phenomenological** theory of **intentionality** and deny the reality of existential **freedom**. "Existential psychoanalysis," in contrast, "recognizes nothing *before* the original upsurge of human freedom . . . it rejects the hypothesis of the unconscious; it makes the psychic act co-extensive with **consciousness** . . . all is there, luminous; reflection is in full possession of it" (BN, 727–729). Sartre reasons that if a person's intentions were truly unavailable to conscious-ness, they would not be intentions at all, but only consequences of mechanical causation.

In spite of his antipathy toward psychoanalytic theory, Sartre ad-mired Freud's work and made ample use of psychoanalytic insights into the human personality. His autobiography, *The Words*, as well as his biographical works, such as *Saint Genet: Actor and Martyr*, *Baudelaire*, and the multivolume biography of Gustave Flaubert, tend to emphasize the formative experiences of childhood and owe much to psychoanalytic technique. The central concern of Sartre's "existential psychoanalysis" is thus evident in the biographical works: to discover in the individual's past signs of the "fundamental project" that uniquely defines that individual's existence. *See also* EXISTENTIAL PSYCHOTHERAPY.

EXISTENTIAL PSYCHOLOGY. *See* EXISTENTIAL PSY-CHOTHERAPY.

EXISTENTIAL PSYCHOTHERAPY. Umbrella term for a range of related approaches in 20th-century psychiatry and psychotherapy that incorporate ideas and methods from existentialist philosophy and **phenomenology**. Alternate labels include "existential psychiatry," "existential analysis," "existential psychology," and "humanistic psy-chology." Practitioners in Europe included Ludwig Binswanger and Medard Boss. In the United States, **Victor Frankl**, Abraham Maslow, Rollo May, and Carl Rogers were important representatives.

While "existential psychotherapy" designates a diverse field of European and American psychiatrists and psychotherapists writing between about 1930 and 1970, the common core of these approaches is a rejection of psychological theories modeled after the natural sci-ences, especially biology. Freudian **psychoanalysis** in particular is criticized for advancing a theory of human nature based on the pre-suppositions of biology, as evidenced by Freud's theory of the drives and what are perceived as other suspect biological constructs. At the same time, Freud's basic insights are often preserved, recast in other terms. For example, drives may be spoken of as "potentialities" for being rather than as physical forces. In place of causal theories, which seek to explain complex behavior in terms of simpler physical and chemical processes, existential psychotherapists propose a phenomenological approach to mental illness that accepts the patient's experience as valid prima facie in its complexity and apparent strangeness, and as irreducible to physical or physiological explanation. Mental illness is thus explained not by reduction downward to a simpler level of physical causality, but by translation into more encompassing categories of explanation unique to human existence, such as the search for meaning, the capacity for suffering, awareness of personal **responsibility**, **finitude**, and mortality. Following **Martin Heidegger**, many existential psychotherapists also appeal to the category of **being-in-the-world** as a corrective to overly individualistic or mentalistic assumptions that reduce the person to a biological organism or isolated intelligence. The idea of a **world** of mental illness—the nexus of a patient's imagined and real personal, social, and cultural relationships—was developed as well in an overlapping trend known as "phenomenological psychiatry," whose representatives included Eugene Minkowski.

A seminal link between existentialist philosophy and psychotherapy occurred in the work of the Swiss psychiatrists Ludwig Binswanger (1881–1966) and Medard Boss (1903–1990). Both took guidance from Heidegger's analysis of *Dasein* in *Being and Time* in their effort to rehabilitate traditional psychiatry and psychotherapy. Binswanger, who knew Sigmund Freud, studied under Carl Jung, and interned with Eugen Bleuler at the University of Zurich, represented a direct tie between classical psychoanalysis and German existential philosophy and phenomenology. Beginning in the early 1940s, Binswanger identified Heidegger's analysis of *Dasein* as an essential corrective to Freudian psychoanalysis and classical psychology, both of which he perceived to be overly individualistic and to ignore the fundamental dimension of human "being-in-the-world." Binswanger named his hybrid approach "existential analysis" (*Daseinanalyse*), and this term was taken up by other German-speaking practitioners. He understood existential analysis as a particular anthropological application of Heidegger's philosophical theories.

Medard Boss read *Being and Time* during **World War II** and soon after struck up a correspondence with Heidegger, who was eager to be understood beyond the confines of academic philosophy. Starting in 1959, Boss invited Heidegger to lecture in Switzerland; these lectures continued until 1969 and were published in German as *Zollikoner Seminare* (1987). Initially, the psychiatrists and physicians Boss gathered for the lectures had the impression that "a Martian was for the first time meeting a group of earth dwellers and trying to communicate with them." Eventually Heidegger was able to explain his view that mental illness can be understood as a failure to remain "open to the world" and that modern technological civilization itself suffers from a generalized pathology, of which mental illness is a heightened expression (Safranski, 404–406). Boss's views are found in *Psychoanalysis and Daseinanalysis* (1963).

Finally, it is important to note the prior endeavors of two existentialist philosophers in the fields of psychology and psychopathology. Trained as a psychiatrist, **Karl Jaspers** himself might qualify as the father of existential psychotherapy, to the extent that his first two books, the monumental *General Psychopathology* (1913; revised in 1941) and *The Psychology of Worldviews* (1919), criticize the naïve use of natural scientific method and attempt to rehabilitate psychology with the help of phenomenology and existential philosophy. **Jean-Paul Sartre**, too, in his early work, sought to bring philosophy to bear on problems of psychology and psychopathology. *The Psychology of* **Imagination** (1940) and **Emotions**: *Outline of a Theory* (1939) draw material from Sigmund Freud's and Pierre Janet's accounts of neurosis and offer critiques of these views as overly deterministic. Sartre developed his criticism of Freudian psychoanalysis in *Being and Nothingness*. The last chapter of Sartre's book is devoted to a reformulation of Freud's concept of the unconscious in the language of existentialist philosophy. *See also* EXISTENTIAL PSYCHOANALYSIS.

EXISTENTIAL THEATER. This term has been applied to the work of certain playwrights produced during and immediately after **World War II**, including, most notably, the plays of **Jean-Paul Sartre**. Sartre's own assessment of young French playwrights in 1946 cites Jean Anouilh's *Antigone*, **Albert Camus's** *Caligula* and *Misunderstanding* (*Le Malentendu*), **Simone de Beauvoir's** *Useless Mouths* (*Bouches inutiles*), as well as his own plays, such as *No Exit*, *The Flies*, and *Dirty Hands*, as examples of a new "theater of situations" rather than a "theater of characters" (Contat & Rybalka, 152–153).

EXISTENTIAL THEOLOGY. An umbrella category for the work of various 20th-century German theologians inspired by the insights of existentialist philosophy. The nature of this influence is diverse, and there is no single common doctrine or approach that defines their work. Generally speaking, existential theologians share an interest in rethinking biblical interpretation and issues of Christian **faith** from the perspective of concrete human **existence**. Principal representatives are **Karl Barth** (1886–1968), **Rudolph Bultmann** (1884–1976), Karl Rahner (1904–1980), and **Paul Tillich** (1886–1965). Of these, Bultmann provides a clear case of direct influence of existentialism on theology. His project of "demythologizing" the New Testament entailed translating the ostensibly "mythological" language of first-century Judaism and **Christianity** into an "existential" vocabulary more compelling for a modern audience. This vocabulary he found in **Martin Heidegger**'s analysis of *Dasein*.

A rough distinction may be drawn between existential theology and **religious existentialism**. Existential theologians are primarily concerned with issues of biblical interpretation and interpretations of religious doctrine, while religious existentialists generally avoid traditional theological vocabulary and arguments. **Martin Buber** and **Karl Jaspers** primarily pursued a form of religious existentialism in this sense. However, the distinction is not always clear-cut. For example, Paul Tillich's language and outlook at times closely approximated that of existentialist philosophy, and Martin Buber addressed issues of religious doctrine and biblical interpretation.

"EXISTENTIALISM IS A HUMANISM." Title of a lecture given by **Jean-Paul Sartre** in Paris on 29 October 1945, marking the beginning of the French existentialist movement. The lecture was delivered to a packed auditorium, and the publicity it generated launched Sartre's career as the "leader" of existentialism. A revised version was published the following year as a short book, *L'Existentialisme est un humanisme* (1946), which sold thousands of copies and disseminated existentialism throughout Europe and abroad. Over the years the book has been translated into numerous languages. Sartre later regretted what he perceived as the book's undue influence, as its popular style lent itself to misinterpretation and allowed critics to take existentialism to task without confronting more rigorous expositions such as *Being and Nothingness*. Nonetheless, it remains one of the most accessible accounts of Sartre's thought. It also introduces social and political concerns that preoccupied Sartre's later work.

The premise for the lecture is to defend existentialism against criticisms, leveled by both conservative **Catholics** and **communists**, of being inherently individualist and morally relativistic. In response, Sartre develops the case that existentialism is in fact a form of "humanism," a philosophy that recognizes the absolute nature of individual **freedom**. Through various examples and anecdotes, Sartre's account gropes toward a conception of freedom as **reciprocal**—based on mutual recognition—and thus in a sense as universally binding. En route to this conclusion, Sartre rehearses many of the claims of *Being and Nothingness* in popular guise. Among these is a phrase that became existentialism's best-known definition: "**existence precedes essence**." In the lecture Sartre explains his meaning fairly clearly:

> [I]f god does not exist, there is at least one being in whom existence precedes essence, a being who exists before he can be defined by any concept . . . this being is man . . . man exists, turns up, appears on the scene, and, only afterwards, defines himself . . . . Man is nothing else but what he makes of himself. Such is the first principle of existentialism. (EHE, 15)

As the lecture proceeds, Sartre further characterizes what it means to *exist* in the technical sense employed by existentialist philosophers: "[M]an . . . is the being who hurls himself toward a future and who is **conscious** of **imagining** himself in the future. Man is . . . a plan that is aware of itself, rather than a patch of moss . . . or a cauliflower" (EHE, 16). Self-consciousness and **projection** toward a future, in turn, are expressions of the fundamental feature of existence, freedom: "[T]here is no determinism, man is free, man is freedom" (EHE, 23). As Sartre had observed in *Being and Nothingness,* freedom is "the permanent possibility of . . . rupture" (BN, 439)—the capacity to stand back from one's self and one's **situation** and to accept or to refuse them, or to reshape them in some way. This power of acceptance or refusal is "permanent" in that it is a necessary component of human consciousness. To be conscious is to endow an object or event with meaning, to assign **value** to something or someone, even if most of the time we are unaware of our meaning-giving activity.

Sartre underlines that as free beings we are "without excuses"; try as we might, we cannot escape our power to reflect on, reshape, or re- fuse the reality we experience. Hence we are responsible for every- thing we do and everything we are: We are "condemned to be free." For while we do not choose the **factical** givens of our identity—race, class, physical appearance, and so forth—we choose the *attitude* we take toward them, deciding to increase or to diminish their impor- tance, to accept or to refuse to be identified by them. My situation is not given, but rather results from the attitude I have chosen to take to- ward the givens of my life.

Sartre's next step has been seen as problematic. With little argu- ment, he proceeds to claim that an individual's freedom is nonethe- less constrained by an obligation to consider the viewpoint of all oth- ers. He draws support for this claim from several directions. From **Immanuel Kant**'s perspective, he explains that the existentially **au- thentic** person, in making a decision—for example, to lie, or to steal—must always ask, "What would happen if everybody [acted or] looked at things that way?" (EHE, 19). Critics have rightly remarked that there is little justification for such a Kantian perspective within Sartre's position as formulated until this point. Indeed, it is difficult to square any standard moral perspective with the claims of radical individual freedom to the extent that such freedom does not recog- nize "values" as binding in themselves, apart from the consent of the individual who chooses them.

Sartre nonetheless suggests a path for response. He invokes G. W. F. **Hegel**'s idea that freedom can be realized only through a "mutual recognition" of self and **other**: "The man who becomes aware of himself . . . also perceives all others . . . as the condition for his own existence. He realizes that he cannot be anything . . . unless others recognize it as such" (EHE, 37). Thus, " in wanting freedom, we dis- cover that it depends entirely on the freedom of others, and that the freedom of others depends on ours" (EHE, 46). This is the first clear avowal in Sartre's writings of the necessarily social dimension of freedom, an idea developed subsequently in *Critique of Dialectical Reason*.

It is not clear whether Sartre's lecture adequately addresses the criticisms leveled against existentialism. However, the lecture does succeed in painting a compelling picture of human existence: responsible yet free, obligated to others yet concerned with self, "anguished" yet optimistic and creative. Such a picture appealed to Europeans in 1945, as it announced to those morally and physically depleted by the war that the past does not determine the present, because the present is continually being remade through human choice.

EXISTENTIALIST LITERATURE. Existentialism is unique among 20th-century philosophies in that it is as often identified with literature as with traditional philosophy. This is due in large measure to the unique literary talents and aspirations of the French existentialists — **Simone de Beauvoir**, **Albert Camus**, **Gabriel Marcel**, and **Jean-Paul Sartre**. Each considered himself or herself first and foremost a writer rather than an academic philosopher. Their novels and plays, published during and after **World War II**, were more accessible and more widely read than their philosophical works, and it was mainly through them that existentialism was initially conveyed to the reading public. This resulted in the misconception of existentialism as a literary movement rather than a form of philosophy, and this idea has cast a shadow over the category of existentialist literature, resulting in nagging ambiguity. Since the 1950s, the existentialist label has been liberally applied to a broad spectrum of literary authors from a range of historical periods, with no clear criteria for distinguishing "genuinely existentialist" works from those only purporting to be so. The scope of "existentialist fiction" is thus indefinitely large. However, it is possible to introduce a distinction between three senses in which a work of literature may be considered existentialist: works of literature written by existentialist philosophers; works of literature influential to the development of existentialist philosophy; and works of literature that express an idea or content associated with existentialism, such as **absurdity** or **alienation**, but that otherwise are unconnected to existentialist philosophy.

Instances of the first case, works of literature *written by* existentialist philosophers, generally have some specifiable content and intention related to existentialist philosophy. Notable in this category are most of the novels, plays, and short stories written by Beauvoir, Marcel, and Sartre. Though there are some borderline cases, it may be stipulated that the existentialist works are those written with a philosophical intention linked more or less explicitly to the author's existentialist philosophy. Classic works that meet this requirement include Sartre's plays *No Exit* and *The Flies*, his novel trilogy *The Roads to Freedom*, and Beauvoir's novel *She Came to Stay*. Camus's novel *The Stranger* is also commonly placed in this category as a masterpiece of existentialist fiction. Yet while Camus's fiction is clearly linked to his philosophical outlook, and while his outlook has clear affinities with existentialism, there are reasons to classify *The Stranger* as a work of the absurd rather than as an existentialist novel. As one might expect, the themes of existentialist fiction reflect the diversity of the authors' philosophical interests. The novels and plays of Beauvoir and Sartre primarily address issues of **contingency**, **freedom**, and **bad faith**; Marcel's plays explore themes of alienation, **faith**, and **love**; and Camus's fiction treats of the absurd and the overcoming of **nihilism**. The literary work of **Miguel de Unamuno** presents difficulties of classification similar to that of Camus.

The second case of existentialist literature comprises works of fiction influential to the development of existentialism but not written by existentialist philosophers. Widely cited examples include works by the great 19th-century Russian novelists **Fyodor Dostoevsky** (1821–1881) and Leo Tolstoy (1828–1910). Tolstoy and Dostoyevsky were certainly not discovered by existentialists; both were broadly influential in Germany and in France by the late 19th century. Nor can either author be plausibly classified as "existentialist" in his own right. Nonetheless, specific works, such as Dostoyevsky's *Notes from Underground* and Tolstoy's *The Death of Ivan Ilyich*, were significant in the evolution of the **philosophy of existence**, particularly in Germany, as **concrete** models of the human experience of **death**, guilt, and suffering.

The third case of existentialist literature—works that, while lacking clear philosophical intention or affiliation, forcefully exhibit an idea central to existentialist philosophy such as human alienation, **finitude**, or freedom—is the broadest, most historically variable, and most difficult to circumscribe. In the 1950s and 1960s, works like **Samuel Beckett**'s play *Waiting for Godot* and **Franz Kafka**'s novel *The Trial* were frequently cited as examples of "existential fiction" due to their vivid atmosphere of alienation and absurdity. **Ernest Hemingway** (especially for his story "A Clean, Well-Lighted Place") and **William Faulkner** were also at times placed in this category, as were writers as diverse as Herman Hesse, Norman Mailer, and J. D. Salinger.

This capacious view of existentialist literature reflected a liberal interpretation of existentialism, widespread in the 1950s and 1960s, when leading commentators such as **William Barrett** and **Paul Tillich** portrayed existentialism as a broad cultural trend rather than a narrowly defined form of European philosophy. For Barrett, existentialism was defined by a "radical feeling of human finitude" (Barrett, 36), whose roots could be discerned in the prophets of the Old Testament, Socrates, and Saint Augustine. Tillich understood existentialism as a generalized cultural phenomenon he called "the expression of the anxiety of meaninglessness." On this basis Tillich could praise existentialism as "the great art, literature, and philosophy of the 20th century" (*The Courage to Be*, 139, 143), a judgment that today seems hyperbolic.

This schema for discussing existentialist literature is by no means comprehensive or exhaustive. It is clear that certain works and authors plausibly associated with existentialism do not fit neatly into any of the three categories mentioned. An interesting case is the British novelist and philosopher Iris Murdoch, who was influenced by existentialism both as a philosopher and as a writer. Nonetheless, in her philosophy Murdoch maintained a critical distance from Sartre's existentialism, and in her fiction she approached existentially flavored themes in her own fashion. Murdoch's novels, such as *Under the Net*, *An Unofficial Rose*, and *A Severed Head*, explored psychological dimensions of freedom in a manner reminiscent of the novels of Sartre and Beauvoir, yet not beholden to them. *See also* SURREALISM; THEATER OF THE ABSURD.

EXISTENZ (Ger. "existence"). In the philosophy of **Karl Jaspers**, *Existenz* refers to the spiritual dimension of a human being in contrast to sensorial and physical existence (*Dasein*) and to **consciousness** in general (*Bewusstsein überhaupt*), the dimension of abstract and rational **understanding**. *Existenz* for Jaspers is the most **authentic** dimension of the person, and as such it is not simply given but must be achieved through transformative acts of thinking, decision, and self-reflection. Through these "inward actions," that is, through a personal struggle with the **ciphers** of the divine and with the limits of human knowledge, but also through feelings of identification with humanity and participation in the history of thought and reason, I discover that my true being emerges in relationship to nonempirical reality or **transcendence**. "Existenz is the self-**being** that relates to itself and thereby also to transcendence from which it knows that it has been given to itself and upon which it is grounded" (PE, 21). Jaspers emphasizes that *Existenz* is not intended as a precise, objective concept. Rather, the term is meant to function as a "reminder" of the potential for spiritual self-realization present in each person, and of the transformative experience under which this self-realization takes place.

EXISTENZPHILOSOPHIE. *See* PHILOSOPHY OF EXISTENCE.

EXISTING INDIVIDUAL. For **Søren Kierkegaard**, the existing individual is the actual living person who **exists** in **time**, suffers, enjoys, decides, acts, feels **responsible** for himself or herself, and feels **anxiety** over his or her **death**. The existing individual is contrasted to the "speculative philosopher," who acts as if he or she were a disembodied mind, able to comprehend **existence** from a perspective outside of it, without participating in it. **G. W. F. Hegel** is for Kierkagaard the exemplary speculative philosopher. *See also* KNOWING SUBJECT.

– F –

FACTICITY (Ger. *Faktizität*). Technical term introduced by **Martin Heidegger** in *Being and Time* to refer to the manner in which human beings apprehend the concrete social, historical, and physical givenness of their **situation**. The term is employed by subsequent existentialists in a sense close to Heidegger's. Heidegger contrasts facticity with objective "factuality," the manner in which facts about ourselves and the world are ostensibly true independent of how we experience them. In Heidegger's account, ***Dasein***'s facticity stands in tension with its essential **freedom**—its capacity to determine itself according to its own **choices** and possibilities. Facticity is, further, closely linked to what Heidegger calls **"thrownness,"** the manner in which the individual is thrust into a given family, culture, nationality, and time period, which it has not chosen yet which constitute part of its being. The language of thrownness and facticity is meant to point up the way such relationships are from a human perspective never simply neutral facts but aspects of **existence** that matter deeply to us and about which we must take a stand.

FAITH. An existentialist conception of faith is distinguished by at least two assumptions. First, genuine faith must affect the total person, one's **actions** as well as one's beliefs, attitudes, and aspirations. Second, faith can be arrived at only through a "leap" of personal **commitment** and never through reasoning or theoretical reflection alone. **Søren Kierkegaard** starkly defended such a view of faith as an exceptional personal achievement premised on an acceptance of the **absurd**. An exemplar of faith was **Abraham**, who was prepared to sacrifice his only son in order to confirm his belief. Abraham was able to renounce his earthly happiness at the same time he believed it would be restored, "by virtue of the absurd." Abraham thus embodies Kierkegaard's view of faith as an antirational achievement. Kierkegaard criticized the aspiration of **Hegelian** philosophy to "go beyond faith," that is, to arrive at a more sophisticated understanding of God and the human relation to the divine through philosophical concepts. While philosophy may articulate the "thought content" of religion, it cannot explain how an individual enters into faith in the course of his or her life; this remains mysterious, and may be adumbrated through analogies and allegories, but not rationally explained. Kierkegaard also criticized the perceived complacency and hypocrisy of the **Christian** church, which he felt had strayed from the teachings of Christianity expressed in the New Testament. He was particularly disturbed by the idea of a Christian state religion (as in his native Denmark), which he thought deprived being a Christian of meaning since all citizens were understood to be "persons of the Christian faith." **Martin Buber** echoed Kierkegaard's position when he recalled that "the so-called religious man . . . is only imagining that he believes unless the heart of his life is transformed by it, unless . . . what he believes in determines his essential attitude from the most secret solitude to public action" (BMM, 192).

FALLING (Ger. *Verfallen*). Technical term in the philosophy of **Martin Heidegger** that designates the way human beings tend to interpret themselves inauthentically, misunderstanding their essential **freedom** and **responsibility**, in large part by identifying themselves with social roles and the expectations and opinions of others. In *Being and Time*, Heidegger characterized falling in terms of "idle talk," "curiosity," and "**ambiguity**." These are ways in which ***Dasein*** "loses itself" by conforming its thought and behavior to "what everyone thinks" and "what everyone does." According to Heidegger, philosophy and science contribute to falling by underwriting the tendency of human beings to understand themselves on the model of nonhuman things, that is, by encouraging the misapplication of static, impersonal categories such as **substance**, property, object, subject, and state to human **existence**, which is essentially dynamic, **historical**, and in a profound sense subjective. At the same time Heidegger insists that falling is not a purely negative condition that might be overcome or avoided; it is integral to *Dasein*'s **being-in-the-world** as **being-with-others**.

Heidegger denies that the concept of falling contains any moral or religious content. Yet it is difficult to ignore the resonance with the "fall of man" in **Christian** theology, and equally hard not to read Heidegger's general characterization of inauthenticity as a condemnation of the superficiality of social existence. Heidegger's account of falling and inauthenticity is indebted to the critique of modern social life presented by **Søren Kierkegaard** in *The Present Age*. *See also* AUTHENTICITY AND INAUTHENTICITY; LEVELING.

FANON, FRANTZ (1925–1961). French psychiatrist and political theorist, born and raised in Martinique. Fanon was one of the first theorists of decolonization and an active supporter of the Algerian nationalists in the French–Algerian War. He maintained that native populations across the developing world, in particular in Africa and Latin America, should rebel against control by Western colonial powers and forge their own societies, employing violence as a legitimate means to social revolution. He regarded the rural masses, rather than intellectuals trained in the West, as the prime agents of social change. **Jean-Paul Sartre** endorsed Fanon's revolutionary socialism and wrote the preface to his best-known work, *The Wretched of the Earth* (1963).

FAULKNER, WILLIAM (1897–1962). American novelist and short-story writer, awarded the Nobel Prize for Literature in 1949. Faulkner is tied to existentialism in two respects. As a literary model for French writers in the 1930s, Faulkner, along with writers like **John Dos Passos** (1896–1970), John Steinbeck (1902–1968), **Ernest Hemingway** (1899–1961), and Erskine Caldwell (1903–1987), introduced a direct, colloquial tone and a rawness of subject matter that had considerable influence on the style of *The Stranger*, **Albert Camus**'s first novel, as well as on **Jean-Paul Sartre**'s first novel, *Nausea*, and on his *The Roads to Freedom* trilogy. Sartre discussed Faulkner's work in a 1939 essay, "On *The Sound and the Fury*: Time in the Works of Faulkner" (LPE, 79–87), in which Faulkner's obsession with the past and with the **moment** of **consciousness** is contrasted with what Sartre claims is a more modern, and more **authentic**, "**metaphysics** of time," represented by **Martin Heidegger**'s claim that human beings are essentially oriented toward future possibilities.

In another respect, Faulkner's attention to themes of **alienation**, isolation, and mortality, with special attention to the lived, first-person consciousness of these experiences, is clearly linked to existentialist concerns. *See also* EXISTENTIALIST LITERATURE.

FEAR. *See* ANXIETY.

FEAR AND TREMBLING (*Frygt og Bœven*, 1843). In this complexly layered exploration of the biblical story of **Abraham** and Isaac, **Søren Kierkegaard** brings to life the psychology of Abraham, treating the story not as a myth but as a real human experience, "as if it happened yesterday" (FT, 34). Kierkegaard's analysis of the story, presented under the pseudonym Johannes de Silentio, defends a view of **faith** as suprarational and ultimately incommunicable. One of Kierkegaard's motives is to oppose the rationalist **metaphysics** of G. W. F. **Hegel**, according to which religious belief may be rationally articulated within a philosophical framework. While Abraham is recognized as the "father of faith," Kierkegaard insists that his experience, upon careful consideration, remains impenetrable to reason: It is not sourced in any calculation or deliberation we might follow. Rather, Abraham has faith "by virtue of the **absurd**." That is, Abraham believes both that he must sacrifice his son and at the same time that his son will be restored to him, for his trust in God's wisdom and goodness is absolute. The state of mind of a person who clearheadedly maintains such contradictory beliefs cannot be readily grasped; it is a source of awe and wonder, which we contemplate with trepidation. Psychologically, the core of Abraham's experience—the feeling that Isaac must be sacrificed yet that at the same time that he will not be lost—is a paradox, strictly private and incommunicable. The reader who recognizes this grasps that faith is not a state of complacent belief nor even a type of philosophical wisdom, but something awesome and even terrifying. *Fear and Trembling* was Kierkegaard's favorite book, the one he thought would earn him "an imperishable name as an author."

FEELING. *See* EMOTION; MOOD.

FEMINISM. The sole existentialist to have a clear interest in feminism was **Simone de Beauvoir**, whose 1949 study *The Second Sex* was a foundational work of modern feminist theory. In that book, Beauvoir offered an account of how women are constituted as the **other** to men in Western societies, as passive and dependent subjects who reflect back men's superior intellectual and moral status. Beauvoir was one of the first writers to discuss the social construction of feminine identity and problems that arise when women's secondary moral and economic status is internalized. She reasoned that, because of women's inferior status in society, their very conception of themselves often differs from that of men. Hence women and men cannot be said to be equally free, for women are conditioned to misapprehend their own powers and possibilities. By focusing on the **concrete situation** of women in French society, Beauvoir arrived at a conception of situated **freedom** that served as a corrective to **Jean-Paul Sartre**'s conception of freedom as absolute. Freedom is situated in that it is necessarily differentiated by the basic social and economic position of the individual. It is not an ahistorical constant.

Beauvoir's work began to have a significant impact starting in the 1970s, when her ideas, along with those of Sartre and other existentialists, were developed by feminist philosophers and theorists from various disciplines. The ideas of objectification by the look of the other, the **master-slave dialectic** and the struggle for recognition, **reciprocity**, and the essential role of the **body** in the constitution of subjectivity have been broadly influential. Beauvoir's notion of woman as other has also been important in race and identity theory, where it has been applied to understand the asymmetrical status of racial and ethnic minorities and other subgroups.

FEUERBACH, LUDWIG (1804–1872). German materialist philosopher. Feuerbach evolved from being a student of **G. W. F. Hegel** to being a leading critic of Hegelian idealism. In the development of 19th-century German philosophy, Feuerbach is thus a crucial bridge figure between Hegel and **Karl Marx**. Feuerbach's materialist critique of Hegel provided Marx and Friedrich Engels with a philosophical starting point for their doctrine of **historical materialism**. Feuerbach's **naturalistic** view of the human being also anticipated the perspective of **Friedrich Nietzsche** and **Sigmund Freud** later in the century. Finally, his writings anticipated certain themes of existentialism, such as the primacy of embodied agency over theoretical knowing.

Among Feuerbach's central insights was the claim that religion (and idealist philosophy, which he saw as having a fundamentally religious motivation) is produced historically by the **alienation** of human **consciousness**, that is, by the unconscious projection of human powers onto a super-human being. This view was expressed notably in *The Essence of Christianity* (1841), his best-known work. Like Hegel, Feuerbach recognized **Christianity** for its unique identification of the divine and the human. Yet unlike Hegel he argued that Christianity had fulfilled its role—to bring to awareness what is highest in human nature—and must be superseded by a secular, naturalistic society. In such a society of the future, human powers will be reclaimed by human beings, and love of God will be replaced by true love of humanity. Feuerbach's utopian aspirations for human beings were echoed by Marx's conception of **communist** society.

FINITUDE. The existentialist conception of finitude may be elucidated in comparison with the nonexistentialist concept of finiteness. Traditionally, to say that human understanding, for example, is *finite* is simply to say that it has limits and is not infinite in power or scope.

In similar fashion, one may speak of numbers, space, or time as finite or infinite. In contrast, existential finitude involves an emotional apprehension of one's own finiteness as an existing individual. Finitude is thus often accompanied by **anxiety** and is revealed primarily through an awareness of **death**, for death brings into focus the finite span of time in which one's life occurs. Without such awareness, existentialists maintain, life would lack urgency and directedness, as possibilities would seem open-ended and indefinite. *See also* BEING-TOWARDS-DEATH; THROWNNESS.

FLIES, THE (*Les mouches*, 1943). Play in three acts by **Jean-Paul Sartre**, his first staged production. Produced during the German occupation of France, *The Flies* is a retelling of Aeschylus's story of Orestes, which is passed through the filter of Sartre's existentialism. The play was approved by wartime censors, yet is evidently intended by Sartre as an allegory of resistance to the German occupation. Orestes returns to his native Argos to find his mother, Clytemnestra, ruling the city with her lover, Aegistheus, the two having murdered the rightful king, Agamemnon. Electra, Orestes's sister, has been enslaved, and the city is subjected to a plague of flies, which symbolize the town's compromised moral condition. Like Mathieu, the hero of Sartre's novel *The Age of Reason*, Orestes has hitherto known that he is free, but only in the abstract sense of **freedom** from **responsibility** and constraint. His decision to kill Aegistheus and Clytemnestra allows him to experience his freedom for the first time through **concrete** and personal **commitment**: "I have done *my* deed. . . . The heavier it is to carry, the better pleased I shall be; for that burden is my freedom" (Act II, scene ii). Orestes's final **action** is to take the plague of flies away with him, leaving the people of Argos to confront their own freedom "without excuses," unclouded by self-serving **guilt** and fear. The play's intended allegorical meaning and its thinly veiled criticism of the collaborationist Vichy government were not apparent to audiences of the time.

FLORE, CAFÉ DE. This café in the heart of **Saint-Germain-des-Prés** became the base of operations for **Jean-Paul Sartre** and **Simone de Beauvoir** starting in the winter of 1941. There was a fuel shortage in Paris during **World War II**, and the well-heated Flore was an attractive place to work. Sartre and Beauvoir arrived in the morning, wrote for several hours at separate tables, and returned after lunch for several more hours of work in the afternoon. Sartre spent so much time there that the owner, Pierre Boubal, had a separate phone line installed for Sartre's use.

FOR-ITSELF. *See* BEING-FOR-ITSELF AND BEING IN-ITSELF.

FOUNDERING (Ger. *scheitern*). Technical term in the philosophy of **Karl Jaspers** that refers to the inevitable failure of human **understanding** to grasp the **world** and human being as they are in themselves and as a totality. When philosophy, science, or religion attempts such a totalization of knowledge, it *founders* (or alternately is "shattered" or "shipwrecked") for two principal reasons: The nature of the human being cannot be objectively represented but only experienced and reflected on in moments of **authentic** self-awareness Jaspers calls *Existenz*; and the world as a totality is never given to human inquiry because each inquiry-perspective is of necessity limited and excludes other points of view. Foundering is positive in that it gives one an experience of the limits of objective knowledge and thus reminds one that there is something beyond these limits, toward which spiritual and **metaphysical** striving is directed. This Jaspers calls **transcendence.**

FRANKFURT SCHOOL. This name refers to a group of dissident **Marxist** theorists (by training primarily philosophers, social scientists, and cultural and literary critics) associated with the Institute for Social Research of Frankfurt University in Germany during the 1920s and 1930s. The particular Frankfurt School brand of Marxism was known as "critical theory," theory aimed at the emancipation of human beings from the **alienating** effects of modern technological capitalism. In contrast to classical Marxists, Frankfurt School theorists questioned the revolutionary potential of the working class. In modern capitalism, they believed, all individuals tend to accept the **values** of individualism and consumerism, and all are under the sway of technology. The goal of criticism is thus not to establish a utopian society but to continually "**negate**" existing norms and institutions by pointing up their contradictions and inconsistencies.

Major Frankfurt School figures included **Theodor Adorno**, Walter Benjamin, Erich Fromm, Max Horkheimer, and **Herbert Marcuse**. The leading philosopher to inherit the theoretical perspective of the Frankfurt School was **Jürgen Habermas**. When the Institute for Social Research closed in 1934 in response to the rise of Nazism, many members immigrated to the United States. There, in New York City, it was reestablished as the New School for Social Research. The School's major theoretical statements appeared at this time, including Horkheimer and Adorno's *Dialectic of Enlightenment* (1947) and the collective work *The Authoritarian Personality* (1950). In 1952, Horkheimer and Adorno returned to Frankfurt and established a second incarnation of the institute, while Marcuse remained in the United States and became a naturalized citizen. Adorno directed the Institute until his **death** in 1969.

Though basically Marxist in outlook, Frankfurt School thinkers saw traditional Marxism as beholden to deep prejudices like the belief in the supremacy and objectivity of science, and promotion of the human domination of **nature**. They maintained that traditional Marxist theory, because it was formulated in the era of industry, had focused almost exclusively on economic factors. In contrast, they argued for the relative independence of theory from economic conditions. They drew freely upon various theoretical perspectives, including philosophy, sociology, and, **psychoanalysis**, in their effort to understand modern capitalist society. Using these diverse resources, they identified features of modern technological culture that traditional Marxists had largely ignored, such as the insidious effects of the media, advertising, and mass communication on individual **consciousness**. After **World War II**, they painted a grim picture of Western democracies as fully "administered" consumer societies governed by anonymous forces and "false needs" to consume and to acquire which individuals feel compelled to fulfill.

On the whole the Frankfurt School was hostile to existentialism. In *The Jargon of Authenticity*, Adorno was a vociferous critic of the philosophy of **Martin Heidegger**, which he portrayed as an expression of German **Nazism**. Adorno was also critical of the existentialism of **Jean-Paul Sartre**, in particular Sartre's notion of "**committed literature**." Marcuse was the exception in this regard. He studied philosophy with Heidegger in Freiburg University in the late 1920s and early 1930s. Though he came to criticize Heidegger's political involvements and the failure of his philosophy to respond to social and historical realities, Marcuse acknowledged the revolutionary character of Heidegger's critique of technology.

FRANKL, VIKTOR (1905–1997). Austrian neurologist, psychiatrist and psychotherapist, founder of "logotherapy," and survivor of the **Nazi** concentration camp at Auschwitz. Though independently conceived and practiced, Frankl's logotherapy is an instance of a broad range of 20th-century psychotherapeutic approaches designated by the heading **existential psychotherapy**.

In his autobiographical account of his experiences at Auschwitz, *Man's Search for Meaning* (1962; originally *From Death Camp to Existentialism*), Frankl recounts how he learned to turn the horrors of camp life into a challenge for "inner triumph" and growth. Part of his triumph lay in the realization that suffering and **death** are not meaningless events but essential features of human life, in that they allow one to exercise moral courage and dignity. Though few are able to rise to this challenge, the few who do, including Frankl, "offer sufficient proof that everything can be taken from a man but one thing: the last of the human **freedoms**—to choose one's attitude in any given set of circumstances" (65).

Frankl's view of human freedom—that the attitude a person (concentration camp inmate, mental patient, or otherwise) takes toward an event in his or her life (physical suffering, mental illness) is the result of a free decision—is thus quite close to that of **Jean-Paul Sartre**. Frankl's view of the meaning of suffering, in turn, bears comparison to that of **Albert Camus**, for whom absurd suffering is an occasion to struggle against **absurdity** and to act with dignity.

Like other versions of existential psychotherapy, Frankl's psychotherapeutic method, "logotherapy," distinguishes itself from **Sigmund Freud**'s psychoanalysis and Alfred Adler's individual psychology. Instead of a will-to-pleasure (Freud) or a will-to-power or will-to-overcome-inferiority (Adler), logotherapy is premised on "man's will-to-meaning . . . his deep-seated striving and struggle for a higher and ultimate meaning to his existence" (97). This quest for purpose and meaning, rather than the desire for sex, wealth, or power, is the most fundamental human motive, and when it remains unfulfilled there results an "existential frustration," for which pathological striving for sex, wealth, or power may try to compensate. Writing in 1946, Frankl believed that "existential frustration" plays "at least as . . . important a part in the formation of neuroses as sexual frustration once did" (*Man's Search for Meaning*, 99).

FREE WILL. *See* FREEDOM.

FREEDOM. For existentialists, freedom is the defining characteristic of human **existence**, and a distinctive conception of freedom stands at the heart of existentialist philosophy. In general terms, existential freedom refers to the capacity to shape one's life according to one's chosen **projects** and **commitments** rather than being determined by external factors such as heredity, society, family, or fate. Freedom is thus not limited to a specific "faculty" of the will; rather, it is a general power of **choice** and self-determination, evident in a range of behaviors and **actions**, that lends existence its human character. Existentialists tend to accept the truth of metaphysical freedom or "freedom of the will" prima facie as a given of human self-experience; they are not generally concerned with traditional arguments in favor of free will versus determinism. Their main objective is to understand why human beings tend to avoid acknowledging their freedom, and, correlatively, what it means to live in full acknowledgment that one is free. Fleeing from one's freedom rather than owning up to it is referred to as the basic strategy of inauthenticity. Facing up to and taking **responsibility** for one's freedom is the normative goal of existence. A life lived in awareness of existential freedom is an **authentic** life, one that realizes the most genuine possibilities of human existence.

Jean-Paul Sartre was particularly preoccupied with the notion of freedom, and his insistence on the absolute character of free choice is often taken as representative of the existentialist position. In fact, however, it represents only one end of a spectrum of opinion. In *Being and Nothingness*, Sartre identified freedom with the **negating** power of **consciousness**, the power to interpret and assign meaning to things and thus to "negate" things as given. Specifically, this meant the power to revise the past in the service of future **projects** and to continually remake oneself through one's choices. Later, however,

Sartre's view evolved from the notion of absolute freedom toward a conception of *situated freedom*, the idea that freedom is necessarily constrained by social and **historical** conditions. This position was outlined by **Martin Heidegger**'s account of *Dasein* as **thrown** into a historical situation. It was further developed by **Maurice Merleau-Ponty** in the final chapter of his *Phenomenology of Perception*. Here Merleau-Ponty criticized Sartre for falling prey to a rationalist dilemma, according to which human action must be either absolutely free or externally determined. Viewed from the perspective of **concrete** existence, Merleau-Ponty argued, this is a false dilemma, because human experience is never wholly free, nor is it simply determined. Rather, freedom is experienced as a dialectical give-and-take between self and **world** in which the individual takes up possibilities offered by the **situation** without creating them *ex nihilo*. Freedom is thus not radical creation of meaning but *modification* of existing meanings. The illusion of absolute freedom arises only when one assumes the perspective of a disembodied **consciousness** lacking intrinsic relatedness to a world.

A further, important existentialist claim is that, while people at all times are essentially free and self-determining, most are not willing or able to face up to this fact. The strategy of avoiding freedom is referred to variously as "fleeing" from the task of "becoming a self" (**Søren Kierkegaard**), "**bad faith**" (Sartre), and "inauthenticity" (Heidegger). In each case, freedom provokes an experience of **anxiety**, which the individual seeks to overcome. Anxiety in turn is linked to the realization that one is responsible for the person one is and for what one has made of oneself, yet that there is no ultimate justification for one's choices. Thus existential freedom is complexly bound up with a cluster of concepts—authenticity, anxiety, and responsibility—which stand at the core of existentialist accounts of the human being.

A somewhat different approach to freedom was proposed by **religious existentialists** like **Karl Jaspers**. Where Sartre and Merleau-Ponty tended to identify freedom with social and political choices, such as committing oneself to a revolutionary cause, resisting torture, or overcoming political oppression, Jaspers saw freedom as an expression of the spiritual and religious nature of the human being. Jaspers's view of freedom may be traced back to figures like **Immanuel Kant** and **Friedrich Schelling**. While spiritual freedom may not be empirically known or verified, it may be immediately experienced, for example, in moments of personal crisis and moral decision and in genuine **philosophizing**.

FRENCH RESISTANCE. This term refers to individuals and groups during **World War II** who resisted the **Nazi** occupation of France in more or less organized fashion. The core of French Resistance fighters were organized by the French **Communist** Party, the success of their efforts boosting the political power of French communists after the war. Among existentialists **Albert Camus** stands out as an active participant in Resistance activities, though even Camus has been criticized for waiting too long to commit himself. From the fall of 1943 through the summer of 1944, Camus helped to publish the clandestine newspaper *Combat*. Sartre's role in the French Resistance was commonly overstated after the war, in part due to his own romantic view of the Resistance hero: "Each of us . . . who had some knowledge of the resistance operations was led to ask himself the agonizing question: 'If they torture me, will I hold out?' Thus the very question of **freedom** was posed, and we were brought to the edge of the deepest knowledge that man can have about himself" ("The Republic of Silence" [1944]). Sartre made the question of torture and resistance the center of his play *The Victors* (1946); in *The Flies* (1944), he used the Greek legend of Orestes as an allegory for resistance to the German occupation. However, Sartre's actual involvement in Resistance activity was relatively insignificant. In 1941, with **Maurice Merleau-Ponty**, he attempted to organize a Resistance group of French leftist intellectuals, but the endeavor, called "Socialism and **Freedom**," stalled before it could produce results. Toward the end of the war Sartre contributed articles to *Combat*.

FREUD, SIGMUND (1956–1939). Austrian neurologist and founder of **psychoanalysis**. Freud is to be credited with the momentous discovery that neuroses or "nervous disorders" are not caused by an organic disfunction of the nervous system but by repressed desires and **emotions**. This aspect of Freud's thought made him attractive to French **philosophers of existence** in the 1930s, when his works became available in French translation. To **Maurice Merleau-Ponty** and **Jean-Paul Sartre**, Freud's theory was appealing in that it explained apparently random organic disturbances as the product of **intentional** acts (wishes, thoughts, and so forth) linked to a person's identity. Moreover, Freud's frank analysis of sexuality offered a **concrete** approach to human behavior. At the same time, Freud's concept of the unconscious mind conflicted with their **commitment** to **phenomenology**, which assumed that all mental contents must be presented to **consciousness** in some form. Thus, while they referred to Freud's theories approvingly in their published writings, both Sartre and Merleau-Ponty were inclined to interpret the Freudian unconscious as a type of tacit or **prereflective** consciousness and not as a distinct mental realm or agency.

Sartre discussed Freud's theories in a chapter of his book on emotion and at several points in *Being and Nothingness*. In the latter book, Freud's views served as a foil for Sartre's discussion of **bad faith** and the fundamental **project** and provided the model for a new type of inquiry that Sartre named **existential psychoanalysis**, of which Sartre's study of **Jean Genet** was a prime example. Sartre's interest in hidden motives and conflicts, childhood fantasies, and sexual perversions suggests a general influence of Freudian theories. Merleau-Ponty discussed Freud's theory of sexuality in a chapter of *Phenomenology of Perception* entitled "The Body in Its Sexual Being." Here, Merleau-Ponty suggested that psychoanalytic research reveals sexuality to be a kind of symbolic "atmosphere" that suffuses human **existence**, a generalized manner of existing through the body, related to language, perception, and other persons, and not restricted to physical arousal.

Freud's work was less appreciated among German existentialists. **Karl Jaspers**, who was trained as a psychiatrist, was familiar with Freud's theories and made reference to Freud in his early writings, notably in *General Psychopathology*. However, in Jaspers's mature work, Freud was perceived as a reductionist who dangerously distorts the moral and spiritual dimensions of the human being.

FROMM, ERICH. *See* EXISTENTIAL PSYCHOTHERAPY; FRANKFURT SCHOOL.

FUNDAMENTAL ONTOLOGY. In the philosophy of **Martin Heidegger** as expounded in *Being and Time*, this refers to the claim that the study of human **existence** has priority over other forms of scientific and philosophical inquiry because the fundamental categories of **being** (the object of **ontology**) are properly revealed only through analysis of existence. The sciences give an account of various "regions of being," such as *nature*, *language*, *history*, *space*, and *time*, but they leave untouched the ontological meaning of these regions. How are they related? In what types of experience are they confirmed? Are they fundamental, or can they be traced back to more basic categories? The only way to assess the status of diverse ontological categories and concepts, Heidegger claims, is to take up a stance within existence itself, or, alternately put, to take up the perspective of the sole being that employs these concepts and categories: ***Dasein***. *Dasein* necessarily operates with a tacit ontological **understanding** of itself and the **world** it relates to, an immediate sense of the kind of being it is and the kind of being of other things. According to Heidegger, this **everyday** understanding of being is presupposed by theoretical science and traditional philosophy. Hence the task of examining the most fundamental categories of being, or fundamental ontology, falls to existential philosophy, which Heidegger understands as ***phenomenology*** properly understood.

– G –

GADAMER, HANS-GEORG (1900–2002). German philosopher. Gadamer was a student of **Martin Heidegger** from 1923 to 1929. On the basis of Heidegger's teaching, Gadamer developed a systematic approach to **hermeneutics**, the theory of human **understanding** and interpretation. This is expressed in his major work, *Truth and Method* (*Wahrheit und Methode*, 1960). Gadamer stresses the historical **situatedness** and the open-ended character of hermeneutical understanding (*Verstehen*). Like Heidegger, he views ostensibly ahistorical applications of reason, such as scientific theories, as **historically** conditioned: Theories can be formulated only on the basis of background assumptions relative to a specific cultural and historical tradition. Fortunately, background assumptions, or **horizons** of understanding, are not entirely closed and static. They remain open and flexible to a degree, allowing for a "merging" of one's horizons with those of the other—text, person, or artwork—one seeks to understand. Gadamer's emphasis on the finite and perspectival nature of understanding, and his view of the history of philosophy as an ongoing conversation between self and other, bear comparison with the philosophy of **Karl Jaspers**.

GENERAL PSYCHOPATHOLOGY (Allgemeine Psychopathologie, **1913).** **Karl Jaspers**'s first published work was written while he was pursuing an academic career in psychology at the University of Heidelberg, several years before his discovery of the **philosophy of existence**. The book is a catalogue of psychiatric theories and mental disorders. Nonetheless, it is distinguished by its **phenomenological** descriptions of various mental illnesses and its suggestion that first-person experience (i.e., that of the patient) may be essential to proper diagnosis and classification. **Jean-Paul Sartre** helped to translate Jaspers's book into French as a philosophy student in the late 1920s.

GENET, JEAN (1910–1986). French novelist, diarist, and poet. Genet met **Jean-Paul Sartre** and **Simone de Beauvoir** in the mid-1940s and became a member of Sartre's circle in Paris. A petty criminal and homosexual who had served time in prison, Genet was attractive to Sartre for his underworld aura, individualism, and psychological complexity as well as for his adventurous prose. Sartre devoted a 600-page study to Genet, *Saint Genet: Actor and Martyr* (1952), an outstanding example of what Sartre called **existential psychoanalysis**. The book probed Genet's writing for clues to his past and his inner life, the "original **choice**" that made him into the person he is. It also explored in **concrete** detail notions of **freedom**, **bad faith**, and **authenticity** sketched more abstractly in *Being and Nothingness*.

According to Sartre, Genet exemplifies the tension between subjectivity and objectivity, **being-for-self** and being-for-others that is constitutive for **existence**. An orphan taken in as a young child by French peasants, Genet was a bright student who aimed to please others, yet he remained unsure of his identity. At age 10, he was caught stealing and was told, "You are a thief." According to Sartre, this objectifying judgment is a "cruel punishment," which became the key to Genet's identity and the source of unresolvable conflicts that are played out in his writing. Genet is torn between the objectifying gaze that "petrifies" him in his **being** (as a thief and a social misfit) and his experience of himself as a free **consciousness** without fixed nature or **essence** (in addition to stealing, he is attracted to beauty, suffering, and the idea of saintliness; Sartre observes that he is not intrinsically "evil," only society's judgment makes him so).

Sartre recognizes that Genet is not free to create himself *ex nihilo*; he is free only *to make something of what others have made of him*. This is an important clarification of the idea of radical **freedom** expounded in *Being and Nothingness*, for it acknowledges the power of social relations and institutions in the constitution of personal identity. Genet is not free to remake the entire system of **values** that judges him (to do so would require stepping outside of this system, and doing this would leave significant parts of himself behind). He is free, however, to modify these values. He accomplishes this by actively and passionately choosing the identity society has assigned to him: to be a thief and a social deviant. This choice represents his fundamental **project**. By willfully accepting society's judgment and celebrating a life of crime and homosexuality in his fiction and his memoirs, Genet asserts his freedom within the limits of his **situation**—he "creates himself" not *ex nihilo* but from the materials of his past. For Sartre, this makes Genet "one of the heroes of this age" (599). Genet represents one version of authenticity, for he affirms his freedom by direct engagement with his situation.

GESTALT PSYCHOLOGY. Form of modern psychology developed primarily in Germany in the 1920s through the 1940s, based on the insight that perception operates by grasping meaningful wholes (*Gestalten*) rather than bits of sense data. According to Gestalt theorists, sense perception is informed by invariable laws—for example, of symmetry, contiguity, and color constancy—and these laws cause us to perceive things in terms of meaningful patterns and to assimilate new information to habitual categories. For example, a dotted line is perceived as continuous rather than fragmented, objects close to each other are perceived as a group, and a piece of white paper continues to be perceived as white even when cast in shadow. A further Gestalt principle is that of figure and ground. In normal perception, a perceived object (figure) stands out against a background that remains indistinct (ground). The primitive status of the figure–

ground relationship undercuts the atomist assumption that perception originates in the reception of isolated sensory data.

Gestalt theory intersects with existentialism largely through the work of **Maurice Merleau-Ponty**. Merleau-Ponty was attracted to the Gestaltist critique of perceptual atomism as well as "logicism," the assimilation of perception to intellectual processes. At the same time, he criticized the attempt to provide a causal account of perception in line with biological and psycho-physiological science. Like **Edmund Husserl**, Merleau-Ponty regarded causal accounts of human experience as reductive and **naturalistic**. Instead, he maintained that perception represents an "originary" level of meaning, a kind of "silent language" that cannot be reduced to either intellectual processes or physiological events. On Merleau-Ponty's account, perception is inherently **situational** and subjective; the subject of perception is not the organism, as the Gestaltists believed, about which universal laws may be postulated, but the "*lived body*," guided by emotional dispositions, intentions, and habits. Merleau-Ponty makes extensive use of the findings of Gestalt theory in both *The Structure of Behavior* and *Phenomenology of Perception*. In the latter work, he refers particularly to the research of Kurt Koffka and Wolfgang Köhler.

GIACOMETTI, ALBERTO (1901–1966). Swiss modernist sculptor and painter. Associated with the **surrealists** in the 1920s and 1930s, Giacometti befriended **Jean-Paul Sartre** and **Simone de Beauvoir** in Paris in the early 1940s during the German occupation of France. In her memoirs, Beauvoir recalls the "deep bond of understanding between [Giacometti] and Sartre: they had both staked everything on one obsession—literature in Sartre's case, art in Giacometti's—and it was hard to decide which of them was more fanatical" (PL, 387). For Sartre, Giacometti's approach to sculpting the human face recalled **phenomenology**: Both sought to capture the expressive meaning of the **world** "as it existed for other people . . . and . . . so . . . to avoid the pitfalls both of subjective idealism and pseudo-objectivity" (PL, 387–388). Giacometti's tortured, elongated sculptures of the human form were often characterized as "existentialist" in that they expressed a mood of **anxiety** and **alienation**.

GIDE, ANDRÉ (1869–1951). French novelist, essayist, and diarist. Gide's lucid prose style and his interest in issues of human **freedom**, social conformity, and individuality were influential on the literary endeavors of **Albert Camus** and **Jean-Paul Sartre**. Gide's 1914 novel *Les caves du Vatican* (*The Vatican Swindle*) introduced the idea of the "gratuitous act," an act that is purely unmotivated and inexplicable. For no apparent reason, the novel's protagonist pushes a complete stranger to his **death** from a moving train. Gide's notion of the gratuitous act may have provided a model for Camus in his novel *The Stranger*, whose protagonist also murders a man for no apparent reason. Gide published a collection of critical essays on **Fyodor Dostoevsky** and helped to introduce Dostoyevsky's work to the French public. In the 1930s, appalled by the exploitation of African workers by French colonial corporations, he became a **communist**. A trip to the Soviet Union in 1936, however, changed his mind, and Gide published his criticisms of the Soviet system in *Return from the U.S.S.R.* (1936), the first book by a French intellectual of the Left to repudiate **communism**. In 1947, he was awarded the Nobel Prize for literature.

GINSBERG, ALLEN. *See* BEAT MOVEMENT.

GOD. *See* CHRISTIANITY; EXISTENTIAL THEOLOGY; KIERKEGAARD, SØREN; NIETZSCHE, FRIEDRICH; RELIGIOUS EXISTENTIALISM.

"GOD IS DEAD." *See* DEATH OF GOD.

GRÉCO, JULIETTE. French pop singer associated with **Jean-Paul Sartre** and the existentialist movement in Paris in the late 1940s and 1950s. Dark-haired and dramatic, Gréco was the reigning diva of the nightclubs of **Saint-Germain-des-Prés** for several years. Because she knew Sartre (he had written a song for her, "La Rue des Blancs-Manteaux") and **Simone de Beauvoir**, she was often misidentified by the press as an "existentialist," lending credence to the myth that existentialism was a kind of bohemianism. As commentator **David Cooper** observes, Gréco was the embodiment of the **café existentialist**: "Film of Juliette Gréco singing in the late 1940s gives an idea of the chic appeal which feigned *ennui* and despair apparently had for young Parisians of the time. Few of them, presumably, waded through the six hundred pages of *Being and Nothingness*, and their interpretation of existentialist **freedom** as a license to act as unconventionally as possible . . . was a complete distortion of Sartre's and Beauvoir's notion" (Cooper, 12).

GREEKS. *See* HELLENISM.

GRENE, MARJORIE (1910–). American philosopher and early interpreter of existentialism. As an exchange student in Germany in the early 1930s, Grene attended the lectures of **Martin Heidegger** and **Karl Jaspers**. Her 1948 book, *Introduction to Existentialism* (originally entitled *Dreadful Freedom: A Critique of Existentialism*), was among the first and most philosophically astute discussions of existentialist philosophy by an American philosopher. Grene went on to write a book on the philosophy of **Jean-Paul Sartre** and on the thought of Heidegger.

GUILT. An existentialist conception of guilt is tied to the notion of existential **responsibility**: To be guilty is not primarily to "owe something" to others but to be aware that one is responsible for oneself. Alternately, it is to be aware that one must exist without external foundation or cause, that is, that one is free. **Martin Heidegger** linked various psychological and religious manifestations of guilt to the fundamental "nullity" of **existence** itself. Existence is "guilty" in that it lacks a **metaphysical** foundation or **essence**. True existential guilt thus has nothing to do with the judgment of others; it is a matter of owning up to one's own **freedom**.

    Karl Jaspers was the sole existentialist to apply a philosophical conception of guilt to **historical** circumstances. In *The Question of German Guilt* (1946), Jaspers examined the issue of the collective guilt of Germans for the actions of the **Nazi** government during **World War II**.

GURVITCH, GEORGE (1894–1965). Russian-born French sociologist. Gurvitch's 1930 book *Tendences actuelles de la pensee allemande* (*Contemporary Trends in German Thought*) was among the first works to introduce French philosophers to the thought of

Edmund Husserl and **Martin Heidegger**. **Jean-Paul Sartre** and **Maurice Merleau-Ponty** were both familiar with Gurvitch's work.

GURWITSCH, ARON (1901–1973). Lithuanian-born American philosopher and phenomenologist. Gurwitsch was a leading student of **Edmund Husserl** in Germany in the 1920s and early 1930s. He was also well-versed in **Gestalt psychology**, and his original work combined the findings of Gestalt theory with Husserlian **phenomenology**. As a Jew, Gurwitsch was forced to abandon his studies in Germany in 1933. He fled to France, where he became a respected scholar and teacher of Husserlian phenomenology from 1933 to1939. While in Paris he befriended **Maurice Merleau-Ponty**, who was already familiar with his work, and Merleau-Ponty attended Gurwitsch's lectures on phenomeonology and Gestalt psychology. Gurwitsch, who had conducted research in Germany with the psychologists Adhémar Gelb and Kurt Goldstein on deficits in abstraction and language, communicated to Merleau-Ponty unpublished observations on Goldstein's famous brain-injured patient "Schneider," material that Merleau-Ponty made use of in *Phenomenology of Perception*. Gurwitsch was also familiar with **Jean-Paul Sartre**'s phenomenological study of **consciousness**, *The Transcendence of the Ego*, and he was the first to publish an article on Sartre's philosophy in English, "A Non-Egological Conception of Consciousness" (*Philosophy and Phenomenological Research* I [1941]: 325–338). In 1940, Gurwitsch immigrated to the United States, where he held a variety of academic positions before finding a permanent post at the New School for Social Research in New York. He became a naturalized American citizen in 1946. His works include *The Field of Consciousness* (1964) and *Studies in Phenomenology and Psychology* (1966).

– **H** –

HABERMAS, JÜRGEN (1929–). German political philosopher and social theorist. As a graduate student at the University of Frankfurt in the early 1950s, Habermas studied with Max Horkheimer and **Theodor Adorno** and thus became associated with the **Frankfurt**

School. In 1953, while still in graduate school, he became one of the first to criticize **Martin Heidegger** for his involvement with German National Socialism. The incident that provoked Habermas's criticism was the appearance of Heidegger's 1935 lecture course *Introduction to Metaphysics*, which was revised for publication in 1953. Habermas was disturbed to find that Heidegger had included passages from 1935 that extolled the "inner truth and greatness" of National Socialism (IM, 199). In his article, Habermas argued that this, compounded by lack of an explanatory footnote or apology, left the impression that Heidegger had never repudiated his views. Heidegger responded in a letter to the newspaper *Die Zeit* that he was only respecting the historical integrity of the course. For Habermas, however, Heidegger's position was evidence that German intellectuals were unable to come to to terms with the legacy of **Nazism** and **World War II**.

HAMANN, JOHANN GEORG (1730–1788). German philosopher and critic of Enlightenment rationalism. Hamann was influential on **Søren Kierkegaard**, who shared his view that reason cannot be divorced from **concrete** experience and that religious truth cannot be adequately translated into philosophical concepts. Kierkegaard also found in Hamann a model of how to criticize the language and content of German Idealism—that is, the philosophy of **G. W. F. Hegel**, **Immanuel Kant**, and **Friedrich Schelling**—from a position outside of philosophy. Like Hamann, Kierkegaard used wit, irony, and intentional ambiguity as critical tools, turning the language of German philosophy against itself: "I, following Hamann's example, 'express myself in various tongues and speak the language of sophists, of puns, of Cretans and Arabians . . . and babble a confusion of criticism, mythology, *rebus*, and axioms, and argue now in a human way and now in an extraordinary way'" (FT, 149).

HEGEL, GEORG WILHELM FRIEDRICH (1770–1831). German idealist philosopher, and the most influential German philosopher of the first half of the 19th century. Hegel was significant in the development of existentialism first as an object of criticism and subsequently, in the 20th century, as a source of inspiration. **Søren Kierkegaard** saw in Hegelian idealism the epitome of philosophical arrogance, especially Hegel's view that reason is the highest expression of human personality and that subjective experience depends for its meaning and validity on the possibility of translation into a universal objective system. A particularly noxious instance of this idea for Kierkeggard was the assumption that **Christianity** must be brought into harmony with philosophical reason by transposing its "mythical" contents into the conceptual language of philosophy.

Hegel's Philosophy. Hegel's particular brand of idealism, called "absolute idealism," was an attempt to demonstrate that the ultimate nature of everything that exists—human subjects, beliefs, and institutions, along with nonhuman **nature** and the entire material universe—is "rational." To say that the universe is rational is to say not only that it is governed by intelligible laws, but also that it is guided by intrinsic purpose. This fundamental intelligibility and purpose, which Hegel called "the Idea," remains latent at the level of nonhuman nature. In human beings, however, the Idea becomes **conscious** and active. Through the progressive development of human culture, evident in the practice of philosophy, science, art, and religion, humans gradually discover the deep intelligibility in things and understand themselves as necessary participants in the revelation of truth.

Hegel's absolute idealism defined itself in contrast to the idealism of **Immanuel Kant**, for whom human reason has intrinsic limits which philosophy is required to set forth and justify. Hegel rejected Kant's thesis that reason is constrained to operate within the limits of space and time and that reality beyond the spatial-temporal world must remain an unknowable "**thing-in-itself.**" Disposing of Kant's distinction between appearance and thing-in-itself, Hegel boldly proclaimed that reason knows no limits, and that everything that exists must eventually receive the imprimatur of human **understanding**.

The process according to which reality is progressively understood, gradually but following a necessary logic throughout human history, is called "dialectic." The dialectic of human history is at the same time a dialectic of reason, or alternately of "**consciousness**," as the same logic operates both in the objective unfolding of events and in our subjective apprehension of them. Importantly, the dialectic is a collective and not simply an individual accomplishment; it is fueled by the distinctive manner of understanding that typifies whole cultures and eras, and thus undergirds individuals' thoughts and actions. To this collective manner of understanding Hegel gave the name "spirit" (*Geist*) (Hegel's most famous work is entitled *The Phenomenology of Spirit*). Thus, for example, for Hegel the discoveries of Isaac Newton were the fruit of the modern scientific spirit, while the exploits of Napoleon were the crowning achievement of the age of revolution, guided by the spirit of **freedom** and equality.

Hegel's dialectic is governed by a logic of "sublation" (*Aufhebung*), whereby each subsequent form of spirit or consciousness negates the claims of the preceding form at the same time that it preserves their truth at a higher level. Thus, for example, while the discovery of scientific laws negated the medieval notion of divine providence (God's inscrutable plan) that sees natural events as an expression of God's will, at the same time it preserved the idea that God is active in the world in the assumption that the laws of nature are created by God to be amenable to human understanding. This for Hegel is an improvement over the idea that God is a **transcendent** and inscrutable power. From Hegel's dialectical perspective, religion is not simply negated by science. Rather, its claims are "mediated," made more intelligible, consistent, and thus palatable to human understanding.

Kierkegaard's Critique. Kierkegaard's disagreement with Hegel can be brought into focus by examining their differing views of the proper relationship between philosophy and religion, reason and **faith**. As noted, Hegel rejected the idea of a transcendent God to the extent that it conflicts with the absolute nature of reason: If God is transcendent to human understanding, then reason is limited, not absolute, relative to the divine mind, which stands outside of it. Accordingly, Hegel saw **Christianity** as the highest form of revealed religion, in that it succeeded in resolving the opposition between the divine and the human, the infinite and the finite. There is significant difference of opinion among scholars as to Hegel's view of Christianity. However, the view that Kierkegaard seems to reject is one that has ample textual support in Hegel's writings. This is the view that, in Christianity, God is revealed to be immanent to the world of human affairs, and thus not a transcendent, superhuman entity. The Christian religion, in this reading, is a resolution of the apparent opposition between the infinite and the finite, the universal and the particular. It is a reminder of how human beings must come to grasp their own moral and intellectual powers and aspirations as divine.

Kierkegaard rejected all aspects of Hegel's position. Faith, he maintained, is without rational foundation; it is premised on **the absurd**. The **essence** of Christianity, in turn, is subjective passion, not a truth communicable in objective terms. Finally, God is wholly transcendent to human understanding. Human reason and morality are essentially finite and limited and cannot be identified with the divine.

Hegel's Positive Influence on Existentialism. Hegel's positive role in the development of existentialism is linked in the first place to his conception of history. His insistence on the importance of historical understanding and on the development of consciousness according to historical stages was evident in **Wilhelm Dilthey**'s conception of **hermeneutics** and in his approach to the human sciences. Dilthey's views in turn were crucial to **Martin Heidegger**'s understanding of human **historicality** in *Being and Time*.

In the 1930s, Hegel's philosophy played an important role in the development of French philosophy of existence, particularly thanks to the lectures of **Alexandre Kojève**. Kojève brought the Hegelian dialectic to life for a generation of French intellectuals, including **Raymond Aron**, **Maurice Merleau-Ponty**, and **Jean-Paul Sartre**. His reading focused on the "struggle for recognition" enacted in the dialectic of master and slave, which Hegel had discussed in a chapter of the *Phenomenology of Spirit*. Kojève assigned the **master–slave dialectic** central importance in Hegel's thought. Further, he supplemented Hegel's rather brief analysis with elements from the philosophies of **Martin Heidegger** and **Karl Marx**. Sartre's conflictual view of interpersonal relationships in *Being and Nothingness* was similar to Kojève's. In the same work, Sartre freely appropriated Hegelian vocabulary such as **"being-in-itself"** and **"being-for-itself."**

HEIDEGGER, MARTIN (1889–1976). Preeminent 20th-century German philosopher and seminal theorist of existentialism. Though Heidegger did not consider himself an existentialist, his 1927 masterwork **Being and Time** became the foundational statement of existentialist philosophy. Most notably, it served as a model for **Jean-Paul Sartre**'s *Being and Nothingness*. In *Being and Time*, Heidegger transformed **Edmund Husserl**'s **phenomenology** into **existential phenomenology**, an analysis of **concrete historical existence**. Heidegger's work also stimulated existential approaches to theology (**existential theology**) and psychopathology (**existential psychotherapy**) and gave new direction to **hermeneutics**.

Life. Heidegger was raised in a Catholic household of modest means in the southwestern German village of Messkirch. His father, a master cooper and sexton at the town's Catholic church, died in 1924. His mother, a cheerful woman from a well-to-do farming family, died in 1927. His only brother, Fritz, five years his junior, lived in Messkirch his whole life, where he was well-loved as the town "card." Fritz Heidegger typed 30,000 pages of his brother's manuscripts and kept them safe during **World War II** in the vault of the bank where he worked.

Heidegger's early education was sponsored by the Catholic Church. Between the ages of 14 and 20 he prepared for the Roman Catholic priesthood, first as a high school seminarian in Constance and then as a college student at the University of Freiburg. He spent two weeks in a Jesuit novitiate in 1909 but was dismissed for health reasons. In 1911, he abandoned the seminary altogether and turned to the study of mathematics and philosophy at Freiburg University, graduating in 1913 with a philosophy dissertation, "The Doctrine of Judgment in Psychologism." Between 1913 and 1916 he was groomed to occupy the Chair of Catholic Philosophy at Freiburg, receiving a grant from the Catholic Church to write his *Habilitationsschrift* (qualifying dissertation for university teaching), whose topic he was advised to change from "The Logical Essence of the Concept of Number" to a thesis in medieval philosophy, "The Doctrine of Categories and Signification in Duns Scotus." His training in medieval and classical philosophy provided a firm historical foundation for his later thought, which was characterized by careful historical and textual analysis of seminal philosophical works. In 1916, Heidegger was gravely disappointed when the teaching position went to another candidate. The following year he broke with the Catholic Church, whose dogmatic antimodernism conflicted with his interests in contemporary philosophy.

Heidegger married Elfride Petri, an economics student, in 1917, and they had two sons, Jörg, in 1919, and Hermann, in 1920. In 1918, Heidegger was called to active military service and served on the Western Front. The end of **World War I** marked the start of Heidegger's career as an original philosopher, which began under the aegis of **Edmund Husserl**'s **phenomenological** movement. Husserl had joined the Freiburg philosophy faculty in 1916, and Heidegger worked as his teaching assistant between 1919 and 1923. Heidegger was deeply influenced by Husserl's view of the autonomy of philosophical inquiry vis-à-vis the sciences and by his enthusiasm and dedication to the philosophical life. Up until 1929, Husserl regarded Heidegger as his brightest student and eventual successor. Yet, from the start, Heidegger was critical of Husserl's privileging of the theoretical attitude of the worldless **ego** and was clear in his intention to "radicalize" Husserl's approach by applying phenomenological insights to concrete, historical existence. From 1923 to 1928, Heidegger taught at Marburg University, and then in the fall of 1928 he returned to Freiburg to assume Husserl's chair after his retirement. Heidegger remained at Freiburg through the end of World War II, when he was banned from teaching due to his participation in **Nazism**. He was reinstated in his teaching position in 1950 and in 1951 was given emeritus status.

Heidegger's single foray into politics was his tenure as rector of Freiburg University under Nazi rule, from April 1933 to April 1934. He had joined the Nazi party in 1932, attracted to the message of romantic German nationalism, antimodernism, and community. His writings in the early and mid-1930s reflected his perception that National Socialism represented the "authentic spirit of the German nation." Chastened somewhat by his experience as university rector, where he began to see the dogmatic narrow-mindedness and irrationality of the Nazi bureaucracy, he became disillusioned with political action and returned to university teaching and writing. Eventually he saw the same "technical will to mastery" that guided American capitalism and Soviet **communism** at work in German National Socialism. However, he never expressed regret or apologized for his actions, and many commentators have come to take a harsh view of his Nazi involvement.

Existentialism and Ontology. Heidegger's central philosophical concern was not human existence per se but **ontology**, the study of **being**. However, in *Being and Time* the analysis of human existence is given priority over other forms of ontological inquiry because "being" is understood as the manner in which things appear to and are grasped as significant by human beings. Heidegger thus insists that ontology must be understood as more than an enumeration of formal categories of being; it is a matter of "re**awakening**" the "question of the *meaning* of being," the manifold ways things are "disclosed" by the range of human activities, **moods**, and purposes. A defining feature of Heidegger's existentialist stance, accordingly, is the belief that the nature of things cannot be understood apart from human involvements with them. Put more strongly, it is the thesis that things can be said "to be" only to the extent that they are taken up in a world of human "**projects**" and "possibilities." Subsequent existentialists like Sartre and **Maurice Merleau-Ponty** subscribed to this thesis.

Another feature of Heidegger's account crucial for subsequent existentialists is the distinction between **authentic and inauthentic** existence. Inauthentic existence or inauthenticity (*Uneigentlichkeit*) designates an **everyday** mode of existing in which the meaning of the **world** is taken as a matter of course, social norms and practices are uncritically accepted, and one loses sight of one's **freedom** as a **finite** individual. Authenticity (*Eigentlichkeit*) is a manner of "taking hold" of one's existence in terms of possibilities consciously **chosen** rather than facts passively accepted. It is occasioned by a lucid attitude toward one's own **death** and toward one's historical **situation**, as these bring about an **anxious** awareness of one's true nature as a "being of possibility."

Existentialist Period. The existentialist phase of Heidegger's thought may be defined as the period during which he subscribed to the thesis of the privileged status of human existence for philosophical inquiry. This phase began in the winter semester of 1919, with his first university lecture course after World War I, and reached its high point in lectures and publications in the two or three years following the publication of *Being and Time* in 1927. In the 1930s, Heidegger began to question the existentialist thesis, and his focus shifted away from human existence toward an account of "the event" (*das Ereignis*) of being, which he attempted to approach from a nonanthropological perspective. This shift away from an anthropological perspective is referred to as Heidegger's "turn" (*Kehre*). The turn began around 1930 and appears to have been complete by the end of the decade. Heidegger's turn is generally accepted as the boundary between his early and later philosophy. The same distinction may thus serve to delineate the period of his existentialist thought.

The decline of Heidegger's existentialism coincided with his disillusionment with **politics** and with the possibility of human agency in general following his service as the rector of Freiburg University in 1933–1934 under the Nazi regime. By the mid- to late 1930s, Heidegger came to view a bias toward subjectivity as symptomatic of a deep "will to mastery" that infected modern philosophy and lay at the root of modern technological society. Heidegger's later (i.e., postexistentialist) writings, published mainly after World War II, centered around a critique of Western **metaphysics** and technological society. The later writings extolled the powers of **poetry** and art in preserving an authentic, nontechnological appreciation of the world and of human beings.

Being and Time. The publication of *Being and Time* in 1927 in Husserl's **Yearbook for Philosophy and Phenomenological Research** earned Heidegger a coveted chair of philosophy at Freiburg University, the position that Husserl had vacated the year before. When it appeared shortly thereafter in book form, it was an immediate success and made Heidegger something of a star in German philosophical circles as well as a thinker of interest in France and elsewhere in Europe. What follows is a general summary of Heidegger's argument and intentions. (For a detailed discussion, *see BEING AND TIME.*)

Heidegger's strategy in *Being and Time* is to conduct a radical reappraisal of the meaning of human being that will allow for a corresponding reappraisal of the meaning of being in general. In other words, by revising our understanding of what it means to exist as a human being, Heidegger hopes to come to a renewed understanding of what it means for anything to exist. The question of human being thus receives priority in this inquiry because, it is assumed, only by confronting our own existence are we granted access to the nature of other things.

The body of the book proposes an original account of ***Dasein*** — human existence as it is revealed in everyday practical activities and relationships rather than in ideas, theories, and other mental representations, the focus of traditional philosophical accounts. Heidegger develops the thesis that the world we experience is necessarily the correlate of everyday moods and actions, and that for this reason it has been overlooked by scientific and theoretical observation. He sets forth an extensive critique of the primacy of the theoretical attitude, according to which reality consists in an "external world" of physical objects to be known or manipulated by the "internal world" of human **consciousness**. In doing so, he rejects the assumption that the basic constituents of reality are **substances**, essentially mental things and physical things that stand in no intrinsic relation to each other or to a broader context of meaning. This assumption gains validity only from the perspective of theoretical observation. However, humans are not primarily **knowing subjects**, but engaged agents; we are subject to moods, attuned to **others**, aware of the past, and anxious about the future. In sum, we are **being-in-the-world**. The world in turn is not an array of external objects but a network of things **ready-to-hand** that matter to us.

As noted, Heidegger's ultimate concern in *Being and Time* is ontology, not existence; the probing analysis of existence is not meant to stand as an end in itself but as a necessary stage in the critical reappraisal of the traditional understanding of being as **presence-at-hand**. Specifically, the stirring account of *Dasein*'s struggle for authenticity in its confrontation with anxiety and death is intended to "reawaken the question of the meaning of being" by bringing readers into contact with an experience of themselves uncontaminated by traditional prejudices. Nonetheless most interpreters—and virtually all existentialists, including **Karl Jaspers**, Merleau-Ponty, and Sartre—regarded *Being and Time* mainly as a contribution to the philosophy of existence, or more narrowly as a work of **philosophical anthropology**. Thus by the late 1930s, *Being and Time* was widely perceived as a manifesto of existentialist philosophy, while the project of **fundamental ontology** remained Heidegger's alone.

Heidegger's Status as an Existentialist. The discrepancy between Heidegger's self-conception as an ontologist and his reputation as an existentialist, or existential phenomenologist, remains a source of ongoing controversy, particularly in regard to his relationship to Sartre. It is common for Heidegger scholars to deny that Heidegger was an existentialist, on the grounds that he clearly rejected this classification. Heidegger repudiated any similarity between his thinking and that of Sartre, which he appeared to hold in low regard. If Sartre was an existentialist—and clearly he was—then, the reasoning goes, Heidegger cannot be one. To overcome this interpretive dilemma, several points must be recalled. First, Heidegger's explicit rejection of existentialism in 1947, in his *Letter on Humanism*, occurred during the height of the French existentialist movement and thus was based on a narrow identification of existentialism with Sartre's philosophy of the time. It is understandable that one philosopher would refuse a label that attempted to assimilate his thought to that of another. It must also be recalled that Heidegger's judgment took place 20 years after the publication of *Being and Time*, at a time when his thinking had already made its "turn" away from the analysis of existence; evidence suggests that his conception of his work in 1946 was quite different from his view of things in 1927. Finally, one must bear in mind that Heidegger tended to reject *all* labels applied to his thinking, not only that of existentialism. Heidegger repudiated attempts to characterize his work in terms of other philosophical endeavors to which it was related, such as Husserlian phenomenology, Karl Jaspers's philosophy of existence, **Max Scheler**'s philosophical anthropology, and **Wilhelm Dilthey**'s **philosophy of life**. *See also* HEIDEGGER AND NAZISM.

HEIDEGGER AND NAZISM. The primary link between existentialism and **Nazism** occurred in the career of **Martin Hedeigger** in the early and mid-1930s, when between April 1933 and April 1934 Heidegger served as rector of Freiburg University under Nazi rule. Heidegger implemented Nazi policies at the university, gave speeches defending Nazi ideology, and alienated former friends and students, including **Edmund Husserl** and **Karl Jaspers**. Heidegger's motivation for joining the Nazi Party and serving as rector was his belief that National Socialism represented the rebirth of German culture, a reawakening of the human spirit akin to that which had occurred in ancient Greece 2,400 years earlier. German renewal, he believed, would lead to the salvation of Western culture from the effects of **nihilism** and mass technological civilization. Heidegger believed, moreover, that his own philosophy of **being** had an important role to play in bringing this renewal to fruition. After **World War II**, Heidegger was convicted by a university denazification committee and was banned from teaching until 1951, when he was granted emeritus status. In his later reflections on events, Heidegger did not repudiate or apologize for his actions. Rather, he stood fast in his belief in the transformative potential of National Socialism, explaining that the movement had been derailed from its true **metaphysical** mission by Nazi fanaticism and reductive biological thinking. The degree to which Heidegger's **political** beliefs may be linked to the philosophy of *Being and Time* remains a matter of controversy.

An important text for understanding Heidegger's position at the time was the 1935 lecture course *Introduction to Metaphysics (Einführung in Die Metaphysik*,1953). Here Heidegger set forth his view of the "crisis" affecting Europe as a manifestation of a broader historical and metaphysical crisis of the "forgetting of being." To his students in the summer of 1935, he bemoaned the "spiritual decline of the earth": "the darkening of the world, the flight of the gods, the destruction of the earth, the transformation of men into a mass, the hatred and suspicion of everything free and creative" (IM, 38). In response, he spoke of the need to "repeat" (*wiederholen*) the beginning of Western culture as it had occurred in ancient Greece "with all the strangeness, darkness, insecurity that attend a true beginning" (IM, 39). The vehicle of this repetition, he asserted, was philosophy itself. Yet, in contrast to *Being and Time*, philosophy was no longer understood in the context of individual **existence**, but rather in a political context, as the expression of "a people." The German *Volk*, he held, were in a state of crisis, "caught in a great pincers" between Russia and the United States. Still, Germany remained "the most metaphysical of nations" (IM, 38), and the German tongue the most authentic of modern languages. Hence the renewal of modern Europe could come about only through German renewal. *See also* WORLD WAR I.

HELLENISM. Hellenism refers to a broad tendency, widespread in Europe in the 18th and 19th centuries, to idealize and emulate the thought and culture of Ancient Greece. Admiration for the Greeks was especially pronounced in 19th-century Germany among philosophers and men of letters, such as Johann Wolfgang Goethe, Johann Gottfried Herder, **G. W. F. Hegel**, and **Friedrich Nietzsche**, who came to greatly admire the culture of the ancient *Hellenes*, as they called themselves. Homer's epics, the tragic plays of Aeschylus, Sophocles, and Euripides, Greek statuary and temples, and the figure of Socrates were especially valued. The virtues ostensibly exemplified by the Greek peoples included a sense of harmony and moderation, an appreciation of art and science, and a noble stoicism in the face of suffering.

Classical scholar and archeologist Johann Winckelmann (1717–1768) stood at the forefront of Hellenizing trends in Germany. His influential "Thoughts on Imitation in Greek Painting and Sculpture" (1755) identified a "noble simplicity and quiet grandeur" as the essence of Greek art and the definition of classical beauty. A century later, Friedrich Nietzsche, another German classicist, disputed this view. In *The Birth of Tragedy Out of the Spirit of Music* (1872), Nietzsche argued that Greek tragedy arises out of conflicting principles rather than solely out of a quest for simplicity and order. Beneath the **Apollonian** tendency toward order and restraint Nietzsche saw a more primitive **Dionysian** tendency toward intoxication and unrestrained passion. In his analysis, the genius of Greek tragedy is to allow the Dionysian elements of life to be expressed and enjoyed through the formal measure of poetry and art. What Nietzsche admired in the Greeks in all their endeavors was the ability to confront the conditions of human existence, including **death** and senseless suffering; Greek tragedy represents the impulse to transform suffering into something joyous and life-affirming.

In the 20th century, **Albert Camus** held a romantic view of ancient Greek culture similar to Nietzsche's. Camus contrasted the **values** of the "Mediterranean world" with those of northern Europe. The latter tend toward doubt, despair, and denial of the human condition, the former toward affirmation of life and appreciation of beauty. For Camus, the Mediterranean world, which found paradigmatic expression in the culture of ancient Greece, is defined by "sunlight": It celebrates the pleasures of the body along with powers of the mind, the beauty of the changing earth along with the beauty of the unchanging heavens. In contrast, the European world, which resulted from the repression of the Greek sensibility by **Christianity**, is centered around death and denial of the human condition. Hence, for Camus as for Nietzsche, the ultimate Greek virtue is a type of "strength" or "courage" to affirm life's value without denying the reality of death and suffering.

Among German existentialists, a pronounced Hellenism is found in the philosophy of **Martin Heidegger**. Heidegger's attitude toward the Greeks, however, is not unequivocal. In particular, it is pre-Socratic thought and culture that Heidegger admires; in his view, philosophy after Plato is vitiated by a restrictive **metaphysics** of **substance**.

HEMINGWAY, ERNEST (1899–1961). American novelist. In the 1930s and 1940s, Hemingway's terse, direct style was influential on the literary endeavors of **Simone de Beauvoir, Albert Camus**, and **Jean-Paul Sartre**, Camus's *The Stranger* bearing the clearest signs of this influence. In her memoirs, Beauvoir explained the nature of Hemingway's appeal to her and Sartre: "His individualism and his concept of human nature were both very close to ours: there was no split in his heroes between head, heart, and body" (PL, 114). Unlike James Joyce and Marcel Proust, modernists who in Beauvoir's view "opted for a form of subjectivism," Hemingway achieved a uniquely concrete realism: "He managed to endow physical objects with extraordinary reality, just because he never separated them from the action in which his heroes were involved . . . . A great number of the rules which we observed in our own novels were inspired by Hemingway" (PL, 114). *See also* EXISTENTIALIST LITERATURE.

HERMENEUTIC CIRCLE. Originally, in the **hermeneutics** of Friedrich Schleirmacher, an idea referring to the circular relationship between **understanding** and interpretation of literary texts. In order to interpret a particular statement in a text, one must already understand, through certain heuristic assumptions, the text's overall meaning and intentions; yet to grasp the overall meaning of the text, one must be able to understand the particular statements. **Wilhelm Dilthey** extended this problematic to all expressions of human culture. In the 20th century, the notion of the hermeneutic circle was given broader existential meaning by **Martin Heidegger**.

In *Being and Time*, Heidegger reasoned that all attitudes and perceptions in which we encounter something as meaningful, and a fortiori any explicit theoretical interpretation, presuppose a prior understanding of the world, a tacit sense of what things are and what they mean. Understanding and meaning are, moreover, not primarily intellectual and linguistic acts but practical attitudes: I "understand" a hammer by picking it up to build a house, not by reflecting on it or making theoretical assertions about it. The circle of human understanding is thus for Heidegger not "vicious" but a structural feature of human **existence** itself: All instances of understanding are conditioned by a prior **projection** of definite possibilities upon the **world**.

Heidegger's conception of **existential phenomenology** was tied to the idea of the hermeneutic circle in that it entailed beginning with the assumptions of **everyday** understanding and then passing to a level of philosophical awareness where these tacit assumptions may be analyzed and made explicit. For Heidegger, the ideal of rigorous knowledge without presuppositions was untenable. Here Heidegger broke clearly with **Edmund Husserl**'s conception of phenomenology as pure and presuppositionless intuition of **essences**.

HERMENEUTICS. Traditionally, the science of interpretation of biblical and classical texts. The modern conception of hermeneutic as the philosophical study of human **understanding** and interpretation is particularly relevant to existentialism. This conception began in Germany in the early 19th century, when Friedrich Schleiermacher (1768–1834) offered a systematic treatment of issues surrounding textual and historical interpretation. How—based on what type of presuppositions—can we understand an ancient text or a foreign culture? How does the past become intelligible to us, given that we cannot remove ourselves from history in order to judge it "objectively"? Schleiermacher's work was significantly expanded in the late-19th and early-20th centuries by **Wilhelm Dilthey**, who provided a direct theoretical link to existentialism. Specifically, Dilthey set the stage for **Martin Heidegger**'s view of philosophy as a kind of hermeneutic **phenomenology**: a rendering explicit of tacit **everyday** assumptions about ourselves and the **world**. Because everyday assumptions inevitably include certain misinterpretations of who we are and what the world is, phenomenology for Heidegger must proceed by critical analysis of traditional concepts rather than simply by intuition.

HISTORICAL MATERIALISM. Historical materialism, or, alternately, "dialectical materialism," is the philosophical designation of **Karl Marx**'s theory of history. According to **Marxist** theory, human history proceeds through a series of necessary stages, from primitive tribal life to advanced industrial capitalism. The belief and **value** systems of each stage are determined by the material conditions under which people live and work at that stage. "Material conditions" refer primarily to economic relations and correlative basic class divisions of society, such as that between men and women, hunters and gatherers, king and subjects, landowners and peasants, or factory owners and factory workers. Marx's theory is *materialist* rather than *idealist* in its insistence that ideas, including technical as well as ordinary theories and schemes of evaluation, are by-products of underlying physical and economic facts rather than primary causes of human behavior. It is *historical* or *dialectical* in its claim that social and economic tensions in existing society necessarily produce new forms of society.

According to Marx, the *telos* of this dialectical development is the production of a classless society in which economic resources and means of production are held in common; greed, envy, and human conflict are largely abolished; and thus **alienation** is overcome. To achieve such a **communist** society, however, a revolution is required in which workers, united as a class Marx calls the proletariat, overthrow existing political institutions, such as parliamentary democracy, which narrowly serve the interests of the middle and upper classes at the expense of the interests of the working classes. The Russian Revolution of 1917 was intended as such a revolution of the proletariat. Among existentialists, **Simone de Beauvoir**, **Maurice Merleau-Ponty**, and **Jean-Paul Sartre** became increasingly attracted to Marx's theory of historical materialism after **World War II**.

HISTORICALITY (Ger. *Geschichtlichkeit*). A technical term in the vocabulary of **Martin Heidegger**'s *Being and Time*. Historicality refers to the existential character of human **temporality**. For Heidegger, time is not lived as an indefinite series of "nows" but always as a unity "stretched between birth and **death**." The unifying element of any human **understanding** of time is our fundamental awareness of death, which gives time its directedness and its form. On the basis of an **authentic** attitude toward death, the individual may go on to appropriate his or her past as a set of definite, historical possibilities, which may be reawakened by individual action and **commitment**. That *Dasein* always exists with some understanding of its historical possibilities is the sense of Heidegger's claim that the human being is "historical" in its very **essence**.

HISTORICISM. Loosely, the view that truth and **understanding** are historically conditioned. In traditional philosophy, a historicist perspective is often seen as relativist and thus as a fallacious viewpoint, to be avoided. Existentialists embrace historicism, however, to the extent that they see social and historical presuppositions as necessary for human understanding. Without presupposed **horizons** of understanding, no act of understanding would be possible. The positive character of historical understanding is captured in the existentialist conception of **hermeneutics**. Critics of this perspective include **Edmund Husserl**, the founder of **phenomenology**. In his essay "Philosophy as Rigorous Science" (1911), Husserl criticized the historicist philosophy of **Wilhelm Dilthey** as a form of self-refuting relativism that undermines philosophy's quest for objective and universal truth. Later Husserl was disturbed to find an even more radical version of Dilthey's hermeneutic position elaborated by his former student, **Martin Heidegger**, in *Being and Time*.

HÖLDERLIN, FRIEDRICH. *See* POETRY AND PHILOSOPHY.

HOPE (Fr. *espoir***).** In the **religious existentialism** of **Gabriel Marcel**, hope is a basic human attitude of affirmation of life's **value** and purpose. "Hope consists in asserting that there is at the heart of **being**, beyond all data and all calculations, a mysterious principle which is in connivance with me" (PEM, 28). To hope, for example, that someone I love will recover from a deadly cancer is to believe that reality is not indifferent to my desires and to what I understand as good. Hope is not a matter of objective knowledge but an active affirming of life's ultimate value despite appearances to the contrary; to experience hope is thus to enter into a **mystery**. For Marcel, hope as a fundamental existential attitude is opposed to, and often emerges out of, "despair," resignation to life's apparent lack of value and purpose. "Hope is the act by which [the temptation to despair] . . . is overcome" (HV, 36). Maintaining itself in the face of possible despair, hope requires that one pass beyond self-affirmation, "desire," or "pride" to a state of "humility," in which one consents to acknowledge values beyond the self. In this sense, hope for Marcel is linked to love, **commitment**, and **reciprocity**. To love another is to commit oneself to a future that cannot be known; it is to have hope in one's own and the other person's ongoing capacity to love and be loved. Holding out this expectation, love allows both the other and the self to rise to the occasion and fulfill it.

Marcel's conception of a "**metaphysics** of hope" attempts to remain within the human experience of hoping and to avoid explicit theological argument. Yet it is clear that "absolute hope" is grounded ultimately in **faith** in God. In this regard, Marcel's view bears comparison with **Søren Kierkegaard**'s notion of faith; both maintain that faith (absolute hope) is "beyond the reach of objective criticism" (HV, 66).

HORIZON (Ger. *Horizont).* In the **phenomenology** of **Edmund Husserl**, "horizon" refers to an aspect of an object or act of **consciousness** that is presupposed and not given. Every object has a horizon, or multiple horizons, which, like the horizon of the landscape, may recede and shift with changes in **action** and attention. For example, presupposed by my perception of a red apple is the understanding that the apple is "edible," that I could take a bite out of it. Being "edible" is part of the horizon of my perception, a content not fully "given" but "anticipated" and presupposed. However, if I attempt to bite the apple and find out that it is made of wax, the horizon may shift to encompass the idea of "being on display in a museum." A crucial aspect of Husserl's concept of horizon is thus that consciousness is not a static apprehension of things but a **temporal** process whereby various possibilities for action and **understanding** are **projected** into the future.

Martin Heidegger makes extensive use of the phenomenological conception of horizon in *Being and Time.* To say that *Dasein* exists by "projecting possibilities onto the **world**" is to say that action and understanding are guided by one's particular affective and pragmatic horizons. Alternately, Heidegger speaks of the world as the horizon for all of *Dasein*'s particular involvements. In this sense, the world is the "horizon of all horizons"; it is what Husserl calls the "**life-world.**"

HORKHEIMER, MAX. *See* FRANKFURT SCHOOL.

HUMAN CONDITION. Some existentialists distinguish between **human nature**, understood as an invariable and universal **essence** of human beings, and the human condition, understood as certain general circumstances under which human life is pursued. According to **Jean-Paul Sartre**, for example, the human condition consists of such general requirements as the need to work, to live among others, and to die, yet it does not entail any specific content of character or mind such as moral goodness or moral evil, rationality or irrationality. In *The Human Condition* (1959), **Hannah Arendt** proposed a detailed **phenomenological** account of the human condition as that of an intrinsically social and political being.

HUMAN CONDITION, THE. *See* ARENDT, HANNAH.

HUMAN NATURE. A strong thesis of human nature, one that assigns a specific content or essence such as moral goodness or rationality to all human beings, conflicts with the existentialist conception of **freedom**. For existentialists, a human being is the result of freely chosen **projects** and thus cannot be properly understood as an instance of a universal category. On this basis, **Jean-Paul Sartre** denies that there is a human nature. **José Ortega y Gasset** makes a similar assertion independently of Sartre.

HUSSERL, EDMUND (1859–1938). German philosopher and founder of **phenomenology**. Husserl exerted a profound effect on existentialism, both through his teaching and writing and through the example of his devotion to philosophy. **Martin Heidegger** was Husserl's teaching assistant at the University of Freiburg from 1919 to 1923 and for a time was expected to succeed Husserl as the leader of the phenomenological movement. **Jean-Paul Sartre**'s early work proceeded under the aegis of Husserlian phenomenology, and **Maurice Merleau-Ponty** maintained an active interest in Husserl's thought throughout his life. Husserl's conception of philosophy as a "rigorous science," however, ran counter to the assumptions of **existential phenomenology**. Hence, as a general rule, when existentialists appropriated Husserl's ideas they transformed them significantly.

Husserl was committed to the idea that philosophy could be a foundational "science," a method of clarifying the basic presuppositions of all knowledge. Following in the footsteps of **Immanuel Kant**, he envisioned that philosophy must concern itself solely with "**essences**," universal and necessary meanings, rather than with empirical "facts," which are particular and **contingent**. He came to seek these essences in the invariable features of **consciousness**, the basic assumptions and patterns that give shape to a consciously experienced world. Following **René Descartes**, Husserl believed that philosophy must also be grounded in moments of self-evident truth gained through introspection. The method of arriving at the essential meanings and laws upon which knowledge was founded he came to call "phenomenology" starting around 1906. However, Husserl was a self-proclaimed "perpetual beginner" in philosophy; he revised and refined his ideas throughout his life, aiming for exactness and clarity rather than an overarching system. Thus, of the several distinct versions of phenomenology he proposed between 1907 and his **death** in 1938, there is disagreement among scholars over which is to be taken as authoritative. Another complication is the role of such philosophers as **Max Scheler**, who developed a divergent conception of phenomenology, related to but distinct from Husserl's.

Having begun his academic career in mathematics, Husserl turned to study philosophy with **Franz Brentano**. From Brentano Husserl learned the practice of "descriptive psychology," an attempt to clarify the nature and basic types of conscious experience irrespective of its causal origin. He also learned the doctrine of **intentionality**, that mental states are directed toward specific mental objects, by which they may be distinguished from physical or physiological events, which lack this intrinsic reference. Husserl's distinctive approach to psychological and philosophical issues first gained expression in the second volume of his *Logical Investigations* (1901). The first volume of this work had proposed a critique of "psychologism," the view that mathematical notions are founded on psychological processes, for example, the concepts of arithmetic on the process of counting—a position Husserl himself had defended in his earlier work. In the second volume, *Phenomenology and the Theory of Knowledge*, Husserl presented six investigations on topics such as linguistic expression, universals, intentionality, judgment, and truth, whose scope indicated the broadening of his philosophical horizons. Here readers encountered Husserl's philosophical motto, to return "to the things themselves," that is, to consider matters of philosophical importance directly rather than through the lens of traditional theories. The promise of making a fresh start in philosophy, "without presuppositions" and thus unbeholden to existing schools and prejudices, had considerable appeal for young German philosophers at the time. It was during this period (around 1910) that Heidegger first became attracted to Husserl's thought. In 1913, Husserl published *Ideas*, the first mature statement of the methods and aims of phenomenology. This work introduced major concepts such as the **phenomenological reduction**, eidetic variation, **horizon**, and the transcendental **ego**.

The starting point for Husserl's phenomenology was that **consciousness** itself holds the key to the problem of justifying and clarifying knowledge, for all things about which we may form judgments must initially "appear to" or be "presented" in consciousness as *phenomena* of some type—that is, as objects perceived, imagined, remembered, felt, or conceived intellectually. Like his contemporaries **Henri Bergson** and **William James**, Husserl saw consciousness as an active force, an ever-shifting mental "stream" that nonetheless preserves its unity and coherence as it effortlessly turns its gaze from objects in the world, to "other minds" present with it, to its own inner life. However, Husserl was not interested in the empirical nature of consciousness but rather the "transcendental conditions" according to which objects are experienced by any conscious subject. Husserl came to believe that careful description of the various forms of conscious experience (perception, imagination, memory, consciousness of time, consciousness of spatial relations, and so forth) would reveal the invariant structures essential to each form of consciousness. These "eidetic" structures in turn, he believed, would outline an unchanging substructure of reality itself, for all possible objects of thought ("intentional" objects) must conform to them.

Throughout his career, in a continual effort to articulate how this essentialist program should be accomplished, Husserl sought to avoid the pitfalls of an a priori rationalism divorced from experience. Yet at the same time he remained a severe critic of philosophy too closely bound to historical and psychological contingencies. This criticism was strongly expressed in "Philosophy as Rigorous Science" (1911), in which Husserl attacked the **worldview** philosophy of **Wilhelm Dilthey** as a form of relativism; it continued in his rejection of Heidegger's *Being and Time* as a **historicist** and anthropological perversion of phenomenology. In the crisis-laden political atmosphere of the 1920s and 1930s, however, Husserl came to take more seriously the social and historical dimensions of consciousness. A late work, *The Crisis of European Sciences and Transcendental Phenomenology* introduced the notion of the **life-world**, the rich domain of pretheoretical experience, which, Husserl argued, provides an irreducible foundation for scientific thought. In this regard, Husserl's later thought approximates that of Heidegger and other existentialists, which he had previously rejected.

HYPPOLITE, JEAN (1907–1968). French philosopher and leading translator and interpreter of the philosophy of **G. W. F. Hegel**. Along with **Alexandre Kojève**, Hyppolite was largely responsible for introducing Hegelian thought into the milieu of French **philosophy of existence** in the 1930s and 1940s. He produced the first complete French translation of Hegel's *Phenomenology of Spirit*, in two volumes (1939–1941), and a significant study of the same work, *The Genesis and Structure of Hegel's "Phenomenology of Spirit"* (1946).

– I –

I AND THOU. See BUBER, MARTIN.

IDEALISM. See REALISM AND IDEALISM.

IMAGINATION. **Jean-Paul Sartre** devoted considerable attention to the philosophical analysis of imagination in two early works, *Imagination: A Psychological Critique* (1936) and *The Psychology of Imagination* (1940). The former book is based on Sartre's doctoral dissertation and was originally intended as the introductory section of *The Psychology of Imagination.* This latter book is an original **phenomenological** study of "imaginative consciousness," which anticipates many of the positions of *Being and Nothingness*, in particular the idea that **consciousness** entails a **"negation"** of reality, and that this negating power is the **essence** of human **freedom**. Following the analyses of **Edmund Husserl**, Sartre portrays the act of imagination as exemplary of the freedom of human consciousness: Through imagination I "withdraw from the world" as it is in order to imagine it as it might be. This negating power is evidence of the freedom of consciousness, for a determined consciousness would remain "engulfed by the real," enmeshed in detailed responses to psychological stimuli and thus never capable of "withdrawing" from reality in order to re-create it. Sartre's treatment of imagination as the power to negate provided the core of his account of consciousness as **being-for-itself** in *Being and Nothingness*.

INAUTHENTICITY. *See* AUTHENTICITY AND INAUTHENTICITY.

INDIRECT COMMUNICATION. Phrase applied to the writings of **Søren Kierkegaard**, whose goal is not to directly state a set of objective truths but to stimulate a process of self-questioning in the reader. The aim of indirect communication is explicitly Socratic: to lead one to question the foundation of one's own beliefs, often by deflating the received view of things and so shaking the reader out of complacency. To effectively disguise his authorial position and to avoid the appearance of making direct assertions, Kierkegaard employs a variety of distancing techniques, including the use of literary pseudonyms, persistent irony, and paradox. Kierkegaard also, by and large, disguises the autobiographical origins of his work—for example, his broken engagement to Regine Olsen, his aestheticism and literary ambitions, and his relationship to his father—by integrating them into larger fictional and theoretical structures in which the reader may consider various possibilities unencumbered by an overly personal, hence limited, authorial perspective.

INDIVIDUALIZE. The process by which a person becomes an **authentic** self is described by existentialists as a process of becoming *individualized*, removed from the impersonal anonymity of **everyday existence**, where one acts and thinks in conformity with others, and is placed before one's essential **responsibility** for oneself. For **Martin Heidegger**, individualization occurs through an awareness of one's own **death** as a "non-relational possibility" that cannot be shared with others, thus that must be confronted alone, as an individual. **Søren Kierkegaard** speaks in similar fashion of the process of "becoming an individual" as the process of assuming a truly first-person perspective. For Kierkegaard, such a perspective is not simply given but must be achieved through acts of **ethical commitment** and religious decision.

INFINITE RESIGNATION. *See* KNIGHT OF FAITH AND KNIGHT OF INFINITE RESIGNATION.

INTENTIONALITY. As formulated in the **phenomenology** of **Edmund Husserl**, intentionality refers to the quality of conscious states that "aim at" or "intend" objects distinct from themselves. Most mental states are intentional; they are *of* or *about* something. For example, I perceive "that it is raining," I imagine "how the party was," I think "about the Pythagorean theorem." Reflection on the intentional nature of conscious experience led Husserl to discover that different mental states or attitudes have distinctive types of intentional objects, for example, that perceiving a thunderstorm is qualitatively different from imagining a storm, or from remembering it. Inquiry into essential "structures" of different intentional states became a central interest of phenomenology. However, whereas Husserl understands intentionality primarily as the relationship between the **mind** and the "**essences**" or "meanings" it intuits, existentialists understand it as a direct contact with things as they are immediately experienced, a contact with the **world**. **Situated** or embodied intentionality is thus a central insight of **existential phenomenology**: that meaning is produced through a range of interpretive and evaluative relations between embodied individuals and the world they inhabit.

Husserl analyzes conscious, intentional experiences into three terms: the act of intending (*noesis*) , the object intended , real or unreal (*noema*), and the self that does the intending (**ego**). He maintains further that each form of intentional consciousness (e.g., perceiving, remembering, imagining, etc.) has its own necessary and invariant structure. For example, perceiving requires an intentional object that stands spatially outside of the perceiver; remembering, in contrast, requires an object that is not spatially external yet that is not simply a product of the act of remembering, the latter being a feature particular to acts of imagining.

Several implications of Husserl's view of intentionality prove crucial for existentialists. First, because **consciousness** cannot be understood apart from its relations to a host of real and imagined objects, it cannot be reduced to a flux of sensations, as in empiricism, nor to an array of purely mental ideas, as in idealism. The notion of consciousness thus contains an irreducible reference to a world of objects thought, perceived, imagined, and so forth. As noted, proponents of existential phenomenology amend Husserl's view to say that consciousness relates to the actual empirical world, not merely the invariant "essences" of such a world.

A further implication provides a central premise of existentialism: Consciousness is not a passive recipient of stimuli but actively structures and organizes the world it relates to. Again, for existentialists consciousness must be understood to encompass practical, emotional, and bodily dimensions of the human being and not simply cognitive and intellectual elements. **Emotions**, **moods**, and practical activity rather than logical thought or theoretical contemplation reveal the nature of the world as a correlate of one's intentional attitudes toward it. Through my **projects** and attitudes, I invest the world with meaning and **value**. At the same time, I project possibilities upon the world only to the extent that I find myself in a meaningful situation that is not of my making.

Finally, it may be noted that existentialists deny the possibility of a **phenomenological reduction** of consciousness that is central to Husserl's phenomenology. According to existentialists, such a bracketing out of empirical concerns is neither desirable nor possible, since intentionality accrues to engaged, historical individuals rather than to detached, transcendental **egos**.

INTERSUBJECTIVITY. *See* BEING-WITH-OTHERS; OTHER, THE.

INTERNAL TIME CONSCIOUSNESS, THE PHENOMENOLOGY OF (1928). This book consists of a series of lectures on the **phenomenology** of **time** given by **Edmund Husserl** between 1905 and 1910. The lectures were compiled by Husserl's assistant, Edith Stein, and later edited for publication by **Martin Heidegger** in 1928. Drawing inspiration from the writings of St. Augustine and **William James** on time, Husserl developed a phenomenology of internal time **consciousness** that describes the experience of past, present, and future as structured by **intentionality** (the meaning-intending activities of consciousness). Husserl argued that objective clock-time, the concept of a series of abstract "now-points," presupposes the lived experience of time that he described as constituted by the retention of an intended past and the anticipation of a ***projected*** future. Every present has a temporal "thickness" that is defined by these temporal modes of possibility.

Husserl showed that the experience of time is essential to (constitutive of) the structure of consciousness itself, and moreover that time is organized according to the structures of intentionality. Heidegger developed these insights in ***Being and Time***, where the **understanding** and experience of temporality is the defining feature of human existence. For Heidegger, the **"being"** of human being is temporally structured, and to exist as a human being is in a profound sense to experience time in certain ways, though not primarily in the manner of a self-reflective consciousness, as Husserl had supposed.

INTRODUCTION TO METAPHYSICS. *See* HEIDEGGER AND NAZISM.

IONESCO, EUGÈNE. *See* THEATER OF THE ABSURD.

IRON IN THE SOUL. See *ROADS TO FREEDOM, THE.*

ITALIAN EXISTENTIALISM. Under the guidance of **Nicola Abbagnano**, existentialism in Italy from the 1930s through the1950s took on a different cast than its French and German counterparts. Abbagnano accepted **Søren Kierkegaard**'s and **Martin Heidegger**'s critiques of rationalist **idealism** and of the hegemony of the **knowing subject** as well as their insistence on human **finitude**. Yet he regarded their work as part of an initial, negative phase of existential philosophy that was to be followed by what he termed "positive existentialism." By positive existentialism he meant a constructive analysis of what he took to be the central concept of existential philosophy: possibility as it applies to "man in his concrete, natural, and historical experience" (*Critical Existentialism*, 12). Influenced by the work of John Dewey, Abbagnano thus distanced Italian existentialism from the French and German traditions and brought it in line with

American **pragmatism**. Both were **action**-oriented and strongly anti-metaphysical, distinguished philosophical thinking from scientific knowledge yet accepted the validity of science, and maintained an optimistic view of the application of philosophy to empirical problems.

IVAN ILYICH, THE DEATH OF. See *DEATH OF IVAN ILYICH, THE.*

– J –

JAMES, WILLIAM (1842–1910). Preeminent American psychologist and philosopher of the late 19th and early 20th centuries. With John Dewey and Charles Sanders Peirce, James was a leading figure of American **pragmatism**. His groundbreaking *Principles of Psychology* (1890) was known to **Edmund Husserl**, and James's account of the dynamic nature and spontaneity of the "stream of **consciousness**" played a role in the development of **phenomenology**. James's views were also known to **Henri Bergson**, and there are significant similarities between the theories and perspectives of the two thinkers. In *The Emotions: Outline of a Theory* (1939), **Jean-Paul Sartre** rejected the James-Lange theory of **emotion**, which held that emotions are conscious experiences of physiological disturbances.

JANET, PIERRE (1859–1947). French psychologist and neurologist. In his early work, Janet advanced a view of the unconscious causation of hysterical disorders that paralleled, and in some cases predated, the theory of **Sigmund Freud**. Like Freud, Janet held that hysteria was caused by "fixed ideas" that become dissociated from consciousness yet remain active on an unconscious level. Janet's views were discussed by **Jean-Paul Sartre** in his 1939 book *The Emotions: Outline of a Theory*. According to Sartre, Janet's account of **emotion** as a "sudden agitation" and disadaptation of the organism is ambivalent in its physiological description of a phenomenon that is nonetheless recognized as psychological. Janet portrays emotional symptoms as "automatic" responses of the organism, yet at the same time he describes them as "set-back behaviors" motivated by the patient's desire to avoid painful situations. For Sartre, Janet's account exemplifies the tendency, present among even the most acute observers, to reduce human behavior to impersonal mechanisms; the same tendency is expressed for Sartre in the **psychoanalytic** theory of the unconscious. Sartre's theory nonetheless preserved elements of Janet's account, notably the idea that emotions are at bottom strategies to avoid or resolve painful or difficult situations. Commenting on one of Janet's patients, Sartre observed that a hysterical woman on the verge of a confession who suddenly bursts into sobs is crying "*in order not to say anything.*" This, for Sartre, is the true meaning of emotion, which Janet glimpsed but could not clearly articulate: Allowing herself—that is, **choosing**—to become overwhelmed by emotion is a strategy to avoid the more painful act of confessing to the doctor.

JAPANESE EXISTENTIALISM. *See* NISHITANI, KEIJI.

JASPERS, KARL (1883–1969). German psychologist and philosopher. Jaspers was among the earliest proponents of the **philosophy of existence** in Germany—his first work in the field predated that of **Martin Heidegger** by several years. Jaspers's existentialism is distinguished by its focus on interpersonal, **ethical**, and **transcendent** dimensions of **existence**, in contrast to Heidegger's **hermeneutic** and **ontological** approach. He also emphasized the lived character of philosophy, distinguishing between philosophy as objective knowledge and **philosophizing** as a process of personal transformation issuing from confrontation with the paradoxes of life. Essential to the experience of philosophizing, he maintained, is open and sincere **communication** with an **other**. His major mature work, *Philosophy* (1932), in three volumes, is a relatively systematic account that outlines a dialectical progression from **everyday consciousness** and scientific and philosophical **understanding** of the **world**, to lived awareness of personal **freedom** and **finitude**, and finally to recognition of transcendent reality. The dialectical nature of Jaspers's conception owes something to the thought of **G. W. F. Hegel**. His chief philosophical debt, however, is to **Immanuel Kant**, and much of Jaspers's work can be described as an attempt to elaborate an existential basis for Kant's **metaphysics**. After **World War II**, Jaspers emerged as a leading voice for democratic reform in Germany, and during this time his political writings, such as *The Question of German Guilt* (1946) and *The Atom Bomb and the Future of Man* (1958), overshadowed his philosophical accomplishments. The existentialist phase of Jaspers's thought may be roughly circumscribed between 1919 and 1949.

Life and Works. After completing a doctorate in medicine in 1908, Jaspers turned to the study of psychology. His work as an assistant at the psychiatric ward of Heidelberg Hospital from 1908 to 1915 provided the basis for his first book, **General Psychopathology** (1913), an inventory of psychiatric theories that proposed an early **phenomenological** account of mental illness. In 1910, he married Gertrud Mayer, a young Jewish woman from a pious family, who was preparing for graduate studies in philosophy. With Gertrud Jaspers's interests shifted toward philosophy. In 1922, largely on the basis of his widely read **Psychology of Worldviews**, he received a professorship in philosophy at the University of Heidelberg, where he remained until 1937. In 1932, Jaspers published the most detailed statement of his philosophical position, *Philosophy*, in three volumes, and began to achieve international recognition. In 1937, however, Jaspers was banned from teaching by the **Nazis** because his wife was Jewish. Jaspers and Gertrud spent the war years in Heidelberg, fearful of deportation, "careful and cautious, heedful of the . . . Nazi authorities, determined to commit no act and to utter no word we could not justify" ("Philosophical Autobiography," in PKJ, 62).

After the war, Jaspers revived his reputation with works like *The Question of German Guilt* (1946), which raised the issue of collective German responsibility for the Holocaust. Jaspers was considered for the post of German minister of education, but declined due to a congenital heart condition. Disillusioned with the persistence of reactionary elements in German society, he left Germany in 1949 to accept a teaching position at the University of Basel and became a Swiss citizen. He remained at Basel until his retirement in 1961. Jaspers's postwar publications in philosophy are voluminous. They include the monumental tome *On Truth* (1947), *The Perennial Scope of Philosophy* (1948), *Reason and Anti-Reason in Our Time* (1950), and an ambitious history of world philosophy, *The Great Philosophers* (1957–1981), left incomplete at his death.

Overview of Jaspers's Philosophy. Historically, Jaspers's existentialism developed in tension between Kant's transcendental **idealism**, the **historicism** of **Wilhelm Dilthey**, and the subjectivism of **Søren Kierkegaard** and **Friedrich Nietzsche**. From Kant Jaspers inherits a concern for "reason" and for objectivity and universality, a respect for the limits of philosophical speculation, and an awareness of reason's inherent "restlessness," its ceaseless quest to surpass the limits of experience. From Dilthey he receives an understanding of the multiplicity of **historical** perspectives, the inherent limits of one's historical **horizon**, and the need to rethink intellectual categories in terms of "categories of life." From Kierkegaard and Nietzsche he acquires a concern for subjectivity—for the irreducible uniqueness of the individual, the quest for **authentic** existence, and the concrete, subjective dimensions of philosophical truth. Jaspers's distinctive view of philosophizing as an open-ended search for transcendent truth pursued by existing individuals within particular historical horizons is a synthesis of these perspectives.

Many of Jaspers's ideas are nonetheless self-conscious elaborations of Kantian insights. Philosophy for Jaspers begins with a "basic operation of thought" in which one becomes existentially aware of the Kantian distinction between **phenomenon and noumenon**—that is, between the world as it appears to us and the world as it is "in itself." My awareness that knowledge is limited by a human perspective within space and time is not simply an intellectual acquisition, but an existential event that "shifts the posture of consciousness": "I get an inner jolt that will effect a change . . . in my attitude toward everything objective" (BPW, 24). It is this shift in perspective that for Jaspers inaugurates philosophical thinking. In becoming aware of the limits of knowledge, I also become aware that something stands beyond those limits, and it is to this nonobjective and noncognizable realm of **being** itself that genuine philosophy is directed. Objectively, in reference to the world, nonobjective being is what Jaspers calls "transcendence"; subjectively, in reference to my own being, it is ***Existenz***. Each term is understood as an aspect of "the **Encompassing**," the indefinitely open horizon of possibilities that I sense beyond the limits of any perspective (historical, scientific, philosophical, religious) I assume. The Encompassing is Jaspers's term for the most fundamental manner in which being is experienced by human beings.

It becomes clear that philosophy for Jaspers is less an intellectual analysis of the conditions of knowledge (as it is for Kant) than an exhibition of how knowledge "**founders**" under given existential circumstances. Jaspers's most influential account of how knowledge founders centers on the notion of **limit situation**, first introduced in *Psychology of Worldviews*. Limit situations arise when I confront an existential, and not just an intellectual, antinomy—opposing **values** that cannot be avoided yet cannot be reconciled. Therewith I am thrown into a state of cognitive suspense, being unable to understand the nature of that which I am called on to evaluate. **Death**, guilt, and suffering constitute limit situations. The positive result of confronting such situations is an expansion of awareness and self-awareness, a heightened sense of individual **freedom** and possibility that for Jaspers characterizes *Existenz*.

Elucidation of Existenz. A good deal of Jaspers's work was devoted to "elucidating" the concept of *Existenz*. Jaspers insisted that *Existenz* was to be understood "with the accent that Kierkegaard gave it: everything essentially real is for me only by virtue of the fact that I am I myself" (PE, 3). In other words, *Existenz* refers to what makes me into a *self* rather than simply an instance of a universal category (e.g., *homo sapiens*, rational animal) whose properties can be known and described from an external perspective. *Existenz* is an irreducibly nonobjective idea; it is a *possibility* rather than a property of human being, a capacity for moral **choice** and self-reflection that a person may or may not exercise. When exercised, *Existenz* raises one out of mundane existence to a higher level of moral self-awareness. In this manner, Jaspers's existentialism pressed beyond a Kantian framework, for the task of realizing *Existenz* involves not simply adherence to the laws of reason, but inner struggle, **anxiety**, and decision.

Philosophy plays an important role in **awakening** the impulse to authentic existence. It offers no proofs or definite conclusions. Instead, it simply "illuminates possibilities" and provides "**ciphers**" that point toward transcendence. In Jaspers's view, philosophical terms are analogous to what Kant called "ideas of reason," regulative concepts such as God, **freedom**, and the immortality of the soul, which transcend the bounds of possible experience yet serve as legitimate guides for thought and action. Their purpose is to effect an "alteration of our consciousness of Being," a shift in "our inner attitude towards things" (RE, 75).

Reason and Communication. While he insists on the nonobjective character of philosophy, Jaspers nonetheless preserves a place for reason and for communication in his thought. Authentic *Existenz* does not take place alone; it requires dialogue with an other person, through whom I am called on to plumb the depths of my beliefs and **values**. It also opens out onto the history of human thought in which I feel myself to participate. Jaspers thus attempts to preserve a Kantian element of universality in his existentialism, and, while he insists on the nonobjective character of existence, he resists Kierkegaard's view of the ineffability of inner life. Philosophical reflection occasions an expansion rather than an abandonment of reason, an identification with humanity and participation in the history of thought.

Religion. Jaspers was a profoundly religious thinker, yet he rejected most of the doctrines of organized religion as objectifying dogmas. To exist authentically, he thought, requires acknowledging a relationship to a transcendent reality: "*Existenz* . . . is irreducibly in another . . . it is authentic being before transcendence to which alone it surrenders itself without reservation" (RE, 62). However, God is but a cipher for **transcendence**, not a being that can be known or objectively defined. Hence religious truth lies not in any particular doctrinal faith but in the relation to transcendence, and this relation lies at the heart of all world religions. Alternately, Jaspers believed, an awareness of transcendence may be occasioned by philosophy itself when genuinely practiced. Jaspers thus came to refer to his own position as one of "philosophical faith," a sense of religiosity born out of awareness of the limits of human will and cognition. His view that the self emerges as unique and truly individualized only when it "knows itself before transcendence" (RE, 63) stands at the core of **religious existentialism**.

JAZZ. While jazz was an ingredient in the bohemian milieu of **café existentialism** in the 1950s and so was sometimes associated with existentialist philosophy, the relationship between the two endeavors is largely fortuitous. Both existentialism and modern jazz or "bebop" came to public attention after **Word War II**. With its fast tempos, emphasis on individual creativity, and rejection of tradition, modern jazz was embraced by café existentialists as well as by American **Beat** poets. Though French existentialists were exposed to jazz in the night clubs of **Saint-Germain-des-Prés**, they had limited knowledge about it. **Jean-Paul Sartre** demonstrated this in "Nick's Bar, New York City" (1947), when, like an anthropologist describing an alien culture, he recounted his visit to a jazz club in New York City during his 1946 State Department tour of the United States. The music is "harsh, violent, pitiless [. . .] the cruel shrills of birds of prey [. . .] You yell . . . they blow. . . . You are possessed. You yell out like a woman in childbirth . . . you feel like whirling round and round, howling at **death**" (SP, 183–184). Exceptional among Sartre's circle in the 1940s and 1950s was **Boris Vian**, who was an accomplished jazz trumpeter and jazz critic. Another fortuitous link between jazz and existentialism was **Juliette Gréco**, who had an affair with modern jazz trumpeter and composer Miles Davis during his visit to France in 1949. Apart from such chance connections, French existentialism flourished alongside the jazz clubs of Saint-Germain without reciprocal influence. Contrast may be drawn with Beat authors Jack Kerouac and Allan Ginsberg, who in the 1950s drew inspiration from the free-flowing improvisations of bebop musicians.

Jazz appears to play a significant role in Sartre's semiautobiographical novel *Nausea*. In the novel's conclusion, the hero, Antoine Roquentin, has an epiphany while listening one last time to his favorite "jazz" recording, "Some of These Days," a song he imagines having been written by a "Jew with black eyebrows" to be sung by a "Negress." However, in all likelihood the piece Roquentin refers to was the theme song of Sophie Tucker, a white Jewish vaudevillian, and not strictly speaking a jazz recording at all. It seems that Sartre had a loose understanding of the difference between jazz, an improvisatory music, and various types of popular music that emulated it. This suspicion was inadvertently corroborated by **Simone de Beauvoir**. In her autobiography, Beauvoir reported that Sartre (around 1930) used to sing "*Old Man River* and the current jazz hits." "Ol' Man River" became a popular song after its debut in the 1927 musical *Showboat!* but was never a jazz hit. The version Sartre sang may have been modeled after a well-known recording of the time by the actor and singer Paul Robeson with the Paul Whiteman Orchestra, the leading American society orchestra of the day. The other performers Beauvoir goes on to list, "Sophie Tucker, Layton and Johnstone, Jack Hylton, the Revelers" (MDD, 335–336), were popular white dance bands and singers of the 1920s and 1930s, not jazz musicians.

JEANSON, FRANCIS (1922–). French philosopher and leading interpreter of **Jean-Paul Sartre**'s *Being and Nothingness*. Jeanson's book *Le Problème moral et la pensée de Sartre* (1947) (*Sartre and the Problem of Morality* [1980]) was one of the earliest discussions of Sartre's philosophy by a trained philosopher. Jeanson's critical review of **Albert Camus**'s *The Rebel* (*Les Temps modernes* [May 1952]) provoked an angry response from Camus (*Les Temps modernes* [August 1952], which subsequently led to the end of Camus's relationship with Sartre. Jeanson is also the author of *Sartre par lui-meme* (1955) (*Sartre by Himself*), a collection of conversations with Sartre.

JUDAISM. *See* BUBER, MARTIN; LEVINAS, EMMANUEL; ROSENZWEIG, FRANZ.

– K –

KAFKA, FRANZ (1883–1924). German-speaking Czech novelist. Beginning in the 1950s, Kafka was frequently associated with existentialism due to the vivid atmosphere of **alienation** and absurdity expressed in works such as *The Castle*, *The Trial*, and *The Metamorphosis*. However, Kafka may be more accurately described as an author of the **absurd**. This in fact was how he was understood by **Albert Camus** and **Jean-Paul Sartre**. Kafka's influence on Sartre's and Camus's literary endeavors can be detected in Sartre's *Nausea* and Camus's *The Stranger*. *See also* EXISTENTIALIST LITERATURE.

KANT, IMMANUEL (1724–1804). German philosopher whose "critical philosophy" was the crowning achievement of Enlightenment thought and the foundation of German idealism and Romanticism. Virtually all German philosophers in the 19th and 20th centuries worked in Kant's shadow. Among existentialists, Kant's thought was particularly important for **Karl Jaspers** and **Martin Heidegger**. Both German and French existentialists accepted a qualified version of Kantian idealism according to which human attitudes and **intentions** actively organize and lend meaning to the world.

In *Critique of Pure Reason* (1781), Kant distinguished the world as it appears to us from the **world** as it is in itself. Objects we experience, Kant reasoned, have necessarily been organized by the human manner of sensing things in space and time and thinking about them according to categories like "cause and effect," "**substance**," "quality," and "quantity." Beyond the perspective of human cognition, the world remains an unknowable "X," a "thing-in-itself," off-limits to human understanding. Knowledge of ultimate things like the soul, God, and the ends and origins of the universe remains essentially beyond our reach, as it transcends the limits of space and time set by human cognition. Thus for Kant we cannot successfully conceive of the universe as a totality, understand a nontemporal (divine) perspective, or prove the existence of the soul.

Jaspers proposed existential interpretations of various Kantian ideas. He accepted Kant's view of the limits of knowledge along with the idea that reason is essentially "restless" and will ceaselessly try to surpass these limits. He accepted also Kant's idea that attempts to transcend experience lead to unresolvable "antinomies." These Jaspers characterized as **limit situations**, not merely intellectual paradoxes but situations of deep uncertainty that catalyze existential transformation. *See also* NEO-KANTIAN PHILOSOPHY.

KAUFMANN, WALTER (1921–1980). American philosopher, translator, and early commentator on existentialism. Born in Freiburg, Germany, Kaufmann immigrated to the United States in 1939 and after **World War II** became the dominant American scholar and translator of **Friedrich Nietzsche**. He defended Nietzsche successfully against accusations of anti-Semitism and paved the way for Nietzsche's eventual acceptance in the Anglo–American philosophical community. Kaufmann's best-selling anthology, *Existentialism from Dostoyevsky to Sartre* (1956), helped to introduce existentialist philosophy to American readers. In this book, Kaufmann was highly critical of **Karl Jaspers**'s interpretation of Nietzsche, which he claimed saw Nietzsche's importance in his exemplary *Existenz* rather than in his philosophy. Kaufmann was also an early critic of **Martin Heidegger**'s involvement in **Nazism**.

KEROUAC, JACK. *See* BEAT MOVEMENT.

KIERKEGAARD, SØREN (1813–1855). Danish writer and critic generally considered the principal 19th-century forerunner of existentialism. Kierkegaard's pseudonymously authored works of the 1840s represent the first philosophical treatment of **existence**: the perspective of the **finite individual** existing in time and eminently concerned with his or her own life. However, to call Kierkegaard an existentialist is misleading. He considered himself a writer, not a thinker, and was critical of the abstract exercise of reason required of philosophy, particularly when directed at human existence. His primary concern was religious: to clarify and defend the fundamental precepts of **Christian faith**. These he saw imperiled by the **leveling** tendencies of modern society and by the objectifying impulse of German idealism, in particular the philosophy of **G. W. F. Hegel**, which sought to reduce the existing individual to an instance of universal mind or spirit. Especially pernicious in his view was the assumption that faith can best be expressed in philosophical terms, for example as obedience to the rules of reason.

Kierkegaard borrowed freely from the vocabulary of German idealism, but always in the service of his religious aims. In such works as *The Concept of Anxiety*, *Either/Or*, *Fear and Trembling*, and *Concluding Unscientific Postscript*, he combined theological and philosophical argument, psychological observation, and social critique within complexly layered literary constructions. He also employed the technique of **indirect communication**, encouraging readers to enter imaginatively into different subjective perspectives rather than to remain neutral observers. His goal in this was to **awaken** readers to the urgency of their lives—ultimately, to their awareness of sin and desire for redemption. In addition to these "psychological" and "dialectical" works that represent the core of his legacy to existentialism, Kierkegaard published under his own name a series of "upbuilding discourses" on New Testament themes that pursued the goal of religious awakening more directly.

Becoming a Self. Kierkegaard understood by "existence" not some general property or state but the perspective of the "subjectively existing individual," the person intimately concerned with his or her life, and, ultimately, with the state of his or her soul. This perspective, he reasoned, is irreducibly singular and subjective: One existence cannot stand in for another, and there is no universal concept or standard to which an existing individual can be seen to conform. Accordingly, the meaning of existence cannot be adequately expressed in terms independent of the first-person perspective in which it is lived. Attempts to provide such an objective account of existence, such as the Hegelian system, necessarily distort what they seek to explain: They deprive life of its singularity and subjectivity.

Philosophical accounts of existence also tend to overlook its essential **temporal** character. Existence is ongoing, not static, a kind of "becoming" rather than a state of "**being**." Normatively, it is a striving to "become a self," an attempt to come to grips with one's ineluctably spiritual nature. Kierkegaard saw spiritual striving as definitive of all types of human life, whether or not explicitly religious. He proposed a stage theory of existence where (under one interpretation) the individual moves from one stage to the next in search of self-fulfillment. The lowest stage, termed "the aesthetic," is a life of hedonistic pleasure; such a life is a flight from selfhood rather than an autonomous choice of existence, for it is motivated by the desire to dim the awareness that one is a free, spiritual being. Hence aesthetic life offers only the illusion of satisfaction. Continual pleasure is an unrealizable goal, and it leaves untouched the spiritual element of human desire. Aesthetic existence is thus characterized by *despair*, a fundamental lack of fulfillment caused by an evasion of selfhood. To achieve a sense of true human identity, the individual must make a conscious **ethical choice**. This occurs in the next stage, "the ethical," where one consciously **commits** oneself to a moral ideal (e.g., being a faithful friend, a good citizen, or a loyal spouse). Like the German idealists, Kierkegaard places ethics at the core of human personality: The act of choice brings into relief one's **freedom** as a self-determining being. At the same time, to act ethically is to recognize universal laws as binding on oneself. The ethical is thus linked to the third and highest stage of existence, "the religious." Here the relation to universal and unchanging **values** is made explicit. The individual is brought into conscious relation with God, who is eternal.

Under this interpretation, the self progresses along a dialectical path from sensory particulars (the aesthetic), to the universal (the ethical), to the eternal (the religious). Yet religious existence is not a finalized state. It requires a continual "appropriation" and "repetition" of personal ideals. Kierkegaard describes faith in terms of a tension and a deepening of subjective awareness. It is a "passion" maintained in face of objective uncertainty, that is, in view of the fact that God's existence cannot be proven. He speaks of the "leap of faith" as the passage from the finite to the infinite that cannot be bridged by human reason. Because the human being always has one foot in the finite, the faith commitment must continually be reexamined and renewed and never simply dogmatically accepted.

Self-Forgetting. Kierkegaard also inaugurated the existentialist premise that authentic selfhood is complicated by a tendency toward self-forgetting, a tendency to avoid acknowledging one's freedom. Referred to by subsequent existentialists as inauthenticity or "**bad faith**," self-forgetting operates by various strategies of denying individuality and subjectivity: becoming "just like everyone else" by identifying with social roles and public opinion, effacing one's spiritual self by living only for the moment in the pursuit of aesthetic pleasures, or denying one's subjectivity by losing oneself in abstract speculation. The Hegelian philosopher exemplifies the latter tendency. By endeavoring to freeze existence and to "hover above it" in thought, he "makes an attempt to cease to be a human being, to become a book or an objective something" (CUP, 93).

Kierkegaard rejected no aspect of the Hegelian system more forcefully than the assumption that knowledge is superior to faith, and that philosophy affords a more precise and comprehensive understanding of religious truth. Hegel's claim that philosophy expresses in conceptual thought what Christianity struggles to communicate through feeling and myth he found particularly offensive. For Kierkegaard, the essence of religion is not reconciliation (or what Hegel calls "mediation") but *paradox*: the requirement that the individual accept two apparently contradictory truths. If God is eternal, it is incomprehensible how God may exist in time. Thus the truth of **Christian** faith is not a logical concept, but a paradox that cannot be rationally expressed or communicated. An alternate paradox of faith is the subjective certainty that God exists, which must be held in face of the objective uncertainty of this belief for which no rational proof can be offered.

Kierkegaard's opposition to Hegelian idealism was further articulated by the formula "truth is subjectivity." This was not intended as a denial of objective truth, but an affirmation that the truth of religious and ethical beliefs is evidenced by the passion with which one maintains them and acts according to them, not by external objective standards. Hence, subjective truth is not the correspondence of a belief with outward reality, but the "inwardness" with which a belief is maintained and integrated into one's life. For Kierkegaard, Hegelian philosophy risked obliterating the distinction between subjective and objective truth. He saw this danger present in all philosophy to the extent that it encouraged the illusion that life can be understood from a perspective outside of existence.

Kierkegaard's Existentialist Legacy. After his **death**, Kierkegaard's writings languished in relative oblivion outside of Denmark for several decades. They were rediscovered starting around 1909 when a complete German translation was undertaken, making Kierkegaard available to a generation of German intellectuals starting around the time of **World War I**. Subsequently his notions of the **absurd, anxiety,** choice, and commitment were freely appropriated by 20th-century existentialists. Both **Martin Heidegger** and **Karl Jaspers** incorporated Kierkegaard's insights into their philosophy in the 1920s. A striking example is Heidegger's account of anxiety in *Being and Time*, which may be read as a secularized version of Kierkegaard's. **Martin Buber** and **Franz Rosenzweig** also read Kierkegaard as an early proponent of **religious existentialism**. In the same years, Kierkegaard was instrumental to the development of **existential theology** in Germany as his ideas entered into the thinking of **Karl Barth, Rudolph Bultmann,** and **Paul Tillich**. Kierkegaard was translated into French starting around 1930. French **philosophers of existence** also drew inspiration from him, though this was tempered by a rebirth of Hegel studies in France and by a general wariness toward religion among French intellectuals of the time. *See also* KNIGHT OF FAITH AND KNIGHT OF INFINITE RESIGNATION.

KNIGHT OF FAITH AND KNIGHT OF INFINITE RESIGNATION. In *Fear and Trembling*, **Søren Kierkegaard** advances this distinction to characterize the difference between genuine **faith** and the final stage prior to genuine faith. The knight of infinite resignation renounces something dear to him, following God's **ethical** commandments, but then lives in a state of resignation, awaiting fulfillment in an afterlife. Such a person is akin to the tragic hero of **Greek**

drama, who remains defeated after sacrificing something dear to him in obedience to the law or the command of the gods. The knight of infinite resignation has obeyed the letter of God's command but has not yet attained genuine faith, for the belief that God is good, just, and loving is not applied to temporal existence, only to a beyond. The knight of faith goes a step beyond renunciation to "perform the double movement" of faith: He renounces what is dear to him, but at the same time expects to win it back "by virtue of the **absurd**." For Kierkegaard, **Abraham** is the exemplary knight of faith for "[h]e did not have faith he would be blessed in a future life but that he would be blessed here in the world. God could give him a new Isaac. . . . He had faith by virtue of the absurd" (FT, 36).

KNOWING SUBJECT. Existentialists labored in various ways to overcome the prejudice that the human being is primarily a theoretical knower. In place of the self as knower they stressed the self as embodied agent, engaged in a **world**, and concerned with itself and with others. **Martin Heidegger** offered an extensive critique of the ostensible primacy of the theoretical attitude. In ***Being and Time***, Heidegger argued that the theoretical attitude presupposes a more basic practical and affective engagement in a world. Following Heidegger, **Maurice Merleau-Ponty** defended the thesis of the "primacy of perception," that theoretical knowledge is derivative upon **prereflective** understanding of the world, accomplished through the tacit powers of the **body**.

The bias toward the knowing subject was clearly formulated in the modern period by **René Descartes**, who emphasized the autonomy of the mind from the body, reason from **emotion**. Starting in the late 19th century, philosophers like **Wilhelm Dilthey** and **Friedrich Nietzsche** in Germany, **Henri Bergson** in France, and **William James** in the United States criticized the knowing subject as an artificial abstraction. Dilthey formulated this objection vividly: "No real blood flows in the veins of the knowing subject constructed by Locke, Hume, and Kant but rather the diluted extract of reason as a mere activity of thought. . . . In the real life-process, willing, feeling, and thinking are only different aspects" (Wilhelm Dilthey, *Selected Works*, Volume 1, *Introduction to the Human Sciences*, 50–51). The existentialist critique of the knowing subject has been compared to that proposed by American **pragmatists** like James and John Dewey. *See also* BEING-IN-THE-WORLD.

KOESTLER, ARTHUR (1905–1983). Hungarian-born novelist, journalist, and critic. Koestler was a German-speaking Jew raised in Budapest and Vienna during the Austro-Hungarian empire who later moved to London, becoming a British citizen in 1945. A Zionist attracted to **communism**, Koestler visited the Soviet Union in 1932 and was a member of the German Communist Party from 1931 to 1938. After learning of Joseph Stalin's purges and show trials in the late 1930s, he became an outspoken critic of the Soviet Union, which he believed to have degraded into a regime of totalitarian terror under Stalin. His best-selling 1940 novel, *Darkness at Noon* (1941), which records the experience of a Bolshevik revolutionary imprisoned for treason, is one of the most powerful anti-Stalinist statements of the time. With his British-born wife Mamaine, the French-speaking Koestler befriended **Simone de Beauvoir** and **Jean-Paul Sartre** in Paris in 1946. Hot-tempered and prone to bouts of heavy drinking, Koestler argued fiercely with Sartre over politics, challenging his socialism and sympathy for Soviet **communism**. Sartre appreciated Koestler's warmth and spontaneity. However, Beauvoir grew to strongly dislike him: "[H]is anti-**Communism** made him irrational, maybe even insane. We could find no common, peaceful accord with him in anything" (Bair, 362). Koestler remained on close terms with **Albert Camus**, whose politics were more in sympathy with his own. **Maurice Merleau-Ponty** parodied Koestler's book *The Yogi and the Commissar and Other Essays* (1945) in an article entitled "The Yogi and the Proletariat," published in *Humanism and Terror* (1948).

KÖHLER, WOLFGANG. *See* GESTALT PSYCHOLOGY.

KOJÈVE, ALEXANDRE (1902–1968). Russian-born French philosopher and influential interpreter of the philosophy of **G. W. F. Hegel** and **Martin Heidegger**. Kojève was a charismatic teacher who lectured on Hegel's philosophy at the *École des hautes études* in Paris from 1933 to 1939. His lectures were attended by a host of young French philosophers and intellectuals, including **Raymond Aron**, **Georges Bataille**, **Jacques Lacan**, Claude Lévi-Strauss, and **Mau-**

rice **Merleau-Ponty.** Along with **Jean Hyppolite** and **Jean Wahl,** Kojève was thus largely responsible for the Hegelian atmosphere of French philosophy in the 1940s and 1950s. This was exemplified in the Hegelian tone and vocabulary of **Jean-Paul Sartre**'s *Being and Nothingness.* While Sartre did not attend Kojève's seminar, his approach to human subjectivity was in several respects substantively similar to Kojève's.

Kojève admitted that his reading of Hegel was more of a "transformation" than a strict interpretation. Having studied in Germany with **Karl Jaspers,** Kojève was familiar with German **philosophy of existence,** and he incorporated aspects of **Martin Heidegger**'s philosophy into his reading of Hegel. He also made use of **Marxism,** which he understood as the dominant political vision of his age. According to Kojève, human beings are raised above the animal level by *desire,* that is, essentially a desire to be *recognized* by other human beings. Following **Karl Marx,** he maintained that a dialectical struggle between masters and slaves, in effect a "struggle for recognition," played out between groups, classes, and nations, is the engine of human history. Following Heidegger, he held that humans lack a constitutive **essence** and so are defined by their "nothingness" or "**negativity,**" their ability ever to create themselves anew. In the **master–slave dialectic,** it is the slave who truly confronts **death,** becomes cognizant of essential human "lack" or **finitude,** and transforms the **world** through work. The "end of history," a phrase Kojève popularized, refers to a time when **political** struggles have ended and universal equality and **reciprocity** have been achieved. *See also* KOYRÉ, ALEXANDRE.

KOSAKIEWICZ, OLGA. *See SHE CAME TO STAY.*

KOYRÉ, ALEXANDRE (1892–1964). Russian-born French philosopher who was among the first to introduce modern German philosophy, including the **phenomenology** of **Edmund Husserl** and **Martin Heidegger,** into French intellectual life in the 1920s and 1930s. Koyré specialized in the history and philosophy of science and had studied with Husserl in Germany in the 1910s. He was the editor of *Recherches philosophiques,* the journal that published **Jean-Paul Sartre**'s first extensive work of philosophy, *The Transcendence of* *the Ego*, in 1936. In a series of articles in the early 1930s, he helped to introduce the philosophy of **G. W. F. Hegel** into French intellectual circles. In 1933, his seminar on Hegel at the *École des hautes études* in Paris was taken over by his friend, **Alexandre Kojève.**

– L –

LACAN, JACQUES (1901–1981). French **psychoanalyst** famous for his revisionist interpretation of psychoanalytic theory and practice. According to Lacan, **Sigmund Freud**'s theory of the unconscious is independent of biological facts and theories, even though Freud sometimes couched it in these terms. Rather, the major concepts of psychoanalysis (the unconscious, dreams, repression, the drives or instincts, and so forth) make sense only on the basis of a structuralist theory of language. Lacan maintained that human desire takes shape only once the child's affect is represented in words voiced to an **other**. Prior to representation by symbolic language, the patient's experience is ineffable and strictly inaccessible to the analyst. One of Lacan's most striking claims was to identify linguistic representation with *repression*: When a need or affect is given linguistic expression, it becomes vulnerable to an endless "play of signifiers" and henceforth can only be metaphorically or symbolically expressed, never fully retrieved or experienced as "real." This metaphoric and metonymic play is the stuff of the unconscious. Dreams and neurotic symptoms are organized according to a system of linguistic puns and tropes and not by reference to a prelinguistic content. Concepts like "affect" and "trauma" refer simply to gaps within the discourse of the patient, not to an **emotional** experience that might be relived. The goal of therapy is therefore not to strengthen the **ego** (e.g., by reliving past experiences that have been repressed) but to align the patient with the "discourse" that unconsciously governs his or her behavior. This discourse is "structured like a language," or more accurately like a playful coded message; once it has been correctly interpreted by the analyst, the patient's symptoms cease. In Lacan's view, this is because the desire has been "recognized by the Other."

Lacan's position entailed a rejection of the primacy of **consciousness** and the priviledging of the first-person perspective, which he held to be inimical to psychoanalysis. In the 1950s and 1960s, he became a vocal critic of **existential phenomenology** as practiced by **Maurice Merleau-Ponty** and **Jean-Paul Sartre**. However, Lacan did not arrive at his interpretation of Freud until about 1950. Prior to then his concerns were consistent, and often overlapped, with those of existential phenomenology, and he may well have profited from reading Sartre's early studies on imagination and *The Transcendence of the Ego*, in particular Sartre's thesis that the "ego is an other," an idea that became central to Lacan's postwar interpretation of Freud. In the 1930s, Lacan was also affiliated with the **surrealists** in Paris, particularly with **Georges Bataille**. In the mid- and late 1930s, he attended **Alexandre Kojève**'s seminar on **G. W. F. Hegel**. Kojève had a profound impact on Lacan, and after **World War II** Lacan developed a conception of human subjectivity focused on the desire for symbolic recognition similar to Kojève's. Lacan read all types of contemporary philosophy, including Sartre's *Being and Nothingness* and **Martin Heidegger**'s *Being and Time*, and aspects of both texts were reflected in his own thinking. He translated Heidegger's "Logos" essay into French and in 1955 hosted Heidegger and his wife during Heidegger's first visit to France after the war. By this time Lacan had embraced the antihumanist (and antiexistentialist) position as expressed in Heidegger's *Letter on Humanism*.

LAING, R. D. (1927–1989). Scottish psychiatrist and psychotherapist whose critical approach to mainstream psychiatry was influenced by existentialist philosophy, in particular by **Jean-Paul Sartre**'s account of the **reciprocal** relations between self and **other**. Laing was among the first to take seriously the **phenomenology** of psychosis and to pursue the assumption that psychotic symptoms are meaningful for the patient undergoing them even if they cannot be intelligibly communicated to the therapist. Laing defended the controversial hypothesis that severe mental illness is often occasioned by social and familial factors. When an individual is confronted with contradictory social demands, he reasoned, madness may be a "sane" response to an "insane world." Laing was coauthor with David G. Cooper of *Reason and Violence: A Decade of Sartre's Philosophy, 1950–1960* (1983).

LEAP OF FAITH. *See* KIERKEGAARD, SØREN.

LEBENSPHILOSOPHIE. See PHILOSOPHY OF LIFE.

LEFORT, CLAUDE (1924–). French political philosopher. As a young philosopher of the Left in the 1950s, Lefort contributed articles to **Jean-Paul Sartre**'s journal *Les Temps modernes*. He was particularly close with his mentor, **Maurice Merleau-Ponty**, with whom he shared a conception of socialist politics distrustful of the authoritarian tendencies in Soviet **communism**. In 1953, Lefort published a debate with Sartre in *Les Temps modernes* over the interpretation of **Marxism** Sartre had proposed in *The Communists and Peace* (1968). Lefort's criticism represented Merleau-Ponty's disapproval as well as his own, and Sartre's heated reply signaled the end of Sartre's relationship with Merleau-Ponty. Shortly thereafter Merleau-Ponty resigned from the editorial board of *Les Temps modernes*. Lefort edited Merleau-Ponty's last, incomplete philosophical work, *The Visible and the Invisible* (1968).

LESSING, GOTTHOLD EPHRAIM (1729–1781). German Enlightenment dramatist and critic. In *Concluding Unscientific Postscript to "Philosophical Fragments,"* **Søren Kierkegaard**'s wry comments on "Possible/Actual Theses by Lessing" introduce the distinction between subjective and objective thinking explored by Kierkegaard in the rest of the book.

LETTER ON HUMANISM **(*Brief über den Humanismus*, 1947).** In this, his first publication following **World War II**, **Martin Heidegger** repudiated **Jean-Paul Sartre**'s existentialism as a form of "humanism" and defined his own position as nonanthropocentric and nonexistentialist. Indirectly, Heidegger's essay was a response to Sartre's widely read **"Existentialism Is a Humanism,"** in which Sartre claimed an affinity between Heidegger's thought and his own. More immediately, the 50-page text was prompted by a question posed by French philosopher **Jean Beaufret**, "How can we restore meaning to the word *humanism*?" Heidegger responded by rejecting the conventional view of humanism as a desirable moral good. Instead, he portrayed humanistic thinking as a deep-seated Western prejudice that places human beings at the center of a universe they are destined to dominate.

According to Heidegger, Sartre's existentialism clearly expresses this prejudice by establishing human subjectivity at the center of the world and by excluding any extra-human dimension. In contrast, he observed, his own thought acknowledges human beings as receptive and responsive to **being**: "Man does not decide whether and how beings appear, whether and how God and the gods or history and nature come forward into the lighting of Being. . . . The advent of beings lies in the destiny of Being. . . . Man is the shepherd of Being" (BW, 210). The idea that "man is the shepherd of being"—that the role of human beings is to safeguard and preserve those elements of history, language, and culture that constitute a human world—is characteristic of Heidegger's later thought. It is Heidegger's contention that, because existentialism exalts the individual's powers to act and to create, it misconstrues our proper relationship to being. Hence, to restore meaning to "humanism" would require rethinking the very nature of the "human." Heidegger maintains that this was precisely the project of *Being and Time*, where **Dasein** was understood not as a "mind" or "subject" ranging over a world of external "objects," but as **being-in-the-world**.

Some scholars have accepted *Letter on Humanism* as adequate proof that Heidegger was not an existentialist, neither in 1947 nor in 1927 at the publication of **Being and Time**. However, this judgment is problematic. It must be recalled that Heidegger's rejection of Sartre occurs 20 years after *Being and Time* and reflects a shift in Heidegger's philosophical outlook that began in the 1930s, after *Being and Time*. This shift, known as Heidegger's "turn," entailed an attempt to overcome anthropocentrism, the perspective entailed by his earlier analysis of human existence. The same may be said of Heidegger's assessment in 1947 of his accomplishments in *Being and Time*. The standards he brings to bear on *Being and Time*, in particular his concern not to understand being through the lens of human existence, are not those that guided him during its conception.

LEVELING (Ger. *Einebnung*). In *The Present Age* (1846), **Søren Kierkegaard** referred to the anonymous force of public opinion and social conformity as engendering a process of "leveling." Leveling is that "abstract power" that destroys individuality in modern life by making individuals conform to a common standard, usually a lowest common denominator. Its main agency is "the Press," which creates the illusory entity "the Public," an indefinite collection of "unreal individuals who never are . . . united in an actual situation" (KA, 265). Through daily newspapers and gossip everyone is exposed to the same news and ideas and becomes perpetually caught up in superficial affairs, to the exclusion of matters of the self. The process of leveling can only be stopped by the individual's decision to attain "religious courage" and seek "religious isolation."

Martin Heidegger's discussion of public life was substantively indebted to Kierkegaard's. In *Being and Time*, Heidegger described the way in which the individual's **possibilities** are diminished—"leveled down"—by conformity to tradition and the opinion of others. Heidegger referred to the subject of this abstract leveling as "*das Man*" (the neutral pronoun "one" in German), an anonymous, intangible "anyone." Much like Kierkegaard's Public, *das Man* restricts the individual's options of **choice** to what is "familiar" and "respectable." "Dimming down" a person's awareness of "the possible as such" (BT, 239), Heidegger writes, *das Man* produces a "levelling down [*Einebnung*] of all possibilities of being" (BT, 165). Heidegger's view of **authenticity and inauthenticity** is linked closely to his account of *das Man*, for the process of leveling entails that *Dasein* understand itself in terms inappropriate to the type of being it most genuinely is.

LEVINAS, EMMANUEL (1906–1995). Lithuanian-born French philosopher. Levinas was instrumental in introducing the **phenomenology** of **Edmund Husserl** and the **existential phenomenology** of **Martin Heidegger** into French philosophy in the 1930s. He became a leading interpreter of Heidegger's philosophy among French **philosophers of existence** prior to **World War II**. After the war, he developed an original form of existential phenomenology centered on the **ethical** relation to the other person. He also pursued a dual career as a Talmudic scholar and interpreter of Jewish thought.

Levinas's *The Theory of Intuition in Husserl's Phenomenology* (1930) was the first book-length treatment of Husserl's thought by a French philosopher, and it played a crucial role in the development of existentialism in France. The importance of Levinas's book is reflected in an anecdote concerning **Jean-Paul Sartre**. In 1932, having just heard about phenomenology in a conversation with **Raymond Aron**, Sartre immediately purchased Levinas's book and impatiently began reading it, the pages still uncut, while walking down the sidewalk. Levinas had studied with both Husserl and Heidegger at Freiburg University in the late 1920s, and at the time the difference between their viewpoints was not always apparent. Levinas was thus sympathetic to the idea that Heidegger's approach to phenomenology was a continuation of Husserl's, and the interpretation of Husserl presented in the book was, he admitted, filtered significantly through Heidegger's own philosophy. This fact goes a long way toward explaining the curious admixture of Husserlian and Heideggerean ideas one finds in French accounts of phenomenology of the time. From Levinas, apparently, Sartre learned that phenomenology was concerned with **concrete existence** and not merely with cognitive processes. He also learned that it was concerned with **ontology** or a theory of **being** and not merely, or even primarily, epistemology or the theory of knowledge.

In the 1950s, Levinas developed an original phenomenology of **ethical** experience. He published his ideas in *Totality and Infinity: An Essay on Exteriority* (1960). How does the **ethical** claim of the other person—of the widow, the orphan, or the concentration camp prisoner—fit into the scheme of existence? Can an existentialist ontology such as that proposed by Heidegger in *Being and Time* provide a foundation for **ethics**? Levinas came to view Heidegger's analysis of *Dasein* as essentially monological, concerned only with the "circuit of the self" and unable to take into account the experience of "infinity," that dimension of the other person that exceeds egological understanding and "enjoyment." Following the model of **Franz Rosenzweig** and **Martin Buber**, Levinas saw the experience of infinity, or "transcendence," as embodied in the encounter with the other person. The **other** is encountered in a "face-to-face" relation. The face of the other compels my attention—it seems to request something of me, yet it remains alien to me; it exists "by itself and not by reference to a system." Levinas thus foregrounded an aspect of experience passed over by Heidegger's and by Sartre: the experience of the other person as a "Stranger" who is not an object in my world or modeled on myself. His contention was that the encounter with the other represents the heart of ethics, for without the possibility of such an encounter we would remain captives of limited and selfish perspectives, and thus heedless of moral **responsibility**.

LÉVY-BRUHL, LUCIEN (1857–1939). French philosopher and ethnologist. A contemporary of **Henri Bergson**, Lévy-Bruhl was a professor of philosophy at the Sorbonne, best known for his work on "primitive" or "pre-logical mentality." **Edmund Husserl** admired Lévy-Bruhl's work, and their correspondence in the 1930s documented a shift in Husserl's thought toward an appreciation of the cultural and historical dimensions of **consciousness**.

LIFE, PHILOSOPHY OF. *See* PHILOSOPHY OF LIFE.

LIFE-WORLD (Ger. *Lebenswelt***).** Term coined by **Edmund Husserl** referring to the ordinary **world** of human experience in contrast to the world as constructed by scientific or philosophical theories. In *The Crisis of European Sciences* (1935), Husserl developed the thesis that the world of immediate perception and belief constitutes the necessary foundation for scientific theories about reality. Science can never "go beyond" the life-world because the life-world provides the basic data and assumptions needed to pursue any inquiry whatsoever. Husserl affirmed that the life-world forms a pretheoretical totality. In this regard, his view is similar to **Martin Heidegger**'s conception of "world" in *Being and Time*. However, Husserl had examined the notion of world in various contexts prior to the publication of *Being and Time*, and he denied that his treatment derived from Heidegger. Later, the notion of the primacy of the life-world was elaborated by **Maurice Merleau-Ponty**.

LIMIT SITUATION (Ger. *Grenzsituation***).** In *Psychology of Worldviews*, **Karl Jaspers** describes "limit situations" as experiences of **death**, suffering, struggle, **guilt**, and chance, which in their incomprehensibility may provoke deep existential self-transformation. Through limit situations we transcend our mundane selves and enter into *Existenz*.

The concept of limit situation is Jaspers's application of **Immanuel Kant**'s "antinomies of reason" to the realm of **value** and evaluation. In Kant's *Critique of Pure Reason*, an antinomy is an opposition between two equally valid arguments, one that admits of no concievable resolution. Limit situations arise when I confront an existential, and not just an intellectual, antinomy—opposing **values** that cannot be avoided yet cannot be reconciled. Therewith I am **thrown** into a state of cognitive and existential suspense, being unable to understand the nature of that which I am called on to evaluate, yet being unable to escape it. Reason and purposive **action** thus "founder" in such situations as I come up against the limits of objective knowledge. Through the experience of foundering, I am prompted to move beyond the perspective of ordinary **consciousness** (*"Dasein"*) and to enter into genuine *Existenz*. The experience of the limit situation is thus for Jaspers essentially transformative; it shakes me out of a complacent, mundane perspective and thrusts me into an awareness of **transcendence** and, correlatively, of my own **freedom**.

For example, death, when authentically experienced, constitutes an exemplary limit situation: "Death is something inconcievable . . . really unthinkable"; it is something we know in general yet "at the same time there is something in us which instinctively does not believe it necessary or possible" (*Psychologie der Weltanschauungen*, 261). The tension between my fundamental commitment to life and my awareness of death is an existential antinomy, an unresolvable opposition that brings home to me that "everything is in flux . . . everything is relative, finite, split into opposites" (*Psychologie der Weltanschauungen*, 259).

Jaspers's concept of death as a limit situation was particularly influential for **Martin Heidegger**'s account of **being-towards-death** in *Being and Time*. However, Heidegger was critical of Jaspers's general philosophical approach. In an extended review of Jaspers's book, "Comments on Jaspers's *Psychology of Worldviews*" (*Pathmarks*, 1–38), Heidegger presented an early statement of his view of human being as *Dasein*. This view he proposed against the perceived deficiencies of Jaspers's philosophy of *Existenz*.

LITERATURE. *See* EXISTENTIALIST LITERATURE.

LIVED BODY. *See* BODY AND MIND; MERLEAU-PONTY, MAURICE.

LOGICAL POSITIVISM. Anti**metaphysical**, empiricist philosophy formulated in the 1920s and 1930s by a group of Austrian philosophers and scientists known as the Vienna Circle. Starting around 1926, Rudolph Carnap (1891–1970) became the leading figure of the group. In the 1930s, the group disbanded and their ideas took hold in other European countries. A. J. Ayer (1910–1989) was the chief exponent of logical positivism in Great Britain.

The logical positivists denied that metaphysical statements have meaning, because they refer to entities that cannot be perceived and hence described and known. Statements about "God," "**being**," "the soul," or "the Nothing" have no "truth value"; they can neither be confirmed nor disconfirmed and are strictly speaking meaningless. Philosophically, logical positivists were archenemies of existentialism. Carnap applied this criticism to **Martin Heidegger**'s philosophy; Heidegger's references to "the Nothing" are meaningless, he held. Ayer made a similar point in reference to **Jean-Paul Sartre**'s *Being and Nothingness*: "words like 'nothing' and 'nobody' are not used as the names of something insubstantial and mysterious, they are not used to name anything at all" ("Novelist and Philosopher, J.-P. Sartre," *Horizon* [July 1945]: 19).

LOGOTHERAPY. *See* FRANKL, VICTOR.

LOOK, THE. *See* OTHER, THE.

LÖWITH, KARL (1897–1973). German philosopher. A student of **Martin Heidegger**'s at the University of Marburg in the early 1920s, Löwith, who was Jewish, fled Germany upon Adolf Hitler's rise to power, traveling first to Japan (1933–1935) and then to the United States (1942–1944). In 1952, he returned to Germany to teach as a professor of philosophy at the University of Heidelberg.

Löwith's memoirs, *My Life in Germany before and after 1933*, recount his relationship with Heidegger. For Löwith, Heidegger's magnetism as a teacher lay in his fervent concern with personal **authenticity** rather than in his meditation on the history of **being**. Löwith thus provides evidence that Heidegger was perceived at the time as a **philosopher of existence**. However, Löwith's account was strongly colored by his feelings of betrayal. When he met with his former teacher in Rome in 1936, Löwith claimed, Heidegger did not bother to remove his **Nazi** Party pin from his jacket lapel. Löwith was thus among the first to raise questions about Heidegger's involvement with Nazism. In particular, Löwith made the claim, though with scant evidence or argument, that Heidegger's existentialism itself was essentially fascistic: "Expressions of violence thoroughly determine the vocabulary of both National Socialist politics and Heidegger's philosophy. The apodictic character of Heidegger's emotive formulations corresponds to the dictatorial style of politics" (*My Life in Germany*, 37). For Löwith, Heidegger's thought was an exemplary expression of German **nihilism**. This Löwith understood as an obsession with **death**, destruction, and "nothingness," and a disregard for the **values** of civilization which extended from Martin Luther to **Friedrich Nietzsche**. Löwith was a well-regarded Nietzsche and Hegel scholar. His books include *From Hegel to Nietzsche* (1941) and *Meaning and History* (1957). Portions of Löwith's memoir dealing with Heidegger originally appeared in an article, "The Political Implications of Heidegger's Existentialism," published in *Les temps modernes* (vol. 14 [1946–1947]).

LUKÁCS, GEORG (1885–1971). Hungarian literary critic and **Marxist** philosopher. Lukács's early book *History and Class Consciousness* (1923) was instrumental in the development of Marxist philosophy beyond the orthodoxy of Soviet **communism** and had a strong influence on the political outlook of **Maurice Merleau-Ponty** and **Jean-Paul Sartre**. Both Merleau-Ponty and Sartre appreciated the **Hegelian** perspective on Karl Marx's thought offered by Lukács, as it refused to reduce **consciousness** to an epiphenomenon of economic forces and thus provided a toehold for **freedom** in the dialectic of history. This idea led Lukács to reject the strictly materialist view of history defended by orthodox communists and resulted in his book being banned by the Communist Party. Lukacs soon repudiated his own work, however, and entered into a harsh polemic with Sartre over the meaning of existentialism and Marxism. Lukács launched the first attack in a apolemical book entitled *Existentialism or Marxism?* (1947).

(An excerpt from the book is published in *Existentialism versus Marxism*, edited by George Novak, 134–153.) The situation deteriorated when, in Paris to promote the French edition of his book in 1949, Lukács published an interview in the newspaper *Combat* entitled "Existentialism Indirectly Justifies Capitalism." Sartre responded by calling Lukács a "crypto-existentialist" who had misunderstood Marx. Merleau-Ponty defended Sartre in a short "Commentary" published in *Les temps modernes* (republished as "Marxism and Superstition" in *Signs*, 261–262) (*See* Contat & Rybalka, 221–223).

Merleau-Ponty had been particularly attracted to the dialectical aspect of Lukács's early thought, which recognized the interplay of subjective and objective elements in the evolution of truth, and to the idea that, because we are "immersed" in history, the perspective of totality or of universal history is unavailable to us. Merleau-Ponty agreed with Lukács that truth for Marx is an always "unrealized" totality rather than an absolute state of affairs that can be stated unambiguously. He discussed Lukács's position at length in *Adventures of the Dialectic* (30–73). In *The Destruction of Reason* (1954), Lukacs argued that the embrace of the irrational by *Lebensphilosophie* had paved the way for Adolf Hitler's National Socialist movement.

– M –

MACQUARRIE, JOHN (1919–2007). Scottish theologian and philosopher. Macquarrie was the cotranslator (with Edward Robinson) of **Martin Heidegger's** *Being and Time* and a lucid commentator whose combined interests in theology and philosophy provided him with unique resources for understanding existentialism. His early books, *An Existentialist Theology: A Comparison of Heidegger and Bultmann* (1955) and *The Scope of Demythologizing* (1960), reflect a depth of knowledge in both fields. His 1972 book *Existentialism* was a ground-breaking work that offered a synthetic account that sought to capture underlying commonalities between existentialists rather than simply cataloguing their differences. It remains one of the best general studies of existentialism in English. Macquarrie's translation of *Being and Time* was a work of consummate scholarship and a boon for the study of existentialism in America in the 1960s and 1970s. It remains the standard English translation of *Being and Time*. His other books include *Martin Heidegger* (1968) and *Studies in Christian Existentialism* (1966).

MANDARINS, THE (*Les Mandarins*, 1954). Autobiographical novel by **Simone de Beauvoir** documenting French intellectual life during and immediately after **World War II**. Beauvoir worked on the novel for four years between 1949 and 1953, writing and rewriting passages to unify its three main themes, love, friendship, and politics. It was, she recalled "the book I wrote with most passion. It is the book I found the most important among my novels" (Bair, 424). The novel includes fictionalized portraits of **Nelson Algren**, **Albert Camus**, **Arthur Koestler**, and **Jean-Paul Sartre**.

MARBURG SCHOOL. *See* NEO-KANTIAN PHILOSOPHY.

MARCEL, GABRIEL (1889–1973). French Catholic **philosopher of existence**, playwright, musician, and critic. Marcel may be credited as the earliest French existentialist, having developed his reflections on **concrete**, embodied existence beginning in the 1920s, well before **Jean-Paul Sartre**'s rise to fame. Marcel was an early critic of Sartre and may have been the first to introduce the term "existentialism" (around 1944) as a label for Sartre's thought. He came to dislike being called an "existentialist," however, as the label suggested an affinity with Sartre that he rejected. Marcel's thought shares many common elements with **religious existentialists** like **Karl Jaspers** and **Martin Buber**, in particular the idea that **being transcends** objective knowledge, and that intimations of the divine are found in experiences of love and communion with the other person.

Life and Works. An only child, Marcel had an upper-middle-class upbringing in a Protestant household. After the **death** of his mother when he was only four years old, he was raised by his father and his aunt, both of whom tended toward agnosticism. From an early age he was attracted to the theater and to writing plays, an activity he pursued throughout his life, authoring 30 plays in his lifetime. Marcel was also a gifted musician. During **World War I**, he worked as an administrative director for the Red Cross, locating missing soldiers, and this experience strengthened his religious convictions and led him to question the relevance of abstract philosophy. In 1929, he converted to Catholicism. Having passed the national *agrégation* exam in philosophy in 1910, Marcel taught philosophy periodically at various French high schools. For most of his life, however, he was employed as a drama and music critic and as an editor.

Marcel's early interests in philosophy were related to post-Kantian thought, especially that of **Friedrich Schelling**, and to the idealism of the English philosophers F. H. Bradley and Josiah Royce. Marcel's first extended work of philosophy was a critical study of Royce's philosophy, *Royce's Metaphysics* (1956). His own philosophical perspective emerged in the 1920s via a critique of idealism and philosophical abstraction in general. It is documented first in **Metaphysical Journal** (1927), a kind of philosophical diary of observations and reflections recorded between 1918 and 1925, and continued in *Being and Having* (1935). Marcel rejected the idea of the philosophical system, his preferred forms of expression being the essay and the lecture. These are collected in *Creative Fidelity* (1940); *Homo Viator* (1945); his Gifford Lectures of 1949–1950, published in two volumes as *The Mystery of Being* (1950); and his William James Lectures at Harvard University in 1961–1962, published as *The Existential Background of Human Dignity* (1963). An important early article that sets forth many of Marcel's mature ideas is "On the Ontological Mystery," published in 1933 (PE, 9–46). Among Marcel's numerous plays, his early drama *The Broken World* identifies the problem of **alienation**, which is a central theme of his existentialist writings.

A Philosophy of Participation. Marcels's intentionally unsystematic, exploratory style reflects his belief that philosophy should derive from personal experience and should avoid overly abstract or impersonal theorizing. Such abstraction leads to the false conclusion that philosophy has only to deal with "problems," theoretical puzzles that may be solved without the personal "participation" of the thinker: "[W]e have developed the execrable habit of considering the problems in themselves . . . in abstraction from the manner in which [they are] woven into the very texture of life" (BH, 102). For Marcel, genuine philosophy deals rather with "**mysteries**," problems in which the thinker is essentially implicated. Love, **death**, **freedom**, hope, and fidelity are examples of mysteries explored by Marcel. In each case, one's personal experience of the issue is essential; when the philosopher withdraws to an impersonal perspective the telling-ness of the mystery is lost and it devolves into a mere problem. "A mystery . . . is something in which I find myself caught up . . . whose essence is therefore not to be before me in its entirety" (BH, 100). Thus, where problems call for solution, mysteries call for deepening acknowledgment and reflection.

Marcel makes clear that traditional philosophy and science con-tribute to our alienation to the extent that they endorse the primacy of the **knowing subject** and the ideal of objective knowledge. The con-sequence of this alienation is a general misapprehension of the "**on-tological** weight of human experience" (BH, 103)—that the world, other people, and ourselves are not primarily objects to be known but rather types of ontological "presence," instances of "being" that im-plicate us, make demands on us, incite wonder and respect, and stim-ulate us to create. In other words, the human relationship to being is essentially one of "participation," not that between "spectator" and "picture."

My relationship to my own body is a basic instance of participa-tion: "I *am* my body," it is an "absolute mediator," the perspective I can never withdraw from entirely (BH, 12). The paradigmatic expe-rience of participation for Marcel, however, is found in my relation-ship to others. In relegating the other person to the "problem of other minds," traditional philosophy obscures the **ethical** and practical na-ture of the relationship, that the other is a **concrete** person—friend, parent, lover, or teacher—with whom my identity is intertwined. The problem of the other for Marcel is thus not primarily epistemological or metaphysical but ethical, as it concerns the quality of my partici-pation in this relationship, of my "**availability**" to the other.

Availability and Reciprocity. Much of Marcel's work is devoted to an exploration of basic interpersonal experiences, which for him are the anchoring points of a human life and point the way toward au-thentic spiritual existence. Availability (*disponibilité*) designates for Marcel openness, candor, and genuine receptivity to the other person. To be available is to be present to the other emotionally and spiritu-ally, not only intellectually: "[T]he person who is available to me is . . . capable of being with me with the whole of himself when I am in need" (PEM, 40). In other words, to be available is to relate to the other as subject, not object, as "You," a source of action and thought who remains irreducible to my thought and desire.

Moreover, this relation to the other is strictly reciprocal. To exist for me, the other must be seen as a subject, and, conversely, I must be seen in the same light by the other. Reciprocity is thus characterized by Marcel as a type of "communion," a dialogical relation to a You that stands at the heart of love, fidelity, and **faith**. This view of reciprocity underlies Marcel's belief that existence is essentially collaborative and communal, not egocentric. "If . . . I treat the other . . . *qua* freedom [. . .] I help him . . . to be freed, I collaborate with his freedom" (BH, 107). Alternately, to love someone is "to expect something" from them, to expect them to remain worthy of your love; but at the same time it is "to give" them the opportunity to meet that high expectation (HV, 49–50). For Marcel, freedom, love, hope, fidelity, and faith—central features of existence—are essentially collaborative efforts, requiring reciprocal recognition of self and other, I and You.

Marcel as a Christian Existentialist. Marcel rejects the existentialist label because he refuses the association with Sartre, and, moreover, is "generally . . . repelled by all labels and 'isms'" (TWB, 240). He accepts, however, the idea that he is in a sense a "**Christian** philosopher": "[F]rom the moment I began to think philosophically for myself . . . I was drawn to recognize that there must be an extremely profound reality in Christianity and that my duty as a philosopher was to find out how this reality could be understood" (TWB, 238). If Marcel avoids explicit theological arguments, it is because his writing aims to have universal appeal, regardless of religious affiliation. He expressed this intention toward the end of his life in a conversation with **Paul Ricoeur**: "I consider myself as having always been a philosopher of the threshhold . . . who kept himself . . . on a line midway between believers and unbelievers so that he could somehow stand with believers . . . but also speak to nonbelievers . . . and perhaps . . . help them" (TWB, 240). Marcel's position on the border between Christian theology and philosophy bears comparison with that of **Karl Jaspers**, a philosopher for whom Marcel has great respect. At the same time, by his own admission Marcel's concern for "the sacred sense of being" shares something in common with the philosophy of **Martin Heidegger** (TWB, 243), especially Heidegger's later thought.

MARCUSE, HERBERT (1898–1979). German-born American social and political philosopher, member of the **Frankfurt School** of critical theory. In contrast to his Frankfurt School colleagues **Theodor Adorno** and Max Horkheimer, Marcuse initially found merit in **Martin Heidegger**'s analysis of human **existence** (*Dasein*), which he likened to **Karl Marx**'s analysis, in *Economic and Philosophical Manuscripts of 1844*, of human **alienation** under capitalism. Marcuse studied with Heidegger at Freiburg University in the late 1920s and early 1930s, hoping to unite his interests in **Marxism** and existentialism. At the time, he saw in Heidegger "a new beginning, the first radical attempt to put philosophy on really **concrete** foundations—philosophy concerned with human **existence**, the **human condition**, and not merely with abstract conditions and principles" (cited in Richard Moran, *Introduction to Phenomenology*, 245). Later he came to question the concreteness of Heidegger's thought and its ability to deal with historical reality. However, he continued to recognize the revolutionary character of Heidegger's critique of technology and the Western domination of **nature**. Marcuse's best known books were *Eros and Civilization* (1955) and *One Dimensional Man* (1964). The latter exposed the **leveling** tendencies of capitalist society and explored alternative possibilities for social organization suggested by "subversive" elements like the U.S. student movement. The former was Marcuse's attempt to fuse Marxism and **Freudian** theory, an attempt to imagine the conditions of a psychologically and politically nonrepressive society.

MARX, KARL (1818–1883). German philosopher whose revolutionary social and economic theory, **Marxism,** came to shape the events of the 20th century. As a young man, Marx was associated with a group of German philosophers known as the Young Hegelians, the secular, left-leaning faction of the disciples of **G. W. F. Hegel.** Inspired by **Ludwig Feuerbach**'s materialist critique of Hegelian idealism, Marx proposed a dialectical approach to human history that recognized only material (physiological, social, and economic) causes. In Paris in the early 1840s, Marx encountered Friedrich Engels, who became his lifelong collaborator and friend. Marx worked as a journalist and became active in European socialist workers' movements. By 1848, with Engels, he came to defend a version of socialism known as "**communism**," which posited the abolition of private property and the common (state) ownership of economic resources. Set forth in polemical terms in *The Communist Manifesto* (1848), Marx and Engels's conception of communism was underpinned by "**historical materialism**," a materialist theory of history that had developed via the critique of Hegel. In 1849, Marx was expelled from Prussia and immigrated to London, where he spent the rest of his life working in relative isolation in the British Museum on a monumental critique of capitalism, *Capital*, his major theoretical work. Only one volume of *Capital* was published during Marx's lifetime, in 1867; the other two volumes were edited by Engels and appeared after Marx's **death**.

MARXISM. The social and economic theory of **Karl Marx** and its subsequent philosophical developments. Marxism also refers to political practices and institutions founded on this theory. Marxist theory played an important role in the development of French existentialism after **World War II**, especially in the thought of **Maurice Merleau-Ponty** and **Jean-Paul Sartre**. The centerpiece of Marx's viewpoint was a materialist theory of history, according to which capitalism sows the seeds of its own destruction, setting the stage for a workers' revolution. In Marx's analysis, human societies pass through a series of necessary stages of economic production, from primitive hunter-gatherers, to agrarian societies, to small crafts and manufacturing, and finally to industrial capitalism. Under capitalism, social and economic inequities latent in earlier forms become fully pronounced, producing an **alienated** and impoverished class of workers called "the proletariat." Marx predicts that when the proletariat comes to full awareness of its predicament, revolution will ensue. Private property will be abolished and a **communist** society will be instituted. Therewith, all forms of human alienation shall be overcome, greed, envy, and social strife eliminated. In Marx's major work, *Capital*, this theory is presented as strictly empirical and "scientific," and human behavior is portrayed as subject to inexorable economic laws. However, earlier works, such as *Economic and Philosophical Manuscripts of 1844*, reveal a humanistic and philosophical perspective. Here Marx proposes a type of **metaphysics** according to which human **consciousness** actively participates in its own emancipation. For both Sartre and Merleau-Ponty, the most significant philosophical development of Marx's ideas was the "critical Marxism" elaborated in the 1920s and 1930s by such thinkers as **Georg Lukács** and Antonio Gramsci, who recognized the importance of the early philosophical writings. *See also* HISTORICAL MATERIALISM.

MASTER–SLAVE DIALECTIC. In **G. W. F. Hegel**'s *Phenomenology of Spirit*, a stage in the development of human self-awareness characterized by antagonistic codependence of self and other. In Hegel's account, the master objectifies the slave as inferior but remains dependent on the slave's recognition of his superiority. When through his labor the slave gains the upper hand, the roles are reversed, the slave taking the superior position, and the unstable "dialectic" begins again, neither party being able to receive the fully human recognition it seeks from the other. In historical terms, Hegel suggests that such a dialectic continues until disparity of rank and privilege is abolished.

The master–slave dialectic is important to the history of existentialism largely because **Alexandre Kojève** assigned central importance to it in his lectures on Hegel in Paris in the 1930s. Through Kojève the idea of the master–slave dialectic and of the "struggle for recognition" it represents filtered into French existentialism. The master–slave relationship is particularly significant to **Jean-Paul Sartre**'s account in *Being and Nothingness*, in which interpersonal relations are described in terms of a desire to "objectify" and "subdue" the other, who is perceived as an alien perspective that calls into question the uniqueness and privilege of one's own consciousness. In similar fashion, **Simone de Beauvoir** also sees master–slave antagonisms as central to human relationships. Her novel *She Came to Stay* begins with an epigraph from Hegel, "Each consciousness seeks the **death** of the other." *The Second Sex* generalizes this analysis to normal social relations between men and women, especially that whereby women become an object for men's appreciation and control.

MATERIALISM. *See* HISTORICAL MATERIALISM.

MERLEAU-PONTY, MAURICE (1908–1961). French philosopher and major proponent of **existential phenomenology**. Along with **Jean-Paul Sartre**, his friend and colleague, Merleau-Ponty belonged to the generation of young French thinkers who helped to introduce the **phenomenology** of **Edmund Husserl** and **Martin Heidegger** into French philosophy after **World War II**. His main contribution was a phenomenological account of perception that highlighted the role of the **body** as the anchor of the perceptual **world**. This theme was broached in his first book, *The Structure of Behavior* (1942), and treated in depth in ***Phenomenology of Perception*** (1945), his major philosophical work.

Merleau-Ponty's philosophical interests encompassed a variety of subjects, including psychology, art, language, history, and **politics**. Politically he embraced a version of **Marxism** akin to Sartre's, and he served as political editor of *Les Temps modernes* from 1945 to 1952. In the early 1950s, he broke with Sartre and the French **Communist** Party and distanced himself from political polemics. His later philosophy, less empirical and more speculative in nature, sought to articulate a nondualistic **ontology** of pretheoretical experience.

Life and Works. Born in the small French town of Rochefort-sur-Mer, Merleau-Ponty attended high school in Le Havre before enrolling in the prestigious Lycée Louis-le-Grand in Paris to finish his preparation for the selective entrance exam to the **École Normale Supérieure**. He was accepted into the Ecole Normale in 1926 and graduated in 1930, a year after Sartre, who was three years older than he. Like Sartre, his early work combined interests in empirical psychology and psychopathology with the study of Husserlian **phenomenology**; the combination of these endeavors he understood as offering a **concrete** approach to philosophical problems. Unlike Sartre, however, who abandoned teaching after World War II, Merleau-Ponty remained an academic all his life, progressing through the ranks from lycée teacher to university professor to the Chair of Philosophy at the College de France. Merleau-Ponty had a traditional Catholic upbringing and was a practicing Catholic until suffering a crisis of faith in his late twenties. This may have disposed him more favorably toward **religious existentialists** like **Gabriel Marcel**, one of Sartre's severest critics. While he criticized aspects of the philosophy of such predecessors as **Henri Bergson**, Heidegger, and Husserl, in general Merleau-Ponty sought to preserve rather than to overturn his relation to the philosophical past.

15111111111111111

Sartre and Merleau-Ponty knew each other as students at the École Normale, but they were not close friends. Merleau-Ponty was on closer terms with **Simone de Beauvoir**, his classmate, and it was Beauvoir who provided the most detailed portrait of Merleau-Ponty as a student. In her memoirs, she recounted her friendship with a certain "Jean Pradelle," a pseudonym for Merleau-Ponty: "He had a meditative air and . . . I hastened to lay bare my soul to him . . . he had lost his father, and got on perfectly well with his mother and sister and did not share my horror of family life" (MDD, 246). We learn from Beauvoir that Merleau-Ponty "disapproved of his fellow students' coarse manners, their indecent songs, rude jokes, brutality, debauchery, and cynical dissipations." We also learn that he was classed among the observant Catholic students, whom Sartre derided. While Beauvoir, Sartre, and Merleau-Ponty each enjoyed upper-middle-class upbringings, according to Beauvoir only Merleau-Ponty "remained perfectly adapted to his class and its way of life, and accepted bourgeois society with an open heart" (MMD, 247).

Merleau-Ponty went on to teach high school philosophy at Beauvais (1931–1933) and Chartres (1934–1935), and returned to teach at the École Normale Supérieure (1935–1939). During this period, he began the study of **Gestalt psychology** and behaviorism that resulted in his first book, *The Structure of Behavior*, published in 1942. During this time, he also discovered the philosophy of **Karl Marx**. Like many French intellectuals of the time, from the late 1930s through about 1950 Merleau-Ponty remained a dedicated **Marxist** though never a fully convinced **communist**.

In August 1939, Merleau-Ponty was mobilized into the French army, where he served as a lieutenant until France's defeat by German forces in August 1940. Catalyzed by his experience in the war, upon his return to civilian life in Paris, he joined with Sartre to organize a **resistance** group of leftist intellectuals, **Socialism and Freedom**. In occupied Paris, he composed his major work, *Phenomenology of Perception*, published in 1945. He also worked during this time to help establish archives for Husserl's manuscripts in Paris. Husserl's works had been banned by the **Nazis** due to his Jewish heritage. Just before the war, his voluminous unpublished manuscripts had been moved to Louvain, Belgium, for safekeeping by the Belgian scholar Herman Leo Van Breda. In April 1939, Merleau-Ponty traveled to Louvain to consult Husserl's unpublished writings. From 1942 to 1944, he and several young colleagues labored unsuccessfully to establish a center for Husserl's unpublished writings in Paris. In 1944, typescripts of several of Husserl's later works were smuggled from Louvain to Paris, but no official institution would accept the risk of housing them. Nonetheless, Merleau-Ponty was able to consult them for his research on *Phenomenology of Perception.* A permanent Husserl archive was eventually established in 1958 at the University of Paris library.

Merleau-Ponty's interest in German phenomenology had begun sometime around 1929 when he attended Edmund Husserl's lectures at the Sorbonne, later published as *Cartesian Meditations.* Like Sartre, Merleau-Ponty was influenced in his approach to Husserl by Heidegger's **hermeneutic** phenomenology. At the same time, he was aware of the differences between Husserl's and Heidegger's perspectives, and in his mature work he attempted to reconcile them. From 1945 to 1949, Merleau-Ponty was professor of philosophy at the University of Lyon; from 1950 to 1952, he held the Chair of Child Psychology and Pedagogy at the Sorbonne, a post subsequently occupied by Jean Piaget. In these same years, he served as coeditor with Sartre of *Les Temps modernes.* From 1952 until his premature **death** in 1961, Merleau-Ponty held the Chair of Philosophy at the Collège de France.

The Lived Body. The core of Merleau-Ponty's existential philosophy was his probing account of human embodiment, a theme treated only superficially by most other existentialists and largely ignored by the philosophical tradition. This theme was elaborated in *Phenomenology of Perception.* To begin, the body as observed and explained by science (the objective body) must be distinguished from the body as subject of experience, the "phenomenal body" or "lived body" (*le corps vécu, le corp propre*). The lived body operates generally below a level of explicit awareness but above a level of involuntary physiological reflex. It is illustrated by the type of **prereflective** awareness one has, for example, of one's location in space and of the arrangement of familiar places. For example, without thinking (forming a distinct representation of the world in my mind), I know that my bookcase stands within reach of my desk, how many steps there are from the landing to the second floor, and that I cannot fit through the doorway without stooping. The nonthematized attitudes, habits, and intentions according to which one reckons with such things as one's spatial surroundings Merleau-Ponty characterized as a "tacit *cogito*," or alternately as an "operative **intentionality**," an idea derived from Husserl. Once the nature of embodiment is understood, he maintained, perception cannot be coherently construed as either a purely physiological reaction (the reception of sensory stimuli) or a purely mental act (the synthesis of sense qualities in the mind). Rather, it is an immediate apprehension of meaning through the tacit agency of the body.

Meaning *(sens)* in turn is originally perceptual or "lived" rather than conceptual or linguistic. When I hear the sadness of a melody or see a landscape as threatening, I am grasping a lived meaning in its full bodily import, not merely entertaining an idea in my mind. Moreover, perceived meaning cannot be analyzed into its sensory constituents; the melody (and a fortiori its perceived sadness) disappears as soon as I attend only to the individual tones out of which it is made. From Gestalt psychology, Merleau-Ponty derived the principle that the simplest object of perception entails at least a figure/ground relationship. He thus affirmed that perceived meanings are always the result of the relationships between objects and qualities of objects and cannot be further simplified. Hence the notion of atomic "sense data," the ostensible building blocks of perception, is a theoretical construct rather than a true ingredient of experience.

The Primacy of Perception. Merleau-Ponty defended the thesis of the *primacy of perception*, an idea derived from Husserl's concept of the **life-world**. This is the idea that perception is ontologically and epistemologically primitive in human experience, and that scientific and philosophical thought are "founded" on prior perceptual understanding. Like Heidegger, he argued that the givenness of the perceptual world cannot be gainsaid by philosophy and is not subject to the **realism**/idealism debate: "[T]he perceived world . . . is simply there before us, beneath the level of the verified true and the false" (PrP, 3). Because science and philosophy must take perceptual experience for granted, they should not be accepted as independent sources of truth. Rather, they should be seen as distinct modes of symbolic expression that give voice to the "silent language" of perception. Accordingly, the goal of philosophy is "to re-establish the roots of the mind in its body and in its world" (PrP, 3), not to clarify the contents of mind by separating them from bodily contaminants.

Critique of Sartre. Merleau-Ponty's account of perception as embodied engagement in a world lacked the drama of **anxiety** and **authenticity** characteristic of much existentialism. However, it provided an important counterpoise to Sartre's voluntarism, in particular to his view of **consciousness** as absolute **freedom**. In the last chapter of *Phenomenology of Perception*, Merleau-Ponty proposed a critique of Sartre's position. He argued that, in Sartre's view, consciousness is effectively disembodied, unconstrained by physical circumstances, society, and the past. Yet embodiment furnishes necessary conditions for freedom, for without a bodily perspective, consciousness would float effortlessly above the world, executing its will and encountering no "resistance" in things. To such a consciousness every thought and every act would appear equally "free," hence the very idea of freedom becomes unintelligible. In place of Sartre's view of freedom as absolute, Merleau-Ponty advocated a conception of *situated* freedom. According to this view, a free act is an "exchange" between self and world in which the self takes up and modifies previously given meanings but does not create them ex nihilo. Merleau-Ponty's view of freedom thus emerged from his understanding of the perceptual world as a field of given possibilities within which the body may act. It also drew upon the **ambiguity** of perception, according to which boundaries of self and world, and self and **other**, remain fluid and indeterminate.

Marxism and Politics. Merleau-Ponty devoted considerable attention to political questions, in particular to a clarification of Marxist theory as it applied to the events of the day. His attraction to Marxism was based, like Sartre's, on the ideal of a socialist transformation of society. At the same time, it was tempered by skepticism in regard to Marx's more crudely materialist and reductionist claims, which deny the reality of human freedom. Because his theoretical engagement with Marxism preceded Sartre's by several years, Merleau-Ponty was elected to serve as political editor of *Les Temps modernes*, a role he exercised from 1945 to about 1950. In this period, he aligned himself with the politics of the French Communist Party and was hostile to what he perceived as the unilateral imperialism of the

United States. Nonetheless, he remained critical of orthodox Marxism, especially the doctrine that the dialectic of history proceeds independently of human agency and choice. His essays on politics were collected in *Sense and Non-Sense* (1948) and *Humanism and Terror* (1948).

In 1950, Merleau-Ponty learned of the concentration camps in the Soviet Union and he ceased his affiliation with communist politics, though he continued to "share the **values**" of socialism. In 1952, he surmised that North Korea, led by the Soviet Union, had provoked the Korean War, and he became disillusioned with Marxism. He resigned from the editorial board of *Les Temps modernes* and broke off relations with Sartre, whose commitment to **communism** had deepened. In 1955, Merleau-Ponty published *Adventures of the Dialectic*, a critique of Marx's dialectical theory of history that included a lengthy analysis and repudiation of Sartre's interpretation of Marx.

METAPHYSICAL JOURNAL (*Journal métaphysique*, **1927**). **Gabriel Marcel**'s first philosophical work is plausibly the earliest published statement of French existentialism. The book records Marcel's philosophical observations and reflections in a series of journal entries dated between 1918 and 1925. Its intentionally unsystematic, exploratory style reflects Marcel's belief that philosophy should derive from personal experience and avoid overly abstract, impersonal theorizing. The theme of embodiment (*incarnation*) as developed in Marcel's *Journal* was particularly influential for **Maurice Merleau-Ponty**. Merleau-Ponty commented on the importance of Marcel's thought to the **philosophy of existence** in a 1959 lecture, "The Philosophy of Existence" (Stewart, 495–496).

METAPHYSICS. Traditionally, metaphysics is the branch of philosophy concerned with the ultimate nature of what exists and with questions that transcend empirical observation, such as the existence of God, the soul, and **freedom** of the will. Existentialists employ the term in different ways, both negatively and positively. **Martin Heidegger** tends to see metaphysics as vitiated by an ontology of **substance** that obscures the **embodied** and **historical** character of human **existence**. At the same time, metaphysics for Heidegger informs the very language of Western philosophy and so cannot be simply dismissed; rather, the possibilities of metaphysical thinking must be retrieved and reappropriated in accordance with a renewed understanding of existence. In contrast, **religious existentialists** like **Karl Jaspers** and **Gabriel Marcel** speak of metaphysics positively as involving a relation to **transcendence**. The **philosophy of existence**, Jaspers writes, "gains space for its own unconditioned activity through conjuring up Transcendence (as metaphysics)" (MMA, 159). In similar fashion, Gabriel Marcel defines metaphysical thought as "reflection trained upon **mystery**" (BH, 101).

MIND–BODY DUALISM. *See* BODY AND MIND.

MINENESS (Ger. *Jemeinigkeit*). In *Being and Time*, **Martin Heidegger** observed that human **existence** always has the character of "mineness"; it is necessarily something that "I am" or you are," not merely something that "is," which might be displayed to a neutral observer. Following the example of **Søren Kierkegaard**, Heidegger maintained that a human life is not something that "happens" but that about which each of us is most intimately *concerned*. Alternately, he expressed this by saying that **existence** is essentially "an *issue*" for itself; it cannot be reduced to a neutrally occurrent entity **"present-at-hand."** An important related claim made by Heidegger is that existence, because it is essentially characterized by mineness, necessarily involves one in the choice to "be oneself" or "not to be oneself," that is, to exist authentically or inauthentically. In Heidegger's analysis, in its **everyday** mode *Dasein* exists inauthentically, uncritically accepting possibilities dictated by society and losing sight of itself as a "being of possibility." In the exceptional **moment** of vision, *Dasein* attains to **authenticity** by taking hold of its existence in terms of possibilities consciously chosen and affirmed.

MOMENT (Greek *kairos*, Dan. *Øieblikket*, Ger. *Augenblick*). **Søren Kierkegaard** introduced the idea of the moment in his *Philosophical Fragments* to describe the paradoxical **temporality** of God's incarnation in human form, which requires the entry of the eternal into time; he maintained that the same incommensurability of the eternal and temporal characterizes genuine religious **faith**. "Such a moment has a peculiar character. It is brief and temporal indeed, like every moment; it is transient . . . it is past, like every moment in the next moment. And yet it is decisive, and filled with the eternal . . . let us call it the *Fullness of Time*" (*Philosophical Fragments*, 22).

Around the time of **World War I**, Kierkegaard was discovered by a generation of young German intellectuals, and the idea of the Moment gained currency in German theology and philosophy, in different forms, during the 1920s. **Existential theologians Karl Barth** and **Paul Tillich** develop the idea of the *Kairos* in their respective theologies.

In a less theistic framework, **Martin Heidegger** employs the notion of the "moment of vision" or the "instant" (*Augenblick*) to characterize the manner in which *Dasein* achieves **authentic** insight into its **situation**: "[B]y shattering itself against **death** . . . [and] by handing down to itself the **possibility** it has inherited . . . . [*Dasein* can] take over its **thrownness** and be **in the moment of vision** for 'its time'" (BT, 437, last bold in text). Heidegger maintains that the moment or "instant" (*Augenblick*) is the primal **phenomenon** of temporality, from which the philosophical and scientific notion of the "now" as the point of present time is derived. In the moment, *Dasein* is **resolute** and orientated toward **action**.

MONOLOGUE. *See* DIALOGUE.

MOOD (Ger. *Stimmung*). From an existentialist perspective, moods are an affective apprehension of the significance of things, a **prereflective** way in which the meaning of the **world** and the **situation** of the self registers in human awareness. Moods are thus always something more than transient subjective states or irrational disturbances. Moods are constitutive of **existence**, not merely incidental to it, for human experience is always mooded in some sense, and moments of awareness are linked to specific existential moods. The latter are discussed in some detail by **Martin Heidegger**. According to Heidegger, moods like **anxiety**, **boredom**, fear, and joy are expressions of an affective "attunement" to the world, an immediate resonating with how things are, captured nicely in an alternate meaning of the German term *Stimmung*, the tuning of a musical instrument. Mood is the basic instance of *Befindlichkeit* or **state-of-mind**, colloquially, "how one is"; literally in German, "how one finds oneself." Heidegger makes the **phenomenological** observation that moods are not known via reflection but rather "assail us" *"prior to* all cognition and volition" (BT, 175). That is, moods are not chosen but often arise against one's will and beyond one's knowledge of their causes. In this way, moods reveal essential human **thrownness** and **facticity**: that we exist under circumstances we do not choose but that nonetheless we must come to terms with as part of our identity. Further, Heidegger argues that moods are not passing psychological disturbances but constitutive possibilities of *Dasein*; one always finds oneself in some mood or other, and through moods the world, myself, and others are disclosed in a certain light.

In a striking reversal of traditional theories, Heidegger argues that mood is not a subjective projection onto an emotionless world but a *"disclosive submission to the world, out of which we can encounter something that matters to us"* (BT, 177). For example, a mood of apprehension allows the silhouette of a mountain to appear as threatening, while a mood of elation "discloses" the blue sky as joyful. It is crucial to Heidegger's view that moods not be understood as mere subjective projections. Rather, the world necessarily appears under some affective aspect or other, and this disclosure is effected by *Dasein*'s mood. A final feature of Heidegger's account is the claim that moods make manifest the "burden" of *Dasein*'s being. That is, in immediately apprehending the meaning of a situation, moods make manifest that one has no choice but to live in it and make something out of it. *See also* EMOTION.

MORALITY. *See* ETHICS.

MOUNIER, EMMANUEL (1905–1950). French personalist philosopher and editor of the Catholic philosophical journal *Esprit*. Mounier's *Introduction aux existentialismes* (1946) endorsed the existentialists' return to **concrete** human **existence** but criticized the perceived tendency of **atheistic existentialists** like **Jean-Paul Sartre** and **Martin Heidegger** to neglect experiences of love, friendship, communication, and **faith** and to unjustly emphasize the role of abandonment, isolation, **absurdity**, and conflict in human life. Mounier championed instead the **Christian** existentialism of **Gabriel Marcel**.

MYSTERY (Fr. *mystère*). A central claim of the philosophy of **Gabriel Marcel** is that the modern **world** is deprived of mystery, a sense that there is an underlying unity to things, in which one participates, yet which cannot be known objectively. Science and philosophy contribute to the lack of mystery by promoting an impersonal, objective stance that removes the existing individual from participation in what is known. From this perspective, all matters are "problems" that can be solved by an impersonal application of reason. For example, the "problem of evil" is treated as a theoretical puzzle in theology and philosophy, to be resolved independently of personal experience. In contrast, the "mystery" of evil is a matter in which I am personally involved—for example, through my experience of unjustified suffering. The line between problems and mysteries cannot be too clearly drawn, however. All problems with a human dimension have a dimension of mystery; yet, when treated theoretically, mysteries may deteriorate into problems. Unlike problems, mysteries do not admit of solutions; rather, they lead to deeper reflection on the nature of **existence**. **Religious existentialists** generally concur that an awareness of mystery is essential to fulfilled human existence.

MYTH OF SISYPHUS, THE. (*Le Mythe de Sisyphe*, **1942**). Along with his short novel *The Stranger*, published the same year, this essay on the the absurdity of **existence** established **Albert Camus's** literary and philosophical reputation in France and abroad. In it, Camus makes the case that the unity of contemporary "existential philosophy" and modernist literature can be found in a shared emphasis on the **absurd**. While the outlook Camus propounds here has often been characterized as existentialist, a more fitting label, favored by Camus at the time, is "absurdist." It is worth noting that in the essay Camus distances himself from "existential philosophers" such as **Martin Heidegger**, **Karl Jaspers**, **Søren Kierkegaard**, and **Lev Shestov**.

The essay opens with the provocative assertion that suicide is the only serious philosophical problem; it raises the question of "whether or not life is worth living" in a universe devoid of purpose (or whose purpose cannot be known). Camus thus evinces what **Friedrich Nietzsche** called the "**death of God**," the decay of religious belief and **transcendent values** in modern secular society. In the modern era, Camus maintains, existence has been revealed as absurd, in that it stands without justification or foundation, and the defining experience of modernity is an apprehension of radical **contingency**.

The aimlessness of history, the futility of daily work, the pointlessness of **death**, war, and murder, and the inscrutability of human motives may each occasion an experience of absurdity. In each case, the absurd results from the gap between the human expectation for meaning—for purpose, order, and intelligibility—and the meaninglessness of the **world**. However, if the absurdity of existence is harsh and unpalatable, it must nonetheless be confronted with honesty rather than ignored or denied. Belief in religious redemption, scientific progress, or **metaphysical** system-building bring solace at the price of intellectual dishonesty; they impute meaning to the world where there is none. Such metaphysical illusions are contradicted by the evidence of human history and by the immediate certainties of existence: that I exist here and now, that existence is purely contingent (that I or any other part of the world could just as readily not exist), and that I will die. Instead of appealing to abstract forces or entities, about which I can never be certain, Camus exhorts his readers to meet the absurdity of existence with "lucidity."

Camus's model of such lucidity is the mythical figure of Sisyphus, and his retelling of the ancient **Greek** myth provides the book's centerpiece. According to Greek myth, Sisyphus was forced by the gods to roll a rock up a mountain for eternity. In Camus's hands, Sisyphus is transformed from a tragic figure into an absurd hero who finds meaning in his struggle despite the futility of his task. "He *is*, as much through his passions as through his torture. His scorn of the gods, his hatred of death, and his passion for life won him that unspeakable penalty in which the whole life is exerted toward accomplishing nothing" (MS, 120). Sisyphus is the exemplar of absurdist **authenticity**. He does not give in to **hope** (that life does have a **transcendent** meaning, despite appearances), suicide (because there is no point in living if life has no transcendent meaning), or a type of unthinking existence that deadens one to the problem. Rather, he understands that existence is "neither sterile nor futile" when approached from a properly human perspective. He invests himself in the immediate purposiveness of his life (pushing the rock over the mountain) while at the same time remaining conscious of the absurdity of his predicament—its lack of transcendent purpose. In the end, it is a lucid consciousness of the absurd that allows one to seize upon one's own **action**, passion, and **freedom** as the source of life's meaning. *See also* EXISTENTIALIST LITERATURE.

– N –

NATORP, PAUL. *See* NEO-KANTIAN PHILOSOPHY.

NATURALISM. In general terms, *ontological* naturalism is the view that everything is made up of natural entities and that there are no supernatural beings such as divinities, spirits, or souls. Often associated with this ontological position, *methodological* naturalism is the assumption that the laws and methods of empirical science are sufficient to explain everything that happens, including all aspects of human thought and behavior. As a rule, existentialists rejected methodological naturalism. Their position in regard to ontological naturalism varied, **religious existentialists** clearly taking exception to it insofar as they recognized God or some transcendent power as active in nature and human affairs. The case of atheistic existentialists is less clear.

While some philosophers in the 17th century (e.g., Thomas Hobbes) and the 18th century (e.g., David Hume) took a naturalist stance toward philosophical problems, naturalism as a general research program came to prominence starting in the middle of the 19th century following advances in physics, physiology, and other empirical sciences. Charles Darwin's theory of evolution by natural selection, **Karl Marx**'s theory of **historical materialism**, and **Sigmund Freud**'s theory of unconscious drives were influential naturalistic accounts of human behavior.

At the start of the 20th century, **Edmund Husserl**'s **phenomenology** emerged as a staunch opponent of a type of methodological naturalism called "psychologism," the attempt to explain thought and logic by referring to physiological and psychological facts about human beings. Existentialism in turn preserved an antinaturalist stance. Following Husserl's lead, the **existential phenomenology** of **Martin Heidegger** and, subsequently, of **Jean-Paul Sartre**, argued for the primacy of philosophical understanding over scientific explanation.

For Heidegger, a naturalistic perspective was inadequate for understanding human **existence** because the categories of empirical science, such as "organism, "**body**," "matter," "life," and "**nature**," were laden with the very metaphysical prejudices (such as the distinction between subject and world and the opposition of mind and body) that obscured the phenomenon of existence in the first place. Genuine philosophical understanding entailed a deeper approach, a "**fundamental ontology**," which, Heidegger believed, derived its categories from existence itself rather than from theoretical (scientific) assumptions about it.

Sartre's early phenomenological works on **imagination**, **emotion**, and **consciousness** were centered around a critique of naturalistic psychology. This critique, which was continued in the arguments against **psychoanalysis** in *Being and Nothingness,* held that to regard a mental state or an action as causally determined by physiological and psychological processes was to deny that it was **freely** produced. According to Sartre, by reducing behavior to subhuman mechanical processes, naturalism deprived human existence of its defining characteristic: the power to act and to interpret the world according to one's own lights, independently of environmental pressures or biological needs. Sartre's antinaturalist position was conveyed in his assertion, in "**Existentialism Is a Humanism**," that "there is no **human nature**."

Though influential in the development of existentialism and for this reason often classed as an existentialist, **Friedrich Nietzsche** had much in common with other great 19th-century naturalists. Like Darwin and Freud, Nietzsche proposed a type of naturalistic explanation that traced human institutions, **actions**, and beliefs back to underlying facts about human nature—physiological and psychological needs and drives—and that was critical of the notion of free will.

NATURE. Existentialists devoted relatively scant attention to nature and the natural (i.e., nonhuman) world as topics of philosophical inquiry. One reason for this was that their focus on the distinctive features of human **existence**—those features not shared with other living things—narrowed their inquiry in advance to exclude more general organic, biological, and mammalian traits. Another reason was that the traditional philosophical concept of nature was understood to be vitiated by the Cartesian premise that nature is simply a collection of *res extensa*, physical things in space to be observed and measured by the rational mind. **Martin Heidegger** saw **Descartes**'s view as exemplary of the modern metaphysical conception of reality, according to which the totality of things that exist, natural and non-natural, human and nonhuman, constitute a universe of things **present-at-hand** rather than a **world** to which we are intrinsically related.

Generally, the existentialist position was that things and events of nature appear within the **horizon** of human **being-in-the-world**; natural things are not normally experienced as neutral, valueless physical objects but rather as things invested with meaning with which we are involved in some way. For example, to the farmer the south wind is not experienced as a "flow of air" in a certain direction but rather as a "sign of rain" (BT, 111). Scientific accounts of nature in turn are, for most existentialists, parasitic on the prior tacit **understanding** of natural things.

NAUSEA (La nausée, 1938). **Jean-Paul Sartre**'s first novel. The novel recounts in diary form the tortured musings of Antoine Roquentin, a historian who has holed up in the provincial town of "Bouville" to research a book on a (fictional) 18th-century diplomat, the "Marquis de Rollebon." Bouville is modeled on the French town of Le Havre, where Sartre was at the time employed as a high school philosophy teacher, and the character of Roquentin, prone to intensive self-reflection, is modeled on Sartre himself. The novel begins with Roquentin beset by a feeling of strangeness, a "nausea" about things whose cause cannot be identified. It builds to a hallucinatory climax in a city park, when Roquentin experiences the "key to **existence**" while contemplating the roots of a chestnut tree: "[T]he root, the park gates, the bench, the sparse grass, all that had vanished: the diversity of things, their individuality, was only . . . a veneer. This veneer had melted, leaving soft, monstrous masses, all in disorder—naked" (127). What Roquentin experiences is that existence is **"absurd"** or "de trop," purely contingent. He becomes viscerally aware that language and thought (the world of **"essences"**) cannot make sense of the brute physical existence of things, including his own existence. Roquentin grasps that the "gratuitousness" of the world and of his own **body** and **consciousness** is the cause of the nausea. He also realizes that most people are in flight from **contingency** and that they combat it by positing illusory necessary causes such as God, fate, or human reason. Roquentin's heroism consists in his ability to confront the contingency of existence.

Nausea was conceived and written between about 1932 and 1936, prior to the formulation of Sartre's mature existentialist position, which was expounded in *Being and Nothingness* (1943) and whose main concern was radical individual **freedom**. Thus, while often identified as a classic of **existentialist literature**, strictly speaking *Nausea* (whose working title was *"factum* on contingency") is a pre-existentialist work. The novel's focus on contingency is in many respects closer to the **philosophy of the absurd** expounded around the same time by **Albert Camus**.

NAZISM. The German National-Socialist Workers Party, or Nazi Party, ruled Germany between 1933 and 1945 under the dictatorship of Adolf Hitler. Nazi ideology was premised on belief in the racial superiority of Germans and their "destiny" to rule Europe and the racial inferiority of Jews, Roma, Slavs, and other non-European groups, who were assigned subhuman status. This led to Hitler's invasion of neighboring European states and the outbreak of **World War II**, and to the systematic extermination of about 6 million Jews and several million others deemed racially inferior. To gain power, Hitler and the National Socialists capitalized on the widespread feeling that Germany should not have lost **World War I** (an implausible "Jewish conspiracy" was often blamed) and that the reparations Germany was forced to pay according to the Treaty of Versailles were excessive and unfair. The Nazis also exploited the fear of **communism** and of a communist takeover of Germany.

Martin Heidegger, infamous among existentialists for his support of National Socialism, shared both of these latter sentiments. Beginning around 1932, Heidegger embraced National Socialism as a revolutionary movement that sought to recapture the "historic greatness" of the German people. Between April 1933 and April 1934, Heidegger served as rector of Freiburg University under Nazi rule. During his tenure as rector, Heidegger implemented Nazi policies at the university, gave speeches defending Nazi ideology, and alienated many former friends and students, including **Edmund Husserl** and **Karl**

Jaspers. Swept up in the nationalistic fervor, Heidegger believed his philosophy could provide the spiritual foundation for National Socialism, while National Socialism would create conditions for a rehabilitation of philosophy and of the German university system. The Nazis removed Jaspers from his teaching post in 1937 because his wife was Jewish, and he and his wife lived out the war quietly in Germany. In *The Question of German Guilt*, which examined the question of collective responsibility for the events of the Nazi period, Jaspers admitted suffering from "metaphysical **guilt**" for not having risked himself to help others. *See also* HEIDEGGER AND NAZISM.

NEGATION/NOTHINGNESS. Many existentialists advance the claim that human **existence** bears a special relationship to nothingness and negation. Their approach to these matters has seemed paradoxical, even nonsensical, to traditional philosophers, for whom negation refers simply to a property of negative judgments, and nothingness does not refer to anything at all but derives from a reification of the term "nothing." **Martin Heidegger** and **Jean-Paul Sartre** make the case that nothingness and negation are essential to human experience; a human world is necessarily shot through with absence and possibility and so cannot be reduced to an array of occurrent entities. They employ a daunting variety of terms to express different aspects of this idea: the nothing (*das Nichts*), nullity (*Nichtigkeit*), negation (*Verneinung*), nothingness (*néant*), nihilization (*néantisation*), lack (*manque*), abyss (*Abgrund*), and absence are among the most important. Historical precedent for their thinking comes from **G. W. F. Hegel**, who early in the 19th century rekindled philosophical interest in "the negative" and "non-being." In his *Phenomenology of Spirit*, Hegel referred to **consciousness** as a "negative power" that rejects ordinary appearances in search of deeper underlying truth, negating what is merely actual in favor of what is possible. In similar fashion, Sartre maintains that human desires and **projects** introduce a sense of "absence" or "lack" into the world, a sense of what may be or might be, of what ought to be, and an apprehension of what is no more. Heidegger was inspired by Hegel to reconsider the nature of nothingness as an **ontological** category. He contends that the concept of **being** is itself linked intrinsically to nothingness. Because being is not a determinate entity or concept of the type recognized by science and traditional philosophy, it appears to be "nothing at all," pure indeterminacy or nonsense. Further, he suggests that human beings have a peculiar relationship to nothingness, for only human beings can grasp the *groundlessness* of their own being, their lack of essential cause or content.

Sartre discusses a host of negative phenomena in *Being and Nothingness*, including absence, lack, distance, repulsion, and regret, which demonstrate the pervasiveness of the negative in human life. Negation is not merely a property of negative judgments but an integral component of consciousness. For example, when I walk into a café expecting to find my friend Pierre, I experience his "not being there" immediately and intuitively; each face I inspect, each table, and each conversation is perceived in terms of its "not being Pierre." Prior to human involvement, reality (**being-in-itself**) is solid and undifferentiated and strictly speaking unknowable. It is my intention of finding Pierre that introduces a "flickering of nothingness" (BN, 10) into the "plenitude" of **being**. Like Hegel, Sartre thus celebrates the negative power of consciousness; by introducing absence into the plenum of being, consciousness is "the origin of nothingness." Further, consciousness in general is defined by Sartre as a power of "nihilation" (*néantisation*), that is, an ability to modify the world as given in service of the world as imagined or desired. This is precisely what occurs when I experience Pierre's absence from the café, for it is my expectation of finding him, that is, my conscious intention vis-à-vis Pierre, that adds to the world of positive things an apprehension of nonbeing. Consciousness is the origin of nothingness, because without human projects and intentions, reality would remain mute and impenetrable, not properly speaking a human world at all.

As noted, Heidegger frames the issue of nothingness differently, in terms of the meaning of being. Being for Heidegger is understood not as the totality of things that exist, but as the manner in which things "appear." Particular things—a hammer, a tree, a person—are grasped in their being by taking up appropriate attitudes toward them: I drive in nails with the hammer, I pick fruit from the tree, I speak to the person. In each case, the being of the thing reveals itself to me against a **horizon** of tacit meanings and intentions; taken in the most comprehensive sense, the totality of such horizons is the world itself. This is the sense of Heidegger's assertion that beings are grasped from out of a ground of "non-being," because the conditions under which I perceive the tree as a tree, that is, the world, do not constitute a determinate entity that can be directly apprehended. Instead, the "worldliness of the world" remains hidden from scientific inspection and ordinary understanding; that which is not a determinate *something* appears to be "almost like nothing" (IM, 35).

Heidegger's essay "**What Is Metaphysics?**" and his book *An Introduction to Metaphysics* discuss these issues at length. The philosophy of "nothingness" is intended not simply to provoke controversy but to "reawaken the question of the meaning of being." The question, "Why are there beings rather than nothing?" is, according to Heidegger, the fundamental question of philosophy, for it raises the question of the ground (or cause) (*Grund*) of everything that exists. The ground of the totality of beings, however, cannot itself be a determinate being, for example a super-entity such as God, because such a being remains itself subject to the question. The ground of being must rather be understood as an abyss (*Abgrund*), a lack of determinate cause or foundation. Critics have held that Heidegger's approach to nothingness seems unnecessarily to court paradox. Yet its rhetorical intention is clearly to stimulate reflection: How can such a "non-ground" be encountered? If nothingness is not an entity, then how can it be apprehended or thought? Heidegger's answer here, as in *Being and Time*, is that nothingness is encountered via the fundamental mood of **anxiety**. Anxiety is a precognitive apprehension of the groundlessness of the world in tandem with the groundlessness of the self. On the plane of reflection, the correlate of anxiety is philosophy. Genuine **philosophizing** calls into question the received meaning of things and **awakens** a sense of wonder and **mystery** in the world.

NEO-KANTIAN PHILOSOPHY. The dominant academic philosophy in Germany between roughly 1870 and 1920, centered around an elaboration of the philosophy of **Immanuel Kant**. Neo-Kantianism also exerted a general influence on the culture of Wilhelmine Germany, where it played the role of a kind of "state philosophy." Following Germany's defeat in **World War I** and the ensuing loss of faith in traditional institutions, *Lebensphilosophie* (**philosophy of life**), **phenomenology**, and, finally, *Existenzphilosophie* (**philosophy of existence**) gradually weakened the authority of neo-Kantian

244 • NIETZSCHE, FRIEDRICH

philosophy in the university and diminished its popularity in intellectual culture.

Neo-Kantian philosophy was practiced by a range of independent and often rival movements and figures in different German universities, and there is no unified neo-Kantian position. At the heart of neo-Kantianism was the belief that a "return to Kant" was needed to combat, on the one hand, the excesses of **Hegelian** philosophy and post-Kantian Romanticism, which claimed privileged knowledge of "the absolute" and "the transcendent," and, on the other, the threat of positivistic science and **naturalism**, which claimed that all truth can be apprehended by science, and hence that there is no need for philosophy at all. It was argued that a return to Kant demonstrates there are truths proper to philosophy, and that these are neither mystical apprehensions of the absolute nor explanations and descriptions of empirical facts, but rather transcendental facts. **Edmund Husserl**'s phenomenology was in close sympathy with these concerns. A main difference between Husserl's approach and that of the neo-Kantians was Husserl's assumption, after 1913, that the **thing-in-itself** can be given in intuition through the technique of eidetic variation.

The Marburg School of neo-Kantianism was founded by Herman Cohen (1842–1918) and continued by his student, Paul Natorp (1854–1924). **Ernst Cassirer** (1874–1945) was the last representative of the Marburg School, and by the 1920s Cassirer was one of the preeminent philosophers in Germany. A historic debate took place in 1929 in Davos, Switzerland, between Cassirer and a youthful **Martin Heidegger** concerning the status of neo-Kantian philosophy and their divergent interpretations of Immanuel Kant's *Critique of Pure Reason*. A transcript of the debate is published as an appendix to Heidegger's *Kant and the Problem of Metaphysics*. The Southwest German School of Neo-Kantianism, centered at the University of Heidelberg, was founded by Kuno Fischer and represented successively by Wilhelm Windelband (1848–1915) and Heinrich Rickert (1863–1936). Rickert, who was Heidegger's teacher and dissertation adviser at the University of Freiburg, developed a philosophy of **value** that Heidegger came to criticize.

NIETZSCHE, FRIEDRICH (1844–1900). German classicist, poet, and philosopher. Nietzsche's influence on European ideas and letters is immense and defies simple summary. He was the most widely read German writer during the late 19th and early 20th centuries, and his writings left their mark on a range of endeavors, from literature, art, and philosophy to history, **politics**, psychology, and **psychoanalysis**. His role in the development of existentialism was also significant, particularly among German **philosophers of existence**. Martin Heidegger and **Karl Jaspers** each devoted books to Nietzsche's philosophy, though Heidegger's interest in Nietzsche was subsequent to the existentialist period of Heidegger's thought. French existentialists were less indebted to Nietzsche, though they were certainly familiar with his ideas and generally favorable toward them. An exception was **Albert Camus**, whose approach to philosophical issues was modeled closely on Nietzsche's.

Nietzsche's Status as an Existentialist. Nietzsche has frequently been classified as an existentialist or protoexistentialist. Support for this classification is found in his critique of social conformity and conventional morality, his emphasis on individual creativity and "self-overcoming," and his suspicion of the objectivity of philosophical reason and the project of rationalism. A serious obstacle to this characterization, however, is Nietzsche's denial of **free** will. A related obstacle is his acceptance of a **naturalistic** perspective, according to which human beings are understood on the model of other living things, as organisms motivated by drives that promote their own flourishing, rather than sui generis. Nietzsche's status as an existentialist thus should not be accepted as a matter of course. While it may be possible to construe his philosophy as consistent with, or complementary to, existentialism, to do so requires significant interpretative labor.

Nietzsche's Thought. Nietzsche heralded a new beginning in philosophy and culture, to be achieved by overcoming two principal metaphysical "errors": belief in God and belief in the universality and objectivity of reason. Linked to these errors, he maintained, were the institutions of morality that, since the advent of **Christianity**, had required individuals to conform to rules of unselfish conduct and obedience to authority and had fostered the assumption that moral goodness (understood as pure selflessness) represents the highest human good. Nietzsche's mature writings, produced in the decade between 1880 and 1889, amount to a sustained critique of morality and of the metaphysical premises on which it rests. In place of traditional moral **values** of unselfishness, conformity to reason, and subservience to God, his dense, aphoristic books announced a new "table of values" based on the flourishing of creative drives and expression of what Nietzsche called the "**will to power**."

Thus Spoke Zarathustra (1882–1885), his most popular book, expressed this critique in the form of a religious allegory. The sage Zarathustra has retreated to a mountaintop for 10 years. Now, "overfull" with wisdom, he decides to descend among men to share his message of the **death of God** and the "overman," the overcoming of human dependence on God and conventional morality. The overman is Nietzsche's symbol for the "higher" human being who, liberated from the yoke of religion and morality, is able to accept earthly existence without metaphysical support. Significantly, in Nietzsche's fable the overman is not an empirical reality but a future possibility, an ideal of human achievement that may or may not be realized.

Nietzsche's subsequent books addressed similar themes in nonallegorical terms. *Beyond Good and Evil* (1886) and *On the Genealogy of Morality* (1887) presented a sustained critique of traditional moral values and philosophical beliefs. Chief among these was the belief in an autonomous self: a self governed by free will. Nietzsche suggested that the autonomy of the self is a fiction created, among other reasons, to allow for the assignment of moral blame and punishment. In reality, he maintained, a person is a system of competing, often conflicting, "drives," not a unified self or **ego**. A related premise Nietzsche sought to demerit was belief in the objectivity of reason and in a realm of eternal truths that reason discovers. In Nietzsche's account, reason, or the "will to truth," is never purely "disinterested" or objective, but is motivated by ulterior interests like the drive to establish superiority over others, to justify one's preferences, or to suppress the passions.

This idea was expressed by Nietzsche in metaphysical form in the claim that, at bottom, all drives are an expression of an underlying, amoral *will to power*. In response to the Darwinian model of evolution as a struggle for survival, he speculated that living things seek not merely to survive and reproduce but primarily to "*discharge* their strength," to enhance their power. The will to power in human beings is rarely an unimpeded display of force but generally takes more nuanced forms. The artist or philosopher who shapes reality in the image of his or her ideals, or the martyr or statesmen who forgoes self-preservation for the attainment of a higher purpose, is expressing a will to *power*, albeit in the guise of a concern for "truth," "justice," "beauty," or "goodness."

The doctrine of the will to power raises serious philosophical problems for Nietzsche's position. If all human actions express the same will to power, then on what basis can one action be deemed "better" or "higher" than another? How is one value perspective to be justified over another? While Nietzsche was aware of these problems, he did not often address them squarely in his writings. One response offered is that certain values "affirm life" and promote "health," while others deny life and promote "decadence" and decay. The repudiation of the body by Christian morality is for Nietzsche a classic case of a life-denying value, because it denies a necessary condition for human flourishing: bodily health, pleasure, and sensory stimulation. In contrast to the existentialists, Nietzsche's value perspective resembles a form of philosophical naturalism: What is "good" is what tends to help us flourish as natural, sentient, earth-bound beings; what is "bad" is what interferes with our natural flourishing in some way. *See also* PHILOSOPHY OF LIFE.

NIHILISM (from Lat. *nihil,* "nothing"). In philosophy, the view that life lacks meaning or purpose, or alternately, that nothing meaningful can or should be affirmed. The term was first popularized in the 19th century by the Russian novelist **Ivan Turgenev**, with whose work **Friedrich Nietzsche** was familiar. The meaning of the term in existentialism derives from Nietzsche's usage. For Nietzsche, nihilism is occasioned by the **death of God**, the loss of transcendent sources of value in human affairs. Is it possible to live without a transcendent source of value or guarantor of truth? Nietzsche's response is affirmative. Philosophy and religion tend toward nihilism to the extent that, as they evaluate this **world** on the model of an "other world," they devalue earthly existence. To fully overcome nihilism, then, a system of value is needed that makes no reference to other-worldly (eternal, unchanging) existence. This is the task of the "higher men": not simply to negate the **values** of the past but to create *new* values.

Albert Camus rehearsed similar arguments in the 20th century. In *The Myth of Sisyphus*, he reasoned that the main task of philosophy is to ascertain whether life is worth living given that it is **absurd**. Later, in *The Rebel*, he shifted his focus to consider the social and historical causes of nihilism, which he traced to revolutionary political movements that seek to negate the past and to remake the world anew. This was the impulse he saw at work in **Nazism** and Soviet totalitarianism. Thus the proper response to modern nihilism, Camus concluded, was not simply the injunction to "create new values," but to respect the values of solidarity and human dignity as universal human goods.

Many Germans in the 1920s and early 1930s took Nietzsche's diagnosis of nihilism to apply to their historical situation. This was the context for **Martin Heidegger**'s acceptance of German National Socialism as a revolutionary remedy for European decline. *See also* HEIDEGGER AND NAZISM.

NISHITANI, KEIJI (1900–1990). Prominent 20th-century Japanese philosopher influenced by existentialism, in particular by the work of **Martin Heidegger**. Nishitani was conversant with the major currents of modern Western philosophy, including the philosophy of **Immanuel Kant**, **Søren Kierkegaard**, **Friedrich Nietzsche**, and **Friedrich Schelling**, and his original work formed a bridge between Eastern and Western viewpoints, translating Western philosophical insights into the vocabulary of Zen Buddhism and traditional Japanese thought. Nishitani studied with Heidegger at the University of Freiburg from 1936 to 1939. Following the path suggested by Heidegger, he devoted himself to the problem of "**nihilism**," which he understood as the defining issue of 20th-century philosophy. However, Nishitani's approach to nihilism was distinctively non-Western. He understood nihilism in its etymological sense as an experience of "nothingness," and this he linked to the Buddhist concept of "emptiness" (*sunyata*). *Relative* nihilism, or "nihility," he linked to the loss of meaning occasioned by the scientific domination and objectification of nature, the loss of religious faith Nietzsche called the "**death of God**," and the loss of belief in external reality occasioned by philosophical skepticism and idealism. *Absolute* nihilism he equated with the Buddhist concept of emptiness. Absolute nihilism emerges out of a radicalization of nihility that occurs when false dualisms—of self and **world**, spirit and matter, life and **death**, and self and **other**—are overcome through the Buddhist insight into the essential unity of emptiness (or nothingness) and **being**. In this way, Nishitani arrived at a creative synthesis of Buddhist thought and existentialist philosophy, elaborating upon such shared concerns as the problem of **alienation** and of preserving the nonobjectifiable character of **existence** and of being itself.

NIZAN, PAUL (1905–1940). French Marxist political philosopher and novelist, and a close friend of **Jean-Paul Sartre**. Nizan joined the French Communist Party at a young age and quickly rose to become one of its most outspoken intellectual defenders as well as one of the most trenchant critics of the French bourgeoisie, especially the complacent milieu of philosophy professors, which he parodied savagely in the novel *Les Chiens de garde* (1935) (*The Watchdogs*). Nizan resigned from the **Communist** Party after Joseph Stalin signed the German–Soviet Pact of Nonaggression in 1939. Thereafter, he was painted as a traitor by the French communist press. He was killed by the Germans during the retreat to Dunkirk in 1940; his books soon fell out of print, and he was largely forgotten until the republication of his novel *Aden Arabie* (1931) in 1960, for which Sartre provided a moving preface (published in English in *Situations*, 115–173).

Nizan was Sartre's closest friend between about 1921 and 1926 and exerted a lifelong influence. From their high school days at the Lycée Henri IV and the Lycée Louis-le-Grand through their college years at the prestigious **École Normale Supérieure**, the two, referred to playfully by friends as "Nitre and Sarzan," were inseparable. Sartre admired Nizan for his worldliness, his biting sense of irony, and his facility and early success as a writer.

***NO EXIT (HUIS CLOS,* 1944).** This one-act play by Jean-Paul Sartre, an allegory for Sartre's conception of **being-with-others**, remains one of the most widely read works of **existentialist literature**. Sartre wrote the play as a vehicle for two of his female friends, and original rehearsals included **Albert Camus** as director and in the role of Garcin, the male lead. When these plans fell through, the play was staged with a professional cast and director and became a dramatic success, opening in Paris in May 1944. The play is set in hell and takes place in a drawing room decorated with overstuffed "Second Empire" furniture and devoid of mirrors. The three characters, Garcin, Inez, and Estelle, enter one by one and slowly come to terms with their situation. They are dead, have been consigned to hell for their sins, and are to remain together in the same room for eternity, each serving as a mirror to reflect back the qualities of the others. Philosophically, the play is a dramatization of the condition of being-for-others, which Sartre analyzes in **Being and Nothingness**. The **other** "wrenches away" my **freedom** through the look, conferring qualities on me for which I must assume **responsibility** but which I have not chosen and cannot control: "[M]y being-for-others is a fall through absolute emptiness toward objectivity. And this fall is an *alienation*" (BN, 274–275). Garcin's realization at the end of the play that "Hell is other people" should thus be understood to mean, in light of this, not that relations with other people are necessarily antagonistic, but that others tend to fix my identity by their judgments, obscuring my freedom. Garcin realizes that the deplorable "punishment" of being dead is that he is now entirely at the mercy of others whose judgments he can no longer revise through future actions. Sartre makes the same point clearly in *Being and Nothingness*: "[T]o die is to be condemned . . . to exist only through the Other, and to owe to him one's meaning" (BN, 544).

NON-THETIC CONSCIOUSNESS. *See* PREREFLECTIVE CONSCIOUSNESS.

NOTHING/NOTHINGNESS. *See* NEGATION/NOTHINGNESS; "WHAT IS METAPHYSICS?"

– O –

OBJECTIFICATION. *See* OTHER, THE.

OLAFSON, FREDERICK A. *See* ETHICAL VOLUNTARISM.

ONTIC VERSUS ONTOLOGICAL. *See* ONTOLOGICAL DIFFERENCE.

ONTOLOGICAL DIFFERENCE. An expression that refers to the distinction in **Martin Heidegger**'s philosophy between beings and **being**. Beings (*Seinde*) are particular things apprehended through the range of human activities and dispositions; a hammer, a tree, a melody, the past, nature, and God are all beings in the relevant sense. Being (*Sein*) refers to the manner in which things "appear" or are apprehended, the **horizon** against which they emerge as the things they are. Central to Heidegger's argument is the claim that the concept of being is intrinsically indeterminate from the perspective of traditional philosophy and science, eluding attempts at definition and theoretical formulation. Alternately put, both science and philosophy tend to ignore the difference between being and beings, as they seek to reduce being to a determinate entity. Historically, philosophers and theologians have understood being on the model of something **present-at-hand**, the paradigm of which is an unchanging substance or a superentity like God, Nature, or reason. Thus, it is crucial for Heidegger that philosophy be performed in such a way that the **ontological** difference is kept in sight. One example of how this is to be done is, predictably, Heidegger's own philosophy of existence in *Being and Time*. Here, by centering his inquiry around "non-entitative" beings such as *Dasein* and **world**, Heidegger endeavors to approach the question of the meaning of being—that is, in effect, the question of the ontological difference—without falling prey to the reifying tendencies of traditional **metaphysics**.

ONTOLOGY. Traditionally, the branch of **metaphysics** concerned with elucidating types of **being**, of what is "real" or what "exists." The overriding concern of existentialism is **ontological**: to elucidate the nature of human **existence**. Existentialists maintain that an appropriate account of the human being requires categories distinct from the categories of natural science applied to the physical world or the categories of theology applied to God. They also generally insist that ontological questions (concerning the nature of the human being) have precedence over other philosophical questions, in that all other philosophical issues presuppose a conception of the human being. Until this conception is clarified, epistemological and **ethical** questions remain tainted by uncritical ontological assumptions—for example, the assumption that a person is primarily a **knowing subject**.

252 • ORIGINAL CHOICE

The seminal treatment of these issues is found in **Martin Heidegger's** *Being and Time*.

ORIGINAL CHOICE. *See* FUNDAMENTAL PROJECT.

ORTEGA Y GASSET, JOSÉ (1883–1955). Spanish philosopher and essayist. With **Miguel de Unamuno**, Ortega is the main representative of Spanish existentialism. Ortega's account of human existence as embodied and historically **situated** bears similarities to the existentialism of **Martin Heidegger** and **Jean-Paul Sartre** but apparently was developed independently of Heidegger and several years before Sartre published *Being and Nothingness* in 1943. Parallels between the thinkers may derive in part from common intellectual influences such as **Edmund Husserl** and **Wilhelm Dilthey**.

These parallels are at times striking, especially the proximity between Ortega's formulation of ideas and those Sartre arrived at during his mature existentialist period. "I am free *by compulsion*," Ortega wrote in *History as a System* (1941), "whether I wish to be or not. **Freedom** is not an activity pursued by an entity that . . . is already possessed of a fixed being. To be free means to be lacking in constitutive identity . . . to be able to be other than what one was, to be unable to install oneself once and for all in any given being" (203).

After receiving his doctorate in philosophy from the University of Madrid in 1904, Ortega studied in Germany for five years, where he became familiar with the work of Husserl and Dilthey and was a disciple of the **neo-Kantian** philosopher Hermann Cohen at the University of Marburg. In 1910, he became professor of philosophy at the University of Madrid and remained there until the outbreak of the Spanish Civil War in 1936. In 1923, he founded the *Revista de Occidente*, a review that helped introduce German thought into Spain. Between 1923 and 1930, he was an active opponent of the dictatorship of Primo de Rivera, and later served in the Spanish parliament and as civil governor of Madrid. He spent the civil war in exile in Argentina and in Western Europe, returning to Madrid in 1948, where he founded the Institute of Humanities.

Ortega had exceptional literary talent and was best known for his essays and general-interest articles. He published few technical philosophical works, and his philosophy was expounded mainly in his university lectures. His existentialist writings include *Meditations on Quijote* (*Meditaciones del Quijote*,1914), *The Modern Theme* (*El tema de nuestro tiempo*, 1923), *Man in Crisis* (*En torno a Galileo*, 1933), and *History as a System* (*Historia como sistema*, 1941).

OTHER, THE. Existentialists offer a range of interpretations of concepts of the other, otherness, and alterity, which does not lend itself to brief summary. A common feature of most existentialist accounts is their derivation from **G. W. F. Hegel**'s treatment of otherness in *Phenomenology of Spirit*, and in particular Hegel's account of the **master–slave dialectic.** For Hegel, the other is another human consciousness who appears as alien to the self and is initially treated as an object to be subdued or destroyed. Eventually, the antagonism of self and other is played out in a "struggle for recognition" in which each confronts the other in an attempt to extract from it acknowledgment of its own subjectivity. **Jean-Paul Sartre** explores the ramifications of this Hegelian paradigm in *Being and Nothingness.* In Sartre's analysis, the encounter with the other is contrasted with the relation to nonhuman objects. Nonhuman objects may be freely **"negated"** and invested with significance by **consciousness.** In contrast, other human beings are alternate centers of consciousness, irreducible to what I think or perceive of them. The **being** of the other is thus primarily evidenced through the phenomenon of what Sartre calls *the look* (*le regard*). The look is the experience of being seen and judged by others, though not necessarily by particular **concrete** individuals. Rather, the look suffuses the interhuman world, where the experience of being praised, blamed, or interpreted in some other way by others is essential to self-understanding. The look is thus a constitutive feature of **existence**, not merely a contingent occurrence. To consider Sartre's example, when, peeping through a keyhole, I hear footsteps down the hall and realize that someone is looking at me, "I am suddenly affected in my being and . . . essential modifications appear in my structure" (BN, 260). That is, through the look of the other, an aspect of my identity becomes "fixed" and "objectified"; I am (in part) an object for the other, a "peeping Tom." Hence, the other "robs me of my **freedom**" in that it represents an element of **facticity** I can neither control nor simply ignore. The look of the other brings home to me that "I *am no longer master of the situation*"

(BN, 265). For this reason, Sartre qualifies the experience of the other as one of "shame," "the original feeling of having my being outside" (BN, 288).

Sartre's antagonistic view of otherness is tempered by the notion of **reciprocity** stressed more effectively by other existentialists. Reciprocity is, in Sartre's own words, the recognition that "I need the mediation of the Other in order to be what I am" (BN, 289). **Simone de Beauvoir** gives voice to such a conception in *The Ethics of Ambiguity*. **Martin Buber** in turn offers a contrasting account of the other premised on the notion of **dialogue** between I and You. Similarly, **Gabriel Marcel** and **Karl Jaspers** understand the other as primarily the other person with whom I enter into intimate **communication**. Despite these differences, existentialists agree on at least two points. First, relation to the other is constitutive of selfhood, and second, the issue of the other cannot be reduced to an intellectual problem, such as the "problem of other minds," which arises from the intellectualist perspective of traditional philosophy.

OTHERS. *See* BEING-WITH-OTHERS.

OVERMAN. *See* NIETZSCHE, FRIEDRICH.

– P –

PARADOX. *See FEAR AND TREMBLING*; KIERKEGAARD, SØREN.

PARTISAN REVIEW. American literary magazine affiliated in the 1930s with the radical and **communist** left. After about 1937, the *Partisan Review* developed an independent political perspective. The magazine published some of the earliest American accounts of existentialist philosophy, among them **Hannah Arendt**'s winter 1946 article, "What Is *Existenz* Philosophy?" and a more extensive treatment, "What Is Existentialism? (series no. 2, 1947), by **William Barrett**, at the time the *Partisan Review* editor. The review also published a distinguished list of literary modernists, including **Samuel Beckett**, T. S. Eliot, and Wallace Stevens.

PASSION. *See* EMOTION; MOOD.

PERCEPTION. *See* MERLEAU-PONTY, MAURICE.

PERSON. *See* DASEIN; EGO.

PHENOMENAL FIELD. For **Maurice Merleau-Ponty**, perception is understood as a **prereflective** constitution of meaning through the agency of the **body**. In *Phenomenology of Perception*, Merleau-Ponty described the subject of perception as the "lived body" or "phenomenal body," in contrast to the "objective body" analyzed by science. The lived body is both subjective and objective, mental and physical; it is essentially **ambiguous** in **ontological** status. In turn, Merleau-Ponty argued that the world revealed in perception is a *phenomenal field*—a tissue of tacit meanings and possibilities activated through the dispositions of the body—and not a system of mental **representations** or an array of isolated physical objects.

PHENOMENOLOGICAL REDUCTION. In the **phenomenology** of **Edmund Husserl**, the process of "leading back" **consciousness**, from an ordinary stance in which the **world** is the focus of attention, to a reflective stance, in which consciousness itself becomes the focus. Husserl saw the reduction as crucial to phenomenology. Its goal is to "bracket" assumptions about the existence of the world in order to bring into focus the necessary features of how the world is experienced by consciousness. The particular processes and "syntheses" through which things are perceived, remembered, felt, imagined, and so forth, Husserl believed to have an invariable and universal form. Describing these is the primary aim of phenomenology.

Husserl proposed different versions of the phenomenological reduction throughout his career, in each case trying to formulate the specific manner in which philosophy can justify its claims to privileged status over the perspective of ordinary experience and that of the sciences. Common to all of these is the idea that phenomenology leads back to an apprehension of **essences**—the essential meanings of conscious acts and the mental objects they intend—through acts of intuition purified of empirical distortions and prejudices such as may be sedimented into our "natural attitude." The dominant view in

Husserl's later thought was that the reduction leads the philosopher back to a transcendental sphere of subjectivity, a vantage point inhabited not by an empirical self but by a transcendental **ego**, the universal perspective of a rational mind. As a rule, existentialists rejected the transcendental reduction as an illegitimate form of idealism. For **Martin Heidegger**, **Jean-Paul Sartre**, and **Maurice Merleau-Ponty**, the notion of the transcendental ego was itself based on the idealist (Cartesian and Kantian) prejudice that a human being is essentially an inner sphere of mental activity, a **knowing subject** independent of **body** and world. Heidegger maintained that because the human being exists in the manner of **being-in-the-world**, no reduction beyond the empirical historical **horizon** of the world is possible. Phenomenology, for Heidegger, thus became **hermeneutic** phenomenology. Merleau-Ponty concurred with Heidegger on this point: "[T]he most important lesson which the reduction teaches us is the impossibility of a complete reduction. This is why Husserl is constantly reexamining the possibility of the reduction. If we were absolute mind, the reduction would represent no problem" (PP, xiv). For Merleau-Ponty, consciousness is irreducibly embodied and so cannot transcend the **situated** historical perspective of an embodied being. Accordingly, for him, the goal of phenomenology was not to suspend concrete empirical involvements but merely to "[slacken] the intentional threads which attach us to the world and thus [bring] them to our notice" (PP, xiii). It should be noted that existentialists nonetheless accepted the general sense in which phenomenological description can "lead back" beyond **everyday** prejudices to a more appropriate **understanding** of the world and of ourselves. *See also* LIFE-WORLD.

PHENOMENOLOGY. Form of early 20th-century German philosophy, founded by **Edmund Husserl** and instrumental in the development of existentialism. The aim of phenomenology was to identify and describe the invariant structures of human **consciousness**, that is, to describe the essential meanings underlying our most basic perceptions and judgments about the **world**. By clarifying the basic components of cognitive experience, phenomenology hoped to provide a foundation for all knowledge. In its mature form, phenomenology was conceived by Husserl as "transcendental phenomenology." From this perspective, objects in the world are understood as correlates of a generalized human consciousness, and the goal of philosophy is to clarify how various types of objects are "constituted" in consciousness. Husserl's project of a transcendental phenomenology was thus aligned with the philosophy of both **Immanuel Kant** and **René Descartes**. Like Kant's, it sought to identify universal laws according to which the mind actively organizes the data received through the senses. Like Descartes's, it sought to ground philosophy in moments of absolute first-person certainty. Existentialists rejected the goals of transcendental phenomenology, in particular the privileging of ostensibly transparent mental awareness of the **knowing subject**. They advocated instead **existential phenomenology**, which recognized the centrality of embodied agency and **moods** in the constitution of the world.

The starting point for the phenomenologist is the premise of the intentionality of consciousness: that mental processes "point to" or "intend" objects outside of themselves, that they are necessarily *of* or *about* something. Because most human mental experience is intentional, it cannot be reduced to sub-mental (physiological and neurological) events, which occur without intentional reference. Perception is necessarily directed to *something perceived*, just as emotion is directed to *something felt*, and imagination to *something imagined*. Divorced from its appropriate intentional reference, mental experience becomes incomprehensible—a meaningless jumble of sensations. Intentionality thus preserves the irreducibility of mental experience. It also renders unnecessary the distinction between "real" and "unreal" or fictional objects; all objects of experience—perceptual, imaginary, or otherwise—are of interest to the phenomenologist, for each reveals what is true of a specific type of mental process. The phenomenologist's goal is to uncover the essential structures of the various possible types of consciousness—the unchanging "meanings" according to which each mental process is organized. Husserl thought it possible to grasp such essential meanings directly in intuition. To do so, he proposed the technique of the **phenomenological reduction**, whereby beliefs about the external world are "bracketed" and attention is redirected to the process of consciousness itself.

Existentialists such as **Martin Heidegger**, **Maurice Merleau-Ponty**, and **Jean-Paul Sartre** saw themselves as pursuing a type of

258 • *PHENOMENOLOGY OF PERCEPTION*

phenomenology in their mature thought. However, they rejected those aspects of Husserl's thought they believed to be vitiated by uncritical intellectualism and idealism. Generally, they accepted the premises that philosophy is descriptive rather than explanatory or evaluative and that it must focus on how things are "given in" human experience, rather than how they are "in themselves," for example, how they are construed from the perspective of scientific **naturalism**. Yet they rejected the privileging of epistemological concerns and the foundationalist premise, according to which knowledge can be grounded in experiences of intellectual certainty. Heidegger argued for the priority of practical and emotional attitudes in the constitution of human **being-in-the-world**. Similarly, Merleau-Ponty presented embodiment as a necessary condition for knowledge and identified "prepredicative" perception as the ground for theoretical judgments. Sartre stressed the "nothingness" of consciousness and the illusory character of the transcendental and empirical **ego**. Thus, while existentialists preserved many of Husserl's insights, they pressed them into service in new contexts, such as the phenomenology of practical attitudes, art, **freedom**, moral **choice**, and sexuality. *See also* SCHELER, MAX.

PHENOMENOLOGY OF PERCEPTION. *See* MERLEAU-PONTY, MAURICE.

PHENOMENOLOGY OF SPIRIT. *See* HEGEL, G. W. F.

PHENOMENON AND NOUMENON. Taken literally, the Greek term *phenomenon* means "something that appears," and *noumenon* means "something that is apprehended by thought." **Immanuel Kant** employs these terms to express a distinction between the **world** as it is experienced through the senses (the world as "appearance" or "phenomenom") and the world as it is "in itself" (the "noumenon" or "thing-in-itself"). According to Kant, the world of human experience, which forms the basis of empirical science, is phenomenal because it is essentially sensory. Objects we perceive must occur in space and time, and the categories of **understanding** that guide our thought apply only to spatial and temporal objects. As we have no access to how things stand outside of space and time, we have no knowledge of noumenal reality. Ideas we form of such reality, such as conceptions of God or of the soul, are illegitimate when passed off as knowledge (as in proofs of God's existence), though valuable as moral guides.

PHILOSOPHICAL ANTHROPOLOGY. The philosophical study of the human being. In a general sense, a form of philosophical anthropology was pursued by various European philosophers in the 1920s and 1930s, including thinkers like **Martin Buber**, **Martin Heidegger**, and **José Ortega y Gasset**, each of whom endeavored to describe the human being in a language distinct from that of natural and social science. In a narrower sense, philosophical anthropology is associated with the German philosopher **Max Scheler**. Scheler's most detailed account of philosophical anthropology was given in *Man's Place in Nature* (1928).

In Scheler's view, philosophical anthropology seeks a concrete yet philosophically nuanced answer to the question, "What Is Man?" Scheler proposes a synthesis of naturalistic accounts, such as those of Charles Darwin and **Sigmund Freud**, which assimilate human beings to other animals, with classical religious and philosophical views about human uniqueness. He arrives at a compromise whereby human "spirit" (*Geist*)—the capacity to reason, to will, and to experience such "higher" **emotions** as love, reverence, and wonder—is in essence distinguishable from the conditions of "life"—physical needs, drives, and desires. In practice, however, spirit requires the energies of life to be effectively expressed, and so spirit is generally expressed in an impure form.

Scheler's concern for human existence, along with his interest in Husserlian phenomenology, overlap significantly with the concerns of German existentialism, especially those of Martin Heidegger, and the two approaches were often not clearly distinguished at the time. For one thing, Scheler's account in *Man's Place in Nature* appears to be indebted to Heidegger's conception of *Dasein* as **being-in-the-world**. Yet Heidegger took pains to distinguish his "**fundamental ontology**" from philosophical anthropology as well as from the "**philosophy of life**." Heidegger maintains that these approaches (the former represented by thinkers like Scheler and Helmuth Plessner, the latter by **Wilhelm Dilthey** and **Henri Bergson**), because they uncritically accept traditional concepts of "body," "mind," "nature," "spirit," and "life," remain within the ambit of traditional science and

metaphysics. Thus, he claims, they "fail to give an . . . ontologically adequate answer to the question about the *kind of Being* which belongs to those entities which we ourselves are" (BT, 50).

Heidegger's distinction between philosophical anthropology and "fundamental ontology," however, is itself open to criticism. How is one to gain concrete understanding of human beings if not through critical reflection upon the empirical study of actual human cultures and individuals, as proposed by sciences like cultural anthropology, history, sociology, and psychology? If fundamental ontology can in fact transcend empirical or "ontical" knowledge, does it not do so at the risk of making empty abstractions and unjustified generalizations? Such criticism was leveled against Heidegger's method by Buber, among others.

PHILOSOPHIZING. For German **philosophers of existence Martin Heidegger** and **Karl Jaspers**, this term refers to the existentially transformative power of genuine philosophical thinking. Philosophy for them is something more than an intellectual exercise or a cultural and historical tradition: to philosophize is to be gripped by the problems one encounters, not merely to contemplate or analyze them at a distance. Removed from the concerns and prejudices of **everyday** life, true philosophizing thus brings one closer to the possibilities of **authentic existence**.

Jaspers employs the German term *Philosophieren*, in place of the standard *Philosophie*, to describe his own thought and all genuine philosophical thought. Use of the verbal form highlights the dynamic, open-ended, and **communicative** character of philosophical inquiry, in contrast to nonphilosophical (e.g., scientific) justification of theses or doctrines. According to Jaspers, philosophizing is an "appeal to possibilities" that aims to "generate something in the thinker by way of movements of thought" rather than to persuade him or her of the truth of particular positions or arguments. The authentic aim of philosophy, for Jaspers, is thus not simply to describe but to enact the conditions of *Existenz* in oneself and in others: "to incite the thought-acts which teach one to see and to converse with oneself" (PKJ, 824, 836). Alternately, "Philosophic thinking, leads me to my very self . . . it awakens the sources within me which ultimately give meaning even to science itself" (PKJ, 38). Philosophizing is thus contrasted to scientific inquiry, which seeks certain, verifiable, objective knowledge of the **world**, independent of the condition of the knower. Yet science "cannot understand why it itself exists" and thus "does not reveal the meaning of life, provides no guidance." Finally, philosophizing for Jaspers has an **ethical** dimension. It is an appeal to others that **awakens** an appreciation of their own **freedom**, rather than "seducing" them to "evade" their freedom by identifying themselves with impersonal theories and propositions. Philosophy accomplishes this appeal not by trying to explain the world but simply by illuminating its possibilities.

At the height of his existentialist period, during the late 1920s, Heidegger shares a similar view of the transformative power of philosophy. Philosophy is not an activity in which the human being can maintain a detached, neutral perspective on the subject of inquiry. Rather, philosophy takes hold of the philosopher, implicating the inquirer in the inquiry and occasioning reflection on its very **being**: "[I]n the philosophical concept [*Begriff*], man . . . is in the *grip of an attack* [*Angriff*]—driven out of everydayness and driven back into the ground of things" (FCM, 21). For Heidegger, all genuine philosophizing occasions a **mood** of both wonder and **anxiety**, from out of which the whole of being, including human being, appears in a new light, freed from the objectifying prejudices of science and the stultifying conventions of society. Philosophizing is thus linked importantly to **authenticity**: "[P]hilosophizing . . . constitutes the fundamental occurrence of **Dasein**" (FCM, 22), and the "setting-free of the Dasein in man must be the sole and central [thing] which philosophy as philosophizing can perform" (KPM, 178).

PHILOSOPHY OF EXISTENCE (Ger. *Existenzphilosophie*). "Philosophy of existence" is the common label for German existentialism, which flourished primarily in university circles in Weimar Germany during the late 1920s and 1930s. Its major representatives were **Karl Jaspers** and **Martin Heidegger**. *Existenzphilosophie* sought to reorient the predominantly epistemological and **metaphysical** concerns of German philosophy around problems of **concrete**, personal human **existence**.

The term is associated particularly with Karl Jaspers. Starting in the 1930s, Jaspers employed this rubric to refer to his own thought and to a range of thinkers, such as **Søren Kierkegaard** and **Friedrich Nietzsche**, for whom philosophy is essentially a personal quest for meaning rather than an impersonal search for objective knowledge. According to Jaspers, *Existenzphilosophie* "is the way of thought by means of which man seeks to become himself . . . . [It] does not cognize objects, but elucidates and makes actual the being of the thinker . . . . It **awakens** what it itself does not know; it elucidates and gives impetus, but it does not fixate" (MMA, 159, 161). The distinctive character of the philosophy of existence is brought out in contrast with positive sciences such as sociology, psychology, and anthropology. While the latter seek to objectify human beings as instances of universal laws and patterns of behavior, Jaspers asserts, the philosophy of existence brings into focus the essentially nonobjective dimensions of human being: individual **freedom** and spontaneity, which Jaspers calls "*Existenz*," and the relation to "**transcendence**," an awareness of something greater than oneself, the horizon **encompassing** all possible experiences. It is worth noting that Jaspers's account of the historical development of the philosophy of existence in **Friedrich Schelling**, Kierkegaard, and Nietzsche has been preserved by most later accounts of existentialism.

According to F. H. Heinemann, the origins of the term in print can be traced back to Heinemann's 1929 book *Neue Wege der Philosophie* (*New Paths in Philosophy*), in which *Existenzphilosophie* was employed as a label for the then emergent thought of Jaspers and Heidegger on the basis of their shared debt to **Søren Kierkegaard** (*Existentialism and the Modern Predicament*, 1). Jaspers corroborates Heinemann's account in the appendix of his own book of the same name, *Philosophy of Existence*, originally published in 1938 (PE, 95). During the 1930s, the phrase "*philosophie de l'existence*" gained currency among French philosophers to refer to thinkers like Jaspers, Heidegger, Nietzsche, and Kierkegaard, as well as to emerging French philosophers such as **Gabriel Marcel**.

PHILOSOPHY OF LIFE (Ger. *Lebensphilosophie*). *Lebensphilosophie*, philosophy of life, coincides in many respects with what in English is commonly called *vitalism*. Broadly, it refers to a trend in late 19th- and early 20th-century European philosophy, especially German and French philosophy, distinguished by its focus on "life," "lived experience" or "vital force" as the fundamental motor of human experience and as a feature of organic nature that defies explanation by mechanical causes. The philosophy of life flourished during the last decades of the 19th century until about the first decade of the 20th century. It was the immediate predecessor to the **philosophy of existence**, and the concerns of the two movements overlapped significantly. Both proposed a critique of philosophical and scientific abstraction, and both attempted to provide an alternative conception of human life to that offered by scientific materialism, on the one hand, and by philosophical **idealism** and rationalism, on the other.

The philosophy of life, however, was not an organized movement but a rubric that linked together certain philosophers, based on shared interests and assumptions. **Henri Bergson**, **Wilhelm Dilthey**, and **Friederich Nietzsche** are generally recognized as its major proponents. Each devoted himself to the study of life as immediately experienced, and each held that life in its immediacy, spontaneity, and **historical** particularity is beyond the purchase of positive science and abstract philosophy. Their viewpoint was anticipated earlier in the 19th century by **Arthur Schopenhauer**, who maintained that all organisms are guided by an unconscious will to live; Schopenhauer was particularly influential on Nietzsche, especially in Nietzsche's early works.

Continuities between the philosophy of life and the philosophy of existence are apparent. Dilthey's experiential "categories of life," Bergson's "*élan vital*," and Nietzsche's view of life as **will-to-power** each exerted influence on subsequent existentialist thinkers. A point of difference between the two trends was life philosophers' interest in organic nature beyond the human sphere and their general concern for biological and physiological aspects of human life, areas in which existentialists generally showed little interest. In contrast to existentialists, philosophers of life directly confronted challenges of Darwinian biology that were pressing at the end of the 19th century. This was the context, for example, of Bergson's and Nietzsche's identification of a "life force" or "will to power" essential to organic processes yet irreducible to mechanical laws of nature. In contrast, existentialists regarded human **existence** as unique and incomparable to other forms of life.

Dilthey's central contribution to philosophy of life was his distinction between the so-called human sciences (*Geisteswissenschaften*) such as anthropology, psychology, history, and philosophy, whose object is to account for human life as it is experienced by conscious human beings, and the natural sciences, whose object is to explain phenomena, including human consciousness, in terms of nonconscious physical processes. In contrast to the causal explanation (*Erklärung*) employed by natural science, human science requires **hermeneutical understanding** (*Verstehen*), that is, a grasp of the lived meanings of ideas, acts, and artifacts experienced by the inhabitants of particular cultures and historical periods. Because the lived experiences (*Erlebnisse*) of these meanings is constantly changing and developing in the lives of particular individuals and in the historical growth of cultures, no laws can formalize human consciousness, and a formal science of human life and culture modeled on natural science is a grievous mistake. Dilthey's defense of the autonomy of the human sciences based on hermeneutical understanding, lived experience, and **historicality** exerted a profound influence on **Martin Heidegger**'s analysis of human existence in *Being and Time*. In particular, Dilthey provided a framework for Heidegger's recasting of **phenomenology** in terms of hermeneutic understanding, the **hermeneutic circle**, and historicality as constitutive components of existence.

Bergson's major statement of life philosophy, *Creative Evolution* (1907), proposed a theory of biological evolution based on a nonmaterial life force (*élan vital*), which contested the ability of mechanistic theories such as Darwin's theory of natural selection to account for unpredictable or "creative" developments in human evolution and culture. Bergson's view of the fluid, nonsubstantial character of **consciousness** as well as his emphasis on intuition over intellect in the account of mind are influential for French existentialists such as **Jean-Paul Sartre**, **Maurice Merleau-Ponty**, and **Gabriel Marcel**.

Nietzsche's influence on the philosophy of existence was pervasive and profound. In particular, one may single out his conception of life as an expression of "will-to-power," his critique of philosophical rationalism, and his notion of the **death of God**.

PHILOSOPHY OF THE ABSURD. This phrase was applied to **Albert Camus**'s thought of the early 1940s to distinguish it in particular from **Jean-Paul Sartre's** existentialism, with which it was frequently identified. At the core of Camus's conception of **the absurd** was a notion of the radical **contingency** of the universe and of the heroism required to confront it. These ideas may be contrasted with existentialism's focus on human **freedom**, the power to revise and interpret the world according to one's lights, and on **authenticity**, the ideal of fully coming to grips with one's freedom and **responsibility**. While there are similarities between the two viewpoints—for example, concepts of absurdity and contingency play a role in existentialist thought—the emphasis Camus placed on the absurd as an irremediable feature of the **world** and on the tragedy of the **human condition** as a confrontation with absurdity distinguishes his perspective from that of the existentialists.

Camus elaborated his philosophy of the absurd in *The Myth of Sisyphus*. While we seek to understand ourselves and the world, we can discover no reasons for our **existence** and are haunted by a feeling of absurdity. Morality, religion, science, and philosophy purport to discover unchanging, universal principles and **values**; however, **death**, chance, and the impenetrability of human motives render life essentially incomprehensible and controvert claims for **transcendent** meaning. The experience of the absurd thus brings into focus what Camus calls the "fundamental question of philosophy": "whether life," stripped of its illusions, "is or is not worth living" (MS, 3).

An affirmative answer to this question is outlined in Camus's retelling of the Greek myth of Sisyphus. In Camus's hands, Sisyphus becomes the exemplary "absurd hero." Condemned to roll a rock up the same mountain for eternity, Sisyphus acknowledges the absurdity of his condition—that life's goals and accomplishments may be erased (e.g., by death) at any moment and with no justification—at the same time that he derives motivation from it. Instead of being crushed by his predicament, he lives passionately in defiance of the absurd.

A more problematic portrait of the absurd hero was given in Camus's novel *The Stranger*, also published in 1942. Meursault, the novel's protagonist, is an unrepentant murderer. Having senselessly killed an Arab man "because of the sun" on a hot beach, Meursault is in prison awaiting his execution when he is stirred by a priest's harangue for repentence: "I was . . . sure of my life and sure of the death I had waiting for me. . . . I had lived my life one way and could just as well have lived it another . . . nothing mattered, and I knew why"

(*The Stranger*, 120–121). What Meursault knows is that life is absurd. The problem, which Camus attempted to address in subsequent works like **The Rebel**, is that, if life is absurd, then it would appear that "all is permitted": "If one believes in nothing, if nothing makes sense, if we can assert no value whatsoever, everything is permissible and nothing is important" (*The Rebel*, 13). This problem was seized on by critics like **Gabriel Marcel**, who criticized Camus's conception of the absurd as "pure and simple imposture . . . [a] . . . blinding gesture by which all that humanity has ever acquired is swept away and we are thrust headlong into . . . a Narcissism of nothingness" (HV, 211–212).

An avenue of response was suggested by Camus's contention that the struggle against absurdity is itself intrinsically valuable because it endows life with dignity and purpose. If this is the case, then the philosophy of the absurd can at least defeat the charge of **nihilism**, the view that there are no intrinsic values. Indeed, Sisyphus and Meursault are not nihilists, in that they cling to the happiness of earthly existence as an ultimate good. The more difficult question is how the absurdist position overcomes moral relativism—the view that "everything is permissible," even, for example, killing another person. In writings subsequent to *The Stranger*, such as **The Plague** (1947) and *The Rebel* (1951), Camus acknowledged the limits of the absurdist position. He reframed his philosophy of the absurd in terms of a philosophy of "rebellion" that recognized courage, freedom, dignity, compassion, and solidarity with others as universal human values.

PHYSIS (Greek "nature"). **Martin Heidegger** contrasts the modern **understanding** of **being** as **presence-at-hand** with the ancient Greek understanding of being as *physis* (nature). A key to the meaning of the Greek term is found in its Latin translation, *natura*, which derives from *nasci*, "to be born," "to grow," "to spring forth." Similarly, for Heidegger the core meaning of the Greek *physis* is "growth," "emerging forth." Heidegger insists that *physis* should not be understood in terms of modern conceptions of nature, for example, as the object of natural science or as a contrast term to what is human. Rather, the ancient Greek experience of *physis* refers to a range of patterns of growth and change in both human and nonhuman domains: the growth of plants and animals, the changing of the seasons, and the movement of the sun and moon, as well as patterns of human procreation, birth, aging, and **death**. *Physis* is thus a fundamental category for ancient Greek experience, one that captures the manner in which things maintain themselves in existence by a certain effort, standing out from a background of darkness and mystery into which they eventually return. In Heidegger's definition, *physis* is the "prevailing of beings as a whole . . . which prevails through and around [human beings]" (*The Fundamental Concepts of Metaphysics*, 25–26).

When, around the time of Plato, Greek philosophy comes to judge being by a standard of unchanging presence, exemplified in philosophical concepts of **substance** and **essence**, the emergent and mysterious character of *physis* is lost. Moreover, according to Heidegger, once the experience of *physis* is replaced by that of unchanging presence, human beings come to understand themselves as unchanging rational souls or minds that stand apart from the processes of **nature**. In Heidegger's view, the "forgetting" of ancient Greek experience is completed in the modern scientific conception of nature as the realm of physical things moved by purely mechanical forces. Heidegger's interpretation of *physis* is an example of what he refers to as **authentic** "repetition" of the past, one that recuperates past possibilities in the service of a deeper understanding of the present.

POETRY AND PHILOSOPHY. Martin Heidegger was unique among existentialists for his appreciation of the philosophical power of poetry: its ability to reveal truth, or alternately, to disclose **being**. Heidegger was also attentive to the poetic nature of philosophy, maintaining that "the ultimate business of philosophy is to preserve the *force of the most elemental words* . . . to keep the common understanding from **leveling** them off" (BT, 262). In his later thought, Heidegger recognized poetry as a mode of **authentic** speech that bears comparison to philosophy in its capacity to preserve the force of elemental words and disclose the significance of things. Specifically for Heidegger, poetry bears witness to the interrelationship of human beings, **world**, and being, a nexus of relationships that Heidegger comes to refer to as the "event" (*Ereignis*) of being. Unlike the scientist who remains blinkered by merely "calculative" thinking, the poet is attuned to the **mystery** of the event of being and to the resonance of language in which this mystery is attested. Thus, as much or more so than the philosopher, the poet is able to "bring the world to presence," creating for the reader a palpable experience of the mystery and significance of things. In this manner, poetry is the antidote to the "idle chatter" of everyday life; it "has always so much world space to spare that in it each thing—a tree, a mountain, a house, the cry of a bird—loses all indifference and commonplaceness" (IM, 26). While in philosophy a similar goal may be accomplished through analysis and interpretation, in poetry it is realized directly and spontaneously. In Heidegger's estimation, the poets most successful at this task include the German Romantic poets Friedrich Hölderlin (1770–1843), Rainer Maria Rilke (1875–1926), and Georg Trakl (1887–1914).

POLITICS. It is not surprising that existentialists express little interest in a theory of politics, given their focus on individual **freedom**, **responsibility**, and **authenticity** and their corresponding appraisal of collective life as generally inhibiting authentic **existence**. An exception is **Maurice Merleau-Ponty**, who devotes considerable attention to **Marxist** philosophy starting in 1945, with the aim of effecting a *rapprochement* between Karl Marx's views and his own version of **existential phenomenology**. **Jean-Paul Sartre**'s references to Marxism are somewhat abstract until his "conversion" to **communism** in 1952, after which he immerses himself for a time in the empirical details of French politics and abandons philosophical writings. However, when Sartre resumes his theoretical **project** in *Critique of Dialectical Reason* (1960), his own attempt at a synthesis of Marxism and existentialism, his concerns have shifted beyond those of existentialism. On the whole, Sartre's and Merleau-Ponty's forays into political philosophy remain fairly general and abstract, neither thinker ever advancing, for example, a specific theory of the state, citizenship, or justice. The same must be said of **Albert Camus**'s treatment of political issues in *The Rebel*, for, despite an ostensibly historical framework, Camus's empirical references serve mainly to illustrate an a priori conception of rebellion, which he understands as a universal and ahistorical human possibility.

Beyond Sartre's and Merleau-Ponty's critical engagement with communism, the most notorious existentialist involvement in politics is **Martin Heidegger**'s membership in the **Nazi** Party and his tenure as rector of Freiburg University. Heidegger's case in particular has received extensive critical treatment. Especially since the publication in 1986 of Victor Farias's book, *Heidegger and Nazism*, Heidegger's rectorship at Freiburg University between April 1933 and April 1934, and his apparent endorsement of Nazi ideology in his "Rectoral Address" and texts of the time such as *An Introduction to Metaphysics*, have raised important questions about the relationship between his existentialist philosophy and his politics. Was Heidegger's Nazi involvement merely the result of poor judgment, or was it linked internally to his philosophy in some fashion? Some critics who attempt to defend the latter view have suggested that the notion of **authenticity** proposed in *Being and Time* is tainted with a kind of romantic nationalism, antidemocratic spirit, and even immoralism consistent with Nazi ideology. Such critics point to Heidegger's appeal to fate and to the collective destiny of a people, his rejection of the social conventions of *das Man*, and his celebration of the "groundlessness" of authentic decision as evidence for this view. However, it must be recalled that similarly radical ideas were not uncommon among German intellectuals in the 1920s and early 1930s, when an atmosphere of social and economic crisis led many to question the efficacy of the Weimar democracy. Moreover, while Heidegger's account of authenticity may have **decisionist** elements that support the critique of moral conventions, it also assigns important roles to concepts of **guilt**, **conscience**, **responsibility**, and **freedom**, which suggest a type of moral framework. *See also* HEIDEGGER AND NAZISM; MARXISM.

POSITIVISM. In a general sense, the term "positivism" in French and German designates what in English is usually called "scientific materialism," the attempt to reduce all phenomena to physical facts that can be confirmed by scientific observation. In a narrow sense, positivism refers to the French tradition of scientific empiricism founded by Auguste Comte in the mid-19th century, which looked to science as the model of plain or "positive" facts according to which all else should be explained. In the 20th century, French positivism became a more diffuse trend and the term was used loosely to describe any view that sought to reduce philosophy to science, or to model the human sciences, like sociology or psychology, after the natural sciences. For **Jean-Paul Sartre**, positivism's denial of **freedom** is so deeply flawed that it may be rejected out of hand as a philosophical position.

POSSIBILITY. *See* PROJECT/PROJECTION.

PRAGMATISM. Pragmatism became the dominant form of American philosophy by the early 20th century. Each of the three major American pragmatists, Charles Sanders Peirce, **William James**, and John Dewey, defended a version of the idea that the truth is "what works" in practical experience. According to the pragmatists, because truth cannot be attained by abstract reasoning based on a priori principles, all forms of philosophical idealism and rationalist **metaphysics** that claim to attain certainty prior to and independent of verification in experience are fundamentally misguided. Interpreters have long noted similarities between pragmatism and existentialism, particularly their shared criticism of idealism and rationalism as illegitimate abstractions from **concrete** experience. In this regard, William James, whose influential book *Pragmatism: A New Name for Some Old Ways of Thinking* (1907) first popularized the doctrine in America, and who was publicly recognized as the spokesman for the movement, has been seen as the most existentialist of the pragmatists. In contrast to Peirce, for whom pragmatism referred to objective confirmation by empirical observation of an idea or statement, as in a scientific experiment that proves a prediction, James developed a more subjective version of pragmatism that acknowledged **emotional** experiences—moral, aesthetic, religious—as indexes of truth and **value**.

James's understanding of the "stream of **consciousness**" is another point of connection with existentialism, especially with Sartre's understanding of consciousness as a pure spontaneity that re-creates itself at every moment. James's view, developed in *Principles of Psychology* (1890), was familiar to Sartre, who understood it as analogous to **Henri Bergson**'s conception of the duration of consciousness (BN, 610).

One of the earliest French appraisals of the trend toward **existence** in contemporary philosophy, **Jean Wahl**'s *Toward the Concrete*, examines the thought of William James alongside that of Alfred North Whitehead and **Gabriel Marcel**. Wahl perceives in all three thinkers a common concern for concrete, lived experience and a common discontent with the primacy of the **knowing subject**, issues that also characterized the **philosophy of existence** then on the rise in Germany. **Karl Jaspers** recognizes American pragmatism as "a sort of preliminary stage" in the philosophy of existence. "In its assault against traditional idealism, Pragmatism seemed to be laying new foundations." However, Jaspers's assessment is ultimately critical: "[W]hat it built thereon was nothing more than an aggregate of crude analysis of life and cheap optimism" (MMA, 160).

PREREFLECTIVE CONSCIOUSNESS. For **existential phenomenologists**, such as **Martin Heidegger**, **Maurice Merleau-Ponty**, and **Jean-Paul Sartre**, a fundamental error of traditional philosophy and science is to take the reflective attitude characteristic of philosophical thinking and scientific theorizing as the norm of human awareness. Simple **phenomenological** observation suggests, rather, that reflection is a special case derived from a more basic prereflective awareness. Variously referred to as the "prereflective cogito," "nonthetic consciousness," "prepositional consciousness," or the "tacit cogito," prereflective consciousness designates an ordinary, unselfconscious mode of awareness that existentialists take to predominate in human activities. Much of the time we are immersed in the meaning of the things with which we are involved, without becoming reflectively aware of what we are doing. In Sartre's example, if I count the cigarettes I have in my case, I am aware of the cigarettes being counted, not of the activity of counting. Yet when asked what I am doing, I can say immediately that I am counting. Sartre concludes that this suggests the primacy of a "pre-reflective *cogito*," an "immediate, non-cognitive relation of the self to itself," which cannot be confused with reflective awareness or knowledge (BN, liii). Heidegger takes a more extreme stance. In *Being and Time*, he rejects the language of consciousness altogether as hopelessly subjectivist. Instead, he characterizes human **being-in-the-world** as an immersion in practical tasks "**ready-to-hand**," an attunement to **moods**, and an orientation to future **projects**, none of which ordinarily involve explicit self-awareness. Merleau-Ponty synthesizes aspects of both Heidegger's and Sartre's accounts. His refers to the "tacit cogito" as "a comprehensive and inarticulate grasp upon the world" (PP, 404), evidenced particularly in perceptual experience. In perception, the significance of the world is grasped immediately through the affective and practical dispositions of the **body**.

An interest in prereflective experience is shared by American **pragmatists** as well as by **philosophers of life**. A representative of the latter category, **Wilhelm Dilthey**, offers an illuminating description of the prereflective consciousness of a theater-goer: "The more purely, soundly, deeply I am engrossed in the object, the more I forget myself in it. If on the stage in front of me I see Brutus in his tent before the battle of Philippi as the ghost of Julius Caesar appears to him, nothing is there for me but this tent and Brutus in it . . . . My self is, so to speak, extinguished in this moment. . . . I am not aware of the process of my perceiving" (*Introduction to the Human Sciences*, 247).

PRESENT, THE. *See* TEMPORALITY.

PRESENT AGE, THE. *See* LEVELING.

PRESENT-AT-HAND (Ger. *vorhanden*). Technical term in the philosophy of **Martin Heidegger**'s *Being and Time*. Presence-at-hand designates the status of things apprehended as isolated physical objects, sense data, or other constructs of the theoretical attitude. Heidegger's contention is that things present-at-hand are derivative from things grasped according to their ordinary uses and purposes: things **ready-to-hand**. Historically, Heidegger argues, a **metaphysical** idea of presence has exercised control over our understanding of nature and ourselves. A pernicious instance of this is the philosophical conception of the human being as a **knowing subject**. A primary goal of *Being and Time* is to replace such traditional views with an account of human being as **existence**.

PRÉVERT, JACQUES (1900–1977). French poet and screenwriter who was a fixture in the cafés of **Saint-Germain-des-Prés** during and after **World War II**. Prévert's lyrical, populist poems praised pleasures of ordinary life and ridiculed middle class conformity and hypocrisy. His **poetry** became extremely popular after the publication of *Paroles* (1946), and Prévert poems such as "Les feuilles mortes" ("Autumn Leaves"), which were set to to music, became popular hits. Prévert collaborated with singer **Juliette Gréco** and was an acquaintance of **Jean-Paul Sartre** and **Simone de Beauvoir**.

PROJECT/PROJECTION. A central idea in existentialism is that the human being exists by "projecting possibilities" into the world, or, alternately put, that the world is experienced as meaningful because it is the correlate of particular human attitudes and purposes (projects). To say a human life is a "project" or that it is essentially involved in "projecting possibilities" is not to say that we are continually involved in deliberate planning, though planning may be an instance of projection. Rather, the language of projection is a technical way to describe how the world is organized and takes on meaning according to specific goals and capacities of existing individuals. A corollary to the thesis of projection is thus that the world cannot be said to exist "in itself," that is, as neutral matter, independent of human purposes.

   Martin Heidegger introduced the vocabulary of projection (*Entwurf, entwerfen*), which was subsequently taken up by **Jean-Paul Sartre** and **Maurice Merleau-Ponty**. Heidegger speaks of *Dasein*'s "projective **understanding**" of the world in terms of a pragmatic and affective "projection of possibilities" onto things. For example, when a hammer is picked up and used to hammer in a nail, it is "understood" in terms of the nexus of purposes involved in, or the "project" of, building a house; only in such a context can its "**being**" as a serviceable tool become disclosed. For if I were simply to contemplate the hammer, I might never grasp what it is used for. The ultimate possibility guiding the disclosure of the hammer is the purpose for which the house is being built—to provide shelter for myself and my family—though, as I don't normally keep this explicitly in mind while hammering, projection is not an intellectual act but a practical attitude and activity. Heidegger stresses that projective understanding is essentially futural, in that it is guided by life goals yet to be realized and, moreover, under continual revision.

   Sartre presents the example of climbing a rocky cliff. A cliff takes on meaning as something to be climbed, rather than, say, an object to be studied geologically, in virtue of the goal of climbing it. Its being "an obstacle," "intimidating," "challenging," or "impossible," is strictly a correlate of the "project" of climbing it. At the same time, the project of climbing it depends in turn on the **facticity** of the **situation**: that the rock face has certain physical characteristics, is approachable on foot, has been climbed before, and so forth. Heidegger captures this idea by speaking of *Dasein* as a "**thrown** project" (*geworfener Entwurf*), meaning that projects may be freely pursued only within a situation whose basic features are pregiven and not of one's making.

A further sense of project is Sartre's view that particular goals, like climbing a cliff or becoming a great writer, are expressions of a more general "fundamental project" that represents one's most basic attitudes toward the world, others, and oneself. A paradox arises when Sartre speaks of the fundamental project as the product of an "original **choice**." In this case it is hard to say what such a choice amounts to, since it precedes the being-in-situation that gives a sense of meaningful possibilities in the first place. Another paradox is that a person is often unaware of the nature of his or her fundamental project. Here Sartre appeals to **existential psychoanalysis** as a method of deciphering the fundamental project of another, the method he applied in his biographical studies of Charles Baudelaire, **Jean Genet**, and Gustave Flaubert.

One further paradoxical sense of project is intended by Sartre. This is the idea that the goal of human existence in general is the "impossible" project of becoming a unity of **being-for-itself** and **being-in-itself**, a stable synthesis of **freedom** and facticity. Such a project is impossible because, in order to exist as a human being, one must continually project oneself toward future possibilities, revising and reevaluating one's actions and commitments throughout one's life. To imagine that one could freeze this dynamic process while still existing is to imagine a perspective of freedom outside of existence, a perspective attainable only by God.

PSYCHIATRY. *See* EXISTENTIAL PSYCHIATRY.

PSYCHOANALYSIS. Method of psychotherapy developed around 1900 by **Sigmund Freud** that postulates unconscious mental conflicts as the cause of hysterical and obsessional neurosis. By closely analyzing the speech of his patients as they described their problems to him, Freud concluded that thoughts and desires deemed unacceptable by the conscious mind have been repressed from **consciousness** yet remain active on an unconscious level, where they may interfere with conscious behavior. He surmised that neurotic symptoms (as well as dreams and slips of the tongue) are the result of a compromise between censoring forces and repressed desires, a bargain that allows an unacceptable desire to be expressed in disguised form, much like a coded message or a story with hidden meaning. Conflicts underlying neurosis Freud most often traced back to sexual experiences and fantasies in early childhood. In this way, he arrived at a view of **human nature** in which the past determines the present, and reason is in the service of underlying passions.

While German existentialists expressed little interest in psychoanalysis, French existentialists, in particular **Jean-Paul Sartre**, devoted considerable attention to it. In *The Emotions: Outline of a Theory* and again in *Being and Nothingness*, Sartre rejected as incoherent the psychoanalytic idea of unconscious motivation. If desires can act on me in a causal fashion, without my awareness, in what sense can they be said to belong to "me"? In what sense can I be held **responsible** for them? Unconscious desires that operate as physical causes are, like an irregular heartbeat, not part of who I am and what I am responsible for. For this reason, Sartre interpreted the unconscious desires revealed by psychoanalysis as expressions of an underlying choice of self or fundamental **project**.

PSYCHOLOGISM. *See* NATURALISM.

PSYCHOLOGY OF WORLDVIEWS, THE (*Psychologie der Weltanschauungen*, 1919). Karl Jaspers's first book to press beyond the boundaries of psychiatry earned him wide recognition in German intellectual circles, especially after its second edition appeared in 1922. In his "Philosophical Autobiography," Jaspers referred to it as "the earliest writing in . . . modern existentialism" (PKJ, 28). Written while Jaspers was still a lecturer in psychology at Heidelberg University, the book proposed a typology of *worldviews*—general human attitudes and cognitive perspectives—such as **nihilism**, pessimism, and optimism. A worldview is at once a necessary means of understanding the world and a restrictive "shell" (*Gehäuse*) used to protect **consciousness** from experiences and ideas it cannot make sense of. Jaspers's existentialist concerns, first awakened by his discovery of **Søren Kierkegaard** around 1914, are in evidence here. Like Kierkegaard, Jaspers maintains that philosophical **understanding** remains empty and abstract unless underpinned by **concrete** personal experiences of **freedom** and **finitude**. Jaspers proposes that such transformative experiences are occasioned by confronting the "limits" of **existence**. "**Limit situations**," such as **death**, **guilt**, and suffering, reveal the limits of one's personal and cultural perspective, for regardless of one's worldview, they resist being rationally articulated and justified. Beginning with this text, the notion of the limit plays a central role in Jaspers's thought. Only by existentially experiencing the limits of my perspective do I become aware that there is something beyond my perspective, something that cannot be readily explained by traditional science or philosophy, yet that demands philosophical articulation.

The book's importance for the development of existentialism derives mainly from Jaspers's idea of the limit situation. According to Jaspers, limit situations arise when one confronts basic existential antinomies, opposing **values** that cannot be avoided yet cannot be reconciled. One is personally implicated in such situations and must confront them, yet one cannot distance oneself from them to understand them objectively. Jaspers identifies five types of limit situation: death, guilt, suffering, struggle, and chance. In each of these **concrete** experiences, I am unable to understand the nature of that which I am called on to evaluate, yet I am also unable to escape it. Jaspers's discussion of death as a limit situation influenced **Martin Heidegger** in *Being and Time*. Jaspers's book was also significant for suggesting a linkage between **Søren Kierkegaard** and **Friedrich Nietzsche** as the major 19th-century forerunners of existentialism.

PSYCHOTHERAPY. *See* EXISTENTIAL PSYCHOTHERAPY.

PUBLIC, THE. *See* LEVELING.

– Q –

QUENEAU, RAYMOND. French novelist, essayist, and linguist. Associated with **surrealism** in the 1930s, during the 1940s and 1950s Queneau was a friend of **Jean-Paul Sartre** and was affiliated with Sartre's circle in Paris. Queneau was the editor of **Alexandre Kojève**'s *Introduction to the Reading of Hegel* (1947), which he transcribed from Kojeve's lectures. He was also the author of *Derniers jours* (1936), a novel that anticipated themes of Sartre's *Nausea* (1938).

QUESTION OF GERMAN GUILT, THE **(1947). Karl Jaspers**'s book *Die Schuldfrage* (1946) was one of the first attempts to come to grips with the issue of the collective **guilt** of German citizens for the actions of their government during **World War II**. Referring to the Nuremberg Trials, which were poised to begin, and to the threat that Germany would become a "pariah nation, degraded below all others" in the eyes of **world** opinion, Jaspers cautions against collectivist judgments that assign guilt to the entire "German people" without discrimination. Instead, he proposes to distinguish among four types of guilt. *Criminal guilt* results from breaking a law and is judged by the appropriate authority in a court of law. It accrues only to individuals, even when they may have acted as part of a collective or corporation. Few German citizens—specifically, only those **Nazis** convicted by the Nuremberg tribunals—are criminally guilty. *Political guilt* applies to all citizens of a state that, for example, has engaged in war and lost. It is judged by "the victors" and imposed on all citizens without distinction, such as via reparations. All Germans must share in the political liability for having started World War II. *Moral guilt* results when an individual feels that he or she has done something wrong. Jaspers insists that one person may not judge the moral guilt of another; **conscience** alone is the judge of moral guilt. The consequence of moral guilt is penance and personal self-transformation. Many Germans will suffer from moral guilt of some type if they participated in harming or oppressing others in some way. Finally, *metaphysical guilt* is guilt felt "before God" for "crimes committed in my presence or with my knowledge" that I did not try to prevent.

Metaphysical guilt may be felt by survivors who wonder why they have survived while others have suffered and perished. Jaspers admits that he himself feels metaphysically guilty for having remained in Germany through the war and not having risked his life to help others.

While Jaspers offers a nuanced discussion of criminal guilt and political liability, his main concern is with the moral and metaphysical dimensions of guilt. Guilt for Jaspers is ultimately a "vital question for the German soul," a matter of "inner regeneration" rather than external judgment. Each German is thus called upon to assess his or her innermost feelings. Jaspers's advice to intellectuals who in 1933 fervently embraced Nazism for false or self-deluded reasons is to openly confront their moral guilt through an "act of self-renewal." While the name of **Martin Heidegger** is never mentioned, Jaspers's remarks are clearly applicable to the case of his former friend.

– R –

RAHNER, KARL. *See* CATHOLICISM; EXISTENTIAL THEOLOGY.

RASSEMBLEMENT DÉMOCRATIQUE RÉVOLUTIONAIRE (Revolutionary Democratic Rally [RDR]). Short-lived French political movement joined by **Jean-Paul Sartre** in 1948. Intended as a democratic alternative to the French Communist Party, the RDR was a loosely knit organization of socialists and disaffected communists whose goal was to build a united socialist Europe to stand up against the Soviet Union and the United States. **Maurice Merleau-Ponty** was also a member, but less active than Sartre. Sartre and Merleau-Ponty quit the movement after about a year.

READY-TO-HAND (Ger. *zuhanden*). A fundamental **ontological** category, according to **Martin Heidegger**'s *Being and Time*. The world of **everyday** human **concern** is a world of things ready-to-hand: things apprehended as immediately meaningful according to their ordinary uses. In Heidegger's example, a hammer is **understood** as ready-to-hand by being picked up and used to drive in nails and not by being perceived or conceived by the mind. The **being** of the ready-to-hand thus corresponds to human activity and cannot be accessed theoretically: "The hammering itself uncovers the specific 'manipulability' [*Handlichkeit*] of the hammer" (BT, 98). Examined from a theoretical perspective, the manipulability of the hammer vanishes. It becomes a mere occurrent object, a thing with objective physical properties indifferently **present-at-hand** (*vorhanden*). In Heidegger's argument, readiness-to-hand (*Zuhandenheit*) is the primary manner in which the world is apprehended and thus a fundamental mode of being itself. Presence-at-hand (*Vorhandenheit*), in contrast, is a derivative manner of understanding the world; it arises when things ready-to-hand are divorced from their primary contexts of meaning and use.

REALISM AND IDEALISM. Existentialists tend to be suspicious of the problem of the "**existence** of the real **world**" as formulated by traditional philosophy for, from the standpoint of existence, the skeptical problem of the "external world" and related epistemological concerns simply do not arise; they are pseudoproblems. The existentialist contention is that self and world are given together in an irreducible sense. This is recalled most forcefully by **Martin Heidegger**'s definition of *Dasein* as "**being-in-the-world**." For Heidegger, the problem of the existence of the external world arises only on the basis of the false assumption that the human being is a worldless, **knowing subject**. Realism, understood as the view that the world exists independently of human beings, is thus to be rejected, as it is based on a fundamental distortion of the meaning of *world* and of *human being*.

Existentialists are more sanguine in regard to idealism, though they also remain wary of certain pitfalls associated with the idealist position. Generally, they maintain that idealism is correct in recognizing the irreducible link between human intentionality and world. Idealism is false, however, when it construes the world merely as a construct of the human mind or an "object" for **consciousness**. If idealists are right to see the world as shot through with human ideas and purposes, they must at the same time recognize human ideas and purposes as dependent on engagement with a world. Moreover, they must acknowledge the pragmatic and affective dimensions of this engagement as primary: When cognition is assumed to be primary, the world loses its density and **concreteness** and reverts to being merely a correlate of human thought, an array of things **present-at-hand**.

REALITY. *See* REALISM AND IDEALISM.

THE REBEL (*L'Homme révolté*, 1951). In this essay on the nature and limits of political rebellion, **Albert Camus** moves beyond a **philosophy of the absurd** to a stance of universal humanism characteristic of his mature thought. Camus's absurdist position had been elaborated before **World War II** in *The Myth of Sisyphus*. Here the central question is whether, and how, the individual can find meaning in an **absurd** universe. Camus's response is that the individual must confront the absurdity of existence by passionate affirmation of his or her own life, finding meaning immanent within life's pleasures and independent of the demands of society. **Suicide** is rejected as an unacceptable attempt to abolish absurdity rather than to test one's mettle and achieve a measure of dignity by struggling against it. From the perspective of the absurd, **values** are immanent to this individual struggle, and there is little indication of what transindividual values may exist and how they may be justified.

Conceived and written between about 1946 and 1950, *The Rebel* represents a significant shift away from the moral individualism of absurdism. Camus has taken stock of the horrors of **World War II**— **Nazi** concentration camps, the American bombing of Hiroshima and Nagasaki, Joseph Stalin's purges and the revelation of prison camps in the Soviet Union, and France's "purging" of its own collaborators, such as Robert **Brasillach**. Consequently, the issue is no longer suicide but *murder*. For Camus, murder is the definitive political question of the postwar period, one that concerns every citizen of the modern state. Through war, capital punishment, and various forms of **political** oppression and "reform," modern governments regularly kill human beings in the service of ostensibly civilized ideologies. Camus realizes that the absurdist position offers little guidance here; while it encourages us to revolt, it sets no clear limits to that revolt because it provides no clear indication of how we ought to treat or care for others and no clear moral condemnation of murder. Thus, *The Rebel* begins with a consideration of the moral and social implications of political rebellion; this allows Camus to stake out moral ground for his argument and so to advance beyond the **nihilistic** skepticism of the absurdist position. "An act of rebellion is not, essentially, an egoistic act," (22–23) he observes, for it appeals to transpersonal standards of right and wrong and is motivated by a sense of solidarity with other people, whose suffering as well as my own I perceive as unjust. Strictly speaking, Camus reasons, an act of rebellion is always part of a social movement, a stance shared by a group. Rebellion thus finds its own rule of conduct within itself: While I am obligated to rebel against injustice and oppression, I am also obligated to respect the lives and well-being of other people, or else I contradict the original motivation of my rebellion. In this way, the humanism one finds at the core of *The Plague* (1947) and to which Camus was always personally committed emerges for the first time as the basis for his philosophical stance.

"Metaphysical revolt" is Camus's term for the effort, beginning in the late 18th century, not to redress a specific human injustice but to reject the entire human condition and remake it anew. In metaphysical revolt, human beings play at being God. The French Revolution and the Russian Revolution are prime illustrations of such an attitude; they seek to overcome injustice once and for all and to make the world anew, a perfect world of order and justice. For Camus, the ideal of a perfect world is a dangerous utopian illusion; absolute and yet unattainable, all means to its realization come to be perceived as legitimate, even the sacrifice of human lives. Nazism and Stalinism are two extreme expressions of metaphysical revolt for Camus. In each case, revolt against actual injustice is perverted into an absolute desire to remake the world. This in turn, because it is an impossible task and recognizes no limits to its **action**, becomes simply the desire to destroy. Camus's assessment of Soviet **communism** as a form of utopian revolt was unpopular with French existentialists, and it precipitated the end of his friendship with **Jean-Paul Sartre**. In an extended "Reply to Camus" published in *Les Temps modernes* (August 1952), Sartre accused Camus of mistaking politics for morality and of trying to remove himself from history in order to judge it.

While Camus's critical position in *The Rebel* moves beyond absurdism, it remains **Nietzschean** in character in certain respects. Like Nietzsche, Camus maintains that the root problem of the evils of modern society is a form of nihilism characteristic of the European tradition. In Camus's analysis, nihilism is based in a rejection of the conditions of life, and it is this attitude that leads to "inhuman excesses." At the conclusion of *The Rebel*, Camus's recommendation for a return to Mediterranean "moderation" as a remedy for nihilism is also Nietzschean in spirit. The classical Greek virtue of moderation is defined by Camus as the ability to live on the basis of acceptance of human limits rather than by their denial. This includes acceptance of suffering and **death** as ingredients in happiness and life and affirmation of the concrete, natural world as the basis for the world of ideas and human culture. Through moderation, rebellion remains attuned to the condition of actual living human beings and is less susceptible to utopian abstraction. *See also* EXISTENTIALIST LITERATURE.

REBELLION. *See REBEL, THE.*

RECHERCHES PHILOSOPHIQUES. French philosophical journal that published many early studies of existentialist philosophy. Founded in 1931 by **Alexandre Koyré** and others, the journal featured articles by existentially oriented thinkers such as **Jean Wahl** and **Gabriel Marcel**. The journal also published original works of existentialist philosophy, including **Martin Heidegger**'s "On the Essence of Ground" and **Jean-Paul Sartre**'s *The Transcendence of the Ego*.

RECIPROCITY. The idea that self and other stand in a reciprocal relation, for example, that one's knowledge of oneself is gleaned significantly through the judgments of others, or that one's attitude toward others significantly influences others' attitudes toward oneself. The reciprocity of **ethical** and social relations is an important theme in the writings of **Martin Buber** and **Gabriel Marcel** as well as in the work of **Simone de Beauvoir**, **Maurice Merleau-Ponty**, and **Jean-Paul Sartre**.

Buber maintains that the "I" attains to full self-awareness only in relation to a "You," an open, receptive **dialogue** with another person. Moreover, in order to fully realize the I–You relation, I must make myself fully present to the other, giving myself without reserve; in the words of Gabriel Marcel, I must be **"available"** to the other both mentally and emotionally. Marcel's account of the experience of love captures nicely the element of reciprocity:

> To love anybody is to expect something from him, something which can neither be defined nor foreseen; it is at the same time . . . to make it possible for him to fulfill this expectation . . . to expect is in some way to give . . . no longer to expect is to deprive [the other of] . . . a . . . possibility of inventing and creating. (HV, 49–50)

Despite his tendency to construe interpersonal relations as antagonistic, Sartre also describes the reciprocity of self and other as constitutive of the self. "In order to get any truth about myself, I must have contact with another person. The other is indispensable to my own existence, as well as to my knowledge about myself" (EHE, 37–38). Commentator **David Cooper** clarifies Sartre's point: "Only if I regard and treat others . . . as loci of existential **freedom** will I receive back an image of myself as just such a locus" (Cooper, 187). Reciprocity can thus be seen as a condition of authentic self-awareness. As such, an ideal of reciprocity tempers, and complicates, the ideal of individual **authenticity**, which suggests that one must extricate oneself from the false judgments of others in order to seize hold of one's own possibilities.

REFLECTIVE CONSCIOUSNESS. *See* PREREFLECTIVE CONSCIOUSNESS.

RELIGIOUS, THE. *See* KIERKEGAARD, SØREN.

RELIGIOUS EXISTENTIALISM. Umbrella category for a diverse group of existentialist thinkers from Protestant, Catholic, and Jewish traditions. The central concern of religious existentialists, both **Christian** and Jewish, is the human experience of the divine, in contrast to theological arguments about God's nature or God's existence, or questions of religious doctrine, which may be addressed apart from **concrete** human experience. The major religious existentialists are **Martin Buber** (Jewish), **Karl Jaspers** (Protestant), and **Gabriel Marcel** (Catholic). Secondary figures include **Franz Rosenzweig** (Jewish). Though trained as a Protestant theologian, **Paul Tillich** may also be classified as a religious existentialist, in that he rejected most traditional theological conceptions of God in favor of concrete human experience of the divine. *See also* EXISTENTIAL THEOLOGY.

REPRESENTATION (Ger. *Vorstellung***, Fr** *représentation***).** In traditional philosophy and science, the mind is often understood as a kind of nonmaterial place where ideas or "representations" of things are apprehended, stored, and manipulated. Representations are generally understood as thoughts, images, sensations, and so forth, that stand proxy in the mind for something in the world. For example, according to representational theory, when I perceive a tree, I form in my mind a mental image of the tree, which I may combine with other representations, for example, *thoughts* about the tree: that it is a silver maple tree, that it is beautiful, that it is in need of water. The perceptual image is a representation of the physical object, while the thoughts are representations of various states of affairs concerning the object.

Most existentialists reject representational theories of mind on the grounds that they encourage false assumptions about the human being and its relations to the **world** and to others. These theories lend support to the idea that the mind is a self-enclosed subjective sphere and thus that it has no intrinsic relation to an "external" world or to other minds, whose representations remain unavailable to it. If my mind can exist with or without external objects or other minds, it may be conceived as a self-sufficient **substance**, for example, a Cartesian "thinking thing."

Moreover, as **Maurice Merleau-Ponty** observes, once mind and world are disconnected in this way, it is difficult to bring them back together without falling prey either to **idealism**, according to which the mind constitutes the world, or empiricism, according to which the mind passively receives the world as it is, with little or no human contribution.

The existentialist critique of representational theories involves a rejection, or at least a critical reappraisal, of the language of "mind," "subject," and "**consciousness**" in which they are usually conveyed, a strategy that is pursued most decisively by **Martin Heidegger** in *Being and Time*. Characterizing *Dasein* as **being-in-the world**, Heidegger effectively "empties" the "contents of the mind" into a world of shared meanings and involvements, a "**life-world**" where thoughts and **emotions** ordinarily take place. "Dasein . . . does not somehow first get out of an inner sphere in which it has been proximally encapsulated, but its primary kind of Being is such that it is always 'outside' alongside entities which . . . belong to a world already discovered" (BT, 62). Meaning in the life-world is given immediately or "pre-theoretically" in the form of general "**horizons** of understanding" that need not be explicitly grasped in order to guide behavior and thought. Thus, Heidegger argues, an "average, everyday **understanding**" of the world is prior to and serves as the basis for theoretical and scientific judgments, according to which things are observed and known (represented), truly or falsely, in the mind.

REPRIEVE, THE. *See ROADS TO FREEDOM, THE.*

RES COGITANS. *See COGITO ERGO SUM*; DESCARTES, RENÉ.

RES EXTENSA. *See* DESCARTES, RENÉ; SUBSTANCE.

RESIGNATION. *See* KNIGHT OF FAITH AND KNIGHT OF INFINITE RESIGNATION.

RESISTANCE, FRENCH. *See* FRENCH RESISTANCE.

RESOLUTENESS. (Ger. *Entschlossenheit*). In ***Being and Time***, **Martin Heidegger** employs this term to designate the **authentic** manner of being a self, in contrast to inauthentic **existence** governed by the dictates of ***das Man***. To be resolute is to fully accept one's status as a **thrown** being of possibility, that is, as **being-in-the-world**. It is to respond to the call of **conscience** and to accept **responsibility** for oneself. In all of these characterizations, Heidegger retains the sense of a willful decision to accept one's **finite** nature and the task of choosing one's own path in life. Heidegger insists that only on the basis of such willful self-acceptance can ***Dasein*** relate authentically to others.

RESPONSIBILITY. Existentialists generally approach responsibility as primarily a matter of responsibility for the *self*: In becoming aware that I am a **free** and self-determining being, I also become aware that

I am fundamentally responsible for the person I have chosen to be. The insight that one is ultimately responsible for oneself is thus the core of existential responsibility. In this sense, it may be distinguished from various forms of legal and moral responsibility that may be determined externally—for example, the judgment of a police officer that I have rolled through a red light and so am legally obligated to pay a fine, or the judgment of my children that I have not spent enough time with them over the weekend and so am morally obligated to make it up to them. Existentialists portray coming to grips with responsibility as a momentous event, not an everyday occurrence; it is the **moment** in which one accepts one's life as the product of one's own **choices** and **actions** and not the result of environmental circumstances or the decisions of others. In this way, responsibility is linked to the realization that human life is without foundation, that it is "nothingness" or "pure possibility" rather than the unfolding of a predetermined content or **essence**.

An alternate conception of existential responsibility is proposed by thinkers like **Martin Buber** and **Emmanuel Levinas**, for whom ethics is modeled on **dialogue** with the **other**. In their view, responsibility to others is primary and self-responsibility is derivative on relations with others and with God, in which the self comes to fruition. In contrast to thinkers like **Martin Heidegger** and **Jean-Paul Sartre**, who conceived **authenticity** as the struggle of the self to come to terms with its own **finitude**, Buber and Levinas maintained that the obligation to respond to the claim of another person is the foundation of **ethical** experience.

RICOEUR, PAUL (1913–2005) French philosopher. Ricoeur was an original philosopher whose thought developed in tandem with, though distinct from, the mainstream of existentialism in France in the 1940s and 1950s. He had a lifelong interest in **Husserlian phenomenology** and was an early advocate, translator, and interpreter of the **religious existentialism** of **Gabriel Marcel** and **Karl Jaspers**. He participated with **Emmanuel Mounier** in the journal *Esprit* and became associated with **Christian** existentialism. For this reason, Ricoeur was viewed with suspicion by **Jean-Paul Sartre**.

Ricoeur's primary philosophical concern was the nature of selfhood and the formation of personal identity. His philosophical approach to these themes in his early work resembled the **existential phenomenology** of **Maurice Merleau-Ponty**. Both men shared a common debt to Marcel's treatment of embodiment and passivity; both viewed the self as embodied and socially and historically **situated**. Unfortunately, Ricoeur never developed a dialogue with Merleau-Ponty, though both lived in Paris at the time. Neither was he invited to make contact with Sartre and his circle at *Les Temps modernes*, due to what were perceived to be overly conservative religious and political views.

While interred in a German prisoner of war camp during **World War II**, Ricoeur completed a French translation of Edmund Husserl's *Ideas I* (1950), which had considerable influence on Husserl scholarship in France. In the 1960s, he developed an interest in psychoanalysis and the **hermeneutic** theory of **Hans-Georg Gadamer**. In subsequent books, he proposed a nuanced philosophical understanding of the **Freudian** unconscious and of the symbolic and narrative conditions of self-understanding.

RILKE, RAINER MARIA. *See* POETRY AND PHILOSOPHY.

ROADS TO FREEDOM, THE (*Les Chemins de la liberté*). Title of a trilogy of existentialist novels by **Jean-Paul Sartre**. A fourth novel, *La dernière chance*, was projected but never completed. Conceived in 1939 and published between 1945 and 1947, the three novels, *The Age of Reason* (*L'Âge de raison*, 1945), *The Reprieve* (*Le sursis*, 1945), and *Troubled Sleep* (*La mort dans l'âme*, 1947; British title *Iron in the Soul*), take place in Paris in the years leading up to World War II. The novels follow the daily lives of four or five central characters from the rise of fascism in Europe in the late 1930s through the outbreak of the war and the German invasion of France in 1940. In contrast to his first novel, *Nausea*, Sartre here portrays his characters engaged in the social and political problems of their times, reflecting the ideal of "**committed literature**" he elaborates at the time in *What Is Literature?* The books also present concrete illustrations of the problematic of **freedom**, which complement the more abstract exposition presented in *Being and Nothingness*.

As the trilogy's title suggests, the novels dramatize various paths to freedom, various ways in which its characters struggle to realize or to repudiate their **situation** and the need for **choice** and **action** within it. Loosely autobiographical, the first novel, *The Age of Reason*, is centered around the predicament of Mathieu, a young philosophy professor in Paris who must find means to arrange an abortion for his pregnant mistress, Marcelle. Mathieu's inability to commit himself in the relationship, like his indecision over whether to fight in the Spanish Civil War or to join the **Communist** Party, is indicative of his merely abstract understanding of freedom. He strives "to retain [his] freedom" by never fully committing himself to any person or cause. In the end, his brother, Jacques, a decidedly bourgeois lawyer, better understands the nature of existential freedom: "[F]reedom [consists] in frankly confronting situations into which one has deliberately entered, and accepting all one's responsibilities" (*The Age of Reason*, 138). This reflects the philosophical position of *Being and Nothingness*, in which to realize its freedom, **consciousness** must enter into the world and commit itself in some way: "[T]here is freedom only in a *situation*" (BN, 488). Without a world of concrete alternatives, freedom remains an empty power.

Throughout the trilogy, Sartre takes pains to show how becoming aware of freedom is an ongoing struggle, never finalized, not merely an intellectual accomplishment. Each of the characters suffers from a form of **bad faith**. Brunet, the committed communist, appears to be more real than Mathieu, "a whole man, nothing but a man" (154). Yet Brunet's commitment is grounded on an identification with the Communist Party, which absolves him of his responsibility to think and act for himself. Daniel, who has sex with young men, finally admits he is a homosexual, yet in doing so he understands himself as determined by his nature, an instance of a generic type of "invert." It is significant for Sartre's treatment of freedom that each character remains largely blind to his self-deception until it is mirrored back to him through the eyes of another. The **reciprocity** of self and other is presented as an underlying truth of freedom. Daniel expresses this truth to Mathieu toward the end of *The Reprieve* : "Without me, you would be that same insubstantial entity that I am for myself. It is by my agency that you can at times get an occasional . . . glimpse of yourself" (406). *See also* EXISTENTIALIST LITERATURE.

ROSENBERG, HAROLD. *See* ABSTRACT EXPRESSIONISM.

ROSENZWEIG, FRANZ (1886–1929). German Jewish existential philosopher and theologian. Like his friend **Martin Buber**, Rosenzweig developed an existentialist perspective within the framework of Jewish theology and history. Raised in a secular upper-middle-class Jewish household, Rosenzweig was on the verge of converting to Protestantism in 1913 when he had a transformational religious experience in a small Berlin synagogue that convinced him of the relevance of the Jewish faith to everyday **existence**. From this time on he dedicated himself to Judaism, learning Hebrew and becoming a noted Jewish scholar and teacher. From 1922 until his **death**, Rosenzweig suffered from a rare disorder that left him almost completely paralyzed. Nonetheless, he maintained good spirits, learning to type on a specially built typewriter and communicating with his wife through a system of signals. In 1925, he began a modern German translation of the Hebrew bible with Martin Buber, which Buber completed after his friend's death.

Rosenzweig's major philosophical work, *The Star of Redemption* (1921), was a hybrid of theology, history, and philosophy expressed in dense, poetic language. The book's ultimate goal appears to be to defend a vision of philosophy founded necessarily on **faith** and revelation, a "new philosophy" that recognizes the ultimate **mystery** of the world instead of trying to reduce it to purely rational terms. The book begins with the experience of death as an encounter with nothingness; in this Rosenzweig's work has been compared to **Martin Heidegger**'s *Being and Time*. Rosenzweig argues that, while philosophers have attempted to deny death by positing some form of unchanging or absolute truth, such a truth lies necessarily beyond the power of human comprehension. Thus ultimate truth can only be accepted on faith. Rosenzweig's view bears similarities to that of **Søren Kierkegaard**. For both thinkers, **G. W. F. Hegel**'s absolute idealism exemplifies the need for philosophy to be founded on a (hidden) leap of faith.

– S –

SAINT GENET: ACTOR AND MARTYR. *See* GENET, JEAN.

SAINT-GERMAIN-DES-PRÉS. Bohemian neighborhood on the Left Bank of Paris that emerged as the geographical center of French existentialism after **World War II**. Saint-Germain was already a gathering place for French artists and writers in the1930s. **Jean-Paul Sartre** and **Simone de Beauvoir** worked and lived there starting in the early 1940s, attracted by its numerous cafés and bars, bookstores, publishing houses, cheap hotels, and charming narrow streets. Starting in the winter of 1941, at a time when heating fuel was scarce due to the war, Sartre and Beauvoir used the well-heated **Café de Flore** on the Boulevard Saint-Germain as their base of operations, writing there each morning and afternoon as well as socializing and receiving visitors. By the autumn of 1945, the café was recognized as the center of the French existentialist movement, and through the late 1940s tourists flocked to the Flore and to the neighboring Café les Deux Magots to catch a glimpse of Sartre and Beauvoir. **Boris Vian** parodied the Bohemian life of Saint-Germain in his novel *L'Écume de jours*.

SARTRE, JEAN-PAUL (1905–1980). French philosopher, novelist, and playwright. Sartre was the chief representative of existentialism after **World War II**, and it is difficult to overestimate his importance, both for his philosophical and literary contributions as well as for the social and **political** dimensions he introduced into existentialist debates.

The term "existentialism" itself was coined around 1944 as a label for Sartre's philosophy, possibly by **Garbriel Marcel**, one of his staunchest critics. Beginning in the fall of 1945, Sartre and his colleague and companion **Simone de Beauvoir** became famous in the French media as the leaders of an "existentialist movement." Through their journal, *Les Temps modernes*, as well as through their numerous plays, novels, and philosophical works, Sartre and Beauvoir advocated a conception of radical individual **freedom**, **choice**, and **responsibility** that held up to French citizens an ideal of continual self-creation without **metaphysical** foundation. Freedom became the watchword of Sartre's philosophy, and it was in the service of an increasingly political understanding of freedom that Sartre strove through his writings to transform postwar French society. Like many French intellectuals of the time, Sartre was attracted to the **Marxist** ideal of a classless, egalitarian society, yet he remained skeptical of orthodox Marxism and the politics of the Communist Party. However, with the heating up of the Cold War in the early 1950s, Sartre came to regard **communism** as the only viable alternative to Western capitalism, which he perceived as the greatest threat to world peace and social justice.

It should be recalled that Sartre was not an existentialist at every stage of his career. The core of his existentialist writings was conceived and written between 1939 and 1952, starting with *Being and Nothingness* (1943), his major work of philosophy and the primary statement of his existentialism. Nonetheless, aspects of this systematic work were anticipated in shorter **phenomenological** studies Sartre published between about 1937 and 1940. These include studies of **consciousness** (*The Transcendence of the Ego* [1937]), **emotion** (*The Emotions: Outline of a Theory* [1939]), and **imagination** (*The Psychology of Imagination* [1940]). Thus, the boundaries of Sartre's philosophical career, while real, must not be drawn too sharply. Ideas formulated in *Being and Nothingness* continued to inform Sartre's later thought, whose primary goal was a synthesis of existentialism and Marxism. This Sartre attempted in his second major philosophical work, *Critique of Dialectical Reason* (1960).

Life. Sartre's childhood was documented in his playful autobiography, *The Words* (1964). He was a pampered, only child, raised by a doting mother in the home of his maternal grandparents. His father, Jean-Marie Sartre, a French naval officer, died when Sartre was only a year old. His mother, Anne-Marie Schweitzer, was Albert Schweitzer's cousin. Sartre's first and deepest ambition was to become a great writer. From an early age he wrote often and copiously, producing a stream of stories, poems, letters, and lyrics. From 1924 to 1929 Sartre was enrolled as a philosophy student at the prestigious **École Normale Supérieure** in Paris, where his fellow students included **Raymond Aron** and **Jean Hyppolite**. His commitment to philosophy was awakened by **Henri Bergson**'s *Time and Free Will* (*Les données immédiates de la conscience* [1889]). Bergson oriented him toward the study of consciousness and convinced him that through philosophy "you could learn the truth." In 1929 he met Simone de Beauvoir, who was studying philosophy at the Sorbonne, and she became his lifelong companion and collaborator. Having failed his first attempt at the competitive *agrégation* exam for university teachers in 1928, in 1929 Sartre took first place and Beauvoir second. The same year he met **Maurice Merleau-Ponty**, who remained a friend and collaborator for more than 20 years. From 1931 to 1939, Sartre was a high school philosophy teacher, first in Le Havre, then in Laon and in Neuilly. His earliest literary recognition came with the publication of his novel *Nausea* in 1938, followed by a well-received collection of short stories, *The Wall*, in 1939.

Drafted into the French army in September 1939, Sartre was captured by the Germans in June 1940 and spent nine months in a German prisoner-of-war camp, an experience that gave him his first taste of social solidarity. Here he first read carefully **Martin Heidegger**'s *Being and Time* and began to conceive *Being and Nothingness*. In March 1941, Sartre was released on the basis of a falsified medical excuse and spent the rest of the war working productively in occupied Paris, where he completed *Being and Nothingness*, two novels, and the plays *The Flies* and *No Exit*, which premiered in Paris at the time. In 1941, Sartre organized a clandestine group of writers and intellectuals, **Socialism and Freedom**, intended to resist the German occupation, but which disbanded due to internal disagreement. Toward the end of the war he contributed articles to **Albert Camus**'s underground Resistance newspaper, *Combat*.

Sartre emerged from World War II with a heightened political awareness, which found expression in his subsequent thinking and writing. An October 1945 lecture, published subsequently in book form as *Existentialism Is a Humanism*, marked the birth of existentialism as a cultural phenomenon and the start of Sartre's celebrity. This short book set the tone for the French existentialist movement by emphasizing **ethical** and political dimensions of freedom largely absent from Sartre's earlier work. A new political orientation was also evident in the first issue of *Les Temps modernes* (October 1945), in which Sartre, as editor, introduced the idea of "**committed literature**," and in Sartre's critical analysis of anti-Semitism, *Anti-Semite and Jew* (1946). *The Age of Reason* and *The Reprieve*, the second and third novels in Sartre's *Roads to Freedom* trilogy, also appeared at this time (September 1945); they offered **concrete** illustrations of the problematic of **freedom** expounded in *Being and Nothingness*. Taken together with Beauvoir's second novel, *The Blood of Others*, this deluge of publications constituted what Beauvoir referred to as an "Existentialist offensive" (FC, 38).

Starting in the late 1940s, Sartre became more embroiled in political controversies, especially with the communists, and spent less time on philosophy and literature. In 1948, he participated in the formation of a political movement, **Rassemblement Démocratique Révolutionaire**, which lasted about one year. In the same year Sartre's works were placed on the Index of Forbidden Books by the Vatican. In 1950, Pope Pius XIII issued an encyclical that identified existentialism as one of the "False Opinions Threatening to Undermine the Foundations of Catholic Doctrine." The final work of Sartre's existentialist period was a biographical study of the writer **Jean Genet**, *Saint Genet: Actor and Martyr* (1952), which, like his earlier study, *Baudelaire* (1947), put into practice the method of **existential psychoanalysis** outlined in *Being and Nothingness*. In 1952, Sartre broke with Albert Camus over Camus's increasingly critical attitude toward the Soviet Union. In 1953, he broke with Merleau-Ponty over Merleau-Ponty's support for U.S. involvement in the Korean War. Sartre became a staunch supporter of the French Communist Party until the 1956 Soviet invasion of Hungary, which disabused him of his hopes for Soviet **communism** and turned him toward his last philosophical work, *Critique of Dialectical Reason*, which he began in 1957 and published in 1960. In 1964, Sartre refused the Nobel Prize for Literature. His last intellectual project was a monumental biography of Gustave Flaubert in three volumes (1970–1971). Sartre remained active in politics until his **death**, supporting various radical and revolutionary movements in France and around the globe. His funeral procession in Paris in 1980 attracted some 50,000 people.

Phenomenological Phase. Sartre's aim in each phase of his thought was to defend human freedom from physiological and psychological reductionism, and at the same time to demonstrate how consciousness, through which freedom is revealed, is necessarily engaged in the world. In the first phase of his career, his approach to the question of freedom was guided by his understanding of **Edmund Husserl**'s phenomenology, particularly the theory of the **intentionality** of consciousness. Sartre's introduction to phenomenology, recounted in an anecdote by Beauvoir, took place in a Parisian café with Beauvoir and Raymond Aron in 1932:

Aaron said, pointing to his glass: "You see my dear fellow, if you are a phenomenologist, you can talk about this cocktail and make philosophy out of it!" Upon hearing this, Sartre turned pale with emotion. (PL, 112)

Phenomenology seemed to promise the approach to **concrete** experience that Sartre had been hungering for, one that would avoid the pitfalls of idealism ("digesting" the object within consciousness) and **realism** (making the object stand on its own, irrespective of consciousness) as well as materialism (reducing consciousness to a physical object in the world).

Sartre refined his understanding of Husserl in a year spent as a fellow at the Maison Académique Française (French Academic Institute) in Berlin (1933–1934). Here he carefully read Husserl's *Ideas* and developed his own critical position, which was published in 1936–1937 as *The Transcendence of the Ego*. Studies of emotion and imagination that followed rounded out Sartre's phenomenological inquiries. Taken together, their conclusions paved the way for the existentialism of *Being and Nothingness*. The key to phenomenology for Sartre was the thesis of intentionality: that consciousness is essentially "directed to" or "intends" objects outside of itself. However, where Husserl understood intentionality as the relationship between the mind and the "meanings" it intuits, Sartre understood it as a direct apprehension of things as they are immediately experienced, a contact with the world. This was a central insight of **existential phenomenology** as formulated by Martin Heidegger in *Being and Time*. While Sartre had by his own admission not yet read *Being and Time* carefully, his debt to Heidegger was already apparent in a short article from 1939 entitled "Intentionality: A Fundamental Idea of Husserl's Phenomenology." Here Husserl's staid vocabulary is replaced by torrid Heideggerean metaphors: Consciousness is a "being beyond itself," a "refusal to be a substance"; Sartre compares it to a "whirlwind," a "bursting" out beyond ourselves "into the dry dust of the world, on to the plain earth, amidst things." "Imagine us," he writes, " thus rejected and abandoned . . . in an indifferent, hostile, and restive world—you will then grasp the profound meaning" of Husserl's doctrine of intentionality ("Intentionality," 5).

While Husserl had focused primarily on perception, memory, and logical thought, Sartre's concern for concreteness led him to study emotion and imagination as exemplary intentional attitudes. In this Sartre may have been influenced by the work of **Max Scheler**. Fear, anger, love, and imaginative fantasy are not merely subjective states of mind but intentional acts that disclose the world as a correlate of my attitude toward it; through emotions "things . . . abruptly unveil themselves to us as hateful, sympathetic, horrible, lovable" ("Intentionality," 4–5). For Sartre, the doctrine of intentionality established an intrinsic link between consciousness and world; through my projects and attitudes I invest the world with meaning and value, yet the world remains "transcendent" to my experience of it, for it is a concrete world, not a world of my invention, a world of ideas. Later Sartre characterized the position he was seeking as a type of realism.

Transcendence of the Ego. The idea of intentionality led Sartre in turn to question the traditional concept of the self or **ego** as a mental subject that remains identical through time. He formulated his thoughts in *The Transcendence of the Ego* (1937). The mind cannot be thought of as a self-enclosed subjective sphere, nor as a substance that produces thoughts. Rather, "consciousness," "mind," and "self" designate a manner of relating to the world, an activity, not a substantial thing. Harkening back to the thought of Bergson, Sartre observed that consciousness is a pure "spontaneity" that "creates itself" anew at each moment; it is "translucence" in that one sees through it to the world while it itself remains "empty" of content and structure. Hence, when I turn my attention to myself, Sartre reasoned, consciousness relates to itself as an object, not as a subject: "The ego is not the owner of consciousness; it is the object of consciousness" (TE, 97). It follows that the ego does not "inhabit" consciousness as its permanent structure or identity. Rather, the ego is an object in the world like any other: "A tree or a chair exist no differently" (TE, 88).

Critics have noted that Sartre's repudiation of the ego poses problems for explaining the apparent permanence and identity over time of a coherent first-person perspective. Yet for the most part Sartre did not respond directly to this problem, as he regarded self-identity and permanence as illusions rather than as necessary conditions of awareness. Because he believed that consciousness is at bottom an "impersonal spontaneity," a power of apprehending and assigning meaning to the world that creates itself anew at each moment, he concluded that there can be no permanent self to which conscious acts and decisions may be attributed. Rather, "each instant of our conscious life reveals to us a creation ex nihilo" (TE, 98–99). Why then do we tend to assign substantial attributes to consciousness? It is because we confuse the *object* reflected on in self-awareness (a particular person with a particular name, physical appearance, past, temperament, and so forth) with the act and source of reflection (consciousness), which remains elusive, nonobjectifiable, and unpredictable. For this reason, consciousness is inherently disturbing to acknowledge: "There is something distressing . . . to catch in the act this tireless creation of existence of which *we* are not the creators . . . man has the impression of ceaselessly escaping from himself, of overflowing himself, of being surprised by riches which are always unexpected" (TE, 99).

Freedom and Situation. Being and Nothingness preserved and expanded upon many of the insights of the phenomenological period but recast them in an existential and "**ontological**" framework inherited from Heidegger's *Being and Time*. The feeling of being "frightened by one's own spontaneity" Sartre now called **anxiety**. The power, previously exemplified by imagination, to "withdraw from the world" and to "**negate**" what is given, he now named "freedom." (For a detailed discussion, *see BEING AND NOTHINGNESS*.)

The central drama of the book concerns the struggle of consciousness (**being-for-itself**) to accept the "nothingness" of its freedom—its lack of adequate cause or foundation. In this, Sartre's analysis is modeled after Heidegger's; both present existence as a struggle to confront one's essential nature as a finite and free being. Missing from Sartre's account, however, is an appreciation of the historical dimension of consciousness, the manner in which the individual is necessarily formed by a specific class, culture, and time period. Sartre insists rather that freedom is absolute; even a slave is free to choose the attitude he or she takes toward slavery. The situation one inhabits may be accepted or denied, and in this sense it is always freely chosen rather than passively suffered. Individuals are responsible for all aspects of themselves "down to the minutest detail."

A shift toward an appreciation of the *situated* character of freedom is perhaps the defining feature of Sartre's later thought. By the mid-1950s, Sartre came to see freedom as legitimately constrained by social, economic, and historical factors, and consequently he came to repudiate the conception of absolute freedom founded in individual choice. His second and final philosophical work, *Critique of Dialectical Reason*, centered on the notion of *praxis* or action as a collective accomplishment. Individual freedom was still affirmed, but as a moment within a broader social and historical enterprise. Sartre's later view thus approximated the account proposed by Merleau-Ponty in the final chapter of *Phenomenology of Perception*. Toward the end of his career, in 1969, Sartre summarized his mature view of freedom in these terms:

> [T]he idea which I have never ceased to develop is that in the end one is responsible for what is made of one. Even if one can do nothing else besides assume this responsibility. For I believe that a man can always make something out of what is made of him. This is the limit I would accord today to freedom: the small movement which makes of a totally conditioned social being someone who does not render back completely what his conditioning has given him. (BEM, 34–35)

SCHELER, MAX (1874–1928). German philosopher who, during and after **World War I**, was one of Germany's leading public intellectuals and most original thinkers. Working at times outside of the university as a freelance scholar, Scheler expanded the scope of **phenomenology** beyond the study of logic and intellectual processes to a consideration of feelings and **emotions** like sympathy, resentment, and love; religious **consciousness**; and the experience of **values**. Scheler thus succeeded in making phenomenology more **concrete**, more closely aligned with the experiences of everyday life. For this reason, and thanks also to his personal charisma and enthusiasm, his thought was attractive to a generation of German and French **philosophers of existence** in the 1920s and 1930s. Scheler was also greatly appreciated by the Spanish existential philosopher **José Ortega y Gasset**.

Central to Scheler's viewpoint was the idea that **values** must be emotionally felt rather than intellectually known or perceived, and that values have an objective status independent of the experiencing subject. The latter idea Scheler derived in large measure from his contact with **Edmund Husserl**, beginning in 1901. Husserl suggested to Scheler that emotional consciousness, just like perceptual and logical consciousness, must follow invariant rules, independent of empirical conditions. In this way, Scheler concluded that values may be understood as transcendental "essences" apprehended by various types of feeling states. Throughout his career he defended the autonomy of moral, intellectual, and religious values vis-à-vis sensorial life and physical impulses.

In 1915, Scheler published *The Genius of War*, an impassioned apology for World War I and German nationalism. The book won him popular acclaim but sacrificed his friendship with several prominent German intellectuals, including Max Brod and **Martin Buber**, who remained pacifists. The book also earned him a position with the propaganda department of the German Foreign Office, giving inspirational speeches to officers, soldiers, and prisoners of war. Later that same year, however, Scheler experienced a change of heart typical of the turmoils of his personal life. In 1916, Scheler published his reflections in a second book, criticizing war as a destructive force, followed by several publications recommending the reconciliation and unification of Europe based on **Christian** ideals. Scheler continued to be engaged in political issues, advocating in his writings and lectures a cosmopolitan **Catholic** perspective that combined ideals of individuality and socialist cooperation. However, in 1924 he once again experienced a radical shift in thinking and broke with the Catholic Church, which he criticized as antiquated and dogmatic.

In his final years, Scheler attempted to formulate a general vision of human **existence** that expressed his new perspective. This **philosophical anthropology** bore similarities to **Martin Heidegger**'s account of *Dasein* in *Being and Time*. Heidegger acknowledged a debt to Scheler's conception of the person as a center of lived experience irreducible to a thing or **substance**. However, he took pains to distinguish his perspective from Scheler's, which he found limited by its uncritical acceptance of traditional **ontological** categories.

SCHELLING, FRIEDRICH (1775–1854). German Romantic philosopher significant in the history of existentialism particularly for his influence on **Søren Kierkegaard**. Beginning with his 1809 "Essay on Human Freedom," Schelling devoted much of his later thought to the problem of **freedom** and to **existence** in its "positive" "actuality" as opposed to how it is "negatively" (merely intellectually) conceived by philosophical **idealism**. In this way, Schelling became a critic of G. W. F. **Hegel**'s system of absolute idealism, the dominant philosophical position of the time in German-speaking countries. While Schelling and Hegel had attended seminary school together and had lectured side by side at the University of Jena, Schelling came to fault Hegel for his deficient **understanding** of human existence. It is thus fitting that Kierkegaard should have been **awakened** to philosophy while attending Schelling's lectures in Berlin in 1841–1842. Following Schelling, Kierkegaard developed an original critique of Hegel. He also inherited from Schelling the distinctive usage of the term *existence* that characterizes existentialism.

SCHOPENHAUER, ARTHUR (1788–1860). German pessimistic philosopher whose unique blend of post-Kantian idealism and **vitalism** was a major influence on the early thinking of **Friedrich Nietzsche** and a youthful influence on **Søren Kierkegaard**. A critical moment in the development of existentialism was Nietzsche's decision to reject Schopenhauer's view of **existence** as inevitable *suffering*. Nietzsche and those who followed him, such as **Albert Camus**, were thus not pessimists. Unlike Schopenhauer, they viewed embodiment, striving, and the relative strength of the **passions** over reason as cause to affirm life rather than to renounce it in favor of "will-less" quietism.

Schopenhauer's major philosophical work, *The World as Will and Representation* (1818; 1844), followed **Immanuel Kant** in distinguishing between things as they appear to the human mind, namely, as mental **representations** (*Vorstellungen*), and things as they are "in-themselves," independent of human cognition. Schopenhauer diverged significantly from Kant, however, in asserting that the thing-in-itself is accessible to human experience, paradigmatically in the experience of *will*, an immediate, nonrepresentational feeling of existence or a striving to exist. Externally, for example, when I look at a photograph of myself, I appear as a physical thing in the world, about which I can form various mental representations. Internally, for example, when I feel hunger, thirst, or sexual appetite, I experience myself immediately as will. Will, the vital drive to exist, is the fundamental nature of reality untrammeled by categories of human cognition. Plants and animals display a similar dual aspect: to the mind they appear as physical things that follow causal laws corresponding to the laws of science, yet in-themselves they are expressions of will, a blind striving to exist. Schopenhauer's metaphysics held that at the deepest level both organic and inorganic nature are **phenomenal** expressions of a single, unitary cosmic striving to exist.

Schopenhauer's pessimism derived from his assumption, influenced by his reading of the Upanishads, that willing entails suffering. Because the goal of willing is the quietude that results from the cessation of will, and because this is not possible while we are alive, life is inherently painful. The striving of will ceases permanently only in **death** or, in the case of the saint or ascetic, in renunciation of the will to live. Nonetheless, suffering may be temporarily relieved in moments of aesthetic contemplation when one appreciates a beautiful object independent of the desire to possess or enjoy it.

It may be noted that, in his first book, *The Birth of Tragedy*, Nietzsche was indebted to Schopenhauer's discussion of artistic creation. Influenced by Hinduism, Schopenhauer identified the function of art with that of a "veil of illusion"—the Veil of Maya—that necessarily cloaks human perception of reality, protecting us from the dark truth of will. In similar fashion, Nietzsche proposed that in Greek tragedy the **Apollonian** principle of order and reason tempers and makes bearable life's Dionysian elements of chaos and destruction.

SEARCH FOR A METHOD. *See CRITIQUE OF DIALECTICAL REASON.*

SECOND SEX, THE. *See* BEAUVOIR, SIMONE DE; FEMINISM.

SELF. *See* AUTHENTICITY AND INAUTHENTICITY; EGO; FREEDOM.

SELF-CONSCIOUSNESS. *See* CONSCIOUSNESS; EGO; PREREFLECTIVE CONSCIOUSNESS.

SHAME. *See* OTHER, THE.

***SHE CAME TO STAY (L'Invitée,* 1943).** **Simone de Beauvoir**'s first novel, begun in 1938 and completed in 1941, during the German occupation of France, is set on the eve of **World War II**. The novel is based on Beauvoir's relationship with **Jean-Paul Sartre** and with her student, Olga Kosakiewicz, who became one of her closest friends during the war. When Beauvoir introduced Sartre to Olga he became infatuated, and for many months Olga, who did not return Sartre's affections, was the subject of Sartre's obsession. This became a source of frustration for Beauvoir, who genuinely liked Olga yet prized her relationship with Sartre above all else. Her intention to remain united with Sartre in mutual enjoyment and instruction of young Olga (Olga was 17 when they first met) backfired when Olga asserted her own subjectivity.

She Came to Stay tells the story of a similar "conflict of **consciousnesses**" among Françoise (based on Beauvoir), Pierre (based on Sartre), and Xavière (based on Olga). Beauvoir understands this conflict in Hegelian terms, as she announces in the epigraph to the book, a quotation from **G. W. F. Hegel**'s *Phenomenology of Spirit*: "Each consciousness seeks the **death** of the **other**." That is, in human relationships each struggles to possess the other, to control, rather than be controlled by, the other's consciousness. The novel develops various permutations of this theme. Initially, Xavière is merely an "annex" to Françoise, a pliable young girl from the provinces whom Françoise hopes to mold in her image by inviting her to Paris to live with her and Pierre. However, when Xavière begins to assert her own subjectivity, Françoise is forced to experience herself through Xavière's eyes. She sees herself as old, rigid and unspontaneous, jealous—an object judged by another and no longer a sovereign consciousness. Pierre becomes attracted to Xavière, and Xavière becomes increasingly hostile and intransigent to both Pierre and Françoise. The formerly hermetic world, in which Françoise and Pierre imagined that they were "as one," has been breached by a "third," who judges them and shatters their illusion of autonomy. No resolution seems possible. The novel ends with Francoise murdering Xavière by turning on the gas in her room while she sleeps.

She Came to Stay clearly has philosophical intentions as well as personal meaning for Beauvoir. **Maurice Merleau-Ponty**, who devoted an essay ("Metaphysics and the Novel") to the novel, praised it as a successful synthesis of philosophy and literature in which abstract ideas are given **concrete** expression through ordinary human relationships. He admired the way in which for Beauvoir "there is no Last Judgment . . . no other side of things where true and false, fair and unfair are separated out." In this way, for Merleau-Ponty the novel embodied a deep "metaphysical" truth: that "[w]e are inextricably . . . bound up with the world and with others" (SNS, 36). It should also be mentioned that *She Came to Stay* anticipated Sartre's treatment in *Being and Nothingness* of themes of desire, shame, the look of the other, and sadism and masochism.

SHESTOV, LEV (1866–1938). Russian philosopher and religious thinker. Along with **Nikolai Berdyaev**, Shestov is often classed as a "Russian **Christian** existentialist," but it should be noted that his views developed prior to and independently of the major currents of existential phenomenology in the 1920s and 1930s. Shestov's real name was Lev Isaakovich Schwarzmann. He migrated to Berlin in 1922 and then to Paris in the early 1930s. His works on **Fyodor Dostoevsky**, **Søren Kierkegaard**, and **Friedrich Nietzsche** were translated into French in the 1930s and won him an audience among French intellectuals.

Shestov had a mystic bent; stressed the **contingency**, arbitrariness, and **mystery** of **existence;** and was suspicious of attempts to formally analyze it. **Albert Camus** identifies him as a philosopher of the **absurd** and comments on him in *The Myth of Sisyphus*. His thought was not otherwise particularly influential in the development of French existentialism.

SIN. See *CONCEPT OF ANXIETY, THE.*

SINCERITY. According to **Jean-Paul Sartre**, being sincere in the sense of "being true to oneself" is a vice, not a virtue, for it requires the false assumption that one has a fixed nature, **essence**, or inner self in accordance with which one ought to live. Sartre analyzes the "ideal of sincerity" (BN, 62–67) as an instance of **bad faith**; in aspiring to sincerity, I must interpret myself as a "thing"—a person with a fixed character or nature—with which I might "coincide." The goal of sincerity is thus to disburden oneself of the **freedom** and **responsibility** of deciding who one is through one's **actions** and **commitments**. For Sartre, the ideal of sincerity is a basic pitfall of inauthentic **existence**.

SISYPHUS. See *MYTH OF SISYPHUS, THE.*

SITUATED FREEDOM. *See* FREEDOM; MERLEAU-PONTY, MAURICE; SARTRE, JEAN-PAUL; SITUATION.

SITUATION. The concept of situation plays an important role in existentialism, closely linked to the concepts of **action**, **commitment**, and **freedom**. In general terms, the situation is the product of an evolving relationship between freedom and **facticity**, that is, between human **projects** and the **world** in which they are engaged. Factical components of the situation include the past, the physical environment, social facts, and cultural artifacts; the "freedom" component refers to goals and intentions as expressed through one's **chosen** attitudes and actions. Existentialists differ somewhat in their interpretation of the concept, assigning more or less weight to facticity or to freedom. Nonetheless, there is general agreement that the concept of situation is ontologically hybrid, reducible to neither an "external world" of things nor an "internal" sphere of thought. Existentialist accounts of situation, like their accounts of freedom, are meant to recall the interdependence of self and world that cannot be further reduced without serious distortion.

    Jean-Paul Sartre provides the most detailed account of these issues. On the one hand, the situation is relative to one's project. To a mountain climber, a mountain is "climbable," a physical challenge to be met, while to a farmer the same mountain may be simply "untillable land." Similarly, the condition of slavery depends on the attitude in which it is "lived"; some slaves may accept enslavement as preordained, while others experience it as cause for revolt (BN, 550). In each case, the situation reveals the "properties" of things as dependent on human projects. On the other hand, Sartre observes that freedom must encounter some "resistance" to its realization, and that the factical givenness of the world provides such resistance. Accordingly, the mountain and the institution of slavery clearly must in a sense exist "in-themselves," independent of my thoughts and intentions. The facticity of the situation provides resistance, but only on the basis of the meaning my project assigns to it (BN, 482–483). Conversely, the goals I freely pursue are not conceived ex nihilo but as the "surpassing" of factical limits encountered in the social and physical environment. With this in mind, Sartre expresses the idea of "situated freedom": that "there is freedom only in a *situation*, and there is a situation only through freedom" (BN, 489).

Maurice Merleau-Ponty and **Martin Heidegger** offer accounts more weighted toward facticity. According to them, the situation is necessarily informed by an inherited "horizon of significance," projects and meanings *already* constituted by society and tradition. However, as Merleau-Ponty writes, if "[the] world is already constituted," it is "also never completely constituted" (PP, 453). Freedom is exercised by taking up possibilities from the past and actively making them one's own.

SKEPTICISM. *See* REALISM AND IDEALISM.

SOCIALISM. *See* COMMUNISM; MARXISM; POLITICS.

SOCIALISME ET LIBERTÉ (Socialism and Freedom). Short-lived **French Resistance** group organized in 1941 by **Jean-Paul Sartre** along with **Simone de Beauvoir**, **Maurice Merleau-Ponty**, and other intellectuals to fight the German occupation of France and prepare the way for a future socialist government, which, they naïvely believed, would take charge after the liberation of France. The group was a loosely knit association of socialist and Marxist intellectuals and writers, who printed clandestine pamphlets but lacked organization, political coherence, experience, and personal resolve. Twenty years later, in 1961, Sartre described the effort in these terms:

> In 1941, intellectuals, more or less throughout the country, formed groups which claimed to be resisting the conquering enemy. I belonged to one of these groups, "Socialism and Freedom." Merleau[-Ponty] joined us. This encounter was not the result of chance. Each of us had come from a *petit bourgeois* background. Our tastes, our tradition and our professional conscience moved both of us to defend **freedom** of the pen. Through this freedom we discovered all the others. But aside from that, we were simpletons. Born of enthusiasm, our little group caught a fever and died a year later, of not knowing what to do. (*Situations*, 167)

SOLICITUDE (Ger. *Fürsorge*). A technical term in the philosophy of **Martin Heidegger**'s *Being and Time*. Heidegger appropriates the ordinary German expression for "caring for others," as in "child care" or "care for the elderly," to designate *Dasein*'s attitude toward other human beings. He observes that relations with other persons are not incidental to but rather constitutive of a human life. Thus *Dasein*'s essential character as **being-in-the-world** is also a "being-with-others"; the world of everyday practical **concern** is a social world, suffused with the presence of other people. Even when, as is often the case in **everyday** existence, I am indifferent to other people and they do not matter to me, I still apprehend them as human beings to whom I am indifferent and never merely as things **present-at-hand**.

Heidegger outlines two extreme possibilities of solicitude: "that which *leaps in* and dominates, and that which *leaps ahead* and liberates." In *leaping in*, the most common mode, I relate to the other as a subject of concern: Perhaps I help to resolve a problem, for example, I loan a friend some money, and thus I "take away his 'care'." In *leaping ahead* of the other, in contrast, I "help the Other to become transparent to himself *in* his care and to become *free for* it." Unfortunately, the distinction remains highly schematic. Nonetheless, it is significant that Heidegger characterizes *leaping ahead* as the **authentic** manner of relating to other persons, one that somehow "frees the Other in his **freedom** for himself" (BT, 159; slightly altered). Heidegger's characterization of authentic solicitude is reminiscent of **Karl Jaspers**'s concept of authentic **philosophizing** as an illumination of possibilities rather than a justification of doctrines, which leads others to confront their freedom as *Existenz*.

SPACE/SPATIALITY. *See* MERLEAU-PONTY, MAURICE.

SPANISH EXISTENTIALISM. *See* ORTEGA Y GASSET, JOSÉ; UNAMUNO, MIGUEL DE.

SPIRIT OF SERIOUSNESS, THE (Fr. *l'esprit de sérieux***).** Jean-Paul Sartre uses this expression to characterize the common view that **values** exist independently of individual **choice** and **commitment**. For Sartre, such a view mistakenly posits values as preexisting facts rather than consequences of human attitudes; hence, objects become "mute demands" while the subject is "nothing . . . but the passive obedience to these demands" (BN, 626). The spirit of seriousness is exemplary of **bad faith** in that it is motivated by the desire to avoid taking **responsibility** for oneself and the **anxiety** that ensues from this realization.

SPIRITUALISM (Fr. *spiritualisme*). Movement in French philosophy whose name derives from the French term *esprit*, "mind." Spiritualism refers to the philosophical position that the higher powers of the mind, including the will and **emotions** such as love, joy, pride, and guilt, are free from physical determination and represent the **essence** of the human being. A spiritualist tradition in French philosophy begins with the 18th-century philosopher Maine de Biran. Spiritualism is continued in the 19th and early 20th centuries by thinkers such as Félix Ravaisson and **Henri Bergson**. The positions of **Jean-Paul Sartre**, in particular his view of the absolute nature of **consciousness** and **freedom**, have spiritualist overtones.

SPONTANEITY OF CONSCIOUSNESS. *See* CONSCIOUSNESS.

STATE-OF-MIND (Ger. *Befindlichkeit*). In the philosophy of **Martin Heidegger**, *Befindlichkeit* refers to the manner in which the meaning of one's **situation** registers in awareness prior to explicit self-reflection. Heidegger coins the term, derived from colloquial German expressions such as "Wie befinden Sie sich?"—"How are you?"—to capture the idea that we standardly find ourselves in a certain **mood** or disposition without (necessarily) knowing why, and without having chosen it. Central to Heidegger's account is the claim that state-of-mind reveals something about the world and not merely about ourselves, that it cannot be reduced to an "internal," "subjective" state that has no bearing on the way things are "externally" and "objectively." The main thrust of Heidegger's argument in Division I of *Being and Time* is to question the assumption that "reason" and "theoretical observation" are the primary human modes of access to reality; the thesis he defends is that, before the world can be objectively observed and rationally reflected on, it must first be apprehended in a more immediate fashion. State-of-mind is one of two basic modes of this apprehension of meaning; the other is "**understanding**" (*Verstehen*).

STRANGER, THE. *See* CAMUS, ALBERT; PHILOSOPHY OF THE ABSURD.

SUBJECT/SUBJECTIVISM. *See DASEIN.*

SUBJECTIVITY. *See* EXISTENCE; KIERKEGAARD, SØREN.

SUBSTANCE. In traditional philosophy, the category of substance refers to that which exists by itself in an unchanging form. According to Aristotle, a thing is a substance in the sense of being a permanent subject to which various properties are ascribed. (In this way, the distinction between substance and property is informed by the distinction between grammatical subject and predicate.) Moreover, substances are said to be ontologically primary in that properties and qualities cannot exist unless predicated of substances. Thus substance in ancient **ontology** indicates what is the most real in the sense of what is unchanging and self-identical.

Existentialists reject substance ontology as inadequate for understanding human **existence**. Human beings, they insist, do not exist in the same manner as nonhuman things like a stone, a planet, or a table. To begin with, a human being does not consist of some unchanging substrate onto which various changing properties are attached; there is no "**essence**" of the human being in the sense of a universal form or definition that is instantiated by individual humans. Rather, in the case of human beings it must be said that **existence precedes essence**, for what a person is (essence) emerges only in the course of **projects** and **commitments** (existence). Existence is thus fundamentally non-substance-like in that it admits of no permanent properties that can be described from an external perspective.

In place of the language of substance and property, the essential features of existence are described by existentialists as possible ways of **being**, chosen ways of relating to the world, oneself, and others. For example, while a table may be properly described in terms of objective properties such as "being made of wood" and "being six feet long," an existing person cannot be said to "have" properties in this sense. If Pierre "is a coward," it is because he has chosen this manner of being. In each case, what looks like an objective property is better understood as an existential project, a manner of committing oneself.

A further criticism of substance ontology is the manner in which primary substances are thought to exist independently of one another. This is particularly clear in **René Descartes**'s substance dualism, where minds or "spiritual substance" (*res cogitans*) are said to exist independently of things or "material substance" (*res extensa*). **Martin Heidegger** develops a sustained critique of Descartes's substance ontology in *Being and Time*. The core of his criticism is that the relationship between human being and world cannot be thought of as that between two independent substances. Instead, Heidegger defines *Dasein* in terms of its relation to the world, and the world in turn is defined in terms of *Dasein*'s historical, pragmatic, and projective character. *See also* ESSENCE; EXISTENCE.

SUICIDE. Albert Camus begins *The Myth of Sisyphus* with the surprising claim that "suicide is the only serious philosophical question." Suicide, for Camus, is tied to the concept of the **absurd**, the realization that life has no ultimate purpose or justification. The question Camus is concerned with is, does the absurd require suicide?

Camus distinguishes between the physical act of taking one's own life and what he calls "philosophical suicide," seeking an intellectual means of escape from life's absurdity in illusory truths of **metaphysics**, religion, or science. Both are, ultimately, inappropriate forms of response to the absurd. Belief in the redemptive power of religion, in scientific progress, or in philosophical system-building brings solace to the individual at the price of intellectual dishonesty, imputing **transcendent** meaning to **existence** where there is none, or where we can never be sure there is any. These are "metaphysical" illusions, contradicted by the evidence of human history and by the immediate certainties of existence: that I exist here and now, that I can find no reason for existing (i.e., that I and any other part of the world are purely **contingent** and could just as readily not exist), and that I will die.

The physical act of suicide is also an inappropriate response, a concession to absurdity that confirms life's futility. In place of physical suicide or appeal to abstract forces or entities about which I can never be certain, Camus exhorts a response of "lucid struggle" or "revolt." In an attitude of lucid revolt, individuals commit themselves passionately and consciously to their **choices** and activities. This is the response of Camus's **Sisyphus**, the exemplary existential hero, who, fully conscious of his futile labors, nonetheless embraces his **situation**, for he realizes that he is free, "master of his own destiny." "The struggle itself toward the heights is enough to fill a man's heart," Camus writes. "One must imagine Sisyphus happy" (MS, 123). In the end, lucid consciousness of the absurd enables one to overcome **nihilism** and to seize upon one's own **action** and **passion** as the source of life's meaning. *See also* DEATH.

SURREALISM. Modernist movement in literature and art that flourished in Paris between about 1924 and 1939. The surrealists' chief concern was to explore the meaning of the **unconscious** mind, that "shadow world" of repressed desires and childhood fantasies analyzed in the work of **Sigmund Freud**. With the publication of his *Surrealist Manifesto* in 1924, André Breton became the movement's nominal leader. Breton celebrated dreams as the finest fruit of human imagination, and he proposed the literary technique of "automatic writing," a spontaneous and undirected flow of written words that allowed authors to access unconscious associations and create unexpected "sparks" of meaning. In similar fashion, painters such as Max Ernst and René Magritte juxtaposed incongruous images to produce haunting, dreamlike canvases. Surrealist writers who later became associated with existentialism include **Georges Bataille** and Michel Leiris. As a college student in the mid- and late 1920s, **Jean-Paul Sartre** was attracted to surrealism and often emulated the surrealist style in his early fiction. His first published novel, *Nausea*, retained surrealist elements such as references to madness and hallucination. Surrealism was largely dead as an artistic movement by the end of **World War II**. *See also* EXISTENTIALIST LITERATURE.

– T –

TELEOLOGICAL SUSPENSION OF THE ETHICAL. For **Søren Kierkegaard**, the idea that in the experience of genuine religious **faith**, **ethical** norms may be superseded by divine directives. The idea is explored by Kierkegaard in *Fear and Trembling* through the biblical story of **Abraham**. In the **moment** that Abraham is commanded by God to sacrifice Isaac, he is faced with an apparently irreconcilable conflict: on the one hand to love his son (and not to commit murder), on the other to obey God. Kierkegaard insists that Abraham's decision to obey God cannot be rationally explained. His faith evokes awe and admiration but remains beyond our comprehension, for "faith begins precisely where thought stops" (FT, 53).

Kierkegaard's notion of the teleological suspension of the ethical is intended to oppose **G. W. F. Hegel**'s view that religion may be fully articulated in rational terms without reference to a **transcendent** reality; it is also opposed to the idea that following universal ethical norms is sufficient for religious faith. If there is no transcendent reality and everything may be explained as immanent to the process of human history, Kierkegaard observes, then Abraham is simply "a murderer." If, however, we are to accept Abraham as the father of faith, then we must accept the possibility that he entered into relation with a transcendent reality.

TEMPORALITY. Existentialists, in particular **Martin Heidegger**, use this term to designate the subjective and anthropological dimensions of time, the varied human modalities of **understanding** and assessing things in time, rather than the objective features of the **time-series**. From the existentialist perspective, time as a theoretical concept is derivative from ordinary processes of temporal interpretation and understanding, which provide requisite background assumptions for philosophical and scientific theories. Heidegger's *Being and Time* devotes considerable attention to these issues. Heidegger distinguishes existential temporality from scientific and traditional philosophical and theological conceptions of time. Existential temporality, lived time, is essentially *futural*, in that a human life is primarily guided by future possibilities (plans, **projects**), which "stand out" as the **horizon** of present concerns without themselves being reducible to contents or experiences present in the mind. It is also characterized as "ecstatic"—literally, "standing outside"—in that one is continually "ahead of oneself" in one's orientation toward future goals and projects. Existential temporality, furthermore, is **finite** in that the ultimate future possibility, in relation to which both past and present come into focus, is the possibility of one's own **death**. Thus

Heidegger speaks of **authentic** temporality as a kind of **being-to-wards-death**, a tacit recognition of one's own finitude that organizes past and present concerns. In authentic being-towards-death, each of the three temporal **ecstases**—future, past, and present—is coimplicated in a process Heidegger calls "primordial **historizing**." Here, "**Dasein** *hands* itself *down* to itself . . . in a possibility which it has inherited and yet has chosen" (BT, 435).

In contrast, traditional philosophical, scientific, and theological conceptions of time are modeled on the idea of unchanging (atemporal) **substance**. The notion of God as perfect and unchanging being is representative of this tradition, as is the notion of intelligible form or essence underlying a variable perceptible world. Heidegger's contention in *Being and Time* is that existential temporality, in particular the authentic temporality revealed through the experience of being-towards-death, provides the horizon for any understanding of being whatsoever. Time is the most basic mode in which things are apprehended and evaluated. The theoretical conception of time as static, unchanging presence is a deformation of a more basic existential understanding of time as dynamic, futural, and historical.

TEMPS MODERNES, LES (*Modern Times*). French journal of ideas founded in 1945 by **Jean-Paul Sartre**, **Simone de Beauvoir**, and **Maurice Merleau-Ponty**. *Les temps modernes* quickly became the leading review of its kind in France and the main vehicle for the dissemination of Sartrean existentialism. It also served as a platform for airing and defending the socialist ideals of its founders. In the editor's introduction to the first issue (October 1945), Sartre announced the controversial ideal of **committed literature**, to which the journal would be devoted. The original editorial board included **Raymond Aron**; Merleau-Ponty served as political editor from 1945 to about 1950, and many of his early essays on **politics** and philosophy were first published there. He resigned from the journal in 1953 due to political differences with Sartre. Several important works of existentialism were first published in *Les Temps modernes*, including Sartre's *What Is Literature?* and *Anti-Semite and Jew*, and portions of Beauvoir's *The Ethics of Ambiguity* and *The Second Sex*. While most of the review's articles focused on politics, economics, and sociology, *Les temps modernes* also featured the work of such literary modernists as **Samuel Beckett**, **Jean Genet**, **André Gide**, and Francis Ponge.

THEATER OF THE ABSURD. Modernist movement in French theater, also referred to as "New Theater" and "Anti-Theater," that flourished in Paris in the 1950s and early 1960s. Plays typical of the genre, such as **Samuel Beckett**'s *Waiting for Godot* and Eugène Ionesco's *The Bald Soprano*, were virtually devoid of traditional plot and character development. They focused instead on linguistically playful dialogue that highlighted the **absurdity** of the characters' situation, including their inability to communicate with one another. Works in the theater of the absurd were at times misleadingly identified as "existentialist" due to their ostensible portrayal of human **alienation** and the "meaninglessness" of the **human condition**. But absurdist playwrights themselves espoused no particular philosophical position and did not see themselves as linked to existentialist philosophy. The critic who introduced the phrase "theater of the absurd," Martin Esslin, had in mind the concept of the absurd espoused by **Albert Camus**, which Esslin believed to be the shared element of these plays. **Jean Genet**, a playwright whom Esslin associated with the theater of the absurd, was the subject of a biographical study by **Jean-Paul Sartre**, *Saint Genet: Actor, Martyr* (1952). *See also* EXISTENTIALIST LITERATURE.

THEISTIC EXISTENTIALISM. *See* RELIGIOUS EXISTENTIALISM.

THEOLOGY, EXISTENTIAL. *See* EXISTENTIAL THEOLOGY.

THEORETICAL ATTITUDE. *See* KNOWING SUBJECT.

THEY, THE. *See* DAS MAN.

THROWNNESS (Ger. *Geworfenheit*). **Martin Heidegger** thematizes the sense in which to exist is to be thrust into a world whose meaning is already constituted and thus to confront circumstances beyond one's control. In ***Being and Time***, Heidegger calls the condition of finding oneself in a preconstituted historical and social world "thrownness": "Dasein is something that has been thrown; it has been brought into its 'there', but not of its own accord" (BT, 329). The term is meant to highlight the way one is "cast" into one's **situation** without having chosen it, and also perhaps to evoke the fortuitous character of existing in a particular place and time. Yet thrownness is not a negative condition that might be overcome, for a human life requires finite parameters within which particular **choices** can take place. Thus, while the notion of thrownness is closely related to that of **facticity** it also stands in a complementary tension with that of **freedom**, *Dasein*'s manner of **projecting** possibilities. Heidegger's description of *Dasein* as a *"geworfende Entwurf"* or "thrown project" captures nicely the complementarity of these ideas.

TILLICH, PAUL (1886–1965). German-born American Protestant theologian and proponent of **existential theology**. Tillich became acquainted with **Martin Heidegger** when both men were professors at Marburg University in the mid-1920s, and Heidegger's thought remained a strong influence on Tillich's thinking throughout his life. When Adolf Hitler took power in 1933, Tillich immigrated to the United States, where he taught religion and theology at Union Theological Seminary, Harvard University, and the University of Chicago. After **World War II**, he became popular as an interpreter of existentialism, mainly on the basis of his book *The Courage to Be* (1952).

Of the theologians influenced by the work of Heidegger, Tillich perhaps remained most faithful to the existential position of Heidegger's *Being and Time*. For Tillich, as for Heidegger, the nature of things is revealed through human experience and cannot be approached by abstract reasoning. Defining features of human **existence** are an awareness of **death** and a unique questioning attitude toward **being**. Death brings home to me my essential **finitude**, my relation to **"nothingness"** or "nonbeing." In the face of death I feel **anxiety**, and in response I am led to raise the **ontological** question of what stands beyond the finite being I experience, the question of what Tillich calls "being-itself." Traditionally, this is the question of God. Yet Tillich, once again following Heidegger, rejects the idea of God as a type of superentity. The traditional **Christian** view of God as a personal being is mistaken, he believes, because it conflates what is truly "ultimate" with a "symbol" for the ultimate. Existentially,

God is experienced as "the ground of being," a power greater than myself and my world that cannot be further articulated or explained. Thus, religious doctrines are true when taken as symbolic statements, false when taken as **representations** of reality. In this regard, Tillich's theological position is similar to that of **Karl Jaspers** and other **religious existentialists**.

Tillich's most widely read book, *The Courage to Be*, offers a wide-ranging synthesis of existentialist philosophy focused around the experience of anxiety. In his analysis, anxiety is a disturbing yet transformative **emotion** provoked by the experience of death, meaninglessness, and guilt. Anxiety Tillich defined as "the existential awareness of nonbeing," the awareness of finitude and mortality. Courage he saw as the ability to "affirm being" in the face of nonbeing, in spite of anxiety. Courage is a power of self-affirmation and affirmation of the world that transcends finite human capacities. Thus courage is evidence that we are capable of being "grasped by the power of being-itself" (*The Courage to Be*, 156).

TIME. *See* TEMPORALITY.

TOLSTOY, LEO. *See DEATH OF IVAN ILYICH, THE*; EXISTENTIALIST LITERATURE.

TOTALITY AND INFINITY (*Totalité et l'infini*, **1961**). Original work of **existential phenomenology** by **Emmanuel Levinas**. Subtitled "An Essay in Exteriority," the book is a rejoinder to what Levinas takes to be the egocentric accounts of **existence** proposed by **Martin Heidegger** in *Being and Time* and **Jean-Paul Sartre** in *Being and Nothingness*. Employing dense poetic language reminiscent of the style of the Jewish existentialists **Franz Rosenzweig** and **Martin Buber**, to whom he is consciously indebted, Levinas outlines a "**phenomenology** of the **other**" in which the encounter with the other person disrupts the complacent life of the **ego**. The face of the other person—the widow, the orphan, "the Stranger"—compels me to respond yet remains distant from me, irreducible to my perspective. Levinas maintains that this encounter with otherness is the very foundation of **ethics**: Without otherness, the self would remain within its circuit of beliefs, needs, and desires.

A major shortcoming of Heidegger and Sartre's accounts, according to Levinas, is their failure to acknowledge the foundational role of the other within existence. In Levinas's terminology, they remain wedded to **ontology**, the study of **being**. But the other exists "beyond being," that is, outside of any conception I can form of him or her. The **transcendence** of the human other is an analogue of the human experience of the "absolute other," God. Levinas echoes many of the criticisms of Heidegger's philosophy voiced by Martin Buber. His treatment of the other may be understood as a development of Buber's philosophy of the "I" and the "You."

TOWARDS THE CONCRETE. See CONCRETE, TOWARDS THE.

TRAGEDY. *See* APOLLONIAN AND DIONYSIAN; HELLENISM; SCHOPENHAUER, ARTHUR.

TRAGIC SENSE OF LIFE, THE. See UNAMUNO, MIGUEL DE.

TRAKL, GEORG. *See* POETRY AND PHILOSOPHY.

TRANSCENDENCE OF THE EGO, THE. See SARTRE, JEAN-PAUL.

TRANSCENDENTAL EGO. *See* EGO; HUSSERL, EDMUND.

TRANSCENDENCE. The concept of transcendence, expressed also by the related forms "to transcend" and "transcendent," has several distinct meanings in existentialism, though all are linked to the basic sense of the term, "to go beyond" or "to surpass." Traditional philosophy understands transcendence as the state of being beyond experience or outside of the empirical world, in contrast to "immanence," the state of being immediately present or given to experience. God, understood as standing beyond the empirical world, is a traditional example of a transcendent being. Existentialists reject the idea of a transcendent being to which we have no experiential access, including the idea of transcendence (such as God) that can be known only through intellectual contemplation. They propose instead a range of idiomatic usages, the primary sense of which is the idea that the human being is always "beyond itself" or "transcends itself" by striving toward future possibilities. **Jean-Paul Sartre** in particular characterizes **consciousness** in terms of a power of "transcendence," the capacity to continually **negate** and press beyond the actual toward the possible.

A contrasting usage is **Martin Heidegger**'s idea of the "transcendence of the **world**," that the totality of human practices and purposes serves as the unthematized **horizon** for our practical engagements, "standing beyond" *Dasein*'s absorption with particular things. This sense of transcendence derives from the **phenomenological** tradition where it refers to that which is not given but is presupposed in a conscious act. For example, the unseen side of an object I perceive is said to be *transcendent to* my perception. Phenomenologists also speak of the *horizon* as transcendent in this sense. Every object has a horizon or transcendent aspect. Thus, Heidegger's usage derives from the idea that the "world" is the horizon of horizons, the ultimate background of intelligibility to which all particular involvements with things refer.

A final sense of transcendence is developed in the philosophy of **Karl Jaspers** and approximates to the traditional meaning of the term as it applies especially to God. Jaspers understands transcendence as nonobjective and noncognizable "**being**." As such, transcendence cannot be objectively defined or named, only indicated by "**ciphers**" like "being," "actuality," or "God." **Concrete** experiences of transcendent being in turn are the source of **authentic** human being or *Existenz*. "Where I am authentically myself, I know that I have been given to myself . . . . I am aware of the transcendence through which I am" (BPW, 175). Jaspers's account thus differs from traditional views in that transcendence must be existentially apprehended and cannot merely be thought or contemplated.

TROUBLED SLEEP. *See ROADS TO FREEDOM, THE.*

TRUTH IS SUBJECTIVITY. *See* KIERKEGAARD, SØREN .

TURGENEV, IVAN (1818-1883). Russian novelist, known to **Friedrich Nietzsche**, whose novel *Fathers and Sons* first popularized the term **nihilism**. In the novel, the student Bazarov claims to deny all traditional **values**, in art and **politics** as well as religion. Furthermore, he claims that he is only required to deny and has no obligation to offer anything constructive in place of what has been denied. Turgenev's usage became the source of political Nihilism, a widespread revolutionary position in 19th-century Russia. The Nihilists sought to remake the world anew, denying not only traditional religious belief but also modern institutions of law and morality as obstacles to personal **freedom** and happiness. Nietzsche's conception of nihilism differed significantly. For Nietzsche, nihilism resulted from the **death of God**, the loss of a **transcendent** source of value in human affairs.

– U –

ULTIMATE SITUATION. *See* LIMIT SITUATION.

UNAMUNO, MIGUEL DE (1864-1936). Spanish novelist, poet, and professor of philology at the University of Salamanca. Unamuno is sometimes classified as an existentialist due to his focus on passion, suffering, **mystery**, and uncertainty in human life. However, his existential concerns receive little systematic or sustained philosophical treatment. Moreover, his work developed independently of the trends in German and French philosophy that contributed to existentialism, notably **phenomenology**. Unamuno was nonetheless familiar with **Søren Kierkegaard**'s work, and his ideas about **faith** and religion bear comparison with those of **religious existentialists** like **Gabriel Marcel** and **Martin Buber**. In *The Tragic Sense of Life* (1913), his most widely read book of ideas, Unamuno endorses the view that one ought to have religious faith despite the fact that one must remain uncertain of God's **existence** and of the possibility of redemption in an afterlife. Only through the passion of **commitment** can meaninglessness be escaped. Similar themes are explored in Unamuno's last novel, *San Manuel bueno, martir* (1933), which describes the agony of a priest who finds it impossible to believe.

UNCANNY (Ger. *Unheimlich*). This term is given special meaning by **Martin Heidegger**, particularly in *Being and Time*, where the "uncanny" or "uncanniness" (*Unheimlichkeit*) is a feeling of "not being at home" that accompanies the experience of **anxiety**. In anxiety, one becomes open to the possibility of **authentic existence**, experiencing oneself as radically **individualized**, **free**, and **responsible**. Authenticity is thus felt as a shock to **everyday** existence where one is "at home" in the world, comfortable with an average understanding of things and human possibilities. In anxiety, Heidegger writes, "everyday familiarity collapses" and one "enters into the existential 'mode' of '*not-at-home*'" (BT, 233), that is, of uncanniness. In this way, Heidegger exploits the etymological meaning of *unheimlich*, "not-homelike," linking it to the term's ordinary German acceptations of "strange," "weird," or "sinister." Characteristically, Heidegger asserts that ordinary experiences of uncanniness are dependent on the deeper existential sense of human groundlessness. Uncanniness for Heidegger thus remains an ever-present possibility for human experience—the possibility of apprehending oneself as lacking internal or external ground or cause—even if for the most part it is suppressed by everyday requirements for cheerfulness and familiarity.

UNDERSTANDING (Ger. *Verstehen*). In the vocabulary of **Martin Heidegger**'s *Being and Time*, understanding is, along with **state-of-mind**, one of the two primary dimensions of *Dasein*'s apprehension of **being**. The thrust of Heidegger's argument is to show that human beings have a preconceptual understanding of the **world** and of themselves, and that the goal of philosophy is in large part to make this understanding explicit and submit it to appropriate analysis and criticism. In Heidegger's analysis, *Dasein* understands the world and itself not primarily through reflective acts of cognition but rather through **prereflective projection** of its plans and purposes. This projection of possibilities is, moreover, largely pragmatic and affective rather than reflective and theoretical. For example, I understand the "being" of a hammer by using it, picking it up, and driving in nails, not by merely contemplating it; similarly, I understand myself through my various professional and personal involvements and not primarily through self-reflection. *See also* UNDERSTANDING AND EXPLANATION.

UNDERSTANDING AND EXPLANATION (Ger. *Verstehen* and *Erklärung*). The distinction between **hermeneutical** understanding

(*Verstehen*) and causal explanation (*Erklärung*) was first made by **Wilhelm Dilthey** to capture the difference between the aims and methods of the social and human sciences (*Geisteswissenschaften*) and those of the natural sciences. While the natural scientist aims to explain an object by describing its physical causes from an external perspective, the historian or philosopher seeks, in addition to causal explanation, to understand by a kind of "sympathetic intuition" how a person or group of people experienced ideas and events *from the inside*, from the perspective of their own history and culture.

The notion of understanding as *Verstehen* is qualified by **Karl Jaspers**, in *General Psychopathology*, in terms of a "static" understanding of subjectively experienced states and acts, which is provided by **Husserlian phenomenology**, and a "genetic" understanding of how particular thoughts, acts, and **emotions** emerge out of past thoughts and acts—that is, of psychological motives as experienced by the individual. **Martin Heidegger**'s account of the "fore-structure" of *Dasein*'s **understanding** is another significant development of Dilthey's view of hermeneutic understanding. *See also* HERMENEUTIC CIRCLE, THE.

– V –

VALUE. The general thrust of the existentialist view is that values cannot be spoken of independently of human **projects**, in whose light they appear, and thus that the traditional fact/value distinction does not apply unproblematically in human experience. **Martin Heidegger** argues that the concept of objective **reality** as a kind of neutral "matter," onto which human meanings are subsequently appended, is an illusion. Rather, the world is irreducibly meaningful; the idea of neutral things "**present-at-hand**" is derivative of a more fundamental experience of things as intrinsically useful and valuable. **Jean Paul-Sartre** is the main existentialist to discuss the issue of value explicitly. His claim that values are "chosen" and not "discovered" does not mean that one's core values may be changed at a moment's notice, or that they may be created ex nihilo. Rather, his point is that there is no single value perspective built into the nature of things that one is thus required to assume; one chooses to accept a given perspective, whether or not one is aware of this **choice**. For example, religious values gain legitimacy not from divine commandments or from other religious authority but from one's choice to accept them as directives for **action**. Being aware that one has chosen one's own directives for action is an essential part of **authentic** existence. In contrast, appealing to values as pregiven facts is symptomatic of what Sartre calls the "**spirit of seriousness**," which underlies a major form of **bad faith**.

VIAN, BORIS (1920-59). French writer. Vian was a true polymath; an accomplished novelist, playwright, and poet, he was also a dedicated jazz trumpeter, song writer, and jazz critic. A friend of **Jean-Paul Sartre** and **Simon de Beauvoir** in the 1940s and early 1950s, Vian was admired as "the most versatile" of Sartre's social entourage. His popular novel *L'Écume des jours* (1947) celebrated the early years of "existentialist" revelry in and around **Saint-Germain-des-Prés**. *See also* CAFÉ EXISTENTIALIST.

VITALISM. The core of vitalism is the idea that life cannot be reduced to material causes. The term is often applied to the position of **Henri Bergson**, **Wilhelm Dilthey**, and **Friedrich Nietzsche**, where it is understood in a sense equivalent to the expression "**philosophy of life**." However, vitalism also may refer to a range of theories in biology and the history of science. Thus "philosophy of life" more accurately describes the intentions of thinkers like Bergson, Dilthey, and Nietzsche, whose interests were primarily philosophical rather than empirical or scientific in a narrow sense. *See also ÉLAN VITAL*; WILL TO POWER.

VOLITION. *See* WILL.

VOLUNTARISM. *See* ETHICAL VOLUNTARISM.

– **W** –

WAHL, JEAN (1888–1974). French philosopher and influential professor of philosophy at the Sorbonne in Paris. Wahl's books and commentaries were instrumental in the introduction of existential philosophy in

France in the 1930s and 1940s and in the propagation of existentialism in France, Europe, and the United States throughout the 1940s and 1950s. **Jean-Paul Sartre** cites Wahl's *Vers le concret* (1932) (*see CONCRETE, TOWARDS THE*) as an important early work for himself and fellow philosophy students who, in the early 1930s, hungered for a philosophical approach to "**concrete**," "lived" experience as an antidote to the complacent academic philosophies of their college professors. Wahl's *Études Kierkegardiennes* (1938) was an extremely influential early study of the philosophy of **Søren Kierkegaard**, and his *Le Malheur de la conscience de Hegel* (1929) helped introduce **G. W. F. Hegel** to a generation of French intellectuals, including Sartre and **Maurice Merleau-Ponty**. Wahl's other books include *A Short History of Existentialism* (1949) and *Philosophies of Existence* (1969).

***WAITING FOR GODOT. See* BECKETT, SAMUEL.**

WEBER, MAX (1864–1920). Preeminent German sociologist of the late 19th and early 20th centuries. Weber's analysis of the bureaucratization and "rationalization of society" provided a strong model of the inauthenticity of modern life (*see* AUTHENTICITY AND INAUTHENTICITY). Weber had wide-ranging influence on intellectual life in Germany in the early decades of the 20th century, including influence on some existentialists.

As the center of an intellectual circle at the University of Heidelberg in the years following **World War I**, Weber was a formative influence on **Karl Jaspers**, then a lecturer in psychology. In *Psychology of Worldviews* (1919), Jaspers transposed Weber's notion of "ideal types" from the sociology of religion to the field of psychology. Along with **Wilhelm Dilthey**, Weber was a proponent of the *Verstehen* (**understanding**) approach to the social sciences, which defended understanding the past on the basis of one's own cultural and historical assumptions, which are taken to be necessary guides for, rather than impediments to, historical understanding. Jaspers's *General Psychopathology*, which had introduced the *Verstehen* approach to the field of psychology, was already indebted to Weber. The notion of *Verstehen* is the foundation for modern **hermeneutics**; as such it is also of central importance for **Martin Heidegger**'s analysis of **existence** in *Being and Time*.

Weber defended a strict distinction between facts and **values**. Science and philosophy are, or ought to be, value-neutral, concerned exclusively with factual description, analysis, and explanation. In contrast, religion, art, and culture reflect particular *Weltanschauungen* or **worldviews** that express particular cultural and historical evaluations of the world; among these there is no one true view but a diversity of different perspectives across time and cultures. In *Psychology of Worldviews*, Jaspers endeavored to respect Weber's fact/value distinction by describing, without evaluating, the structure of various worldviews and the psychological types associated with them.

WEIL, SIMONE (1909–1943). French philosopher, political activist, and mystic. A brilliant philosophy student, Weil was one of the few women to be admitted to the prestigious **École Normale Supérieure** in Paris, where her classmates included **Raymond Aron** and **Maurice Merleau-Ponty**. As a young philosophy teacher, she became obsessed with issues of social justice and worked tirelessly for workers' causes, becoming an influential figure in the French Anarcho-Syndicalist movement through articles in which she challenged **communist** orthodoxy. Out of sympathy for workers and the suffering of the poor, she lived a life of material deprivation that was also a form of self-punishment. She served as a cook on the frontlines in the Spanish Civil War and as a Paris factory laborer, where she disguised her upper-class Jewish identity. A series of mystical experiences prompted her conversion to **Catholicism** around 1938; her subsequent thought combines mysticism with a type of Platonic **metaphysics** that recognizes goodness as an absolute, nonmaterial value. Weil's **death** at age 34 from complications of anorexia has been interpreted by some as a type of martyrdom. Her writings were published posthumously after **World War II**, many in a series edited by **Albert Camus**. Weil's assessment of the moral situation of France in 1940, *The Need for Roots* (1949; *L'Enracinement*), helped Camus "to crystallize his own views on non-violence and . . . anti-history" (Lottman, 374), which he published in *The Rebel*.

WELTANSCHAUUNG . *See* WORLDVIEW.

WHAT IS LITERATURE? See COMMITTED LITERATURE.

"WHAT IS METAPHYSICS?" (*"Was ist Metaphysik?"* 1929). **Martin Heidegger**'s inaugural public lecture on assuming the chair of philosophy at Freiburg University; the lecture was published in German as an essay the same year. Since the publication of *Being and Time* in 1927, Heidegger had developed a reputation in Germany as a revolutionary philosopher of great promise. "What Is Metaphysics?" helped confirm this reputation and introduced his thinking to a wider readership abroad. Heidegger's idiosyncratic reference to "the nothing" and "nothingness" (*das Nichts*) stirred a good deal of controversy at the time. Some found Heidegger's language intentionally mystifying; harsher critics, like Rudolph Carnap, accused Heidegger of speaking sheer nonsense, confusing a grammatical form of negation with a grammatical substantive. But many found Heidegger's ideas provocative and stimulating. **Jean-Paul Sartre** described the 1938 French translation of Heidegger's lecture by **Henri Corbin** (published in the collection *Qu'est-ce que la métaphysique?*) as "providential," providing him with notions of **authenticity** and **historicity** just when he needed them (WD, 182).

Heidegger's general intention in the lecture is to defend the autonomy of philosophy and to establish its foundational role vis-à-vis the sciences, an argument outlined in *Being and Time*. The intent of Heidegger's reference to "the nothing" is to recapture the original depth and significance of philosophical thought. In contrast to science, which recognizes only determinate, positive entities, philosophy maintains at least a peripheral interest in the question of "nonbeing" and "nothingness." "Why is there something rather than nothing?" is the consummate question of **metaphysics**, for it places the matter of nothingness in relation to **being**. Yet when nothingness is approached solely through reflective thought, it appears illusory. Thus, Heidegger reasons, it must be approached through a nonreflective experience, the experience of **anxiety**. Heidegger rehearses his account from *Being and Time*. In anxiety, Heidegger maintains, the everyday world "withdraws," and one is left with an indeterminate apprehensiveness and uneasiness, a sense of **uncanniness**. The source of this uneasiness, however, is no specific thing or state of affairs. Ultimately, it is an apprehension of the groundlessness of one's own being, that one is essentially a **thrown**, finite, "being of possibility," a "being-in-the-world" and not a **substantial** thing in any traditional sense. Anxiety reveals the "nothingness" of human beings hand in hand with the "nothingness" of the world. It allows us to be moved by the "wonder" and "strangeness" of beings themselves, and ultimately provokes us to ask "why." In this way, Heidegger's essay concludes with a remarkable reversal: Far from being illusory and nonexistent, the nothing lies at the root of all human inquiry, for without an apprehension of nothingness we would not be moved to inquire into why things are as they are.

WILL. *See* CHOICE; ETHICAL VOLUNTARISM; FREEDOM.

WILL TO POWER (Ger. *Wille zur Macht*). While he accepted the claim of Darwinian science that living things strive to survive and reproduce, **Friedrich Nietzsche** maintained that desire for self-preservation and reproduction are not ultimate causes of life but rather instances of a more fundamental drive he called the "will to power." The will to power, Nietzsche speculated, is the drive of all living things not merely to preserve themselves but to "discharge their strength," to enhance their conditions for existing, to extend beyond their current limits, and to impress themselves on the world in some fashion. The will to power is thus clearly a metaphysical doctrine. Under one interpretation, Nietzsche is asserting by it the general principle of **vitalism**: that life cannot be reduced to material or mechanical causes. On this basis, Nietzsche may be classified as a **philosopher of life**. But Nietzsche's primary concern was how the will to power may be expressed in *human* life. It was clear to Nietzsche that human beings sometimes act out of a higher purpose than self-preservation. He contended that many apparently benign and selfless behaviors, such as the philosophical pursuit of truth, the defense of religious beliefs, and the enforcement of moral rules, were disguised expressions of power.

In the late 1930s, **Martin Heidegger** interpreted Nietzsche's doctrine of the will to power as the culminating expression of Western **metaphysics**. By assimilating reality to the human act of will, Heidegger claimed, Nietzsche was simply rendering explicit the tacit anthropocentrism of the philosophical tradition, for which all things exist as objects to be known or manipulated by human beings. Heidegger's view of philosophy as dominated by a subjective will to mastery is apparent in his *Letter on Humanism*.

WITTGENSTEIN, LUDWIG (1889–1951). Austrian philosopher, the preeminent analytic philosopher of the 20th century. Wittgenstein's early work, *Tractatus Logico-Philosophicus* (1922), provided a foundation for **logical positivism**. His later work, published posthumously as *Philosophical Investigations* (1953), was the origin of "ordinary language philosophy." Both his early and later positions have been immensely influential in Anglo–American philosophy. Wittgenstein's use of linguistic analysis as a deflationary tool, and his association with the anti**metaphysical** programs of philosophers like Bertrand Russell, A. J. Ayer, Rudolph Carnap, and Gilbert Ryle, have lent credence to the view that his thought is, or at least ought to be, opposed to existentialism. However, he was not particularly hostile to existentialism, and his viewpoint can be construed as complementary to the existentialist perspective in several respects. On at least one occasion Wittgenstein expressed sympathy with the views of **Martin Heidegger** and **Søren Kierkegaard**: "I can readily think what Heidegger means by **being** and **anxiety**. Man has the impulse to run up against the limits of language. Think, for example, of the astonishment that anything exists. . . . This running-up against Kierkegaard also recognized and even designated it in a quite similar way (as running-up against paradox). This running-up against the limits of language is *ethics*" (cited in *Heidegger and Modern Philosophy*, edited by Michael Murray, 80, translation slightly altered). Wittgenstein's appreciation for Heidegger's "astonishment that anything exists" is less surprising when one recalls that their concerns grew, in part, out of the same soil of post-**Kantian** German philosophy. Hence, Wittgenstein's belief that language represents "the limits" of the **world** is linked to the possibility of suggesting (or "showing") by extra-philosophical means (e.g., by poetry or art) an apprehension of what lies beyond the world, for instance, a sense of the world in its totality. "It is not *how* things are in the world that it mystical, but that it exists," Wittgenstein wrote (*Tractatus*, 6.44). Heidegger expressed a similar thought in "**What Is Metaphysics?**" referring to the feeling of wonder "that there is something rather than nothing." In each case it should be noted that, while "the mystical" and "the nothing" defy scientific description and explanation, they are certainly not without meaning in their proper (nontheoretical) spheres. In this way, unlike the logical positivists, Wittgenstein was not critical of religious, "**ethical**," or "mystical" sentiments per se but rather of philosophers' attempts to express and justify them theoretically. In a manner not unlike existentialist philosophers, such as Heidegger and **Karl Jaspers**, he sought to set limits to the theoretical claims of philosophy and science in order to safeguard that which "cannot be put into words."

WORLD. A central concept in **Martin Heidegger**'s *Being and Time*. Heidegger observes that the world is not the totality of objects **present-at-hand** occurring in space but is first and foremost a human world, the total network of human purposes and meanings that *Dasein* understands **prereflectively** in its involvements with things **ready-to-hand**. The world thus does not come into view as a particular entity. Rather, it is an a priori whole: It functions as the **horizon** for **understanding** particular entities. The human being exists "in" the world, not in the sense that the glass is "in" the cupboard, but in the sense of being actively engaged in it, grasping its meaning through immediate practical **concern**. The core of *Dasein*'s being is thus characterized as a **being-in-the-world**.

WORLD AS WILL AND REPRESENTATION, THE. *See* SCHOPENHAUER, ARTHUR.

WORLDVIEW (Ger. *Weltanschauung*). The notion of the worldview was a product of historically sensitive 19th-century German philosophy. A worldview is the general cognitive and evaluative framework according to which groups and individuals perceive the **world**. One may speak, for example, of the "scientific worldview," the "Christian worldview," or the "artistic worldview" to designate the basic perspective from which the scientist, **Christian**, or artist apprehends reality. According to the **hermeneutic** philosopher **Wilhelm Dilthey**, human experience is necessarily filtered through the lens of a particular worldview, and there is no perspective independent of worldviews. Hence there is no absolute, ahistorical truth. Dilthey proposed examining and classifying the worldviews of different cultures and historical periods in order to gain insight into the essential life experiences (*Erlebnisse*) of people inhabiting these cultures and times. He understood philosophy as the **philosophy of life** (*Lebensphilosophie*), an examination and appreciation of the richness and diversity of human experience across culture and history. The notion of world-view in existentialism was developed by **Karl Jaspers**. In *Psychology of Worldviews*, Jaspers identified such worldviews as **nihilism**, pessimism, and optimism as necessary means of understanding the world and at the same time as restrictive "shells" used to protect **consciousness** from experiences it cannot make sense of.

WORLDVIEWS, PSYCHOLOGY OF. *See PSYCHOLOGY OF WORLDVIEWS.*

WORLD WAR I (1914–1918). In certain respects, the conflict of the First World War, and especially the defeat and subsequent humiliation of Germany under the Treaty of Versailles, set the stage for the crises of the 1920s and the call for cultural renewal, among them the German **philosophy of existence**. After the war, Germany was in crisis economically and politically; the rise of socialism and threat of **communist** takeover (evidenced by failed communist uprisings throughout the 1920s), staggering inflation, and continual political instability, not to mention the millions of young men killed in the war itself, occasioned a wave of apocalyptic and messianic literature and prompted a range of radical responses from German intellectuals. "Conservative revolutionaries," such as Carl Schmitt and Oswald Spengler, reacted to the perceived "decline" of German civilization by advocating the abandonment of democratic government; the ineffectualness of the Weimar Republic should, they believed, be replaced by a "new Germany" built on military and nationalistic **values**. While most German intellectuals rejected this conservative revolutionary agenda, some, like **Martin Heidegger**, sympathized with the call for German renewal in an atmosphere of world-historical crisis. For Heidegger and **Karl Jaspers**, German academic philosophy in the 1920s seemed abstract and inadequate, buried in the past and out of touch with present concerns. The **philosophy of existence** they developed sought to overcome these inadequacies and to attend directly to **concrete** problems of human life. Inspired by the writings of **Søren Kierkegaard**, and, in Heidegger's case, by **Edmund Husserl**'s **phenomenology**, each man approached philosophy not merely as a positing of true theories but as a manner of **awakening** his audience to the possibilities of **authentic existence**. For

Jaspers, this entailed exploring "**limit situations**" such as **guilt**, **death**, and suffering, in which the individual is forced to face the contradictory nature of the finite human perspective. **Martin Heidegger**, in turn, called attention to the role of **anxiety** and **resolute** decision. For both, a properly "existentialized" philosophy could itself play a role in the renewal of German culture. *See also* HEIDEGGER AND NAZISM.

WORLD WAR II (1939–1945). The Second World War was transformative for existentialism, especially in France. For **Simone de Beauvoir**, **Albert Camus**, **Maurice Merleau-Ponty**, and **Jean-Paul Sartre**, the experience of the war shifted philosophical concerns from an individual to a collective register and brought into focus **ethical** issues such as collective **responsibility** and **guilt**, the reality of political violence, the power of history, and the impotence of isolated individual action. The task of assimilating these issues into a philosophical perspective preoccupied most French existentialists throughout the 1950s and in effect coincided with the decline of existentialism in France. For Beauvoir and Sartre as well as, initially, Merleau-Ponty, **Marxism** provided the only viable framework for accomplishing this task. After 1945, for Camus, Marxism as embodied in Soviet **communism** represented a collective terror to be combated. In all events, the necessity of confronting issues raised by the war prompted each thinker to reorder his or her philosophical priorities, shifting focus from problems of individual autonomy and **authenticity** to social, political, and ethical questions.

Life under the German occupation, rather than the experience of combat, bombardment, or deportation, was the most **concrete** aspect of the war for French existentialists. Beauvoir, Camus, and Sartre each reported that during the four years of the occupation they learned the meaning of "solidarity," the moral interdependence of individuals within society. This was reflected in postwar writings, such as Sartre's *Anti-Semite and Jew*, Camus's *The Rebel*, and Beauvoir's *The Second Sex*, which directly addressed problems of social injustice and political repression. German existentialists responded to World War II in a somewhat different manner. With the exception of **Karl Jaspers**'s *The Question of German Guilt* (1946), which addressed the issue of collective responsibility for the war, generally the reaction was more oblique. In his first postwar publication, *Letter on Humanism* (1947), **Martin Heidegger** repudiated Sartre's existentialism as a type of metaphysical subjectivism that misconstrues the human agent as the source of **being** rather than "the shepherd of being." He avoided passing judgment on the events of the war; instead, his postwar philosophy focused on a global "forgetting of being" and technological domination of the earth that transcended national boundaries. For both Jaspers and Heidegger, World War II marked the end of their preoccupation with the **philosophy of existence**. Heidegger explicitly distanced himself from existentialist interpretations of *Being and Time* and announced the bankruptcy of philosophy, turning instead to poetry and what he called "meditative thinking." In his postwar writings Jaspers developed more explicitly theological concerns and pursued interests in world philosophy, though he did not repudiate his earlier positions.

WRIGHT, RICHARD (1908–1960). African American novelist, writer, and poet. Having worked for the **Communist** Party in the 1930s, Wright changed his views about the Soviet Union in 1944 but nonetheless was blacklisted after **World War II**. To pursue his career and to avoid the racism he continually experienced in the United States, Wright moved to Paris in 1946, where he spent the rest of his life. There he befriended **Jean-Paul Sartre**, **Simone de Beauvoir**, and **Albert Camus**. For Sartre, Wright's novels, such as *Native Son* (1940) and *Black Boy* (1945), which addressed issues of social injustice and racism through the prism of Wright's personal experience, were outstanding examples of **committed literature**. Wright's novel *The Outsiders* (1953) was a self-conscious experiment in existentialist fiction modeled loosely on Camus's novel *The Stranger*.

– X, Y, Z –

YALE FRENCH STUDIES. The French Department at Yale University was among the earliest and staunchest advocates of French existentialism in the United States, especially of the work of **Jean-Paul Sartre**. The department chairperson, distinguished French literary critic Henri Peyre, brought Sartre to lecture at Yale in 1946 during his second tour of America, and in 1948 the department launched a journal, *Yale French Studies*, whose first issue was devoted to critical discussions of Sartre's literary and philosophical work. Subsequently, the journal published many articles on Sartre, **Albert Camus**, and other French existentialist writers. Yale was also among the first American universities to introduce a course on existentialism, in 1946.

YEARBOOK FOR PHILOSOPHY AND PHENOMENOLOGICAL RESEARCH (Ger. *Jahrbuch für Philosophie und Phänomenologische Forschung*). Primary journal of German **phenomenology**, founded by **Edmund Husserl** in 1913 and edited by Husserl and **Max Scheler**. Between 1913 and 1930, the *Jahrbuch* published several of the major works of German phenomenology. The first volume (1913) contained Husserl's *Ideas* along with the first volume of Scheler's major work, *Formalism in Ethics*. The eighth volume (1927) presented **Martin Heidegger**'s *Being and Time*.

ZARATHUSTRA, THUS SPOKE. See NIETZSCHE, FRIEDRICH.

Bibliography

Readers seeking a concrete introduction to existentialism might well begin with Jean-Paul Sartre's "Existentialism Is a Humanism," the lecture that inaugurated the existentialist era in France and abroad. It is available in English in *Existentialism and Human Emotions* (as "Existentialism," translated by Bernard Frechtman). An earlier British translation is *Existentialism and Humanism* (Trans. Philip Mairet. London: Methuen, 1948). An alternate translation of Sartre's lecture is given by Walter Kaufmann in his anthology *Existentialism from Dostoevsky to Sartre*. A short, elegant introduction to the existentialist perspective that bears comparison to Sartre's lecture is José Ortega y Gasset's essay "History as a System," published in the book of the same name.

The flavor and concerns of early (predominantly German) philosophy of existence may be gleaned from the following texts: Martin Heidegger's 1929 lecture "What Is Metaphysics?" (published in Heidegger, *Basic Writings*); Karl Jaspers's *Man in the Modern Age*, "Part Four: Our Present Conception of Human Existence" (a short introduction to Jaspers's *Existenzphilosophie* that sets Jaspers's project in historical context); and Martin Buber's lyrical *I and Thou*, a classic statement of religious existentialism. Buber's book may be profitably read alongside Gabriel Marcel's 1933 essay, "On the Ontological Mystery" (published in Marcel, *The Philosophy of Existentialism*).

The story of the emergence of existential philosophy in France prior to Sartre is told by Maurice Merleau-Ponty in "The Philosophy of Existence" (in *The Debate Between Sartre and Merleau-Ponty*, edited by Jon Stewart). A shorter work representative of the thought of this period is Sartre's *The Transcendence of the Ego*. The earliest expression of French existentialism is Gabriel Marcel's impressionistic *Metaphysical Journal*, which appeared in 1927. The fundamental statement of French existentialism is Sartre's *Being and Nothingness*; at more than 600 pages, it remains a daunting work even for professional philosophers. Heidegger's *Being and Time* is generally considered the single most important work of existentialist philosophy and one of the most influential philosophical works of the 20th century. It too is a daunting and challenging book, but both works may be read by nonphilosophers with the help of commentaries described below under "Individual Studies."

The earliest commentaries on existentialism date back to the late 1920s and 1930s, when the first assessments of Jaspers's and Heidegger's philosophy of existence, of their debt to Søren Kierkegaard, and of the phenomenology of Edmund Husserl began to appear in German and French. Works of historical importance (which unfortunately are not available in English translation) include F. H. Heinemann's *Neue Wege der Philosophie* (1929), Jean Wahl's *Vers le concret* (1932), and Georges Gurvitch's *Les Tendences actuelles de la philosophie allemande* (1930). The last two books helped to introduce German existential thought into French philosophy.

The golden age of existentialist criticism followed Jean-Paul Sartre's rise to fame in the mid- and late 1940s and lasted through the 1960s. Notable introductory studies from this period include Marjorie Grene's *Introduction to Existentialism* (1948), F. H. Heinemann's *Existentialism and the Modern Predicament*, (1953), and Jean Wahl's *A Short History of Existentialism* (1949). Wahl's book is of particular interest for its transcription of a discussion among several of the leading French philosophers of existence of the time, including Nikolai Berdyaev, Georges Gurvitch, Gabriel Marcel, Emmanuel Levinas, and Wahl himself. An article that assesses existential philosophy from a German perspective, prior to the emergence of Sartre, is Paul Tillich's "Existential Philosophy" (1944).

American readers of the 1950s and 1960s were frequently introduced to existentialism through Walter Kaufmann's anthology *Existentialism from Dostoevsky to Sartre*, which first appeared in 1956. Kaufmann, who immigrated to the United States from Germany in 1939 and became the foremost American scholar and translator of Friedrich Nietzsche after World War II, provides useful introductions to each existentialist author. His anthology covers a spectrum of existentialist literature and philosophy, including Dostoevsky's *Notes from Underground* and selections from Kierkegaard, Nietzsche, Jaspers, Heidegger, Ortega y Gasset, Sartre, and Camus. Other accessible studies from the period include E. L. Allen's highly readable *Existentialism from Within* (1953), James Collins's *The Existentialists* (1952), and Mary Warnock's *Existentialism* (1970). William Barrett's *Irrational Man* (1958) remains perhaps the single best-selling study of the subject in the United States. However, Barrett's view of existentialism as an attempt to grasp the "shadow side" of human nature is dated and potentially misleading, especially for beginners. Paul Tillich, who had taught alongside Heidegger in the 1920s and immigrated to the United States in the 1930s, also became a powerful spokesman for existentialism in the 1950s and 1960s. Tillich's book *The Courage to Be* (1952) provides a good introduction to themes of existential theology as well as an example of how the concerns of existential psychotherapy were engaged by the anxieties of the Cold War era.

Two of the best general scholarly studies of existentialist philosophy from this period are John Macquarrie's *Existentialism* (1972) and Frederick Olafson's *Principles and Persons: An Ethical Interpretation of Existentialism* (1967). These works offer a critical synthesis of the claims of existentialist philosophy rather than a series of independent discussions of individual thinkers. The best recent monograph on the subject is David E. Cooper's *Existentialism: A Reconstruction* (1999). Cooper's book follows the path forged by Macquarrie and Olafson and provides a synthesis of the thinking of the major existentialists on central themes like anxiety, freedom, ethics, and the overcoming of alienation. Cooper thus demonstrates how the concerns of existentialist philosophers, such as the relation of body and mind, self and world, and self and other, are in line with those of the broader philosophical tradition. His book is recommended reading for beginners and experts alike.

Herbert Spiegelberg's *The Phenomenological Movement* (in two volumes) remains the most detailed and informative account of the development of phenomenology, including existential phenomenology, in Germany and France. It includes excellent chapters on Edmund Husserl, Martin Heidegger, Max Scheler, Gabriel Marcel, Jean-Paul Sartre, and Maurice Merleau-Ponty. Spiegelberg provides historical background that carefully documents the diaspora of German phenomenologists who had studied with Husserl as they spread to France and the United States. Publication details for the secondary sources mentioned so far may be found in the "General Studies" section below. Details for primary sources are given under "Original Works" and "Works in Translation."

Several good introductory discussions of existentialist philosophy are published in *The Encyclopedia of Philosophy* (8 vol. Paul Edwards, ed. New York: Macmillan, 1967). These include Frederick Olafson's illuminating articles on Albert Camus, Maurice Merleau-Ponty, and Jean-Paul Sartre. A more up-to-date resource is *The Routledge Encyclopedia of Philosophy* (10 vols. Edward Craig, ed. London: Routledge, 1998), which includes articles by David E. Cooper on existentialist ethics and Gabriel Marcel, and a strong overview of the subject ("Existentialism") by Charles Guignon. A useful online resource is the *Stanford Encyclopedia of Philosophy,* in which readers may (currently) find scholarly articles on Simone de Beauvoir, Martin Buber, Martin Heidegger, Gabriel Marcel, Maurice Merleau-Ponty, and Jean-Paul Sartre, as well as a good overview of the subject ("Existentialism"). The *Internet Encyclopedia of Philosophy* is another helpful, free online resource, though slightly less consistent in quality. Both of these sites are continually adding new articles.

Several historical dictionaries published in the series Historical Dictionaries of Religions, Philosophies, and Movements by Scarecrow Press are available on the thought of individual existentialists and figures associated with existentialism. They include Alfred Denker, *Historical Dictionary of Heidegger's*

Philosophy, Julia Watkin, *Historical Dictionary of Kierkegaard's Philosophy*, Carol Diethe, *Historical Dictionary of Nietzscheanism*, and David E. Cartwright, *Historical Dictionary of Schopenhauer's Philosophy*. These dictionaries provide summaries of major works and concepts as well as useful historical background. *Dictionary of Existentialism,* edited by Hayim Gordon, is a diverse but uneven collection of articles by contributors from several different countries.

Two general points about this bibliography should be noted. First, in regard to "Original Works" and "Works in Translation" (i.e., books written by existentialists), only those works representative of a thinker's existentialist period are included. Thus, for example, most of Jaspers's and Heidegger's postwar writings, Buber's and Levinas's Talmudic scholarship, and some of Camus's early writings are not listed. As a general rule, attention is focused on classic and recent book-length publications in English. Second, because the critical literature on individual existentialists is voluminous, especially in the case of figures like Heidegger and Sartre, whose influence extends to other disciplines and to virtually every area of philosophy, no attempt has been made to be comprehensive in listing secondary sources.

The bibliography is organized as follows. "Original Works" is a list of publications in the original language (German or French) of eight principal existentialists: Simone de Beauvoir, Martin Buber, Albert Camus, Martin Heidegger, Karl Jaspers, Gabriel Marcel, Maurice Merleau-Ponty, and Jean-Paul Sartre. "Works in Translation" is a list of works by existentialists in English translation, organized alphabetically by the author's last name. Pertinent publications of all major and minor existentialists discussed in the dictionary are cited here, along with selected works of nonexistentialist philosophers, such as Hannah Arendt, Wilhelm Dilthey, Emmanuel Levinas, Edmund Husserl, and Max Scheler, who were important to the development of existentialism. Also included are relevant selections from the work of Søren Kierkegaard and Friedrich Nietzsche.

"General Studies" contains general and introductory studies of existentialism in English. Most commentaries from the 1940s, 1950s, and 1960s are, as noted, organized around individual thinkers, though some, like those by Macquarrie and Olafson mentioned above, are thematic. Clear, accurate overviews of the thought of Sartre, Beauvoir, and Merleau-Ponty, and a good historical discussion of French philosophy in the 1930s ("Between the Wars") are available in Gary Gutting's *French Philosophy in the Twentieth Century*. Gutting also provides historically sensitive discussions of the structuralist and poststructuralist thought that usurped existentialism and phenomenology in the 1970s.

Dermot Moran's *Introduction to Phenomenology* is a fine introduction to the form of philosophy most influential for existentialism. In addition to detailed chapters tracing the evolution of Husserl's phenomenology, Moran provides good summaries of the existential and hermeneutic phenomenology of Heidegger, Hannah Arendt, Hans Georg-Gadamer, and Emmanuel Levinas, as well as useful chapters on Sartre and Merleau-Ponty. A recent collection of scholarly articles on existentialism by various authors is Hubert Dreyfus and Mark Wrathall, eds., *Companion to Phenomenology and Existentialism*. *Phenomenology and Existentialism*, edited by Robert Solomon, is an older anthology of essays by a range of well-known 20th-century philosophers.

"Individual Studies" cites critical literature on individual existentialists, who are listed alphabetically by last name. (Bibliographies are given when available at the start of the entry for that author.) As noted, the literature on figures like Heidegger and Sartre is extensive, so no attempt has been made to be complete or comprehensive. Works listed are mainly classic and recent books in English. A few articles and book chapters are given, as well as a very few studies in German and French.

I limit myself here to recommendations for secondary sources on Martin Heidegger and Jean-Paul Sartre, the two principal existentialist philosophers. Recommended commentaries on Heidegger's existentialist philosophy include David Cooper, *Heidegger*; Hubert Dreyfus, *Being-in-the-World*; Charles Guignon, *Heidegger and the Problem of Knowledge*; and Richard Polt, *Heidegger: An Introduction*. Herman Philipse's *Heidegger's Philosophy of Being: A Critical Interpretation* is challenging but rewarding. Rüdiger Safranski's biography *Martin Heidegger: Between Good and Evil* provides an excellent overview of Heidegger's life and thought placed in cultural and historical context. *The Cambridge Companion to Heidegger*, edited by Charles Guignon, offers a strong sampling of essays on *Being and Time* as well as discussions of Heidegger's relationship to theology, ecology, psychotherapy, and Eastern thought.

Heidegger's involvement with National Socialism has provoked a tide of publications since the late 1980s. The subsection "Martin Heidegger and National Socialism" is a selection of works by historians and philosophers on Heidegger's relationship to Nazism. Hugo Ott's *Martin Heidegger: A Political Life* is the best general overview of the subject. Victor Farias's *Heidegger and Nazism*, which reignited the controversy in the late 1980s, is a loosely argued book that represents the extreme case for the prosecution. Richard Wolin's *The Politics of Being* is a more carefully reasoned condemnation of Heidegger as man and as philosopher. Julian Young's *Heidegger, Philosophy, Nazism* is a spirited defense that seeks to exonerate Heidegger's philosophy from the charges of fascist contamination. Primary documents such as Heidegger's speeches, newspaper articles, interviews, and essays, as well as other testimony from the period, are published in *Martin Heidegger and National Socialism:*

Questions and Answers, edited by Günther Neske and Emil Kettering; *The Heidegger Controversy: A Critical Reader* edited by Richard Wolin; and *The Heidegger Case: On Philosophy and Politics* edited by Joseph Margolis.

Helpful introductions to Sartre's existentialism include Joseph Catalano, *A Commentary on Jean-Paul Sartre's Being and Nothingness*; Christina Howells, *Sartre: The Necessity of Freedom*; and Iris Murdoch, *Sartre: Romantic Rationalist*. Francis Jeanson's *Sartre and the Problem of Morality* (originally published in French in 1947) remains an authoritative study by an associate of Sartre's. A good selection of essays on Sartre's philosophy by leading scholars is *The Cambridge Companion to Sartre*, edited by Christina Howells. The two major biographies of Sartre are Ronald Hayman, *Writing Against: A Biography of Sartre* and Annie Cohen-Solal, *Sartre: A Life*. An intimate first-person account of the existentialist era in France can be found in the third volume of Simone de Beauvoir's memoirs, *Force of Circumstance*. The course of Sartre's life is traced through the details of each of his nearly 600 publications—including numerous interviews—in Michel Contat and Michel Rybalka, eds., *The Writings of Jean-Paul Sartre, Volume 1: A Bibliographic Life*.

The section "Anthologies" lists anthologies of existentialism in English. "Dictionaries" is a list of dictionaries on figures and ideas associated with existentialism. "Historical Background" is a selection of recent works that shed light on the cultural and historical contexts in which existentialism developed in Germany and in France. The remaining sections of the bibliography are organized topically: "Existentialism and Aesthetics," "Existentialism and Ethics," "Existentialism, Feminism, and Race," "Existentialism and Literature," "Existentialism and Marxism," and "Existentialism and Psychotherapy." In each section readers will find a sample of the literature in that field.

CONTENTS

ORIGINAL WORKS

Simone de Beauvoir

La Cérémonie des adieux. Paris: Gallimard, 1981.
Le Deuxième sexe. 2 vols. Paris: Gallimard, 1949.
La Force de l'âge. Paris: Gallimard, 1960.
La Force des choses. Paris: Gallimard, 1963.
L'Invitée. Paris: Gallimard, 1943.
"Littérature et métaphysique." In *L 'existentialisme et la sagesse des nations.* Paris: Nagel, 1948.
Mémoires d'une jeune fille rangée. Paris: Gallimard, 1958.
"Merleau-Ponty et le pseudo-sartrisme." *Les temps modernes* nos. 114–115 (1955): 2072–2122.
Pour une morale de l'ambiguïté. Paris: Gallimard, 1947.
Pyrrhus et Cinéas. Paris: Gallimard, 1944.
Le sang de autres. Paris: Gallimard, 1945.
Tous les hommes sont mortels. Paris: Gallimard, 1946.
La vieillesse. Paris: Gallimard, 1970.

Martin Buber

Begegnung: Autobigraphische Fragmente. Stuttgart: W. Kohlhammer, 1960.
Das Dialogische Prinzip. Heidelberg: Schneider, 1973.
Das Problem des Menschen. Heidelberg: L. Schneider, 1948
Der Mensch und Sein Gebild. Heidelberg: L. Schneider, 1955.
Dialogisches Leben: Gesammelte Philosophische Und Pädagogische Schriften. Zürich: G. Müller, 1947.
Die Frage an Den Einzelnen. Berlin: Schrocken, 1936.
Ereignisse und Begegnungen. Berlin: Schocken verlag, 1930.
Gesammelte Werke. Edited by Richard Beer-Hofmann. Frankfurt am Main: Fischer, 1963.
Ich und Du. Leipzig: Insel-Verlag, 1923.
Urdistanz und Beziehung. Heidelberg: L. Schneider, 1951.

Albert Camus

Carnets: Mai 1935–Mars 1951. Paris: A. Sauret, 1965.
La Chute. Englewood Cliffs, N.J: Prentice-Hall, 1965.
L'Étranger. Paris: Gallimard, 1942.
L'Homme révolté. Paris: Gallimard, 1951

Lettres à un ami allemand. Paris: Gallimard, 1948.

Le Malentendu: Pièce En Trois Actes; Caligula: Pièce En Quatre Actes. Paris: Gallimard, 1944.

Le Mythe de Sisyphe: essai sur L'absurde. Paris: Gallimard, 1942.

Œuvres complètes. Edited by Jacqueline Lévi-Valensi and Raymond Gay-Crosier. Paris: Gallimard, 2006.

La Peste. Paris: Gallimard, 1947.

Réflexions sur la peine capitale. Paris: Calmann-Lévy, 1957.

Martin Heidegger

Der Feldweg. Frankfurt am Main: V. Klostermann, 1995.

Die Grundbegriffe der Metaphysik: Welt, Endlichkeit, Einsamkeit. Edited by Friedrich-Wilhelm von Herrmann. Frankfurt am Main: V. Klostermann, 1983.

Einführung in die Metaphysik. Tübingen: M. Niemeyer, 1953.

Gesamtausgabe. Edited by Friedrich-Wilhelm von Herrmann. Frankfurt am Main: V. Klostermann, 1977– .

Grundprobleme der Phänomenologie (1919/20). Frankfurt am Main: V. Klostermann, 1993.

Hölderlins Hymne "Der Ister". Edited by Walter Biemel. Frankfurt am Main: V. Klostermann, 1984.

Holzwege. Frankfurt am.Main: V. Klostermann, 1957.

Kant und das Problem Der Metaphysik. Frankfurt am Main: V. Klostermann, 1991.

Nietzsche. Ed. Brigitte Schillbach. Frankfurt am Main: V. Klostermann, 1996.

Nietzsche Seminare 1937 und 1944. Frankfurt am Main: V. Klostermann, 2004.

Sein und Zeit. Tübingen: M. Niemeyer, 1979.

Über den Humanismus. Frankfurt am. Main: V. Klostermann, 1949.

Was Ist Metaphysik? Frankfurt am Main: V. Klostermann, 1955.

Wegmarken. Frankfurt am Main: V. Klostermann, 1978.

Zollikoner Seminare: Protokolle, Gespräche, Briefe. Ed. Medard Boss. Frankfurt am Main: V. Klostermann, 1987.

Karl Jaspers

Allgemeine Psychopathologie. Berlin: Springer, 1953.

Die Geistige Situation der Zeit. Berlin: W. de Gruyter, 1931.

Die Schuldfrage: Ein Beitrag zur Deutschen Frage. Zürich: Artemis, 1946.

Existenzphilosophie: Drei Vorlesungen. Berlin: W. de Gruyter, 1938.

Nietzsche; Einführung in das Verständnis Seines Philosophierens. Berlin: W. de Gruyter, 1936.

Philosophie. Berlin: J. Springer, 1932.
Philosophie und Welt; Reden Und Aufsätze. München: R. Piper, 1958.
Psychologie der Weltanschauungen. Berlin: J. Springer, 1922.
Vernunft und Existenz: Fünf Vorlesungen. Bremen: J. Storm, 1949.
Vernunft und Existenz: Fünf Vorlesungen. Groningen, Batavia: J. B. Wolters, 1935.

Gabriel Marcel

Cinq pièces majeures. Paris: Plon, 1973.
Du Refus à l'invocation. Paris: Gallimard, 1956.
tre et avoir. Paris: F. Aubier, Éditions Montaigne, 1935.
Fragments philosophiques, 1909–1914. Louvain: Éditions Nauwelaerts, 1962.
Homo viator: prolégomènes à une métaphysique de l'espérance. Paris: Aubier, 1945.
Journal métaphysique. Paris: Gallimard, 1927.
Le Mystère de l'être. Paris: Aubier, 1951.
L'Existence et la liberté humaine chez Jean-Paul Sartre. Paris: J. Vrin, 1981.
Pour une sagesse tragique et son au-delà. Paris: Plon, 1968.

Maurice Merleau-Ponty

Les Aventures de la dialectique. Paris: Gallimard, 1955.
Éloge de la philosophie. Paris: Gallimard, 1953.
Humanisme et terreur. Paris: Gallimard, 1947.
L'Oeil et l'esprit. Paris: Gallimard, 1964.
Phénoménologie de la perception. Paris: Gallimard, 1945.
Résumé des cours, Collège de France 1952–1960. Paris: Gallimard, 1968.
Sens et non-sens. Paris: Nagel, 1948.
Signes. Paris: Gallimard, 1960.

Jean-Paul Sartre

L'Âge de raison. Paris: Gallimard, 1945.
Cahiers pour une morale. Paris: Gallimard, 1983.
Les Carnets de la drôle de guerre: novembre 1939–mars 1940. Paris: Gallimard, 1983.
Les Communistes et la paix. Volume VI of *Situations* Paris: Gallimard, 1964.
Critique de la raison dialectique. Volume I. Paris: Gallimard, 1960.
Critique de la raison dialectique. Volume II. Paris: Gallimard, 1985.

Esquisse d'une théorie des émotions. Paris: Hermann, 1939.

L'tre et le néant. Paris: Gallimard. 1943.

L'Existentialisme est un humanisme. Paris: Nagel, 1947.

Huis-clos. Paris: Gallimard, 1947.

"Une idée fondamentale de la phénoménologie de Husserl: l'intentionalité." *Nouvelle revue française* 52 (1939): 129–132; reprinted in Volume I of *Situations*. Paris: Gallimard, 1947.

L'Idiot de la famille. Paris: Gallimard, 1971.

L'Imaginaire. Paris: Gallimard, 1940.

L'Imagination. Paris: Alcan, 1936.

"Jean-Paul Sartre répond." *L'Arc* 3 (1966): 87–96.

"Merleau-Ponty vivant." In *Situations,* Volume IV. Paris: Gallimard, 1964.

La Mort dans l'âme. Paris: Gallimard, 1949.

Les Mots. Paris: Gallimard, 1964.

Les Mouches. Paris: Bordas, 1974.

La Nausée. Paris: Gallimard, 1938.

Qu'est-ce que la littérature? Volume II of *Situations*. Paris: Gallimard, 1948.

"Réponse à Albert Camus." *Les Temps modernes* no. 82 (August 1952): 334–353; reprinted in *Situations,* Volume IV.

Saint Genet. Paris: Gallimard, 1952.

Sartre par lui-meme. (Transcript of a documentary film directed by Alexandre Astruc and Michel Contat.) Paris: Gallimard, 1977.

Situations. 10 vols. Paris: Gallimard, 1947–1972.

Le Sursis. Paris: Gallimard, 1945.

La Transcendence de l'ego. Paris: Vrin, 1966.

WORKS IN TRANSLATION

Abbagnano, Nicola. *Critical Existentialism*. Translated, edited, and with an introduction by Nino Langiulli. Garden City, N.Y.: Anchor Books, 1969.

Adorno, Theodor. *The Essential Frankfurt School Reader*. Edited by Andrew Arato and Eike Gebbhardt. New York: Continuum, 1982. (Essays by Theodor Adorno, Walter Benjamin, Erich Fromm, Max Horkheimer, Herbert Marcuse, and others.)

———. *The Jargon of Authenticity*. Translated by Kurt Tarnowski and Frederic Will. Evanston, Ill.: Northwestern University Press, 1973.

Adorno, Theodor, and Max Horkheimer. *Dialectic of Enlightenment*. Translated by John Cumming. New York: Seabury Press, 1972.

Arendt, Hannah. *Between Past and Future*. New York: Penguin, 1977.

——. *Eichmann in Jerusalem: A Report on the Banality of Evil*. New York: Viking, 1963.

——. *Hannah Arendt/Karl Jaspers Correspondence, 1926–1969.* Edited by Lotte Kohler and Hans Saner. Translated Robert and Rita Kimber. New York: Harcourt Brace Jovanovich, 1992.

——. *The Human Condition*. Chicago: University of Chicago Press, 1958.

Arendt, Hannah, and Martin Heidegger. *Letters, 1925–1975*. Edited by Ursula Ludz. Translated by Andrew Shields. Orlando, Fla.: Harcourt, 2004.

Beauvoir, Simone de. *Adieux: A Farewell to Sartre*. Translated by Patrick O'Brian. New York: Pantheon Books, 1984.

——. *All Men Are Mortal*. Translated by Leonard Friedman. New York: World Publishing, 1955.

——. *The Blood of Others*. Translated by R. Senhouse and Y. Moyse. New York: Knopf, 1948.

——. *The Coming of Age*. Translated by Patrick O'Brian. New York: Putnam, 1972.

——. *The Ethics of Ambiguity*. Translated by Bernard Frechtman. New York: Philosophical Library, 1948.

——. *L'Existentialisme et la sagesse des nations*. Paris: Nagel, 1948.

——. *Force of Circumstance*. Translated by Richard Howard. New York: Putnam, 1965.

——. *The Mandarins*. Translated by L. M. Friedman. Fontana, 1982.

——. *Memoirs of a Dutiful Daughter*. Translated by James Kirkup. New York: Harper & Row, 1959.

——. "Merleau-Ponty and Pseudo-Sartreanism." In *The Debate between Sartre and Merleau- Ponty,* edited by Jon Stewart. Evanston, Ill.: Northwestern University Press, 1998.

——. *The Prime of Life*. Translated by Peter Green. Cleveland, Ohio: World Publishing, 1962.

——. *The Second Sex*. Translated by H. M. Parshley. New York: Vintage, 1953.

——. *She Came to Stay*. Translated by Peter Green. London: Secker & Warburg, 1949.

Berdyaev, Nikolai. *Christian Existentialism: A Berdyaev Anthology*. Translated by Donald A. Lowrie. New York: Harper, 1965.

——. *The Destiny of Man*. Translated by N. Duddington. New York: Harper & Row, 1960.

——. *Solitude and Society*. Translated by George Reavey. London: Centenary Press, 1947.

——. *Truth and Revelation*. Translated by R. M. French. New York: Harper & Bros., 1953.

Binswanger, Ludwig. *Being-in-the-world: Selected Papers of Ludwig Binswanger*. Translated by Jacob Needleman. New York: Basic Books, 1963.
———. *Sigmund Freud: Reminiscences of a Friendship*. Translated by Norbert Guterman. New York: Grune & Stratton, 1957.
Boss, Medard. *Meaning and Content of Sexual Perversions: A Daseinsanalytic Approach to the Psychopathology of the Phenomenon of Love*. Translated by Liese Lewis Abell. New York, Grune & Stratton, 1949.
———. *Psychoanalysis and Daseinsanalysis*. Translated by L. B. Lefebre. New York: Basic Books, 1963.
Buber, Martin. *A Believing Humanism: My Testament 1902–1965*. Translated by Maurice Friedman. New York: Simon & Schuster, 1967.
———. *Between Man and Man*. Translated by Ronald Gregor-Smith. London: Routledge & Kegan Paul, 2002.
———. *I and Thou*. Translated by Walter Kaufmann. New York: Charles Scribner, 1970.
———. *The Knowledge of Man*. Edited by Maurice Friedman. Translated by Maurice Friedman and Ronald Gregor-Smith. New York: Harper & Row, 1965.
———. *The Martin Buber Reader: Essential Writings*. Edited by Asher D. Biemann. New York: Palgrave McMillan, 2002.
Bultmann, Rudolph. *Existence and Faith: Shorter Writings of Rudolph Bultmann*. Translated by Schubert M. Ogden. London, 1961.
———. *New Testament and Mythology and Other Basic Writings*. Edited and translated by Schubert M. Ogden. Philadephia: Fortress Press,1984.
———. *Theology of the New Testament*. 2 vols. New York: Charles Scribner, 1952–1955.
Bultmann, Rudolph , and Karl Jaspers. *Myth & Christianity: An Inquiry into the Possibility of Religion without Myth*. Amherst, N.Y.: Prometheus Books, 2005.
Camus, Albert. *Caligula and Three Other Plays*. Translated by Stuart Gilbert. New York: Knopf, 1958.
———. *The Fall*. Translated by Justin O'Brien. New York: Vintage International, 1991.
———. *Lyrical and Critical Essays*. Edited by Philip Thody. Translated by Ellen Conroy Kennedy. New York: Vintage, 1968.
———. *The Myth of Sisyphus and Other Essays*. Translated by Juston O'Brien. New York: Vintage International, 1991.
———. *Notebooks 1935–1942*. Translated by Philip Thody. New York: Marlowe, 1996.
———. *Notebooks 1942–1951*. Translated by Justin O'Brien. New York: Marlowe, 1995.

———. *The Plague*. Translated by Stuart Gilbert. New York: Vintage, 1972.

———. *The Rebel*. Translated by Anthony Bower. London: Penguin, 1962.

———. *The Stranger*. Translated by Matthew Ward. New York: Vintage International, 1989.

———. "Three Interviews" (including "No, I Am Not an Existentialist"). In *Lyrical and Critical Essays,* edited by Philip Thody and translated by Ellen Conroy Kennedy. New York: Vintage, 1968.

Dilthey, Wilhelm. *Introduction to the Human Sciences*. Edited by Rudolf A. Makkreel and Frithjof Rodi. Princeton, N.J.: Princeton University Press, 1989.

———. *Poetry and Experience*. Edited by Rudolf A. Makkreel and Frithjof Rodi. Princeton, N.J.: Princeton University Press, 1985.

Frankl, Viktor. *Man's Search for Meaning: An Introduction to Logotherapy*. Boston: Beacon Press, 1962.

———. *From Death-Camp to Existentialism: A Psychiatrist's Path to a New Therapy*. Translated by Ilse Lasch. Boston: Beacon Press, 1961.

———. *The Doctor and the Soul: An Introduction to Logotherapy*. Translated by Richard and Clara Winston. New York: Knopf, 1955.

Heidegger, Martin. *Being and Time*. Translated by John Macquarrie and Edward Robinson. New York: Harper & Row, 1962.

———. *Basic Concepts*. Translated by Gary E. Aylesworth. Bloomington: Indiana University Press, 1993.

———. *The Basic Problems of Phenomenology*. Translated by Albert Hofstadter. Bloomington: Indiana University Press, 1982.

———. *Basic Writings: From Being and Time (1927) to the Task of Thinking (1964)*. Edited by David Farrell Krell. San Francisco: HarperSanFrancisco, 1993.

———. *Early Greek Thinking*. Translated by David Farrell Krell and Frank A. Capuzzi. San Francisco: Harper & Row, 1984.

———. *The Essence of Human Freedom: An Introduction to Philosophy*. Translated by Ted Sadler. London: Continuum, 2005.

———. *The Essence of Reasons*. Translated by Terrence Malick. Evanston, Ill.: Northwestern University Press, 1969.

———. *The Fundamental Concepts of Metaphysics: World, Finitude, Solitude*. Translated by William McNeill and Nicholas Walker. Bloomington: Indiana University Press, 1995.

———. *Hölderlin's Hymn "The Ister"*. Translated by William McNeill and Julia Davis. Bloomington: Indiana University Press, 1996.

———. *An Introduction to Metaphysics*. Translated by Ralph Manheim. New Haven, Conn.: Yale University Press, 1959.

———. *Introduction to Metaphysics*. Translated by Gregory Fried and Richard Polt. New Haven, Conn.: Yale University Press, 2000.

———. *Kant and the Problem of Metaphysics*. Translated by Richard Taft. Bloomington: Indiana University Press, 1997.

———. "Letter on Humanism." In *Basic Writings: From Being and Time (1927) to the Task of Thinking (1964)*. Edited by David Farrell Krell. San Francisco: HarperSanFrancisco, 1993.

———. *Nietzsche*. 4 vols. Translated by David Farrell Krell. San Francisco, Calif.: Harper & Row, 1979–1987.

———. *On Time and Being*. Translated by Joan Stambaugh. New York: Harper & Row, 1972.

———. *Poetry, Language, Thought*. Translated by Albert Hofstadter. New York: Perennial Classics, 2001.

———. *Qu'est-ce que la métaphysique?* Edited and translated by Henri Corbin. Paris: Gallimard, 1938.

———. *The Question Concerning Technology, and Other Essays*. Translated by William Lovitt. New York: Harper & Row, 1977.

———. "What Is Metaphysics?" In *Basic Writings: From "Being and Time" (1927) to "The Task of Thinking" (1964)*. Edited by David Farrell Krell. San Francisco: HarperSanFrancisco, 1993.

———. *Zollikon Seminars: Protocols, Conversations, Letters*. Edited by Medard Boss. Translated by Franz Mayr and Richard Askay. Evanston, Ill.: Northwestern University Press, 2001.

Heidegger, Martin, with Ernst Cassirer. "Davos Lectures." Appendix to *Kant and the Problem of Metaphysics*. Translated by Richard Taft. Bloomington: Indiana University Press, 1997.

Heidegger, Martin, and Karl Jaspers. *The Heidegger–Jaspers Correspondence, 1920–1963*. Translated by Gary E. Aylesworth. Amherst, N.Y: Humanity Books, 2003.

Husserl, Edmund. *Cartesian Meditations: An Introduction to Phenomenology*. Translated by Dorion Cairns. The Hague: M. Nijhoff, 1960.

———. *The Crisis of European Sciences and Transcedental Phenomenology*. Translated by David Carr. Evanston, Ill.: Northwestern University Press, 1970.

———. *Ideas: General Introduction to Pure Phenomenology*. Translated by W. R. Boyce Gibson. New York: Collier Books, 1962.

———. *The Phenomenology of Internal Time-Consciousness*. Edited by Martin Heidegger. Translated by James S. Churchill. Bloomington: Indiana University Press, 1964.

Jaspers, Karl. *General Psychopathology*. Translated by J. Hoenig and M. W. Hamilton. Chicago: Chicago University Press, 1963.

———. *Hannah Arendt/Karl Jaspers Correspondence, 1926–1969.* Edited by Lotte Kohler and Hans Saner. Translated by Robert Kimber and Rita Kimber. New York: Harcourt Brace Jovanovich, 1992.

———. *Karl Jaspers: Basic Philosophical Writings.* Edited and translated by Edith Ehrlich, Leonard H. Ehrlich, and George B. Pepper. Atlantic Highlands, N.J.: Humanties Press, 1994.

———. *Man in the Modern Age.* Translated by Eden Paul and Cedar Paul. London: Routledge & Kegan Paul, 1966.

———. *Nietzsche: An Introduction to the Understanding of His Philosophical Activity.* Translated by C. F. Walraff and F. J. Schmitz. Tucson: University of Arizona Press, 1965.

———. *Notizen zu Martin Heidegger.* Edited by Hans Saner. Munich: R. Piper, 1977.

———. *The Perennial Scope of Philosophy.* Translated by Ralph Manheim. New York, Philosophical Library, 1949.

———. *Philosophy.* 3 vols. Translated by E. B. Ashton. Chicago: Chicago University Press, 1969–1971.

———. *Philosophy of Existence.* Translated by Richard F. Grabay. Philadephia: University of Pennsylvania Press, 1971.

———. *Psychologie der Weltanschauungen.* Berlin: Springer, 1960.

———. *The Question of German Guilt.* Translated by E.B. Ashton. New York, Dial Press, 1947.

———. *Reason and Existenz.* Translated by William Earle. New York: Noonday Press, 1955.

Jaspers, Karl, and Rudolph Bultmann. *Myth and Christianity: An Inquiry into the Possibility of Religion without Myth.* New York, Noonday Press, 1958.

Kierkegaard, Søren. *The Concept of Anxiety: A Simple Psychological Orienting Deliberation on the Dogmatic Issue of Hereditary Sin.* Edited and translated by Reidar Thomte and Albert B. Anderson. Princeton, N.J.: Princeton University Press, 1980.

———. *Concluding Unscientific Postscript to "Philosopical Fragments."* Volume 1. Edited and trans. Howard V. Hong and Edna H. Hong. Princeton, N.J.: Princeton University Press, 1992.

———. *Either/Or.* Parts I and II. Edited and translated by Howard V. Hong and Edna H. Hong. Princeton, N.J.: Princeton University Press, 1987.

———. *Fear and Trembling/Repetition.* Edited and translated Howard V. Hong and Edna H. Hong. Princeton, N.J.: Princeton University Press, 1983.

———. *A Kierkegaard Anthology.* Edited by Robert Bretall. Princeton, N.J.: Princeton University Press, 1973.

———. *Philosophical Fragments or a Fragment of Philosophy.* Translated by David Swenson. Revised by Howard V. Hong. Princeton, N.J.: Princeton University Press, 1967.

———. *The Present Age*. Translated by Alexander Dru. New York: Harper & Row, 1962.

———. *The Sickness Unto Death: A Christian Psychological Exposition for Upbuilding and Awakening*. Edited and translated by Howard V. Hong and Edna H. Hong. Princeton, N. J.: Princeton University Press, 1980.

Emmanuel Levinas. *Ethics and Infinity*. Translated by Richard Cohen. Pittsburgh: Duquesne University Press, 1985.

———. *The Theory of Intuition in Husserl's Phenomenology*. Translated by André Orianne, Evanston, Ill.: Northwestern University Press, 1973.

———. *Totality and Infintity*. Translated by Alphonso Lingis. Pittsburgh: Duquesne University Press, 1969.

Marcel, Gabriel. *Being and Having: An Existentialist Diary*. Translated by Katherine Farrer. New York: Harper & Row, 1965.

———. *Creative Fidelity*. Translated by Robert Rosthal. New York: Farrar, Straus & Giroux, 1964.

———. *The Existential Background of Human Dignity*. Cambridge, Mass.: Harvard University Press, 1963.

———. *Homo Viator: Introduction to a Metaphysic of Hope*. Translated by Emma Crawford. New York: Harper, 1962.

———. *Metaphysical Journal*. Translated by Bernard Wall. Chicago: Regnery, 1952.

———. *The Mystery of Being*. Translated by René Hague. Chicago: Regnery, 1951.

———. *The Philosophy of Existentialism*. New York: Citadel, 1956.

———. *Philosophical Fragments, 1904–1914; and the Philosopher and Peace*. Translated by Lionel A. Blain. Notre Dame, Ind.: University of Notre Dame Press, 1965.

———. *Three Plays*. New York: Hill and Wang, 1965.

———. *Tragic Wisdom and Beyond. Including, Conversations between Paul Ricoeur and Gabriel Marcel*. Translated by Stephen Jolin and Peter Mccormick. Evanston, Ill.: Northwestern University Press, 1973.

Marcuse, Herbert. *Eros and Civilization*. New York: Vintage, 1962.

———. *The Essential Frankfurt School Reader*. Edited by Andrew Arato and Eike Gebbhardt. New York: Continuum, 1982. (Essays by Theodor Adorno, Walter Benjamin, Erich Fromm, Max Horkheimer, Herbert Marcuse, and others.)

———. *One Dimensional Man*. Boston: Beacon Press, 1964.

Merleau-Ponty, Maurice. *Adventures of the Dialectic*. Translated by Joseph Bien. Evanston, Ill.: Northwestern University Press, 1973.

———. *Humanism and Terror: An Essay on the Communist Problem*. Translated by John O'Neill. Boston: Beacon Press, 1969.

———. *In Praise of Philosophy*. Translated by John Wild and James Edie. Evanston, Ill.: Northwestern University Press, 1963.

———. *Phenomenology of Perception*. Translated by Colin Smith. London: Routledge, 1962.

———. "The Philosophy of Existence." In *The Debate between Sartre and Merleau-Ponty*. Edited by Jon Stewart. Evanston, Ill.: Northwestern University Press, 1998.

———. *The Primacy of Perception*. Edited by James Edie. Evanston, Ill.: Northwestern University Press, 1964.

———. *Sense and Non-Sense*. Translated by Hubert Dreyfus and Patricia Dreyfus. Evanston, Ill.: Northwestern University Press, 1964.

———. *Signs*. Translated by Richard McCleary. Evanston, Ill.: Northwestern University Press, 1964.

———. *The Structure of Behavior*. Translated by A. L. Fisher. Boston: Beacon Press, 1963.

———. *Texts and Dialogues*. Edited by Hugh J. Silverman and James Barry Jr. Translated by Michael Smith et al. New York: Proetheus, 1996.

———. *Themes from the Lectures at the Collège de France 1952–1960*. Translated by John O'Neill. Evanston, Ill.: Northwestern University Press, 1970.

Nietzsche, Friedrich. *Beyond Good and Evil: Prelude to a Philosophy of the Future*. Translated by Walter Kaufmann. New York: Vintage Books, 1989.

———. *The Birth of Tragedy, and the Case of Wagner*. Translated by Walter Kaufmann. New York: Vintage Books, 1967.

———. *Daybreak: Thoughts on the Prejudices of Morality*. Edited by Maudemarie Clark and Brian Leiter. Translated by R. J. Hollingdale. Cambridge: Cambridge University Press, 1997.

———. *Ecce Homo: How One Becomes What One Is*. Translated by R. J. Hollingdale. London: Penguin Books, 1992.

———. *The Gay Science*. Edited by Bernard Williams. Translated by Josefine Nauckhoff. Cambridge: Cambridge University Press, 2001.

———. *On the Genealogy of Morality: A Polemic*. Translated by Maudemarie Clark and Alan J Swensen. Indianapolis, Ind.: Hackett, 1998.

———. *The Portable Nietzsche*. Translated by Walter Kaufmann. New York: Penguin Books, 1976.

———. *Thus Spoke Zarathustra: A Book for All and None*. Translated by Walter Arnold Kaufmann. New York: Modern Library, 1995.

———. *Twilight of the Idols, Or, How to Philosophize with the Hammer*. Translated by Richard Polt. Indianapolis, Ind.: Hackett, 1997.

———. *The Will to Power*. Edited by Walter Arnold Kaufmann. Translated by Walter Kaufmann and R. J Hollingdale. London: Weidenfeld & Nicolson, 1968.

Nishitani, Keiji. *Religion and Nothingness*. Translated by Jan Van Bragt. Berkeley: University of California Press, 1982.

——. *The Self-overcoming of Nihilism*. Translated by Graham Parkes and Setsuko Aihara. Albany: State University of New York Press, 1990.

Ortega y Gasset, José. *The Dehumanization of Art; and, Other Essays on Art, Culture, and Literature*. Translated by Helen Weyl. Princeton, N.J: Princeton University Press, 1968.

——. *History as a System and Other Essays towards a Philosophy of History*. Translated by Helene Weyl. New York: W.W. Norton, 1961.

——. *Meditations on Quixote*. Translated by Evelyn Rugg and Diego Marin. New York: Norton, 1961.

——. *The Modern Theme*. Translated by James Cleugh. New York: W.W. Norton, 1933.

——. *The Origin of Philosophy*. Translated by Toby Talbot. Urbana: University of Illinois Press, 2000.

——. *The Revolt of the Masses*. Edited by Kenneth Moore. Translated by Anthony Kerrigan. Notre Dame, Ind: University of Notre Dame Press, 1985.

Rosenzweig, Franz. *Cultural Writings of Franz Rosenzweig*. Edited and translated by Barbara E Galli. Syracuse, N.Y.: Syracuse University Press, 2000.

——. *Philosophical and Theological Writings*. Edited and translated by Paul W. Franks and Michael L Morgan. Indianapolis, Ind.: Hackett, 2000.

——. *The Star of Redemption*. Translated by Barabara E. Galli. Madison: University of Wisconsin Press, 2005.

Sartre, Jean-Paul. *The Age of Reason*. Translated by Eric Sutton. Harmondsworth, UK: Penguin, 1961.

——. *Anti-Semite and Jew: An Exploration of the Etiology of Hate*. Translated by George G. Becker. New York: Schocken, 1976.

——. *Being and Nothingness: An Essay on Phenomenological Ontology*. Translated by Hazel Barnes. New York: Philosophical Library, 1956.

——. *The Communists and Peace, with a Reply to Claude Lefort*. Translated by Martha H. Fletcher. New York: George Braziller, 1968.

——. *Critique of Dialectical Reason*. Volume I. Translated by Alan Sheridan-Smith. London: New Left Books, 1976.

——. *Critique of Dialectical Reason*. Volume II. Translated by Quinton Hoare. London: Verso, 1991.

——. "Existentialism." In *Existentialism and Human Emotions*. Translated by Bernard Frechtman. Secaucus, N. J.: Citadel Press, 1998.

——. *L'Existentialisme est un humanisme*. Paris: Nagel, 1946.

——. *The Family Idiot*. Translated by Carol Cosman. Chicago: University of Chicago Press, 1981.

——. *The Flies*. Translated by Stuart Gilbert. New York: Knopf, 1948.

——. *Imagination*. Translated by Forrest Williams. Ann Arbor: University of Michigan Press, 1962.

——. "Intentionality: A Fundamental Idea of Husserl's Phenomenology." Translated by Joseph Fell. *Journal of the British Society for Phenomenology* I (1970): 4–5.

——. "The Itinerary of a Thought." In *Between Existentialism and Marxism*. Translated by John Mathews. New York: Morrow, 1974.

——. "Kierkegaard: The Singular Universal." In *Between Existentialism and Marxism*. Translated by John Mathews. New York: Morrow, 1974.

——. *Literary and Philosophical Essays*. Translated by Annette Michelson. New York: Criterion Books 1955.

——. *Nausea*. Translated by Lloyd Alexander. New York: New Directions, 1964.

——. *No Exit*. Translated by Stuart Gilbert. New York: Knopf, 1948.

——. *Notebook for an Ethics*. Translated by David Pellauer. Chicago: University of Chicago Press, 1992.

——. *The Psychology of Imagination*. Translated by Bernard Frechtman. New York: Philosophical Library, 1948.

——. "The Purposes of Writing." In *Between Existentialism and Marxism*. Translated by John Mathews. New York: Morrow, 1974.

——. *The Reprieve*. Translated by Eric Sutton. New York: Knopf, 1947.

——. *Saint Genet, Actor and Martyr.* Translated by Bernard Frechtman. New York: Braziller, 1963.

——. *Sartre by Himself.* Translated by Richard Seaver. New York: Urizen Books, 1980.

——. *Search for a Method*. Translated by Hazel E. Barnes. New York: Knopf, 1963.

——. "Self-Portrait at Seventy." In *Life/Situations: Essays Written and Spoken*. Translated by Paul Auster and Lydia Davis. New York: Pantheon, 1977.

——. "Simone de Beauvoir Interviews Sartre." In *Life/Situations: Essays Written and Spoken*. Translated by Paul Auster and Lydia Davis. New York: Pantheon, 1977.

——. *Situations*. Translated by Benita Eisler. New York: Braziller, 1965.

——. *The Transcendence of the Ego*. Translated by Forrest Williams and Robert Kirkpatrick. New York: Noonday, 1957.

——. *Truth and Existence*. Edited by Ronald Aronson. Translated by Adrian van den Hoven. Chicago: University of Chicago Press, 1992.

——. *Troubled Sleep*. Translated by Gerald Hopkins. New York: Knopf, 1951.

——. *War Diaries: Notebooks from a Phoney War 1939–40*. Translated by Quintin Hoare. London: Verso, 1984.

——. *What Is Literature?* Translated by Bernard Frechtman. New York: Philosophical Library, 1949.

———. *The Words*. Translated by Bernard Frechtman. New York: Braziller, 1964.

———. *The Writings of Jean-Paul Sartre Volume 2: Selected Prose*. Edited by Michel Contat and Michel Rybalka. Translated by Richard McCleary. Evanston, Ill.: Northwestern University Press, 1974.

Scheler, Max. *Formalism in Ethics and Non-Formal Ethics of Values; A New Attempt Toward the Foundation of an Ethical Personalism*. Translated by Manfred Frings. Evanston, Ill.: Northwestern University Press, 1973.

———. *Man's Place in Nature*. Translated by Hans Meyerhoff. Boston: Beacon Press, 1961.

———. *The Nature of Sympathy*. Translated by Peter Heath. New Haven, Conn.: Yale University Press, 1954.

———. *On Feeling, Knowing, and Valuing: Selected Writings*. Edited by Harold J. Bershady. Chicago: University of Chicago Press, 1992.

———. *Selected Philosophical Essays*. Translated by David Lachterman. Evanston, Ill.: Northwestern University Press, 1973.

Shestov, Lev. *"All Things Are Possible" and "Penultimate Words and Other Essays"*. Athens: Ohio University Press, 1977.

———. *Athens and Jerusalem*. Translated by Bernard Martin. Athens: Ohio University Press, 1966.

———. *Dostoevsky, Tolstoy, and Nietzsche*. Athens: Ohio University Press, 1969.

———. *Kierkegaard and the Existential Philosophy*. Translated by Elinor Hewitt. Athens: Ohio University Press, 1969.

———. *A Shestov Anthology*. Edited by Bernard Martin. Athens: Ohio University Press, 1971.

Tillich, Paul. *The Courage to Be*. New Haven, Conn.: Yale University Press, 2000.

———. *The Dynamics of Faith*. New York: Harper & Row, 1967.

———. *Systematic Theology*. Chicago: University of Chicago Press, 1951–1963.

Unamumo, Miguel de. *Tragic Sense of Life*. Translated by J. E. Crawford Flitch. New York: Dover, 1954.

GENERAL STUDIES

General

Douglas, Kenneth. *A Critical Bibliography of Existentialism (the Paris School): Listing Books and Articles in English and French by and About Jean-Paul*

Sartre, Simone De Beauvoir, Maurice Merleau-Ponty. Millwood, New York: Kraus Reprint, 1974.
Orr, Leonard. *Existentialism and Phenomenology: A Guide for Research*. Troy, New York: Whitston Publishing, 1978.

Bibliographies

Allen, E. L. *Existentialism from Within*. Westport, Conn.: Greenwood Press, 1974.
Arendt, Hannah, "French Existentialism." *The Nation* (February 23, 1946): 226–228.
———. "What Is Existenz Philosophy?" *Partisan Review* 8/1 (Winter 1946): 34–56.
Ayer, A. J. *Metaphysics and Common Sense*. San Francisco: Freeman, Cooper, 1970.
Barrett, William. *Irrational Man: A Study in Existential Philosophy*. New York: Anchor Books, 1958.
———. *What Is Existentialism?* New York: Grove Press, 1964.
Blackham, H. J. *Six Existentialist Thinkers*. New York: Harper Torchbooks, 1959.
Collins, James. *The Existentialists: A Critical Study*. Chicago: Henry Regnery, 1952.
Cooper, David E.. *Existentialism: A Reconstruction*. 2nd ed. Oxford: Blackwell, 1999.
Descombes, Vincent. *Modern French Philosophy*. Translated by L. Scott-Fox and J. M. Harding. Cambridge: Cambridge University Press, 1980.
Douglas, Kenneth. *A Critical Bibliography of Existentialism (the Paris School): Listing Books and Articles in English and French by and About Jean-Paul Sartre, Simone de Beauvoir, Maurice Merleau-Ponty*. Millwood, N.Y.: Kraus Reprint, 1974.
Dreyfus, Hubert L., and Mark A. Wrathall, eds. *Companion to Phenomenology and Existentialism*. Oxford: Blackwell, 2006.
Flynn, Thomas. *Existentialism: A Very Short Introduction*. Oxford: Oxford University Press, 2006.
Grene, Marjorie. *Introduction to Existentialism*. Chicago: University of Chicago Press, 1959.
Guignon, Charles. *The Existentialists: Critical Essays on Kierkegaard, Nietzsche, Heidegger, and Sartre*. Lanham, Md.: Rowman & Littlefield, 2004.
Gurvitch, Georges. *Les tendences actuelles de la philosophie allemande*. Paris: Vrin, 1930.
Gutting, Gary. *French Philosophy in the Twentieth Century*. Cambridge: Cambridge University Press, 2001.

Harper, Ralph. *Existentialism: A Theory of Man*. Cambridge, Mass.: Harvard University Press, 1958.

Heinemann, F. H. *Existentialism and the Modern Predicament*. New York: Harper & Row, 1953.

———. *Neue Wege der Philosophie: Geist, Leben, Existenz: Eine Einführung in die Philosophie der Gegerwart*. Leipzig: Quelle und Mayer, 1929.

Ireton, Sean Moore. *An Ontological Study of Death: From Hegel to Heidegger*. Pittsburgh: Duquesne University Press, 2007.

Kleinberg, Ethan. *Generation Existential: Heidegger's Philosophy in France, 1927–1961*. Ithaca, N.Y.: Cornell University Press, 2005.

Langiulli, Nino, ed. *European Existentialism*. New Brunswick, N.J: Transaction, 1997.

Löwith, Karl. *Nature, History, and Existentialism, and Other Essays in the Philosophy of History*. Edited by Arnold Levison. Evanston, Ill.: Northwestern University Press, 1966.

Macquarrie, John. *Existentialism*. Philadelphia: Westminster Press, 1972.

MacIntyre, Alasdair. "Existentialism." In *The Encyclopedia of Philosophy*. Edited by Paul Edwards Vol. 3. New York: Macmillan, 1967.

McBride, William L, ed. *The Development and Meaning of Twentieth-Century Existentialism*. New York: Garland, 1997.

———. *Existentialist Background*. New York: Garland, 1997.

Moran, Dermot. *Introduction to Phenomenology*. London: Routledge, 2000.

Mounier, Emmanuel. *Existentialist Philosophies*. New York: Macmillan, 1949.

Nagel, Thomas. *Mortal Questions*. Cambridge: Cambridge University Press, 1979.

Olafson, Frederick A. *Principles and Persons: An Ethical Interpretation of Existentialism*. Baltimore, Md.: Johns Hopkins University Press, 1967.

Olson, Robert G. *An Introduction to Existentialism*. New York: Dover, 1962.

Orr, Leonard. *Existentialism and Phenomenology: A Guide for Research*. Troy, N.Y.: Whitston Publishing, 1978.

Reinhardt, Kurt F. *The Existentialist Revolt*. New York: F. Ungar, 1960.

Rorty, Richard. *Contingency, Irony and Solidarity*. Cambridge: Cambridge University Press, 1989.

Schrag, Calvin O. *Existence and Freedom: Towards an Ontology of Human Finitude*. Evanston, Ill.: Northwestern University Press, 1961.

Solomon, Robert C. *From Hegel to Existentialism*. Oxford: Oxford University Press, 1989.

———. *From Rationalism to Existentialism: The Existentialists and Their Nineteenth-Century Backgrounds*. Lanham, Md.: Littlefield Adams Quality Paperbacks, 1992.

Solomon, Robert C, ed. *Phenomenology and Existentialism*. 2nd ed. Lanham, Md.: Rowman & Littlefield, 2001.

Spiegelberg, Herbert. *The Phenomenological Movement: A Historical Introduction.* 2d ed. 2 vols. The Hague: Nijhoff, 1969.

Tillich, Paul. "Existential Philosophy." *Journal of the History of Ideas* 5 (1944): 44–70. Reprinted in William McBride, ed. *The Development and Meaning of Twentieth-Century Existentialism.* New York: Garland Publishing, 1997.

von Rintelen, J. *Beyond Existentialism.* Translated by Hilda Graef. London: Allen & Unwin, 1961.

Wahl, Jean. *Philosophies of Existence.* Translated by F. M. Lory. London: Routledge & Kegan Paul, 1969.

———. *A Short History of Existentialism.* Translated by Forrest Williams and Stanley Maron. New York: Philosophical Library, 1949.

———. *Vers le concret.* Paris: J. Vrin, 1932.

Warnock, Mary. *Existentialism.* Oxford: University of Oxford Press, 1970.

Wild, John. *The Challenge of Existentialism.* Bloomington: University of Indiana Press, 1955.

INDIVIDUAL STUDIES

Nicola Abbagnano

Langiulli, Nino. *Possibility, Necessity, and Existence: Abbagnano and His Predecessors.* Philadelphia: Temple University Press, 1992.

Hannah Arendt

Benhabib, Seyla. *The Reluctant Modernism of Hannah Arendt.* Thousand Oaks, Calif.: Sage Publications, 1996.

Hinchman, Lewis P., and Sandra Hinchman, eds. *Hannah Arendt: Critical Essays.* Albany: State University of New York Press, 1994.

McGowan, John. *Hannah Arendt: An Introduction.* Minneapolis: University of Minnesota Press, 1998.

Young-Bruehl, Elizabeth. *Hannah Arendt: For Love of the World.* New Haven, Conn.: Yale University Press, 1982.

Villa, Dana Richard, ed. *The Cambridge Companion to Hannah Arendt.* Cambridge: Cambridge University Press, 2000.

Simone de Beauvoir

Arp, Kristana. *The Bonds of Freedom: Simone de Beauvoir's Existentialist Ethics.* New York: Open Court, 2001.

Ascher, Carol. *Simone de Beauvoir: A Life of Freedom*. Boston: Mass: Beacon Press, 1981.

Bair, Deirdre. *Simone de Beauvoir: A Biography*. New York: Touchstone, 1990.

Bergoffen, Debra B. *The Philosophy of Simone de Beauvoir: Gendered Phenomenologies, Erotic Generosities*. Albany: State University of New York Press, 1997.

Card, Claudia. *The Cambridge Companion to Simone de Beauvoir*. Cambridge: Cambridge University Press, 2003.

Cottrell, Robert D. *Simone de Beauvoir*. New York: F. Ungar, 1975.

Crosland, Margaret. *Simone de Beauvoir: The Woman and Her Work*. London: Heinemann, 1992.

Fullbrook, Edward, and Kate Fullbrook. *Simone de Beauvoir: A Critical Introduction*. Cambridge: Polity Press, 1998.

———. *Simone de Beauvoir and Jean-Paul Sartre: The Remaking of a Twentieth-Century Legend*. New York: Harvester Wheatsheaf, 1993.

Heath, Jane. *Simone de Beauvoir*. New York: Harvester Wheatsheaf, 1989.

Holveck, Eleanore. *Simone de Beauvoir's Philosophy of Lived Experience: Literature and Metaphysics*. Lanham, Md.: Rowman & Littlefield, 2002.

Mahon, Joseph. *Existentialism, Feminism, and Simone de Beauvoir*. New York: St. Martin's Press, 1997.

Merleau-Ponty, Maurice. "Metaphysics and the Novel." In *Sense and Non-Sense*. Translated by Hubert Dreyfus and Patricia Dreyfus. Evanston, Ill.: Northwestern University Press, 1964.

Moi, Toril. *Simone de Beauvoir: The Making of an Intellectual Woman*. Oxford: Blackwell, 1994.

O'Brien, Wendy, and Lester E Embree, eds. *The Existential Phenomenology of Simone De Beauvoir*. Dordrecht: Kluwer Academic, 2001.

Sandford, Stella. *How to Read Beauvoir*. London: Granta, 2006.

Scarth, Fredrika. *The Other Within: Ethics, Politics, and the Body in Simone de Beauvoir*. Lanham, Md.: Rowman & Littlefield, 2004.

Simmons, Margaret. *Beauvoir and the Second Sex: Feminism, Race, and the Origins of Existentialism*. New York: Rowman & Littlefield, 1999.

Tidd, Ursula. *Simone de Beauvoir*. London: Routledge, 2003.

Nikolai Berdyaev

Allen, E. L. *Freedom in God: A Guide to the Thought of Nicholas Berdyaev*. Norwood, Pa.: Norwood Editions, 1975.

Clarke, Oliver Fielding. *Introduction to Berdyaev*. London: G. Bles, 1950.

Lowrie, Donald A. *Rebellious Prophet: A Life of Nicolai Berdyaev*. New York: Harper, 1960.

McLachlan, James M. *The Desire to Be God: Freedom and the Other in Sartre and Berdyaev*. New York: P. Lang, 1992.

Ludwig Binswanger

Binswanger, Ludwig. *Being-in-the-World.* Translated and with an introduction by Jacob Needelman. New York: Basic Books, 1963.

Frie, Roger. *Subjectivity and Intersubjectivity in Modern Philosophy and Psychoanalysis: A Study of Sartre, Binswanger, Lacan, and Habermas.* Lanham, Md.: Rowman & Littlefield, 1997.

May, Rollo, Ernest Angel, and Henri F. Ellenberger, eds. *Existence: A New Dimension in Psychiatry and Psychology.* New York: Basic Books, 1958.

Ruitenbeek, Hendrik. *Psychoanalysis and Existential Philosophy.* New York: Dutton, 1962.

Seidman, Bradley. *Absent at the Creation: The Existential Psychiatry of Ludwig Binswanger.* Roslyn Heights, N.Y.: Libra, 1983.

Medard Boss

Craig, Erik. *Psychotherapy for Freedom: The Daseinsanalytic Way in Psychology and Psychoanalysis.* Carrollton, Ga: Division of Humanistic Psychology, American Psychological Association, 1988.

Friedman, Maurice, ed. *The Worlds of Existentialism a Critical Reader.* New York: Random House, 1964.

Ruitenbeek, Hendrik. *Psychoanalysis and Existential Philosophy.* New York: Dutton, 1962.

Scott, Charles E, ed. *On Dreaming: An Encounter with Medard Boss.* Chico, Calif: Scholars Press, 1982.

Martin Buber

Bibliography

Cohn, Margot, and Rafael Buber. *Martin Buber: A Bibliography of his Writings, 1897–1978.* Jerusalem: Magnes Press and K.G. Saur, 1980.

General

Atterton, Peter, Matthew Calarco, and Maurice S. Friedman, eds. *Levinas & Buber: Dialogue & Difference.* Pittsburgh: Duquesne University Press, 2004.

Avnon, Dan. *Martin Buber: The Hidden Dialogue.* Lanham, Md.: Rowman & Littlefield, 1998.

Balthasar, Hans Urs von. *Martin Buber & Christianity: A Dialogue between Israel and the Church.* London: Harvill Press, 1961.

Baum, Gregory. *Nationalism, Religion, and Ethics*. Montreal: McGill-Queen's University Press, 2001.

Bergman, Samuel Hugo. *Dialogical Philosophy from Kierkegaard to Buber*. Albany: State University of New York Press, 1991.

Berry, Donald L. *Mutuality: The Vision of Martin Buber*. Albany: State University of New York Press, 1985.

Boni, Sylvain. *The Self and the Other in the Ontologies of Sartre and Buber*. Washington, D.C: University Press of America, 1982.

Cohen, Arthur Allen. *Martin Buber*. New York: Hillary House, 1957.

Diamond, Malcolm Luria. *Martin Buber, Jewish Existentialist*. New York: Oxford University Press, 1960.

Edwards, Paul. *Buber and Buberism: A Critical Evaluation*. Lawrence: University of Kansas Press, 1971.

Friedman, Maurice S. *Encounter on the Narrow Ridge: A Life of Martin Buber*. New York: Paragon House, 1991

———. *Martin Buber: The Life of Dialogue*. Chicago: University of Chicago Press, 1955

———. *Martin Buber and the Eternal*. New York: Human Sciences Press, 1986.

———. *Martin Buber's Life and Work*. Detroit: Wayne State University Press, 1988.

Gordon, Hayim. *The Heidegger-Buber Controversy: The Status of the I-Thou*. Westport, Conn: Greenwood Press, 2001.

Hodes, Aubrey. *Encounter with Martin Buber*. London: Allen Lane, 1972.

Huston, Phil. *Martin Buber's Journey to Presence*. New York: Fordham University Press, 2007.

Kaufmann, Walter Arnold. *Nietzsche, Heidegger, and Buber*. New York: McGraw-Hill, 1980.

Mayhall, C. Wayne, and Timothy B. Mayhall. *On Buber*. Belmont, Calif: Thomson/Wadsworth, 2003.

Panko, Stephen M. *Martin Buber*. Peabody, Mass: Hendrickson Publishers, 1991.

Rotenberg, Mordechai. *Between Rationality & Irrationality: The Jewish Psychotherapeutic System*. New Brunswick, N.J.: Transaction Publishers, 2005.

Schilpp, Paul Arthur, and Maurice Friedmann, eds. *The Philosophy of Martin Buber*. La Salle, Ill.: Open Court, 1967.

Smith, Ronald Gregor. *Martin Buber*. Richmond, Va.: John Knox Press, 1967.

Susser, Bernard. *Existence and Utopia: The Social and Political Thought of Martin Buber*. Rutherford, N.J.: Fairleigh Dickinson University Press, 1981.

Theunissen, Michael. *The Other: Studies in the Social Ontology of Husserl, Heidegger, Sartre, and Buber*. Translated by Christopher Macann. Cambridge, Mass.: MIT Press, 1984.

Vermes, Pamela. *Buber*. New York: Grove Press, 1988.

———. *Buber on God and the Perfect Man*. London: Littman Library of Jewish Civilization, 1994.

Walters, James W. *Martin Buber & Feminist Ethics: The Priority of the Personal*. Syracuse, N.Y.: Syracuse University Press, 2003.

Rudolph Bultmann

Long, Eugene. *Jaspers and Bultmann: A Dialogue between Philosophy and Theology in the Existentialist Tradition*. Durham, N.C.: Duke University Press, 1968.

Gardiner, Patrick. "Rudolph Bultmann." In *The Encyclopedia of Philosophy*, edited by Paul Edwards. Volume 1. New York: Macmillan, 1967.

Macquarrie, John. *An Existentialist Theology: A Comparison of Heidegger and Bultmann*. Harmondsworth, UK: Penguin, 1973.

Oden, T. C. *Radical Obedience: The Ethics of Rudolph Butlmann*. Philadephia: Westminster, 1964.

Albert Camus

Bree, Germaine. *Camus: A Collection of Critical Essays*. Englewood Cliffs, N.J.: Prentice-Hall, 1962.

———. *Camus and Sartre: Crisis and Commitment*. New York: Delacorte Press, 1972.

Lottman, Herbert R. *Albert Camus: A Biography*. Garden City, N.Y.: Doubleday, 1979.

Olafson, Frederick A. "Albert Camus." In *The Encyclopedia of Philosophy*. Edited by Paul Edwards. Volume 1. New York: Macmillan, 1967.

Sartre, Jean-Paul. "Camus' *The Outsider*" (review of *The Stranger*). In *Literary and Philosophical Essays*. Translated by Annette Michelson. New York: Criterion Books 1955.

Todd, Olivier. *Albert Camus: A Life*. Translated by Benjamin Ivry. New York: Carol & Graff, 1997.

Wilhelm Dilthey

De Mul, Jos. *The Tragedy of Finitude: Dilthey's Hermeneutics of Life*. Translated by Tony Burrett. New Haven, Conn.: Yale University Press, 2004.

Ermarth, Michael. *Wilhelm Dilthey: The Critique of Historical Reason*. Chicago: University of Chicago Press, 1978.

Makkreel, Rudolf A. *Dilthey, Philosopher of the Human Studies*. Princeton, N.J.: Princeton University Press, 1975.

Owensby, Jacob. *Dilthey and the Narrative of History*. Ithaca, N.Y.: Cornell University Press, 1994.

Tuttle, Howard N. *Human Life Is Radical Reality: An Idea Developed from the Conceptions of Dilthey, Heidegger, and Ortega Y Gasset*. New York: Peter Lang, 2005.

Martin Heidegger

Bibliographies

Nordquist, Joan. *Martin Heidegger: A Bibliography. Social Theory*. Santa Cruz: California: Reference and Research Services, 1990.

———. *Martin Heidegger (II): A Bibliography*. Santa Cruz: California: Reference and Research Services, 1996.

Sass, H.-M. *Martin Heidegger: Bibliography and Glossary*. Bowling Green, Ohio: Philosophy Documentation Center, 1982.

General

Arendt, Hannah. "Martin Heidegger at 80." Reprinted in *Heidegger and Modern Philosophy*. Edited by Michael Murray. New Haven, Conn.: Yale University Press, 1978.

Biemel, Walter. *Martin Heidegger: An Illustrated Study*. Translated by J. L. Mehta. New York: Harcourt Brace Jovanovich, 1976.

Buber, Martin. "What Is Man?" ("Section Two: Modern Attempts"). In *Between Man and Man*. Translated by Ronald Gregor-Smith. London: Routledge & Kegan Paul, 2002.

Caputo, John. *The Mystical Element in Heidegger's Thought*. New York: Fordham University Press, 1986.

Carnap, Rudolph. "The Elimination of Metaphysics through Logical Analysis of Language." In *Logical Positivism*. Edited by A. J. Ayer. New York: Free Press, 1966.

Cooper, David E. *Heidegger*. London: Claridge Press, 1996.

Dreyfus, Hubert L. *Being-in-the-World : A Commentary on Heidegger's Being and Time, Division I*. Cambridge: MIT Press, 1991.

Dreyfus, Hubert, and Harrison Hall, eds. *Heidegger: A Critical Reader*. Oxford: Basil Blackwell, 1992.

Dreyfus, Hubert L., and Mark A. Wrathall. *A Companion to Heidegger*. Oxford: Blackwell, 2005.

Gadamer, Hans-Georg. *Heidegger's Ways*. Translated by John W. Stanley. Albany: State University of New York Press, 1994.

Gelven, Michael. *A Commentary on Heidegger's "Being and Time"*. Dekalb: Northern Illinois University Press, 1989.

Grene, Marjorie. *Martin Heidegger*. New York: Hillary House, 1957.

Guignon, Charles. *Heidegger and the Problem of Knowledge*. Indianapolis, Ind.: Hackett, 1983.

Guignon, Charles, ed. *The Cambridge Companion to Heiddegger*. Cambridge: Cambridge University Press, 1993.

Jaspers, Karl. *Notizen zu Martin Heidegger*. Edited by Hans Saner. Munich: R. Piper, 1977.

Kisiel, Theodore. *The Genesis of Heidegger's "Being and Time"*. Berkeley: University of California Press, 1993.

Langan, Thomas. *The Meaning of Heidegger: A Critical Study of an Existentialist Phenomenology*. New York: Columbia University Press, 1959.

Macquarrie, John. *Martin Heidegger*. Richmond, Va.: John Knox, 1968.

Murray, Michael, ed. *Heidegger and Modern Philosophy*. New Haven, Conn.: Yale University Press, 1978.

Okrent, Mark. *Heidegger's Pragmatism*. Ithaca, N.Y.: Cornell University Press, 1988.

Olafson, Frederick A. *Heidegger and the Philosophy of Mind*. New Haven, Conn.: Yale University Press, 1987.

———. *What Is a Human Being?: A Heideggerian View*. Cambridge: Cambridge University Press, 1995.

Philipse, Herman. *Heidegger's Philosophy of Being: A Critical Interpretation*. Princeton, N. J.: Princeton University Press, 1998.

Pöggeler, Otto. *Martin Heidegger's Path of Thinking*. Atlantic Highlands, N.J.: Humanities Press, 1989.

Polt, Richard. *Heidegger: An Introduction*. Ithaca, N.Y.: Cornell University Press, 1999.

Polt, Richard F. H, and Gregory Fried, eds. *A Companion to Heidegger's "Introduction to Metaphysics"*. New Haven, Conn.: Yale University Press, 2001.

Rorty, Richard. *Essays on Heidegger and Others*. Cambridge: Cambridge University Press, 1991.

Safranski, Rüdiger. *Martin Heidegger: Between Good and Evil*. Cambridge, Mass.: Harvard University Press,1998.

Sallis, John. *Echoes: After Heidegger*. Bloomington: Indiana University Press, 1990.

———. *Heidegger and the Path of Thinking*. Pittsburgh: Duquesne University Press, 1970.

———. *Reading Heidegger: Commemorations*. Bloomington: Indiana University Press, 1993.

Sallis, John, ed. *Radical Phenomenology: Essays in Honor of Martin Heidegger*. Atlantic Highlands, N.J: Humanities Press, 1978.

Steiner, George. *Martin Heidegger*. New York: Penguin Books, 1980.

Zimmerman, Michael E. *Eclipse of the Self: The Development of Heidegger's Concept of Authenticity*. Athens: Ohio University Press, 1981.

Martin Heidegger and National Socialism

Adorno, Theodor. *The Jargon of Authenticity*. Translated by Kurt Tarnowski and Frederic Will. Evanston, Ill.: Northwestern University Press, 1973.

Bambach, Charles R. *Heidegger's Roots: Nietzsche, National Socialism and the Greeks*. Ithaca, N.Y: Cornell University Press, 2003.

Derrida, Jacques. *Of Spirit: Heidegger and the Question*. Chicago: University of Chicago Press, 1990.

Farias, Victor. *Heidegger and Nazism*. Edited by Joseph Margolis and Tom Rockmore. Translated by Paul Burrell and Gabriel Ricci. Philadephia: Temple University Press, 1989.

Habermas, Jürgen. "Martin Heidegger: On the Publication of the Lectures of 1935." In *The Heidegger Controversy: A Critical Reader*. Edited by Richard Wolin, 186–197. Cambridge, Mass.: MIT Press, 1998.

Löwith, Karl. *My Life in Germany before and after 1933*. Translated by Elizabeth King. Urbana: University of Illinois Press, 1986.

Neske, Günther, and Emil Kettering, eds. *Martin Heidegger and National Socialism: Questions and Answers*. Translated by Lisa Harries. New York: Paragon House, 1990.

Ott, Hugo. *Martin Heidegger: A Political Life*. Translated by Allan Blunden. New York: Basic Books, 1993.

Rockmore, Thomas, and J. Margolis, eds. *The Heidegger Case: On Philosophy and Politics*. Philadephia: Temple University Press, 1992.

Sheehan, Thomas, ed. *Heidegger: The Man and the Thinker*. Chicago: Precedent, 1981.

Sluga, Hans. *Heidegger's Crisis: Philosophy and Politics in Nazi Germany*. Cambridge, Mass.: Harvard University Press, 1993.

Wolin, Richard, ed. *The Heidegger Controversy: A Critical Reader*. Cambridge: MIT Press, 1998.

———. *Labyrinths: Explorations in the Critical History of Ideas*. Amherst: University of Massachusetts Press, 1995.

———. *The Politics of Being: The Political Thought of Martin Heidegger*. New York: Columbia University Press, 1990.

Young, Julian. *Heidegger, Philosophy, Nazism*. Cambridge: Cambridge University Press, 1998.

Zimmerman, Michael E. *Heidegger's Confrontation with Modernity: Technology, Politics, and Art*. Bloomington: Indiana University Press, 1990.

Karl Jaspers

Allen, Edgar Leonard. *The Self and Its Hazards: A Guide to the Thought of Karl Jaspers*. New York: Philosophical Library, 1951.

Amin, Sonal K. *Karl Jaspers and Existentialism*. New Delhi: Anmol Publications, 1992.

Dufrenne, Mikel, and Paul Ricoeur. *Karl Jaspers et la philosophie de l'existence*. Paris: Editions du Seuil, 1947.

Ehrlich, Leonard H., and Richard Wisser, eds. *Karl Jaspers Today: Philosophy at the Threshold of the Future*. Pittsburgh: Center for Advanced Research in Phenomenology, 1988.

Howey, Richard Lowell. *Heidegger and Jaspers on Nietzsche*. The Hague: Nijhoff, 1973.

Kirkbright, Suzanne. *Karl Jaspers: A Biography: Navigations in Truth*. New Haven, Conn: Yale University Press, 2004.

Koterski, Joseph W., and Raymond J. Langley, eds. *Karl Jaspers on Philosophy of History and History of Philosophy*. Amherst, N.Y.: Humanity Books, 2003.

Long, Eugene Thomas. *Jaspers and Bultmann: A Dialogue between Philosophy and Theology in the Existentialist Tradition*. Durham, N.C.: Duke University Press, 1968.

Olson, Alan M., ed. *Heidegger and Jaspers*. Philadelphia: Temple University Press, 1994.

———. *Transcendence and Hermeneutics: An Interpretation of the Philosophy of Karl Jaspers*. The Hague: M. Nijhoff, 1979.

Salamun, Kurt, and Gregory Walters, eds. *Karl Jaspers's Philosophy: Exposition and Interpretations*. Amherst, N.Y.: Humanity Books, 2006.

Schilpp, Paul Arthur, ed. *The Philosophy of Karl Jaspers*. New York: Tudor, 1957.

Schrag, Oswald O. *Existence, Existenz, and Transcendence: An Introduction to the Philosophy of Karl Jaspers*. Pittsburgh: Duquesne University Press, 1971.

Thornhill, C. J. *Karl Jaspers: Politics and Metaphysics*. London: Routledge, 2002.

Wahl, Jean. *Le pensée de l'existence. Kierkegaard-Jaspers*. Paris: Flammarion, 1951.

Wallraff, Charles F. *Karl Jaspers: An Introduction to His Philosophy*. Princeton, N.J: Princeton University Press, 1970.

Søren Kierkegaard

Adorno, Theodor. *Kierkegaard: Construction of the Aesthetic*. Edited and translated by Robert Hullot-Kentor. Minneapolis: University of Minnesota Press, 1989.

Buber, Martin. "The Question to the Single One." In *Between Man and Man*. Translated by Ronald Gregor-Smith. London: Routledge & Kegan Paul, 2002.

Collins, James. *The Mind of Kierkegaard*. Princeton, N.J.: Princeton University Press, 1983.

Corxall, Thomas H. *Kierkegaard Studies*. London: Lutterworth Press, 1948.

Gardiner, Patrick. *Kierkegaard*. Oxford: Oxford University Press, 1988.

Green, Ronald M. *Kierkegaard and Kant: The Hidden Debt*. Albany: State University of New York Press, 1992.

Hannay, Alastair. *Kierkegaard: A Biography*. Cambridge: Cambridge University Press, 2003.

———. *Kierkegaard*. The Arguments of the Philosophers. London: Routledge, 1991.

———. *Kierkegaard and Philosophy: Selected Essays*. London: Routledge, 2003.

Hannay, Alastair, and Gordon D.Marino, eds. *The Cambridge Companion to Kierkegaard*. Cambridge: Cambridge University Press, 1998.

Lippitt, John. *Routledge Philosophy Guidebook to Kierkegaard and "Fear and Trembling"*. London: Routledge, 2003.

Lowrie, Walter. *Kierkegaard*. London: Oxford University Press, 1938.

Matustik, Martin J., and Merlod Westphal, eds. *Kierkegaard in Post/Modernity*. Bloomington: Indiana University Press, 1995.

Rée, Jonathan, and Jane Chamberlain, eds. *Kierkegaard: A Critical Reader*. Oxford: Blackwell, 1998.

Sartre, Jean-Paul. "Kierkegaard: The Singular Universal." In *Between Existentialism and Marxism*. Translated by John Mathews. New York: Morrow, 1974.

Shestov, Lev. *Kierkegaard and the Existentialist Philosophy*. Translated by E. Hewitt. Athens: Ohio University Press, 1969.

Swenson, David F. *Something about Kierkegaard*. Edited by Lillian Marvin Swenson. Macon, Ga.: Mercer University Press, 1983.

Weston, Michael. *Kierkegaard and Modern Continental Philosophy: An Introduction*. London: Routledge, 1994.

Westphal, Merold. *Becoming a Self: A Reading of Kierkegaard's "Concluding Unscientific Postscript."* West Lafayette, Ind.: Purdue University Press, 1996.

Wyschograd, Michael. *Kierkegaard and Heidegger: The Ontology of Existence*. New York: Humanities Press International, 1954.

Emmanuel Levinas

Atterton, Peter, and Matthew Calarco. *On Levinas*. Belmont, Calif: Thomson/Wadsworth, 2005.

Bernasconi, Robert, and Simon Critchley, eds. *Re-Reading Levinas*. Bloomington: University of Indiana Press, 1997.

Chanter, Tina, ed. *Feminist Interpretations of Emmanuel Levinas*. University Park: Pennsylvania State University Press, 2001.

Cohen, Richard A., ed. *Face to Face with Levinas*. Albany: State University of New York Press, 1986.

Critchley, Simon, and Robert Bernasconi, eds. *The Cambridge Companion to Levinas*. Cambridge: Cambridge University Press, 2002.

Davis, Colin, *Levinas: An Introduction*. Notre Dame, Ind.: University of Notre Dame Press, 1991.

Moyn, Samuel. *Origins of the Other: Emmanuel Levinas between Revelation and Ethics*. Ithaca, N.Y.: Cornell University Press, 2005.

Peperzak, Adriaan Theodoor, ed. *Ethics as First Philosophy: The Significance of Emmanuel Levinas for Philosophy, Literature, and Religion*. New York: Routledge, 1995.

Peperzak, Adriaan Theodoor, and Emmanuel Levinas. *To the Other: An Introduction to the Philosophy of Emmanuel Levinas*. West Lafayette, Ind.: Purdue University Press, 2005.

Treanor, Brian. *Aspects of Alterity: Levinas, Marcel, and the Contemporary Debate*. New York: Fordham University Press, 2006.

Wyschogrod, Edith. *Emmanuel Levinas: The Problem of Ethical Metaphysics*. The Hague: Nijhoff, 1974.

Gabriel Marcel

Appelbaum, David. *Contact and Attention: The Anatomy of Gabriel Marcel's Metaphysical Method*. Pittsburgh: Center for Advanced Research in Phenomenology, 1986.

Cain, Seymour. *Gabriel Marcel*. South Bend, Ind.: Regnery/Gateway, 1979.

———. *Gabriel Marcel's Theory of Religious Experience*. New York: P. Lang, 1995.

Cooney, William, ed. *Contributions of Gabriel Marcel to Philosophy: A Collection of Essays*. Lewiston, N.Y.: E. Mellen Press, 1989.

Keen, Sam. *Gabriel Marcel*. Richmond, Va.: John Knox Press, 1967.

Konickal, Joseph. *Being and My Being: Gabriel Marcel's Metaphysics of Incarnation*. Frankfurt-on-Main: P. Lang, 1992.

Levinas, Emmanuel. *Jean Wahl et Gabriel Marcel*. Paris: Beauchesne, 1976.

Moran, Denis P. *Gabriel Marcel: Existentialist Philosopher, Dramatist, Educator*. Lanham, Md.: University Press of America, 1992.

O'Malley, John B. *The Fellowship of Being: An Essay on the Concept of Person in the Philosophy of Gabriel Marcel*. The Hague: Martinus Nijhoff, 1966.

Ricoeur, Paul. *Gabriel Marcel et Karl Jaspers: philosophie du mystère et philosophie du paradoxe*. Paris: Temps Présent, 1948.

Traub, Donald F. *Toward a Fraternal Society: A Study of Gabriel Marcel's Approach to Being, Technology, and Intersubjectivity.* New York: P. Lang, 1988.
Treanor, Brian. *Aspects of Alterity: Levinas, Marcel, and the Contemporary Debate.* New York: Fordham University Press, 2006.

Maurice Merleau-Ponty

Bibliography

Lapointe, François. *Maurice Merleau-Ponty and His Critics: An International Bibliography, 1942– 1976. Preceded by a Bibliography of His Writings.* Garland Reference Library of the Humanities, Vol. 51. New York: Garland, 1976.

General

Carman, Taylor, and Mark B. N. Hansen, eds. *The Cambridge Companion to Maerleau-Ponty.* Cambridge: Cambridge University Press, 2004.
Dillon, M.C. *Merleau-Ponty's Ontology.* Bloomington: Indiana University Press, 1988.
Dillon, M. C., ed. *Merleau-Ponty Vivant.* Albany: State University of New York Press, 1991.
Hass, Lawrence, and Dorothea Olkowski, eds. *Rereading Merleau-Ponty: Essays beyond the Continental-Analytic Divide.* Amherst, N.Y.: Humanity Books, 2000.
Kruks, Sonia. *Political Philosophy of Merleau-Ponty.* London: Ashgate, 1994.
Kwant, Remigius C. *The Phenomenoloigical Philosophy of Merleau-Ponty.* Pittsburgh, Pa.: Duquesne University Press, 1963.
Langer, Monica. *Merleau-Ponty's "Phenomenology of Perception": A Guide and Commentary.* New York: Palgrave Macmillan, 1989.
Madison, Gary. *The Phenomenology of Merleau-Ponty: A Search for the Limits of Consciousness.* Athens: Ohio University Press, 1981.
Olafson, Frederick A. "Maurice Merleau-Ponty." In *The Encyclopedia of Philosophy.* Edited by Paul Edwards. Volume 5. New York: Macmillan, 1967.
O'Neill, John. *Perception, Expression, History: The Social Phenomenology of Merleau-Ponty.* Evanston, Ill.: Northwestern University Press, 1964.
Rabil, Albert. *Merleau-Ponty, Existentialist of the Social World.* New York: Columbia University Press, 1967.
Sallis, John, ed. *Merleau-Ponty: Perception, Structure, Language.* Atlantic Highlands, N.J.: Humanities Press, 1981.
Sartre, Jean-Paul. "Merleau-Ponty Vivant." In *Situations.* Translated by Benita Eisler. New York: Braziller, 1965.

Schmidt, James. *Merleau-Ponty: Between Phenomenology and Structurualism.* New York: St. Martin's Press, 1985.

Stewart, Jon, ed. *The Debate between Sartre and Merleau-Ponty.* Evanston, Ill.: Northwestern University Press, 1998.

Van Breda, H. L. "Merleau-Ponty and the Husserl Archives at Louvain." Translated by Stephen Michelman. In Maurice Merleau-Ponty, *Texts and Dialogues*, edited by Hugh J. Silverman and James Barry Jr. New York: Prometheus, 1996.

Whitford, Margaret. *Merleau-Ponty's Critique of Sartre's Philosophy.* Lexington, Ky.: French Forum Publishers, 1982.

Friedrich Nietzsche

Allison, David B., ed. *The New Nietzsche.* New York: Dell, 1977.

Ansell-Pearson, Keith. *A Companion to Nietzsche.* Malden, Mass.: Blackwell Pub, 2006.

———. *How to Read Nietzsche.* New York: Norton, 2005.

———. *Nietzsche and Modern German Thought.* London: Routledge, 1991.

Clark, Maudemarie. *Nietzsche on Truth and Philosophy.* Cambridge: Cambridge University Press, 1990.

Cooper, David E. *Authenticity and Leanring: Nietzsche's Educational Philosophy.* Brookfield, Vt.: Avebury, 1991.

Danto, Arthur Coleman. *Nietzsche as Philosopher.* New York: Columbia University Press, 2005.

Hales, Steven D. *Nietzsche's Perspectivism.* Urbana: University of Illinois Press, 2000.

Hayman, Ronald. *Nietzsche.* New York: Routledge, 1999.

Heidegger, Martin. *Nietzsche.* Translated by David Farrell Krell. San Francisco: Harper & Row, 1979.

Jaspers, Karl. *Nietzsche: An Introduction to the Understanding of His Philosophical Activity.* Lanham, Md.: University Press of America, 1985.

Kaufmann, Walter Arnold. *Nietzsche: Philosopher, Psychologist, Antichrist.* New York: Vintage Books, 1968.

Leiter, Brian. *Routledge Philosophy Guidebook to Nietzsche on Morality.* London: Routledge, 2002.

Leiter, Brian, and Neil Sinhababu, eds. *Nietzsche and Morality.* Oxford: Oxford University Press, 2007.

Löwith, Karl. *Nietzsche's Philosophy of the Eternal Recurrence of the Same.* Berkeley: University of California Press, 1997.

Magnus, Bernd, and Kathleen M. Higgins, eds. *The Cambridge Companion to Nietzsche.* Cambridge: Cambridge University Press, 1996.

Nehamas, Alexander. *Nietzsche, Life as Literature*. Cambridge, Mass.: Harvard University Press, 1985.

Poellner, Peter. *Nietzsche and Metaphysics*. Oxford: Clarendon Press, 1995.

Reginster, Bernard. *The Affirmation of Life: Nietzsche on Overcoming Nihilism*. Cambridge, Mass: Harvard University Press, 2006.

Richardson, John. *Nietzsche's System*. New York: Oxford University Press, 1996.

Richardson, John, and Brian Leiter, eds. *Nietzsche*. Oxford: Oxford University Press, 2001.

Safranski, Rüdiger. *Nietzsche: A Philosophical Biography*. New York: W.W. Norton, 2002.

Schacht, Richard. *Nietzsche*. London: Routledge, 1985.

Schacht, Richard, ed. *Nietzsche, Genealogy, Morality: Essays on Nietzsche's "Genealogy of Morals"*. Berkeley: University of California Press, 1994.

Solomon, Robert C., and Kathleen M. Higgins, eds. *Reading Nietzsche*. New York: Oxford University Press, 1988.

Tanner, Michael. *Nietzsche*. Oxford: Oxford University Press, 1994.

Vattimo, Gianni. *Nietzsche: An Introduction*. Stanford, Calif.: Stanford University Press, 2001.

José Ortega y Gasset

Diaz, Janet Winecoff. *The Major Themes of Existentialism in the Work of José Ortega y Gasset*. Chapel Hill: University of North Carolina Press, 1970.

Dust, Patrick H. *Ortega y Gasset and the Question of Modernity*. Minneapolis, Minn.: Prisma Institute, 1989.

Ferrater Mora. *José Ortega y Gasset: An Outline of His Philosophy*. New Haven: Yale University Press, 1963.

Gonzalez, Pedro Blas. *Human Existence as Radical Reality: Ortega y Gasset's Philosophy of Subjectivity*. St. Paul, Minn.: Paragon House, 2005.

Graham, John T. *A Pragmatist Philosophy of Life in Ortega y Gasset*. Columbia: University of Missouri Press, 1994.

Tuttle, Howard N. *The Crowd Is Untruth: The Existential Critique of Mass Society in the Thought of Kierkegaard, Nietzsche, Heidegger, and Ortega y Gasset*. New York: P. Lang, 1996.

———. *The Dawn of Historical Reason: The Historicality of Human Existence in the Thought of Dilthey, Heidegger, and Ortega y Gasset*. New York: P. Lang, 1994.

———. *Human Life Is Radical Reality: An Idea Developed from the Conceptions of Dilthey, Heidegger, and Ortega y Gasset*. New York: P. Lang, 2005.

Franz Rosenzweig

Batnitzky, Leora Faye. *Idolatry and Representation: The Philosophy of Franz Rosenzweig Reconsidered*. Princeton, N.J.: Princeton University Press, 2000.

Cohen, Richard A. *Elevations: The Height of the Good in Rosenzweig and Levinas*. Chicago: University of Chicago Press, 1994.

Glatzer, Nahum Norbert. *Franz Rosenzweig: His Life and Thought*. New York: Schocken Books, 1961.

Gordon, Peter Eli. *Rosenzweig and Heidegger: Between Judaism and German Philosophy*. Berkeley: University of California Press, 2003.

Jean-Paul Sartre

Bibliographies

Belkind, Allen. *Jean-Paul Sartre: Sartre and Existentialism in English: A Bibliographical Guide*. Kent, Ohio: Kent State University Press, 1970.

Contat, Michel, and Michel Rybalka. *The Writings of Jean-Paul Sartre, Volume 1: A Bibliographic Life*. Translated by Richard McClearly. Evanston, Ill.: Northwestern University Press, 1974.

Wilcocks, Robert. *Sartre, A Bibliography of International Criticism*. Edmonton: University of Alberta Press, 1975.

General

Bell, Linda. *Sartre's Ethics of Authenticity*. Tuscaloosa: University of Alabama Press, 1989.

Brosman, Catharine Savage. *Jean-Paul Sartre*. Boston: Twayne, 1983.

Catalano, Joseph S. *A Commentary on Jean-Paul Sartre's Being and Nothingness*. Chicago: University of Chicago Press, 1980.

———. *Good Faith and Other Essays: Perspectives on a Sartrean Ethics*. Lanham, Md.: Rowman & Littlefield, 1996.

Caws, Peter, *Sartre*. London: Roudedge, 1979.

Cohen-Solal, Annie, *Sartre: A Life*. Translated by Anna Cancogni. London: Heinemann, 1987.

Danto, Arthur. *Sartre*. New York: Viking, 1975.

Desan, Wilfrid. *The Tragic Finale: An Essay on the Philosophy of Jean-Paul Sartre*. Cambridge, Mass.: Harvard University Press, 1954.

Fell, Joseph. *Emotion in the Thought of Sartre*. New York: Columbia University Press, 1965.

———. *Heidegger and Sartre*. New York: Columbia University Press, 1979.

Grene, Marjorie. *Sartre*. Lanham, Md.: University Press of America, 1983.

Hartmann, Klaus. *Sartre's Ontology: A Study of "Being and Nothingness" in the Light of Hegel's "Logic"*. Evanston, Ill.: Northwestern University Press, 1966.

Hayim, Gila J. *The Existential Sociology of Jean-Paul Sartre*. Amherst: University of Massachusetts Press, 1980.

Hayman, Ronald. *Writing Against: A Biography of Sartre*. London: Weidenfeld and Nicolson, 1986.

Howells, Christina, ed. *The Cambridge Companion to Sartre*. Cambridge: Cambridge University Press, 1992.

———. *Sartre: The Necessity of Freedom*. Cambridge: Cambridge University Press, 1988.

Jeanson, Francis. *Sartre and the Problem of Morality*. Translated by R. Stone. Bloomington: Indiana University Press, 1980.

Laing, R. D., and D. G. Cooper. *Reason and Violence: A Decade of Sartre's Philosophy 1950–1960*. London: Tavistock, 1964.

Marcuse, Herbert. "Existentialism: Remarks on Jean-Paul Sartre's *L' tre et le néant*." *Journal of Philosophy and Phenomenological Research* Vol VIII, no. 3 (March 1948): 309–336.

McCulloch, Gregory. *Using Sartre: An Analytical Introduction to Early Sartrean Themes*. London: Routledge, 1994.

Merleau-Ponty, Maurice. "Sartre and Ultrabolshevism." In *Adventures of the Dialectic*. Translated by Joseph Bien. Evanston, Ill.: Northwestern University Press, 1973.

———. "A Scandalous Author" and "The Battle over Existentialism." In *Sense and Non-Sense*. Translated by Hubert Dreyfus and Patricia Dreyfus. Evanston, Ill.: Northwestern University Press, 1964.

Murdoch, Iris. *Sartre: Romantic Rationalist*. New York: Viking, 1987.

Natanson, Maurice Alexander. *A Critique of Jean-Paul Sartre's Ontology*. The Hague: Nijhoff, 1973.

Olafson, Frederick A. "Jean-Paul Sartre." In *The Encyclopedia of Philosophy*, edited by Paul Edwards. Volume 7. New York: Macmillan, 1967.

Plantinga, Alvin. "An Existentialist's Ethics." *Review of Metaphysics*, XII (1958): 235–256.

Reisman, David. *Sartre's Phenomenology*. London: Continuum, 2007.

Schilpp, Paul, ed. *The Philosophy of Jean-Paul Sartre*. LaSalle, Ill.: Open Court, 1981.

Stern, Alfred. *Sartre: His Philosophy and Psychoanalysis*. New York: Liberal Arts Press, 1953.

Warnock, Mary. *The Philosophy of Sartre*. New York: Hillary House, 1965.

Max Scheler

Barber, Michael D. *Guardian of Dialogue: Max Scheler's Phenomenology, Sociology of Knowledge, and Philosophy of Love*. Lewisburg, Pa.: Bucknell University Press, 1993.

Frings, Manfred S. *Max Scheler: A Concise Introduction into the World of a Great Thinker*. Milwaukee, Wis.: Marquette University Press, 1996.

———. *The Mind of Max Scheler: The First Comprehensive Guide Based on the Complete Works*. Milwaukee, Wis.: Marquette University Press, 1997.

Frings, Manfred S, ed. *Max Scheler (1874–1928): Centennial Essays*. The Hague: Nijhoff, 1974.

Kelly, Eugene. *Max Scheler*. Boston: Twayne Publishers, 1977.

Nota, John H. *Max Scheler: The Man and His Work*. Quincy, Ill.: Franciscan Press, 1984.

Staude, John Raphael. *Max Scheler: An Intellectual Portrait*. New York: Free Press, 1967.

Lev Shestov

Copleston, Frederick Charles. *Russian Religious Philosophy: Selected Aspects*. Kent, UK: Search Press, 1988.

Martin, Bernard, ed. *Great Twentieth Century Jewish Philosophers: Shestov, Rosenzweig, Buber, with Selections from Their Writings*. New York: Macmillan, 1969.

Shein, Louis J. *The Philosophy of Lev Shestov (1866–1938): A Russian Religious Existentialist*. Lewiston, N.Y.: Mellen, 1991.

Valevicius, Andrius. *Lev Shestov and His Times: Encounters with Brandes, Tolstoy, Dostoevsky, Chekhov, Ibsen, Nietzsche, and Husserl*. New York: P. Lang, 1993.

Paul Tillich

Adams, J. L. *Paul Tillich's Philosophy of Culture, Science, and Religion*. New York: Harper & Row, 1965.

Alston, William. "Paul Tillich." In *The Encyclopedia of Philosophy*. Edited by Paul Edwards. Volume 8. New York: Macmillan, 1967.

Carey, John Jesse, ed. *Kairos and Logos: Studies in the Roots and Implications of Tillich's Theology*. Macon, Ga.: Mercer University Press, 1984.

Cooper, Terry D. *Paul Tillich and Psychology: Historic and Contemporary Explorations in Theology, Psychotherapy, and Ethics*. Macon, Ga.: Mercer University Press, 2006.

Ferrell, Donald R. *Logos and Existence: The Relationship of Philosophy and Theology in the Thought of Paul Tillich*. New York: P. Lang, 1992.

Lyons, James R, ed. *The Intellectual Legacy of Paul Tillich*. Detroit: Wayne State University Press, 1969.

Mahan, Wayne W. *Tillich's System*. San Antonio, Tex.: Trinity University Press, 1974 .

Martin, Bernard. *The Existentialist Theology of Paul Tillich*. New York: Bookman Associates, 1963.

Pauck, Wilhelm, and Marion Pauck. *Paul Tillich, His Life & Thought*. San Francisco: Harper & Row, 1989.

Miguel de Unamuno

Ellis, Robert Richmond. *The Tragic Pursuit of Being: Unamuno and Sartre*. Tuscaloosa: University of Alabama Press, 1988.

Huertas-Jourda, José. *The Existentialism of Miguel De Unamuno*. Gainesville: University of Florida Press, 1963.

ANTHOLOGIES

Friedman, Maurice, ed. *The Worlds of Existentialism: A Critical Reader*. Chicago: University of Chicago Press, 1964.

Guignon, Charles, and Derek Pereboom, eds. *Existentialism: Basic Writings*. Indianapolis, Ind.: Hackett, 2001.

Kaufmann, Walter, ed. *Existentialism from Dostoevsky to Sartre*. Rev. ed. New York : Meridian Books, 1989.

Marino, Gordon, ed. *Basic Writings of Existentialism*. New York: Modern Library, 2004.

MacDonald, Paul S., ed. *The Existentialist Reader: An Anthology of Key Texts*. New York: Routledge, 2001.

Spanos, William V., ed. *A Casebook on Existentialism*. New York: Thomas E. Crowell, 1966.

DICTIONARIES

Burbidge, John W. *Historical Dictionary of Hegelian Philosophy*. Lanham, Md.: Scarecrow Press, 2001.

Cartwright, David E. *Historical Dictionary of Schopenhauer's Philosophy*. Lanham, Md.: Scarecrow Press, 2004.

Denker, Alfred. *Historical Dictionary of Heidegger's Philosophy*. Lanham, Md.: Scarecrow Press, 2000.

Diethe, Carol. *Historical Dictionary of Nietzscheanism*. Lanham, Md.: Scarecrow Press, 2007.

Drummond, John J. *Historical Dictionary of Husserl's Philosophy*. Lanham, Md.: Scarecrow Press, 2008.

Gordon, Hayim, ed. *Dictionary of Existentialism*. Westport, Conn: Greenwood Press, 1999.

Watkin, Julia. *Historical Dictionary of Kierkegaard's Philosophy*. Lanham, Md.: Scarecrow Press, 2001.

HISTORICAL BACKGROUND

Aron, Raymond. *Memoirs: Fifty Years of Political Reflection*. Translated by George Holoch. New York: Holmes & Meier, 1990.

Barnouw, Dagmar. *Weimar Intellectuals and the Threat of Modernity*. Bloomington: Indiana University Press, 1988.

Beevor, Antony, and Artemis Cooper. *Paris after the Liberation: 1944–1949*. London: Penguin, 1994.

Boschetti, Anna. *The Intellectual Enterprise: Sartre and Les Temps Modernes*. Translated by Richard C. McCleary. Evanston, Ill.: Northwestern University Press, 1988.

Davies, Howard. *Sartre and 'Les Temps Modernes'*. Cambridge: Cambridge University Press, 1987.

Drake, David. *Intellectuals and Politics in Post-War France*. Hampshire: Palgrave, 2002.

Durst, David C. *Weimar Modernism: Philosophy, Politics, and Culture in Germany, 1918–1933*. Lanham, Md.: Lexington Books, 2004.

Forth, Christopher E. *Zarathustra in Paris: The Nietzsche Vogue in France, 1891–1918*. Dekalb: Northern Illinois University Press, 2001.

Fulbrook, Mary, ed. *Twentieth-century Germany: Politics, Culture and Society 1918–1990*. London: Arnold, 2001.

Herf, Jeffrey. *Reactionary Modernism: Technology, Culture, and Politics in Weimar and the Third Reich*. Cambridge: Cambridge University Press, 1984.

Jones, Christopher M. *Boris Vian Transatlantic: Sources, Myths, and Dreams*. New York: P. Lang, 1998.

Judt, Tony. *Past Imperfect: French Intellectuals, 1944–1956*. Berkeley: University of California Press, 1992.

Lévy, Bernard Henri. *Adventures on the Freedom Road: The French Intellectuals in the 20th Century*. Edited and translated by Richard Veasey. London: Harvill Press, 1995.

Löwith, Karl. *My Life in Germany before and after 1933*. Translated by Elizabeth King. Urbana: University of Illinois Press, 1986.

Phelan, Anthony, ed. *The Weimar Dilemma: Intellectuals in the Weimar Republic*. Manchester, UK: Manchester University Press, 1985.

Rabinbach, Anson. *In the Shadow of Catastrophe: German Intellectuals between Apocalypse and Enlightenment*. Berkeley: University of California Press, 1997.

Ringer, Fritz K. *The Decline of the German Mandarins: The German Academic Community, 1890– 1933*. Cambridge, Mass: Harvard University Press, 1969.

Wolin, Richard. *Labyrinths: Explorations in the Critical History of Ideas*. Amherst: University of Massachusetts Press, 1995.

EXISTENTIALISM AND AESTHETICS

Fallico, Arturo B. *Art & Existentialism*. Englewood Cliffs, N.J.: Prentice-Hall, 1962.

Fóti, Véronique Marion, ed. *Merleau-Ponty: Difference, Materiality, Painting*. Atlantic Highlands, N.J.: Humanities Press, 1996.

Fraleigh, Sondra Horton. *Dance and the Lived Body: A Descriptive Aesthetics*. Pittsburgh: University of Pittsburgh Press, 1987.

Johnson, Galen A., and Michael B. Smith, eds. *The Merleau-Ponty Aesthetics Reader: Philosophy and Painting*. Evanston, Ill.: Northwestern University Press, 1994.

Kaelin, Eugene Francis. *Art and Existence: A Phenomenological Aesthetics*. Lewisburg, Pa.: Bucknell University Press, 1971.

———. *An Existentialist Aesthetic: The Theories of Sartre and Merleau-Ponty*. Madison: University of Wisconsin Press, 1962.

Ketcham, Charles B. *The Influence of Existentialism on Ingmar Bergman: An Analysis of the Theological Ideas Shaping a Filmmakers's Art*. Lewiston, N.Y.: E. Mellen Press, 1986.

Kockelmans, Joseph J. *Heidegger on Art and Art Works*. Dordrecht: Nijhoff, 1985.

Kuspit, Donald B. *The Philosophical Life of the Senses (Sensibility-Existentialism)*. New York: Philosophical Library, 1969.

McBride, William L., ed. *Existentialist Literature and Aesthetics*. New York: Garland, 1997.

Morris, Frances, ed. *Paris Post War: Art and Existentialism 1945–55*. London: Tate Gallery, 1994.

Ortega y Gasset, José. *Phenomenology and Art*. Translated by Phillip W. Silver. New York: Norton, 1975.

Rosenberg, Harold. *The Tradition of the New*. Freeport, N.Y.: Books for Libraries Press, 1971.

Young, Julian. *Nietzsche's Philosophy of Art*. Cambridge: Cambridge University Press, 1994.

——. *Heidegger's Philosophy of Art*. Cambridge: Cambridge University Press, 2001.

EXISTENTIALISM AND CHRISTIANITY

Earle, William, James M. Edie, and John Wild. *Christianity and Existentialism*. Evanston, Ill.: Northwestern University Press, 1963.

Kingston, Frederick. *French Existentialism: A Christian Critique*. Toronto: University of Toronto Press, 1961.

Lowrie, Donald A. *Christian Existentialism*. New York, 1956.

Macquarrie, John. *An Existentialist Theology: A Comparison of Heidegger and Bultmann*. Harmondsworth, UK: Penguin, 1973.

——. *Studies in Christian Existentialism*. Philadelphia: Westminster Press, 1966.

Maritain, Jacques. *Existence and the Existent*. New York: Pantheon Books, 1964.

Michalson, Carl. *Christianity and the Existentialists*. New York: Scribner, 1956.

Pattison, George. *Anxious Angels: A Retrospective View of Religious Existentialism*. New York: St. Martin's Press, 1999.

EXISTENTIALISM AND ETHICS

Arp, Kristana. *The Bonds of Freedom: Simone de Beauvoir's Existentialist Ethics*. New York: Open Court, 2001.

Barnes, Hazel E. *An Existentialist Ethics*. New York: Knopf, 1967.

Catalano, Joseph. *Good Faith and Other Essays: Perspectives on a Sartrean Ethics*. Lanham, Md.: Rowman & Littlefield, 1996.

Cooper, David. *The Measure of Things: Humanism, Humility, and Mystery*. Oxford: Oxford University Press, 2002.

Daigle, Christine, ed. *Existentialist Thinkers and Ethics*. Montreal: Queen's University Press, 2006.

Fielding, Helen, Gabrielle Hiltmann, Dorothea Olkowski, and Ann Reichold, eds. *The Other: Feminist Reflections in Ethics*. New York: Palgrave Macmillan, 2007.

Guignon, Charles. *On Being Authentic*. London: Routledge, 2004.
Murdoch, Iris. *The Sovereignty of Good*. London: Routledge, 1970.
Olafson, Frederick A. *Heidegger and the Ground of Ethics: A Study of Mitsein*. Cambridge: Cambridge University Press, 1998.
———. *Principles and Persons: An Ethical Interpretation of Existentialism*. Baltimore: Johns Hopkins University Press, 1967.
Plantinga, Alvin. "An Existentialist's Ethics." *Review of Metaphysics* XII (1958): 235–256.
Taylor, Charles. *The Ethics of Authenticity*. Cambridge, Mass.: Harvard University Press, 1991.
———. *Sources of the Self: The Making of the Modern Identity*. Cambridge, Mass.: Harvard University Press, 1989.
Vogel, Lawrence. *The Fragile "We": Ethical Implications of Heidegger's "Being and Time."* Evanston, Ill.: Northwestern University Press, 1994.
Warnock, Mary. *Existentialist Ethics*. New York: St. Martin's Press, 1967.

EXISTENTIALISM, FEMINISM, AND RACE

Appiah, Anthony. *The Ethics of Identity*. Princeton, N.J.: Princeton University Press, 2005.
Bartky, Sandra Lee. *Femininity and Domination: Studies in the Phenomenology of Oppression*. New York: Routledge, 1990.
Bell, Linda. *Rethinking Ethics in the Midst of Violence: A Feminist Approach to Freedom*. Lanham, Md.: Rowman & Littlefield, 1993.
Bordo, Susan. *Unbearable Weight: Feminism, Western Culture, and the Body*. Berkeley: University of California Press, 1993.
Butler, Judith. *Gender Trouble: Feminism and the Subversion of Identity*. New York: Routledge, 1999.
———. *Subjects of Desire: Hegelian Reflections in Twentieth-century France*. New York: Columbia University Press, 1999.
Fielding, Helen, Gabrielle Hiltmann, Dorothea Olkowski, and Ann Reichold, eds. *The Other: Feminist Reflections in Ethics*. New York: Palgrave Macmillan, 2007.
Fraser, Nancy, and Sandra Lee Bartky, eds. *Revaluing French Feminism: Critical Essays on Difference, Agency, and Culture*. Bloomington: Indiana University Press, 1992.
Gordon, Lewis R. *Bad Faith and Antiblack Racism*. Atlantic Highlands, N.J.: Humanties Press, 1995.
———. *Existentia Africana: Understanding Africana Existential Thought*. London: Routledge, 2000.

Gordon, Lewis R., ed. *Existence in Black: An Anthology of Black Existential Philosophy*. London: Routledge, 1997.

Irigaray, Luce. *An Ethics of Sexual Difference*. Translated by Carolyn Burke and Gillian C. Gill. Ithaca, N.Y.: Cornell University Press, 1993.

———. *The Forgetting of Air in Martin Heidegger*. Translated by Mary Beth Mader. Austin: University of Texas Press, 1999.

———. *Speculum of the Other Woman*. Translated by Gillian C. Gill. Ithaca, N.Y.: Cornell University Press, 1985.

Jaggar, Alison M., and Susan Bordo, eds. *Gender/body/knowledge: Feminist Reconstructions of Being and Knowing*. New Brunswick, N.J: Rutgers University Press, 1989.

Olkowski, Dorothea, and Gail Weiss, eds. *Feminist Intrepretations of Maurice Merleau-Ponty (Re-Reading the Canon)*. State College: Pennsylvania State University Press, 2006.

Ojara, Pius. *Toward a Fuller Human Identity: A Phenomenology of Family Life, Social Harmony, and the Recovery of the Black Self*. Bern: P. Lang, 2006.

Simmons, Margaret. *Beauvoir and the Second Sex: Feminism, Race, and the Origins of Existentialism*. Lanham, Md.: Rowman & Littlefield, 1999.

EXISTENTIALISM AND LITERATURE

Baker, Richard E. *The Dynamics of the Absurd in the Existentialist Novel*. New York: P. Lang, 1993.

Berger, Gaston. *Existentialism and Literature in Action: Two Lectures on Present-day Problems in France*. Buffalo, N.Y.: University of Buffalo Press, 1948.

Brosman, Catharine Savage. *Existential Fiction*. Detroit: Gale Group, 2000.

Ellis, Robert Richmond. *The Tragic Pursuit of Being: Unamuno and Sartre*. Tuscaloosa: University of Alabama Press, 1988.

Fallico, Arturo B. *Art & Existentialism*. Englewood Cliffs, N.J: Prentice-Hall, 1962.

Finklestein, Sidney. *Existentialism and Alienation in American Literature*. New York: International Publishers, 1965.

Intrater, Roseline. *An Eye for an "I": Attrition of the Self in the Existential Novel*. New York: P. Lang, 1988.

Lehan, Richard. *A Dangerous Crossing: French Literary Existentialism and the Modern American Novel*. Carbondale: Southern Illinois University Press, 1973.

McBride, William L., ed. *Existentialist Literature and Aesthetics*. New York: Garland, 1997.

Murdoch, Iris. "Part Three: Encountering Existentialism." In *Existentialists and Mystics*. New York: Penguin, 1997.

Patrik, Linda E. *Existential Literature: An Introduction*. Belmont, Calif.: Wadsworth/Thomson Learning, 2001.

Smallwood, Clyde G. *Elements of the Existentialist Philosophy in the Theatre of the Absurd*. Dubuque, Iowa: W. C. Brown, 1966.

Stralen, Hans van. *Choices and Conflict: Essays on Literature and Existentialism*. Brusells: P. Lang, 2005.

EXISTENTIALISM AND MARXISM

Aron, Raymond. *Marxism and the Existentialists*. New York: Harper & Row, 1969.

———. *The Opium of Intellectuals*. Piscataway, N.J.: Transaction Publishers, 2001.

Cooper, Barry. *Merleau-Ponty and Marxism: From Terror to Reform*. Toronto: University of Toronto Press, 1980.

Desan, Wilfrid. *The Marxism of Jean-Paul Sartre*. New York, Anchor Books, 1965.

Flynn, Thomas. *Sartre and Marxist Existentialism: The Test Case of Collective Responsibility*. Chicago: University of Chicago Press, 1984.

Lukács, Georg. "Existentialism or Marxism?" (excerpt). In *Existentialism Versus Marxism: Conflicting Views on Humanism*. Edited by George Novack. New York: Dell, 1966.

Marcuse, Herbert. "Sartre, Historical Materialism, and Philosophy." In *Existentialism Versus Marxism: Conflicting Views on Humanism*. Edited by George Novack. New York: Dell, 1966.

Merleau-Ponty, Maurice. *Adventures of the Dialectic*. Translated by Joseph Bien. Evanston, Ill.: Northwestern University Press, 1973.

———. *Humanism and Terror: An Essay on the Communist Problem*. Translated by John O'Neill. Boston: Beacon Press, 1969.

Novack, George, ed. *Existentialism Versus Marxism: Conflicting Views on Humanism*. New York: Dell, 1966.

Sartre, Jean-Paul. "Materialism and Revolution." In *Literary and Philosophical Essays*. Translated by Annette Michelson. New York: Criterion, 1955.

———. *Search for a Method*. Translated by Hazel E. Barnes. New York: Knopf, 1963.

EXISTENTIALISM AND PSYCHOTHERAPY

Boss, Medard. *Psychoanalysis and Daseinsanalysis*. New York: Basic Books, 1963.

Buber, Martin. *On Psychology and Psychotherapy: Essays, Letters, and Dialogue*. Edited by Judith Buber-Agassi. Syracuse, N.Y.: University of Syracuse Press, 1998.

Bugental, James F. T. *The Search for Authenticity: An Existential-Analytic Approach to Psychotherapy*. New York: Holt, Rinehart & Winston, 1965.

Cohn, Hans W. *Heidegger and the Roots of Existential Therapy*. London: Continuum, 2002.

Cooper, D. G. *Psychiatry and Anti-psychiatry*. London: Tavistock Publications, 1967.

Frie, Roger. *Subjectivity and Intersubjectivity in Modern Philosophy and Psychoanalysis: A Study of Sartre, Binswanger, Lacan, and Habermas*. Lanham, Md.: Rowman & Littlefield, 1997.

Friedman, Maurice, ed. *The Worlds of Existentialism: A Critical Reader*. New York: Random House, 1964.

Fromm, Erich. *Man for Himself: An Inquiry into the Psychology of Ethics*. New York: Rinehart, 1947.

Gunzburg, John C. *Healing through Meeting: Martin Buber's Conversational Approach to Psychotherapy*. London: J. Kingsley, 1997.

Hanly, Charles. *Existentialism and Psychoanalysis*. New York: International Universities Press, 1979.

Laing, R. D. *The Divided Self*. New York: Penguin, 1969.

———. *The Politics of Experience*. New York: Ballantine Books, 1967.

Loy, David. *Lack and Transcendence: The Problem of Death and Life in Psychotherapy, Existentialism, and Buddhism*. New York: Prometheus Books, 2001.

May, Rollo. *The Discovery of Being: Writings in Existential Psychology*. New York: Norton, 1983.

May, Rollo, Ernest Angel, and Henri F. Ellenberger, eds. *Existence: A New Dimension in Psychiatry and Psychology*. New York: Basic Books, 1958.

Rotenberg, Mordechai. *Between Rationality & Irrationality: The Jewish Psychotherapeutic System*. Piscataway, N.J.: Transaction Publishers, 2005.

Ruitenbeek, Hendrik. *Psychoanalysis and Existential Philosophy*. New York: Dutton, 1962.

Yalom, Irvin D. *Existential Psychotherapy*. New York: Basic Books, 1980.

About the Author

Stephen Michelman (B.A. Vassar College, M.A. and Ph.D. Stony Brook University) is an associate professor of philosophy at Wofford College. He has devoted more than two decades to the study of existentialism and phenomenology and has published articles, reviews, and translations in these areas as well on psychoanalysis and contemporary French philosophy. In 1989, he was a Chateaubriand fellow; in 1990, a Belgian-American Educational Foundation fellow; and, in 1998, a summer fellow for the National Endowment for the Humanities. He has lived in France and Belgium and studied with Jacques Derrida, Jean-François Lyotard, and Claude Lefort, and has presented papers and hosted panels at meetings of the Society for Phenomenology and Existential Philosophy, the American Philosophical Association, and the Merleau-Ponty Circle. His current research interests include Freud, Heidegger, and the philosophy of emotion. He is a member of the American Philosophical Association and the Society for Phenomenology and Existential Philosophy. Professor Michelman lives in Spartanburg, South Carolina, with his wife, Karen Goodchild, and their two children.